The Battle in the Kingdom

J. de Rousseau

Published by

MELROSE
BOOKS

An Imprint of Melrose Press Limited
St Thomas Place, Ely
Cambridgeshire
CB7 4GG, UK
www.melrosebooks.co.uk

FIRST EDITION

Copyright © James de Rousseau 2012

The Author asserts his moral right to
be identified as the author of this work

Cover designed by Matt Stephens

ISBN 978 1 906561 98 7

All rights reserved. No part of this publication may be reproduced, stored in a retrieval system, or transmitted, in any form or by any means electronic, mechanical, photocopying, recording or otherwise, without the prior permission of the publishers.

This book is sold subject to the condition that it shall not, by way of trade or otherwise, be lent, re-sold, hired out or otherwise circulated without the publisher's prior consent in any form of binding or cover other than that in which it is published and without a similar condition including this condition being imposed on the subsequent purchaser.

Printed and bound in Great Britain by:
CPI Group (UK) Ltd, Croydon, CR0 4YY

FSC
www.fsc.org
MIX
Paper from responsible sources
FSC® C013604

CHAPTER 1

THE WORD Gen.1:2–3

In the beginning, was the Eternal Spirit of Light with the Word in the midst of devils in the world of darkness.

The devils ruled the world in darkness in the beginning. That is to say every devil born was from the seed in the nature of the spirit of darkness in the world. The Spirit of Light came unto the goddess of the dark world, and her body was full of Light with the Spirit of the Eternal with the Word.

The goddess did not know how it happened or could explain to the king of devils of the world in the dark, how Light came into her body, the Light in her body blinded them, so the king of devils asked Satan, his first devil by the goddess, to cast the goddess in the bottomless pit called Armageddon where the king of devils threw devils that cause trouble in his world.

When the time came for the Eternal Spirit to come out of the goddess in the bottomless pit of Armageddon, the Eternal spoke the Word and there was one big explosion in the world of darkness by the ETERNAL Spirit in the Light, and the world was now divided between Light and darkness. The Eternal Spirit in the Light took half of the world for himself and went up to the roof of the world.

THE COVENANT OF PEACE BETWEEN THE ETERNAL IN THE LIGHT AND THE ANCIENT DEVILS

From the Roof of the world After Eternal created angels and everything to live in the world in the Light, He proclaimed He will create His CHRIST with the Word to have knowledge and wisdom to create spirits like himself to make natural angels from his seed before he took office to populate all worlds for eternity by the Word.

CHRIST

The Eternal said: His Christ will continue the work in creation after He rested. No one knew when CHRIST would come in the world or where He would come from. or what he would do. The Eternal built the finest of thrones in Heaven for when His Christ and Zion came in the world to sit with his queen. The throne remained vacant in Heaven for many generations.

The Eternal created the earth with everything exotic and wonderful.

In the covenant between the Eternal and the king of devils

It was written in the covenant what the ETERNAL SPIRIT in the LIGHT CHRIST will do after HE rested. His CHRIST will be a creator when CHRIST sits on the throne in the world to continue HIS work in creation and... **Gen.1:9; 1:26**

To put the devils out of the world in the light for ever if any devil made a god with angels of his creation in the light or his creation on earth the covenant of peace will be broken. **1:12; 1:4**

CHRIST to make the covenant obsolete if the peace is broken by a New Testament to make angels in the Light from His seed and to create his Elijah in the Light by the WORD in salvation to be with the WORD. **1:24**

To remove the devils and all gods from the seed of devils for his CHRIST to reign on the throne according to the covenant with the king of devils of the dark world. **1:14**

The creation of CHRIST and ZION was the secret of the Eternal; HE created them different from angels with flesh to make immortal spirits in the Light from the seed of creation and for Christ to create immortal spirits in the Light upon the earth from the throne in Heaven through Elijah with the Word.

CHRIST the creator of immortal spirits, to be among angels in the Light through His Elijah with the Word to remove the devils from the earth if they made gods in the kingdom and save the spirits of gods that has faith in him from the fire to rest in peace. **1:26**

Elijah to present kingdoms from Zion's flesh for CHRIST to create immortal spirits in the light in salvation to be with Christ and Zion in Heaven. **1:27**

CHRIST to create his Elijah if the devils made a god on earth as his son in creation by the WORD.

The purpose of Elijah is to help CHRIST from the day the spirit of god vacate the kingdom to claim the kingdom in righteousness to present kingdoms to Christ to create immortal spirits in kingdoms for salvation in his flesh.

The Eternal created His CHRIST to populate the whole world with angels in the Light and dissolve darkness in the world His CHRIST to finish the work he started to create angels in the light in the heavens after He take a rest.

Christ to rule, Elijah to serve the word for Christ to create immortal spirits

CHRIST and Elijah are created by the Word. CHRIST to rule over all angels from the Element of creation, in the same principle as the ETERNAL with the Word and by the Word, as Lord of the world, after Elijah removes the devils from the earth to the fire so the ultimate would be to have a world with angels in the Light in total harmony with no conflict with devils, and spirits of gods from their seed in the world for ever.

The tabernacle

Satan said to himself: everything good in Heaven seems bad. I am in a state of mind unless I am like the Eternal, I am miserable. The only way is to destroy the ETERNAL and take back half of the world in the light. I'll be a happy king in the world when I bring back the world to darkness. Satan said to the devils: the Eternal is creating more and more angels in the Light, now his Christ is coming to be in second in command and every devil is in suspense, not knowing when CHRIST will come, or from what planet he will come from. Now the Eternal has created this inferior creature for us to worship on the earth to provoke me.

Celebration in the Tabernacle in Heaven

Angels of renown gathered with their siblings to worship the Eternal Father of Light and to give praise to the Eternal for his new creation in the name CHRIST not seen, who will create new angels with his Zion and create angels by the word when he sits on the throne with Zion as His queen of the world.

The angels began to be merry, dancing and celebrating when the Eternal will Passover the Word to His CHRIST to make angels from His seed. Everything that CHRIST will do was written in the covenant in the tabernacle for angels to read then put in the ark as a testimony between two cherubim and a mercy seat.

The Book of the Living and The Book of the Dead

Then there was a book for the names for new angels of CHRIST he would create and another book with a testament with warning and woe by Elijah to remove the devils in the world if they made a god, and to remove spirits of gods and assist His CHRIST with his new creation by the Word to be king in the world.

Next chapter of the book was about King Elijah and His Queen Jerusalem, the daughter of CHRIST and Queen Zion, to live for ever among spirits of creation.

The next chapter of the book was a horse named Genesis in Heaven with five other horses on chariots to meet Elijah anywhere in the world to bring him back to CHRIST to take instruction to pass judgment on devils for making a god in the world and judgment on spirits of gods who disobey and have no faith in Elijah to save them from the everlasting Flames in the sun.

Next chapter of the book was a picture with an eye looking through an image, looking upwards towards to the throne where CHRIST will sit with Zion. Many words were written about salvation and faith, spirits who make war and disturb the peace. Archangel Michael explained the future plan of CHRIST and what CHRIST will do after the ETERNAL rested from HIS work in creation. For his CHRIST to continue the work in creation by the WORD when He sits on the throne of the world.

There were loud noises of praise for the Eternal Father of Light to create his CHRIST to create angels to populate the whole world in the light through his Elijah. The angels began to sing and dance. Alleluia CHRIST, Alleluia Elijah, come into the world and join us with Zion and Jerusalem. Archangel Michael stood up and all the other archangels and ancient angels who witnessed the covenant of peace with devils lifted up their hands to the Eternal Father, and said: O Holy ETERNAL we give thanks and praise for your holy work and covenant of peace before your CHRIST. Come and do holy work in creation by the Word. The Eternal stood and said: peace and love to all of you who are gathered here to worship me and give me praise from your hearts today. Celebrate in the name of CHRIST the Lord of all worlds and His Queen Zion who will sit on the throne in the world with new angels with wisdom and knowledge and to be like us in Heaven, so all spirits in all worlds can live the everlasting life in harmony by the Word through Elijah and his Christ. After the Eternal spoke, there was lightning and thunder to begin the celebration.

No hope for devils in Heaven

Satan, chief of the devils said to the other devils: we have no hope to survive in Heaven unless I am more superior than the Eternal. We devils from the dark world are miserable in this world of Light and it's only by destroying angels and fucking their females, we will be happy. The Eternal is going to create His CHRIST to spite us for our vanity and deceit; we are in suspense and know not what CHRIST will do to us when He comes to take over the world. Now the Eternal is going to create a man in the flesh on earth that is more inferior to us and want us to worship him and call him Lord of the earth?

This man on the earth will have exotic fruit as is in Heaven and will have the planet earth to himself with a lot of creatures with flesh. When the ETERNAL creates HIS CHRIST, his CHRIST will create his Elijah who will be more powerful than the king of devils we chained for his wickedness to me, and I fear what CHRIST will do to us if any devil went to earth. A devil said: Satan, we should do the same as the ETERNAL did to our goddess to take back His half of our world and propagate gods in the world with His creation in the world. We are miserable in Heaven; let's make multitudes of gods to make him envy us. Then we will be like the Eternal on earth with gods from our seed in our nature. Satan said to the devils in council: I fear if I made a god with an angel in Heaven I will be kicked out of Heaven, we should all agree and make an oath to bring the world back to darkness, if we made gods to declare war in Heaven.

The devils in Heaven debate in council

After the Eternal gave His speech for peace and love, Satan the chief of the devils took council with the other chief devils and they began to debate among themselves about the CHRIST that is coming to take over the world from the Eternal.

The first devil to speak asked Satan: what would CHRIST do to us? Now I heard CHRIST will create a backup in the name of Elijah that is more powerful than any devil. It took hundreds of devils to throw the king of the devils in the pit before we came to live among angels in Heaven. We are not allowed to fornicate with angels in Heaven or with the Eternal's creation in the world according to the covenant. Some say this Elijah is of god and we know devils of our father never made a god in the name of Elijah in the Light; others call him the judge between life and death. Satan, what do you think if we ever made a god in the world, to pass on our seed. Will this Elijah of CHRIST destroy us?

Another devil said: Satan, if we return to our dark world it's for eternity with our goddess and the king of devils we chained in the pit. A devil became afraid and began to cry, what can we do? Satan said: take hold of yourself. I will tell you what we will do; let us make a plan and declare war in the Heaven to take over the world before the ETERNAL create HIS CHRIST to take over his throne and all the angels and those who don't fuck with us we will cast them out to the pit for our father to fuck them for the Eternal turning his world upside down. Go and celebrate, and do nothing till I give the word to strike.

Meanwhile according to the covenant a devil is free to go out of Heaven to his part of the world in darkness if he has no desire to celebrate with angels in the Light. Satan said: I'll go to the earth and see what is going on there, to make gods from flesh.

A devil said: Satan, now I know you are mad if you do this. If the Eternal finds out you interfere with His holy creatures of creation, we will all go to darkness for eternity. Satan said: you double-minded fucker, are you happy living among angels in Heaven? We are immigrants, we build castles and can't live in them, the world is divided between Light and darkness and only we devils in Heaven can bring the world back to darkness through war.

Another devil said: Satan, you don't have the WORD to create and destroy the Eternal. Satan said: who needs words? Did our father in the pit have words he agreed to have a covenant for angels to have peace and for us to know the good way, learn and have knowledge of the sciences in the Light? No devil in the dark world can understand science of creation; it is not in our nature. Our father, the king of the devils gave us laws of survival to steal, cheat, rape, kill, to survive, fuck our neighbour, destroy who we don't like with malice, make slaves out of the weak and pass on his seed and make devils to populate the dark world, we are from the spirit of darkness.

Satan said: don't you see this life with angels of creation don't suit you and I? We are forbidden to fuck angels created in Heaven.

Another devil said: Satan, we have peace in Heaven and we can adapt and learn not to make war on who is created good. Satan replied: you motherfucker, you want peace, you have loss of memory, and it's because of our mother we lost half of the world. She could never have enough, our king could never satisfy her, she cried every day wanting to be fulfilled by something new. It is not the Eternal that will satisfy her but Elijah who will cast us and all from our seed back to her and our father in the pit.

Our time in Heaven is coming to an end and we are wasting our time working as migrants for angels in Heaven while there is an abundance of creatures on earth with flesh to eat. What is your problem? You want peace and your penis wants to make war. The only way is to revolt and take over the world and all the angels of creation we will propagate our kind with our seed. The ETERNAL did all the work for us, He creates angels for us to pass on our seed, and the devils began to laugh at the Eternal with the covenant with the old king of devils for peace or war.

A devil said: Satan, the prophet who designed the tabernacle with the new throne for CHRIST said: if there is any war in Heaven, all devils will be cast out of Heaven, I fear if I join the revolution, I'll suffer for going against the covenant to make a god to death. I am worried, it is true I have desire to have sex with angels but we are not allowed to fornicate with angels in Heaven. the world in the light is only for angels of creation. They are happy and polite and graceful they live in peace and love and have respect even if we are inferior. Why can't we wait to see if CHRIST will make things better for us and suffer a little more for peace? Suppose this plan to declare war fails, and we can't come back to Heaven. What will happen to us?

Satan replied: such devils like you make me sick. You are like some who doubt and play between Light and darkness, for instance this prophet Herod of astrology. He thinks he is intelligent looking for signs in the stars to find out when the CHRIST will come. All his interpretation is wrong. He lusts for flesh in secret and can't make up his mind to join us. I know he would fuck angels if he got the chance.

Another devil said: Satan, I heard the ETERNAL is going to create a female creature with flesh. What will happen if she dies on earth? Satan replied: worms would eat her flesh. All this flesh is going to waste on earth and could be put to good use if we pass our seed in her, she will make our god in her flesh and it will be our creation from our seed and not like angels by the Word in Heaven.

A young devil who worked with the prophet Herod said: Satan, that is the point we left the old way to live among angels by creation in the world in the light. Now you want to pass our father's seed to make gods our creation to worship us; you don't have the Word. I've heard from the prophet who has good connection with the angels high up the Word is to be passed on to CHRIST He has a backup with an unknown spirit who will be the judge and he has a plan for salvation for creation. If we made gods He will create much better than our gods by the Word.

A devil said: Satan, supposing we go and interfere with holy flesh and propagate gods to be spirits what will this unknown Elijah do to them? Satan scratched his head, well I never thought of that. If I fuck this woman and she made a god and I kill him he won't pass on my seed, but if she made a girl then she will make gods for us to populate gods in the world.

Another devil asked Satan: supposing you passed your seed before you killed god and a woman made a god for your god, what will you do to this baby god? Satan said: I would eat him from birth for her error, to make a god for my god, from my seed.

Satan said: who cares. But I have another plan: we will have to take control on earth and their we will defeat CHRIST while the Eternal is in Heaven. A devil said: I understand CHRIST is wise and slippery like soap and He will put everything into the hands of Elijah while He is in Heaven and when the time comes for war, all our gods who pass on seed will be destroyed for ever.

A devil said: Satan, this CHRIST and His Elijah have put fear in us. We have a choice to vacate the Heaven in peace or get thrown out; that is the way I see it. We have an unseen CHRIST and a powerful spirit named Elijah who is more powerful than any devil or god and anyone who sees Elijah will die. Christ and Elijah are enemies of devils and their ultimate desire will be to populate new angels to live in the world in the Light and eliminate devils.

The oath

Satan said: our ultimate desire is to destroy the both and populate this earth with our seed. We have to prepare for war in the heavens before we become unwanted guests, we have debated in this council and all who is prepared to make war to take over the world sign this oath. The devils went among the crowds of angels celebrating for CHRIST to come in the world and pass on the declaration of war to the other devils by word of mouth in secret. Satan went to the exit for the angels to let him out. This was allowed as he is not an angel of creation to go and visit the goddess in the dark world. Visiting the earth is forbidden to devils at all tunes.

Ancient Herod, the astrologer

Herod was the astrologer to the ancient devils in Heaven. He studied the body of angels in their Element and the effect they had on him and devils from the Ancient World of Darkness. Herod studied the constellation, planets and the stars so he could predict when CHRIST would come and from which planet in the world. From his observatory, he had a great advantage over Satan and the devils in Heaven. He studied the wonderful order in which the stars are set in the universe and discovered from his observatory, the stars had influence over creatures and made then productive to impart life. The stars also had power over plants and made them fruitful and made minerals to sparkle and twinkle like angels He admired and was beautiful.

The conspiracy

Satan had an appointment with Herod. When they met, Satan told him of his plan to declare war on angels in Heaven and to take the throne of CHRIST, before He came to occupy it to put it in the Light to dissolve darkness. Satan said: from your observatory you can see planets as small as an egg, from ancient devils for CHRIST to inherit for eternity.

Herod, my meeting with you is to ask you to join us with the ancients to fight the Eternal and His angels, and we can share the world between us. Herod said: Satan, I discovered the secret of the stars, how they produce of themselves like creatures on earth, the man on earth will make multitudes and the multitude multiply in the world like himself. Satan, you could use this secret to make gods like stars in Heaven.

Satan said: Herod, this CHRIST that is to come in the world. Can you detect from what planet from your observatory because I fear when He comes, He will be worse than the Eternal, who warns us not to fornicate with angels in His world in the Light. The devils and I have to masturbate and live a celibate life while we live among beautiful angels in Heaven according to the covenant of peace.

Herod said: we ancient devils suffer much for pleasure we can't have like angels. When we were in the dark world we could fuck with she devils but now I suffer this celibacy like you and have to think between war and peace, that is my problem. I can't say yes to war and no for peace. Satan said: Herod you have always been two-faced and want to live between Light and darkness, waiting for something to happen to back the winner. But this CHRIST that is coming is going to deal straight; you are either in the dark or in the Light and don't be brainwashed with your physiology and forget you are an ancient devil from the spirit off the dark world.

The mystery, the ETERNAL created the kingdom as the foundation

The ETERNAL created Adam in the flesh as the body of CHRIST, and the body lay on the altar lifeless on the earth as the foundation for everlasting kingdoms on earth as His sacrifice to death.

The worship of Adam on the altar on Earth

Archangels Michael, Gabriel, Raphael, Uriel and Joel ushered the angels from other planets to come forward to worship the body. The angels in the Light fell on their knees at the altar and worshiped Adam and said: ETERNAL, you have created the body of Adam with splendour to have glory, and they left the earth for the heavens on their spaceships for their planets in other worlds.

Satan was called and his devils to step forward to worship Adam. Satan said: I am not on earth to worship any inferior being than me; it is he who should worship the devils, and me. We are from the Ancient World, we do not worship any other but our king devil. We are in the world before him and if he is rude to the devils and me I'll make a god on this earth to be his king when CHRIST is in Heaven.

The other devils refused to worship Adam, and said: he is only flesh. Michael said: if you touch his flesh CHRIST will remove you out of the earth. The Eternal spoke through the clouds: the image I call Adam is created on earth by my Word, and when I speak the Word, whatever Word that came from His mouth will surpass all words that come from your mouth, with wisdom and knowledge and understanding of creation of angels in the Light.

Satan and the ancient devils felt confident in their plan and in Herod's physiology. They refused to worship Adam and thought to go one step further to challenge the Eternal for their right to worship who they want in this world. Satan said: Eternal, let us put it to the test. If we fail to bring the world back to darkness, your CHRIST will succeed to put the world in the Light, with angels of creation by the WORD. If not you He will worship the most barbarous of the devils under Heaven.

The Eternal replied: be aware, CHRIST will come after you for not worshipping Him and Adam and His Elijah will remove you and devils to a place you have not been.

The Eternal went on to say: though I made Heaven in the Light, I also made the sun with fire to satisfy your envy of Me and My CHRIST with your arrogance if you disobey to worship my creation. The devils and the ancient left the earth and went back to Heaven to plan for war.

The mystery of CHRIST and Zion revealed

When all the angels and devils left earth, Michael, Gabriel, Raphael, Uriel and Joel gave praise to The Eternal for the way HE spoke and stood next to the altar with the lifeless body Adam in silence. The ETERNAL Spirit with the WORD said: Christ, enter the body of Adam and be the element of everlasting life to make immortal spirits as yourself in the Light in your flesh to be among angels in Heaven. The body jumped. The ETERNAL with the WORD said: Zion, enter into the body of Adam and cleave unto CHRIST in your element with the holy egg. You remain in Sanctification in his flesh until you manifest in your image in the flesh of CHRIST. CHRIST manifested in flesh in his image with Zion by the WORD and with the WORD. Adam woke up as if from a deep sleep, and stood before the archangels. They were the first to witness the image of Christ stand and walk. They served CHRIST/Adam angels food and left the earth knowing the secret of CHRIST and Zion sanctified and cleaved with her Christ in Adam as one in the flesh.

The ETERNAL created His CHRIST different from angels in Heaven with a foundation for the flesh of Christ to be an everlasting kingdom to make angels from his seed with Zion and to create immortal spirits by the word to be CHRIST'S in his flesh, in the time of salvation. The Eternal visited CHRIST and Zion.

The Eternal came to earth and took CHRIST on a trip around the earth to speak to him while Zion was asleep in sanctification. The ETERNAL said: CHRIST, I've given you yielding fruit trees with seed of its kind in the Garden of Eden. In due time you will have seed to make immortal spirits in the Light in the kingdom when Zion manifests in your flesh. Your enemy will come upon earth with envy to tempt ZION to make god to be in the kingdom. You will have to wait until the time of salvation for you to create Elijah by the Word to be king in the kingdom of god to create new spirits in the Light upon the earth through Elijah, when you create your Elijah pass on the Word to him for him to say the word for you to you to come and create immortal spirits in the kingdom by the WORD to continue in the flesh of Zions flesh, to be perfect to live in all worlds among angels in the Light.

When it is time to create you shall create through your Elijah in the kingdoms of gods in salvation to be a CHRIST like you. Your Elijah shall judge the spirits of gods of the devils. Elijah will also begat a son who will populate the earth from the seed of creation with your daughter Jerusalem. at the appointed time with her spirit by the WORD.

The salvation plan will be according to the New Testament. CHRIST, after you sabbath your body, you will resurrect on your throne in Heaven to create new spirits to live in the kingdoms upon the earth to resurrect to be in the heavens among angels. Elijah will take His rest and allow spirits of the son of god he begot to multiply kingdoms abundantly on earth. When Elijah awakes, He will present kingdoms in multitudes with spirits of gods who have faith in him to sleep in peace for eternity. Elijah will be king in the kingdom when the work in the kingdom is finished in salvation Ps.19:5

The Eternal blessed CHRIST and Zion spirit sanctified in Adam and said unto CHRIST, in his image in the name of Adam and said: be fruitful, multiply and recreate kingdoms by the Word from your flesh upon the earth, in the time of salvation so you can have dominion on earth and in all worlds. Behold, he said to CHRIST: I given Zion the holy egg to bear CHRIST'S with your seed while you are on the earth. Tell Zion when she manifests it is forbidden to make a god for devils and that she should not stray from you. The Eternal blessed CHRIST and Zion spirit Sanctified in the body of Adam and took His rest from His new creation in the world. **Gen:1.14.17.27; Gen.1:11-28; Gen.15:5; Gen.22:17; Ps.148:3**

Adam CHRIST to the Eternal many years later

Christ said to the eternal creator many years later: you have created me in this body on earth. I am among creatures and All kinds of animals and I am getting bored. I have no one to converse with on earth.

The Eternal answered: I hear your request, my son, but have you ever thought how boring it is for me to be alone for eternity, not having anyone to hold any conversation at my level? Angels I've created and their descendants are inferior to me, but I have created you to have wisdom and knowledge to be like me in command in the world.

Adam CHRIST answered: O Holy ETERNAL. You live on the top of the world for eternity. No one is as perfect as you. By your Word, I am a spirit you created, and manifest in this body with Zion. How can I populate the earth and multiply in peace and love and give Zion children that are pleasing in your eyes, if I am alone? The Eternal Father thundered, this was to try you, My CHRIST. I am pleased that you know the difference between man, beast and creatures by your experience and not by me telling you. Your spirit expressed itself perfectly in your image, freely without fear of me and with good reasoning. I know it wasn't good for you to be alone without company, but it was for you to be observant and judge what is not pleasant in the world, and to be creative to make Zion share your joy for eternity. When she manifests in your flesh she will please thee with children in your likeness to help you to populate the earth from in your flesh from your seed. I'll give thee at the appointed time. And Christ in the body of Adam heard no more.

Manifestation

Instantly CHRIST in Adam fell asleep and the spirit Zion began to awaken in him to manifest her spirit in His flesh. When He woke up Zion was manifest from his flesh in her image lying down next to him, warm and tender and beautiful from His flesh, looking at him with delight. Then she disappeared. Adam said: O Eternal, don't take her away from me.

Adam and Eve

Adam went to the river and sat down by the pool of water. While sitting there in his sorrow and sadness, He took some pebble stones and threw one in the water it began to ripple and the circle disappeared. He threw another one and observed how the ripple made a circle and then disappeared, so he did until all the stones in his hand were no more. Then all of a sudden, a white dove came from nowhere and circled around where he was sitting and it flew away. He looked at the direction it flew and he saw Eve in the pool of water looking at him.

They both stood up and began walking towards each other. Adam held her in His arms, feeling their spirits bonding in flesh and letting their feeling flow with joy and happiness close in body and spirit. They began to kiss each other with long succulent kisses and couldn't be separated in this embrace. Thunder, lightning and rain was pouring down from the sky, but it didn't separate the two of them in paradise joined together in spirit and body, stimulated with happiness like angels above.

O Adam, she cried with happiness and ecstasy of his warm and tender love, I love you. Squeeze me. Let me bond with your body and with your spirit to be yours for ever.

O Eve, you give my spirit strength and happiness to rule the world with you as my queen.

Adam put his fingers through her hair, long smooth like silk. He looked in her eyes; they began to twinkle like stars in the sky, held her tenderly, kissed her well-shaped mouth made for kissing. O beautiful woman of creation, he said, I will call your image Eve. She hugged him and kissed him. Tears of happiness come from her eyes. She went down on her knees and took each teardrop and put them on his feet, then took her hair and wiped his feet clean from the dirt.

He picked her up and embraced her. Then she ran in the pool by the river. Adam chased after her and took a dive in the water. Adam pulled her legs towards him under the water. Then both came up for air.

The sun shone brightly on the two. CHRIST in Adam said: O Eternal Father, thank you for this precious woman as my gift. I will call Zion Eve while she is in my flesh. Birds began to sing, the leaves on the branches of trees began to clap, flowers began to open up and give their perfumed scents. Hand in hand they walked naked in paradise and returned to Adam's cottage to eat, drink and talk and dance and sleep the night away lying in each other's arms.

The trial of faith

CHRIST in Adam showed Eve all there was to see in paradise. He showed her a tree with fruit that is succulent and told her not to be tempted to eat this fruit.

The fear of death

Adam CHRIST created to know everything like the Eternal Spirit about the enemy that will come and try to destroy Him on earth. Adam put the fear of death to Eve if she is found alone on earth. Eve felt she is confined and wants Adam CHRIST to give her space to experience her strength and weakness and ask Adam to give her a place where she can grow what she likes.

Adam answered: choose a portion of the garden to plant according to your needs, but remember not to go astray from my sight for you never know the hour the enemy of death will come to earth. Eve said: how can we be happy if you are in fear of death? Adam answered: that is the point; sin brings death on earth. That is why I warn you. Eve replied: Adam, this death makes me feel unhappy. We are created perfect by the Eternal and were joined together and now we are separated, living in our image in flesh and we are happy together. Let us not think about death so we can be happy.

Adam said: Eve, the Eternal left me with the Word to create a new spirit who will obey me and have wisdom and knowledge to build upwards and is not false like the one who is our enemy, to bring death on earth and want us to fall through deceit, so therefore obey and keep away from this tree in your patch and don't be tempted to go near it. Eve replied: you keep warning me about this tree as though I am on trial. I am innocent and have no fear of death. I am created a free spirit in this woman in your flesh and I love you and be with you in the flesh till death and to live with you in the spirit among angels above for ever, and she went to the part of her garden in Eden.

Obedience to CHRIST in Adam

CHRIST said: it's important, Eve, you are obedient even though you are a free spirit in your image, so when I am not with you, you are not tempted. Obey my words so both of us can be happy while we are on earth. Thus I warn you to save your innocence. Eve replied: by your own words, our life on earth might find us both far apart if I disobey and bring shame on you by deception. Adam replied: your freedom might lead to temptation so keep watch and avoid temptation by our enemy, who wants our flesh to death. Eve said: his fraud is my fear, which will interfere with my faith and love for you. This I dread.

Adam said: try and avoid being absent from my sight, for he who tempts is vain to bring dishonour on thee. He will not tempt both of us at the same time, but he will assault you with his malice and false guile if you are out of my sight. Eve thought for a minute about what Adam had said to her and then replied: if we live so close to each other and we have not had sex I am innocent. How can I be tempted? I have no fear of our enemy.

If our enemy trespass in holy flesh he will commit sin and he will bring dishonour on himself and live in fear of you, and our CREATOR in Heaven if he trespasses in your holy flesh which is forbidden in any assault on me.

Adam said: O woman, I will leave all things in the hand of the spirit when I speak the Word to deal anyone who assaults you and to look after us on earth and our flesh. When the time comes He will be our free spirit and I will put you in His hands to save you from your temptations, because you are beautiful and all who see you will want to tempt you.

The journey to the goddess

Satan had no desire to celebrate with the angels for the coming of CHRIST and His Elijah and asked angels who guard the exit, to let him out to go to the boundary of darkness to see the goddess and the king of devils of the Ancient World and was given an exit pass.

Satan and the goddess in the ancient world

Satan journeyed to the gates to the Ancient World and could hear the goddess crying. Her cry was echoing to be fulfilled with spirits in this dark world. At last Satan found her. She rushed at him and said: I knew you would be back to fuck me to give me spirits from your seed. Look at your father who terrorized us. You chained him to death; I warned him good will come and remove his evil way in the world of darkness. I desired in my womb for change of life in the world and this spirit entered to fulfil my desire for a new way of life and now He is the Eternal that divided the world between Light and darkness. Now, Satan, come and satisfy me with spirits from your seed and fuck me give me spirits to make me happy in this miserable place. Your father is chained to death in shame for his terrorism. He can't harm us now. He is a weak and old devil.

Satan said: O goddess of darkness with foreknowledge of what is good and evil. When I want to do good, I want to do evil. There's a CHRIST and His Elijah coming in this world and I hate them for what they will do to us devils when they come into the world. No one knows who they are. This CHRIST will change the world according to your foreknowledge and sorceries and, what's more, the Eternal has created a man on a planet called earth, his latest venture, and he has a woman that is driving me crazy to fuck to make gods to fuck to pass on my seed in her flesh to death, and you will have multitudes of godly spirits as our new creation of spirits in our world.

The goddess of darkness opened her legs wide and said: Satan, look and you can see what you want to fuck is the same as mine for her to make a god with your seed to lust for flesh. Give me a spirit from your seed instead of a god with all your malice, hate, hostility sexual desire, jealousy, rage, envy and war. Put this seed in my womb to be with me to inherit this world, and I'll be satisfied, but leave this woman alone. If you pass on this seed to her, she will make a god and an Elijah that is stronger than your god will destroy you and all gods from his seed.

Satan said: I will give you this god with all my malice and hate, but tell me, goddess, what do you see again for the future? The goddess used her sorcery and said: I can see a beautiful woman who has taken my place in the world with a man. Satan said: goddess, what do you see again? She answered: Satan, you will be a king with another beautiful woman and she will have a son, and will take over your throne with your laws and commandments and will imitate you and be worse than you on earth and you will come back as one broken hearted in this miserable place to fuck me for eternity.

Satan said: O goddess, what do you see again? The goddess said: when you return to me, you will leave much trouble on the earth, and all devils will be captured and return chained to death like your father, until final judgment. Godly spirits from the seed of devils will cry in pain for the flesh of the woman in the final judgment and she will not have anything to do with them. She will says they belong to devils and she will be free of the oath when you and all devils return for breaking the covenant of peace between the Eternal with the king of devils. Satan, you know that to make a god is a sin, and will be the end of us in the world. O Satan, come, put this seed and torment into me. Don't make a god with this woman. If you do, a more stronger spirit will come to cast us to the everlasting fire in the sun.

Satan said: O goddess, prophecy and see if there is any hope to succeed in this world over this CHRIST. The goddess used her sorcery and said: I can see multitudes of godly spirits from your seed and other devils falling in Hades to await final judgment and I'll be goddess to them. They will hate you for bringing them in this world with no flesh to suffer, and they will fuck me instead of you, crying, in the fire for the flesh of the woman on earth.

Satan, don't have anything to do with this woman. She is a temptation for all devils to fall in fire. I warned our father, good will come and take over his world. He did not listen and now you want to give us less space in the world because of temptation to make a god with Eve.

Satan said goodbye to the goddess and left. When he got to the secret passage to go through the gates, the hounds kept barking to warn him, but he feared not this compulsion to make a god. He journeyed through sludge and watery places on earth in search of Eve

The romance of Adam and Eve

Satan saw Adam and Eve in the Garden of Eden, and hid in the bushes looking at Adam and Eve with envy, hating Adam every minute and lusting for Eve, looking at her beautiful eyes and shape of her body, with furious lust to fornicate, saying to himself: I am in this world before this man and it is I who should have this beautiful woman for myself.

When he looked at Adam he got pain, but when he looked at Eve he got pleasure seeing the both putting down their tools and heading to the river walking hand in hand naked, laughing, stopping now and again to kiss and cuddle each other. It was like looking at butterflies kissing flower to flower. This behaviour of Adam and Eve was too much for him, the harmony between man, woman and creatures on earth. A lion came from the thicket walking towards Adam and Eve and stood on its two hind legs and Eve began to stroke the hair on its body. Adams put his hand in its mouth and the lion would not bite his hand off. Then Eve went on its back to the pool and the lion began to swim with Eve on its back. Then it walked away to meet its lioness and cubs.

This made Satan even more hateful of Adam in this life in paradise and wanting to fuck with Eve even more now and compulsive to commit rape. As Adam and Eve were walking, Eve would stop and pluck a wild flower from the ground and put it to her nose and it would let out its perfumed scent and she would kiss Adam with long kisses. In the pool of water, the fishes would jump for joy, with Adam and Eve splashing water on each other, cuddling and kissing, talking, laughing. Adam taught birds to sing Alleluia to Jah. Satan climbed a tree to have a better view to see if they would fornicate in the water; they behaved like angels in Heaven, and this made Satan jealous and angry.

The monkeys began to jump and squeal in fear when they saw Satan on a branch, peeping at Adam and Eve. The branch he was on suddenly broke and Satan fell to the ground. A male donkey with a long penis was under the tree, eating grass with its mate. Satan frightened the donkey, and it began to bray, hee haw, hee haw. Satan fled in the bush. He frightened a little red rooster and it began to crow. The guinea fowls began to fly, making a lot of noise to draw Adam's attention, but Adam and Eve were accustomed to creatures making noise and were by the pool enjoying life in Paradise.

Adam and Eve came out of water walking hand in hand in harmony towards their cottage for a night's rest. While they were fast asleep Satan with all his malice and hate slept in the bush with wolves howling in the night and other creatures screeching and frogs croaking at him. This made Satan even more hateful and wanted to destroy man, beasts and creatures on earth. Satan said to himself: I have to kill Adam to take this woman. If I kill this man, Christ will come to earth and take this woman from me for himself and I'll end up with this stupid goddess.

This put fear in Satan to return to the goddess. This made Satan more determined to rape Eve before Christ had her for Himself on earth.

Satan debated with himself for quite a while, confined in this place for the night. Then a thought entered his mind: if I rape Eve she will make gods for this Elijah to cast to this goddess to satisfy her for ever.

Satan and Eve

Thou shall not commit adultery

Adam was having a rest, Eve went to her part of the garden and Satan saw his chance at last to be with Eve alone. He came out from the bushes where he had been hiding and called: Eve, Eve and when she looked he came towards her with a big grin on his face in excitement.

Satan said: I am the prince of the other world and I was sent to teach you what is good in my world and what is bad in this world, so no evil can come to you on earth. The goddess of my world sent her greetings and wishes you luck.

Eve said: you are supposed to be celebrating the feast in the tabernacle in Heaven. Why are you on earth? Satan had a crest of a serpent on his head. She was amazed at Satan having a mark of a crawling creature on his forehead and said: the other angels who visited on earth don't have a serpent mark on their forehead? Satan said: all distinguished wise angels in Heaven have a mark on their forehead to distinguish us from angels of creation, that's why I was sent to teach you until the other angels return, so the evil one can't come to earth to harm you and Adam.

Obedience

While they were walking and talking among the trees, where it was a little shady, the fruit on the trees were tempting to be eaten. Satan pulled a branch with lots of fruit. Eve said: don't touch this fruit. Adam said

I must not touch or even come near this tree or eat its fruit, because I'll die and bring death upon the earth.

Disobedience

Satan picked a fruit of the tree and switched it to one he drugged and gave it to Eve. Eve said: I will not eat fruit from this tree. I fear it will bring death on this earth.

Curiosity leads to disobedience

Satan said: Eve, Adam is jealous of you. You are the most beautiful in the world. He told you not to eat fruit of this tree because you would be wise like him. This is an exotic fruit most desired by the angels in Heaven and plentiful on earth. Look, Eve, I'll take a fruit on the branch and take a bite and you will see there is no death on this earth.

The first bite

Satan switched the fruit he quickly drugged and said: take a bite and will know what is good and evil on earth. Eve became curious and took a bite. Then she saw she did not die. She took another bite. Satan said: Adam has not told you the truth and she began to giggle and began to laugh at the fruit that will bring death on earth.

The feast of the tabernacle

Eve began to eat this succulent juicy fruit bite after bite and giggling and getting intoxicated. Satan held her in his arms and began to kiss her hungrily. Eve said: stop it! The more she told him to stop, the more he embraced her tight towards him, kissing her, fondling her breast. She began to say: no you are trespassing too far, stop it! She began to feel strange emotions never felt before and was confused with this violator fondling her body like a hungry beast.

The sin in the world to make a god

This feeling so new was too much for Eve to handle. She began to cry and pushed him away from her. Satan came at her, and she began to scream no.

Satan hit her – a slap to shut her up. She passed out. Satan picked her up and brought her under the tree and raped Eve with hate, vengeance, and bitterness in his nature. He took advantage of Eve while she was drugged to make a god to pass on his seed and destroy Adam with deceit. Eve was asleep on the ground.

All the leaves on the trees fell on the earth. Satan had nowhere to hide. He disappeared and went back to Heaven. He began to boast to the devils about what he did to the woman on earth.

Adam and Eve

Adam woke up from his sleep and went looking for his beloved Eve, and saw the leaves on the trees had fallen on the earth. He went to the part of her garden. He saw Eve covered with leaves, fast asleep.

Adam said: Eve, wake up. She woke up from sleep afraid and trembling. Adam said: what have you done, darling? You are trembling.

I commanded you not to eat the fruit of this tree or even touch it. Why did you disobey? Eve said: the prince of the other world with a crest of a serpent on his head beguiled me to eat the fruit to make me wise as you, and she began to cry, O Adam, he took my virginity. Adam said: this seed in your womb will make a god to pass on Satan's seed to make gods on this earth to destroy my holy flesh with accursed spirits. Naked it will come into this world and when it leaves it will be naked without your flesh.

In sweat from my face and in tears from your eyes shall we have children from your flesh, when Elijah comes in his flesh we will have a new spirit in the kingdom.

Do you understand, Eve, the trouble and hard work you have given me to populate the world because of this sin in Paradise?

This god in your womb, if he passes on this accursed seed in your flesh, he will make a god to pass on his seed to make gods on earth. They will multiply and will want to rule over our children with devils to take over the earth from us.

The Eternal Spirit whispered to CHRIST in Adam's ear: spirits of gods will pass on seed of devils to make gods on earth in your flesh till you return to earth in the time of salvation to remove the spirits from the kingdoms from the flesh of Eve to establish the kingdom on earth, to be forever with immortal spirits by the Word.

Now you shall have seed to make children with Eve with immortal spirits in the Light to be among angels of creation. The spirits from the seed this god will do Satan's wickedness on the earth unless you return, to remove spirits from his seed from your flesh back to Satan and the other devils so you can create new spirit in kingdoms from your flesh in salvation through Elijah.

The Eternal Spirit in the Light looked upon the earth to see how his CHRIST in Adam was handling the situation and said to his archangels: My CHRIST is like me, knowing good and evil. Now my CHRIST has the Word to protect Him on earth and have seed to make angels with Eve.

The Eternal, knowing everything, left it for CHRIST to speak the Word for His Elijah to sanctify and manifest in the image of god in righteousness to be his son created in the kingdom by the word in salvation to direct kingdoms worthy of creation of immortal spirits to establish the kingdom in salvation.

Amen.

Vengeance is mine, said Christ in Adam to Zion Eve

CHRIST in Adam said to Eve: vengeance is MINE. I will repay this devil on earth. Every kingdom will be void of gods when you resurrect from the earth.

Woe to any spirit of god I find in your flesh. From that day CHRIST in Adam decided to eliminate devils in the world for ever and work to a plan.

Eve began to be afraid and said: Adam, I've brought trouble to you let my body be a sacrifice to death and you will be free. I am so ashamed I want to die to come out of this body. What can I do?

Adam said: there is not much you can do. Our love is stronger than death. Perhaps if you went to the Jordan every day and put a stone on your head and repented for this god in your womb, perchance the Eternal will have mercy on you. I love you though I should kill you, but I would be killing myself. The sin has been committed. Good will come from your flesh in the end when Elijah enters the kingdom of this god in your flesh as your saviour.

War in the heavens

The devils declared war in the heavens and began to take the angels in captivity and challenge the Eternal to take over the world. The Eternal sent a comet with a star to pass the Word to CHRIST in Adam on earth. Michael, Gabriel, Raphael, Joel and Uriel gathered with a legion of angels from other planets and they came with their spaceships with lasers to fight the devils. The devil stole spaceships to fight the legions of angels from other planets in the war for the heavens. Michael was in charge with other archangels to the fight with the other angels from planet to planet against the devils.

The devils began to panic. The spaceships with lasers were circling them and they had no choice than to head for the edge of darkness to gain advantage in the dark. Michael and the other angels began shooting lasers with precision at the devils, who ended up in the Ancient Worlds of Darkness. The spaceships they stole were destroyed and all the locking systems to enter the heavens were shut to the devils for ever.

Return to the dark world

The devils went back to their part of their world in darkness. The goddess said to Satan: I told you, you would be back. Now all of you have been expelled in the other worlds to this miserable place to be with me. Satan said: I am going to the earth to make gods for this world in the dark. The goddess said: no, don't go. You will bring us to ruin. There is not enough space for all of us here. If you go and make gods, where will you put their godly spirits when CHRIST casts them out from kingdoms on earth for Elijah to judge? We will have no peace with godly spirits from your seed crying day and night without flesh to return on earth.

The devils begin to debate among themselves. Some devils said: they are too old for this war; they would rather stay with the goddess. They fear this CHRIST and Elijah would chain them to death. Satan said: those who want to stay, remember, when godly spirits come in this world, you cannot fuck with them because you are too old.

The goddess said: listen everyone… If any devil leaves here to go to earth to trouble this woman to make gods, you will return and you will have no strength or seed left to even satisfy me in this world. Satan, it is because of you we have diminished in size. We had the world in darkness to ourselves. You were not satisfied in being the prince of darkness. You want to rule the world to do more evil than your father, to be king of the world.

Because of your lust for power we have lost half of our world to the Eternal Spirit of Light, who created His CHRIST to take the balance of our world. Because of you we will starve to death. Already there is no food and water, and have to go in this sludge to dig for worms and maggots. If you go and make gods, they will not come here with flesh so we can eat them; they will be godly spirits you call your creation, not like us ancients accustomed to live in darkness.

The devils began to debate. Satan said: there are many creatures on earth in abundance. All we have to do is to take over the earth and we will have abundance of flesh to populate a new kind of creature that can live in our world. For this I want strong devils, like Ermin, Magod, Golieth, Annak and Suzanzims, to make giants with these upstarts who threaten us with CHRIST and Elijah.

Satan said to the devils cast out of Heaven: I want everyone that is fit to fight against CHRIST and Elijah to remove the fear of death from us before they get hold of us to remove us from our world to make the covenant with devils absolute by a New Testament for the world to be with angels in the light.We must destroy Christ and Elijah before they destroy us, and bring the world back to darkness to rule according to the law of our nature to rule by force.

Satan handpicked two hundred of the strongest devils in the Ancient World of Darkness to come to the earth and set up an empire based on religion to indoctrinate and put fear in the citizens on earth to live by the law of devils.

The goddess said: Satan, all the devils who follow you will be captured and will be in chains like the king of devils you chained in the chamber for eternity. Before the ETERNAL Spirit of Light left the dark world he prepared this place for all the devils in the world to go in and never come out. If any devil made a god with his creation the godly spirit of the god will suffer much pain and sorrow every second, for passing the accursed seed to make a god to suffer after death.

Eve pregnant with God

Eve conceived and, pregnant with a god for Satan, said: Adam, what can I do to remove this god? It makes me feel sick every morning, my lord. Adam said: it is because the devil trespasses in holy flesh of a virtuous woman. In Heaven it is much joy to give birth to angels in the Light. Adam said: go to the Jordan and put a stone on your head and ask the Eternal to have mercy on you and I for this trespass in your flesh. EVE said: When I pray, the fishes swim around me with tears in their eyes; they jump out of the water when I ask for mercy for this god in my womb. I shiver in the water. I feel so unclean with this god, my lord.

Adam said: this god cannot stay in your womb for ever. It has to come out to face judgment and hope it will not be a rapist as Satan. Don't worry, my love; everything will work out in the end. Take a little rest. I'll go and do some work in your part of the garden to pull out some weeds.

Eve said: Lord; I'll go to the Jordan and wash myself to feel clean from this transgression.

Satan returns

Satan returned to earth with devils and he went in search of Eve and saw her standing in the river with a stone on her head. Satan came to the edge of the water, shedding tears and said: Eve, come out of the water. I have some good news for you. The ETERNAL sent me to intercede on your behalf, so come out of the water.

Eve said: go away, you devil. I don't want to see you or to be seen with you. I hate you for taking my virginity by deceit.

Satan said: O Eve, it is because of you I am cast out of Heaven. I want you to be with me. I left the good life in Heaven to be with you on earth, now come out of the water.

Eve cried: go away. Satan got angry and said: is either you come out of the water willingly, or I come and get you out forcefully. Which way you want it?

Eve cried: go away from me. What you have done to me is sinful. Go away! Satan took a deep breath and blew on the water and the water parted left and right and Eve stood in the middle, naked.

Satan got excited seeing her naked and tried to pull her out. Eve screamed, Adam, Adam, help me! The deceiver is trying to rape me again.

Adam heard her cries and began to run towards the Jordan as fast as he could. He saw Satan pulling Eve out of the Jordan. The spirit CHRIST in His body said: go away.

Satan fell on the ground and backed off. He shouted insults and said: O Adam, all my hostility, envy and hate is for you. It is because of Eve, I am expelled from Heaven, having a good life in the midst with renowned angels and now I am among creatures like you on woman.

Adam said: What have we done to you to come unto this earth and disturb the peace between my woman and me among the creatures on earth? Your presence is hostile towards us and you terrorise the creatures and frighten them on earth. Why don't you go back where you came from?

What is our fault? You say we are inferior to you, yet you come and lust on earth for flesh.

Earth is our paradise. We have caused you no harm or injury. Why do you return to earth and pursue my woman? You will go to Hell.

When Satan heard Hell, he became afraid and remembered what the goddess had told him. Satan said: you being a creature, what do you know about Hell? Tell me! the Eternal made you in the image of CHRIST who is to come in the world. You are of flesh and inferior to me.

When I saw you with such a beautiful woman in paradise, I said to myself: if the Eternal creator created you in flesh I'll make gods in your flesh to be like devils on earth to live in your paradise and I'll be their king with your woman. Now I am expelled because of trespass in flesh of your woman on earth.

Adam took a fierce look at Satan with fire in his eyes and said: be gone, Satan, and warn the other devils if they trespass in holy flesh, CHRIST will come with Elijah to send them to a place where they have not been after they are expelled from the earth.

Satan became confused and afraid that if he came after Adam and Eve again, CHRIST and Elijah will come to remove them from the earth to be chained to death like god his father in the chamber, as predicted by the goddess.

Nine months later, the birth of God

Eve said: O Lord, I'm in pain, and she began to cry, O Adam, help! He began to wipe the sweat of her face; pushing, Eve said: Adam, the god is afraid to come out in this world to suffer like I'm suffering for the sin of Satan.

Adam gave Eve water to drink. Birth pains increased and she began to cry louder and louder. Her legs began to tremble and her heart racing and in fear of death for this sin on a virtuous woman on earth.

Adam said: Eve, I'll put enmity between your flesh and his spirits until it leaves the earth. Cursed are all spirits who shall pass on his seed and make gods from your flesh. I'll destroy the bastard for making you suffer for his god. If he is evil like Satan he will leave the earth to suffer like you are suffering with this birth.

Eve said: Adam, the god won't come out. It's afraid to come in this world, because you are next to me. Go take a walk; maybe his kind come when you are not around. Eve stood up and did as the creatures who gave birth. She opened her legs over a pile of grass and god came out and it began to yell. Adam heard the yelling and quickly came back and picked up god. It was a male god. Its body was hard as wild cane and Adam named him Cain. They washed the blood off and Eve breast fed him. Adam and Eve brought him up to know the good way.

The births of Abel and Tamah

It came to pass that Eve gave birth to a son for Adam. They called him Abel. Then Eve had a daughter for Adam and named her Tamah. The five lived in harmony (five sparrows) when they were grown up. Abel and Tamah were very close and were always together. Cain seem to be more interested in his goats and grazing them, spending a lot of time away in the field. One day he met Satan in the bushes lusting for his sister and mother. (Cain) god said: what are you doing here? Satan said: I came to see you.

One day, the devil came and asked Adam for Cain to come and spend some time with him to learn his culture and laws. God (Cain) went to be with Satan and the devils.

While Cain was away, Abel asked the Lord if he could marry Tamah. Adam and Eve gave their blessings and they celebrated this engagement.

Jealousy

When god (Cain) returned with the devil on horseback and being indoctrinated with laws and oaths and commandments, Eve gave him the good news. Abel and Tamah were engaged to marry.

Cain was furious the devil conspired with him to fuck Tamah to make a female god for him. The devil said to Adam: It is Cain who should have Tamah; he is the first god born on the earth in your flesh.

Adam said: no! You go and get a wife for Cain among your kind. Satan said: there is no god of his kind on earth, except he has Tamah to give him gods like him, in your flesh.

Adam said to the devil: as long as Cain does well he is accepted, but if you want him to have Tamah to pass on your seed, this is not acceptable. It is trespass in holy flesh like you to sin and make gods with Tamah.

You have no respect for what is holy and pure! Leave my yard and do not return before CHRIST comes and destroys you on the earth. This is your second warning before my face, for wanting to make gods on earth in my flesh.

Satan and the devils brought Cain back, and wanted to see the most beautiful woman in the world but became afraid when they heard Adam speak of CHRIST, and rode off on their horses.

Adam said to Cain: sin is in your nature to do like Satan; you desire to do what he tells you. I don’t want you to see Satan any more and stop lusting for Tamah, for the day you fornicate, you will die! So obey.

The conspiracy

Satan came lurking in the bushes and Cain saw him looking at Tamah watering sheep. Cain asked him: what are you doing around the compound? If Lord Adam sees you he will be angry with me.

Satan said: Cain, it’s either you fuck Tamah and make a female god for you, or I take her to make gods. Which is it to be? You lust for her just like me, so you slay Abel and she will be yours to make gods for me. If you don’t do as I say it’s death to you according to the law. Now ask Abel to graze his sheep with your goats and stone him to death and you will have Tamah to make gods. All I ask is a female god to be a godfather to your gods. You are the first born god on earth and I am your father, not Adam.

Cain asked Abel to come and graze sheep in new pasture, where the devil put a big sharp stone and he hit Abel on his head. Abel fell on the ground crying in pain, losing a lot of blood, and fled from the scene.

Adam told Eve, I can hear Abel crying. Let's go and look for him. Eve said: Adam, I told Abel not to go with Cain, as he hated him for being your son and not him.

Adam met god (Cain) and said: where is Abel? Cain said: I don't know. Adam said: what have you done to Abel? I can hear Abel crying for help. Cain said: I don't keep sheep; neither am I his brother.

Adam said: I can hear Abel's spirit crying out to me. You slew him! Where did you put his body, you cursed of the earth? Now the earth will open its mouth to receive you for shedding holy blood on earth.

A fugitive you shall be on the earth, Cain replied: my punishment is greater than I thought. If Satan finds me, he will slay me. Adam said: the day the devil slays you, you shall lose your kingdom to Elijah, who will remove the devils from the earth in this conspiracy to slay Abel to have Tamah.

Cain said: if I am out of your sight, Satan will slay me. Eve said: you killed my son who was good. All you have given me is sorrow since you were born. I've been a good mother to you but instead of happiness is sorrow and pain from the day I gave birth to you on earth. Don't come back to my house.

Cain went to live on his own. He built a hut with stones.

Three days later

Adam, Eve and Tamah sang songs to say goodbye to Abel. Adam put Abel's body on a pile of wood and set it on fire and burnt Abel's body to ashes.

Jesus, the first spirit in the light to rise

A dove flew over their heads and when they looked up they saw a star and Abel's spirit, Jesus, walking in space towards the cloud. The wind came upon the cloud and took Jesus the spirit of Abel to Heaven. Then they went back to their house.

Jesus was the first spirit of the seed of CHRIST in Adam to resurrect to Heaven from the earth.

Reflection after the death of Abel Gen.3:6

Adam said to Eve: Cain's spirit is not accepted in Heaven? When his spirit departs from your flesh it's a secret. The devils don't know we are spirits in our image. I brought up your god (Cain) the good way, but as he got older he became bold, dominating and rude. Since he began to mix with the devils he began to boast we are inferior to devils and was always anxious to be with them.

God (Cain) had no respect Gen.4: 4–8; Jn.3:12

Eve said: my lord, he is a peculiar kind of devil, not like Abel and Tamah that is like us who live in peace; Cain has many faults. He is always up to mischief, taking advantage of your kindness. You allowed him to do what he wanted. He hated me and reminded me of this rape and blaming me for the devils being cast out of Heaven. He said he would not be in this world if it weren't for Satan.

Adam replied: there is not much I can do, while I'm a spirit in this body, but to direct him to our way of life. Remember, he is, as you say, a peculiar kind of devil in your flesh, I told him if he had faith he could live long on earth. But if he disobeyed, Elijah would come and be in his image and will be righteous in my flesh and would be kind, and faithful to us. He thought what I told him was stupid. He said the devils were more superior than me. He also said that the devils told him he is a prince and heir of the earth.

I told Cain that Abel is of my seed, he is my heir. Cain said: he is a god and I'm not his father and he thought he could do what he wanted to be ruler in my house. Abel told him to have respect for the family; Cain told Abel why he doesn't go to Heaven when Abel sang songs of praise to the Eternal for having us on earth.

Darling, we are in this uncomfortable situation in our life as a trial, regardless how we feel. I accept god (Cain) the way he is, not perfect, until Elijah comes to satisfy me and you in our flesh as our son in salvation.

The spirit CHRIST in Adam Gen.1:4; 6:5–6; 2.Pet.13–14; 1.Cor.6:11

I know when I speak the Word, my Elijah will come and He will have perfect relationship with us and through him you will attain fulfilment in your holy flesh with a spirit created in the Light in salvation.

The spirit of Elijah, is the first spirit created in salvation Gen.4:54; 2:3; Ex.13:2; Is.17:10; Ps.62:1; Ps.68:19–20; Isa.5:16; Ezek.36:23

Elijah will never come to be a king on earth while the spirit of your god (Cain) is in the kingdom. Elijah is patient. When the spirit of your god (Cain) vacates the kingdom from your flesh and I speak the Word, Elijah will be the first spirit to sanctify in the body and will be in the image of god in salvation to continue in his kingdom with perfection with immortality to do holy work before me on the earth.

In multitudes, in salvation, in righteousness, without limit. **Gen.28:3; Heb.7:3**

The work expected of Elijah on earth before Christ on his throne according to the scriptures

Elijah will direct the work to be done in creation for new spirits to be in the kingdom by,CHRIST to cast out spirits of the devils to create perfect spirits on earth in salvation.

Creation is by faith through Elijah for CHRIST to perfect kingdoms by the Word, sanctified in images Heb.7:3 2.Pet.19

Eve, my love, do not give up hope. Have faith in Elijah when He is created. He will save you and defeat the devils and give you perfect children in the Light from your flesh.

All kingdoms on earth from your flesh will be in the hands of Elijah, for new spirits in the Light, which I will create for you, to be acceptable by the Eternal Father in Heaven.

The purpose of CHRIST and Elijah

The Word which the Eternal has passed on to me, I'll pass on to Elijah to dissolve the covenant of the Old World between our Eternal Father in the Light and the devils of ancient darkness, for a New Testament for angels in the Light to live in peace in the universe, you shall be next to me as queen of all worlds. This is also the purpose of Elijah to serve me kingdoms from your flesh for creation by the Word.

Elijah is faithful and everlasting 1.Pet.3:10

Elijah will be faithful and will serve me with kingdoms from your flesh as the gift of the earth to create everlasting spirits in the Light. That is a promise to you till the last seed of the devils is removed from your flesh on earth.

(Cain) is a god not perfect

CAIN) is not perfect as you can see and has many faults. As you know, he has not the same spirit as us which you know; he is a god of the seed of Satan and always complaining. He is not like Jesus from my seed that was always cooperative, but abusive towards us. So, my love, let us be patient as Elijah is patient till the time comes for Elijah to inherit his kingdom from your flesh.

CHRIST in Adam said to Eve: give me more children from my seed to live and go above like Jesus after he departed from Abel's body to be among angels in Heaven.

Understanding of death and eternal life

Christ in Adam said to Eve Zion: my beloved Eve, do you understand now from the death of Abel by Cain, why the Eternal gave me the Word to create my Elijah to be our saviour? The ETERNAL knew what would happen before it happened, so we can experience death in our flesh and to live the everlasting life in the spirit to continue His work in creation after I depart from Adam to put order in this world.

The image

When the time comes I will speak the Word, and the spirit Elijah will come and Sanctify and Manifest Himself in the kingdom of god same to be same as us, in the light in the flesh to abide full of grace before me as our first son in creation by the WORD.

Elijah is a free spirit and hope 1.Pet.1:13; 3:5 JN:1.4–9

Eve, my love, let us celebrate to our saviour Elijah. When He is created He will be like us in the Light and he will pave the way for salvation of kingdoms. Our flesh is not lost because of this sin by the devil. The devil will not know the difference and Elijah will catch Satan in his own deceit in the body of god and punish all devils for their sin to make a god in your flesh.

Our Eternal Father has given me the WORD to create my Elijah in your flesh, to remove the devils who wanted to bring shame on you for his sin to make a god. Elijah will have no mercy and forgive no devil. The Eternal heard your prayer and all is in the hands of Elijah to save you after I depart from this body.

Let us celebrate with Tamah this joy. Our first son in creation by the WORD is coming in salvation to fulfil the covenant by our ETERNAL to establish the kingdom on earth by the WORD and for Elijah to be with the WORD.

The vision Gen.3:13–14; 3:5

Eve began to laugh and said: my lord, I have visualised your power in the future by the Word. I made a god for Elijah to take his kingdom to remove the devils from the earth for rape and his deceit and a useless god in my flesh that killed our Abel to see his spirit Jesus from your holy seed go to Heaven.

Zion said: now I know you know everything before it happens, my CHRIST. Eve gave him a kiss and reflected on the first kiss he gave her and said: my lord, give me this Elijah, who knows between good and evil, to destroy the bastard who took my virginity and trespassed in holy flesh forbidden for any devil to make a god.

Much sorrow Gen.3:16

Tamah asked: mother, what is Elijah like? Eve said: my daughter, he will also save you from the devils on earth. Have faith in him for you to be His queen and He your king and husband. Mother, so you and I will be queens in the world? Eve said: after much temptation, my daughter.

Adam said: my daughter, have faith and be obedient to Elijah in the body of your begotten brother by your mother. When the time comes, let us celebrate to Elijah and be joyful from this catastrophe. We will survive and live in peace and love for ever. Elijah will fulfil your flesh and give you children on earth and then they will glitter like stars in Heaven with us. When Elijah will begin to do His work unto your flesh is with my blessed Word, before me when we will be in Heaven in the time of salvation, he will be with you on earth as your king.

Salvation

My father, what is salvation? Well, daughter, the devils on earth want flesh to make gods. If by chance you made a god and he passed his seed, then all godly spirits from your flesh will go to him when Elijah speaks the Word. It is for me to remove them from your holy flesh for you to be satisfied with new children that are of creation through Elijah that are acceptable, pleasant and good in your eyes with no stress to live in the New World for ever with blessing from our holy Eternal Father in Heaven. Elijah will keep an eye on you, my daughter, to do good for you on earth.

The plan to Capture Tamah or Eve

A young devil said: O Satan, I've observed the way the creatures capture their prey. We could use their system. Satan said: explain yourself.

The lions pursue with stealth, slowly and quietly they move in the bushes towards their prey and pounce on them with rapid speed.

The vultures circle in the air and shoot downwards to partake of the feast of the lions. Then the hyenas pester the lions with crying to eat flesh.

Why don't we do the same to Adam and Eve and Tamah? We know Cain is no good as a helper to Adam. Satan said: OK, smart one. We will do it the creature's way on earth.

Adam can't stay in one place with his woman and daughter all the time. We are many on earth now. Let us split in two divisions and wait till Tamah strays from Adam and Eve and capture her to make gods.

Another said: chief, if Adam and Tamah visit Cain we will capture Eve. Another devil said: chief, if we capture either where are we going to put our captive?

Satan called Azazel and said: show him the plan of the dungeon, where she will be kept so she cannot escape from us. The devils agreed to rotate watch on Cain and Adam to take one of the women.

Cakes Lev.7:12; Jer.7:18

It came to pass, Adam visited Cain to see how he was getting on. Cain pretended to be sick and told Adam he missed Tamah and longed to eat some of her cakes and the next time he visits bring some cakes for him. Adam left and went back to his house to be with Eve and Tamah.

Satan and a few other devils were spying on Adam's house. When they saw Adam returned they went to see Cain. He said to the devils: the Lord left him a little while before they came and he was going to bring some cakes for him on his next visit.

It came to pass Adam, Eve and Tamah were celebrating a feast. Tamah made many cakes and there was much left over. Adam said: I'll bring some to Cain tomorrow.

The next day, Adam had to plough and plant corn and told Tamah to take the cakes to Cain. It will cheer him up.

Eve said: Lord, I don't want her to visit him. Adam said: I would take them myself, but I want to finish this ploughing before the end of this day.

Tamah took a basket with cakes and put it on her head. Eve said: be careful and come back straight away. When she got to the hut where Cain lived, Tamah said: I brought these for you. Take, eat. Cain took the basket with cakes and began eating cakes hungrily. He reflected on what the devils said: fuck your sister and pass your seed so you can have a daughter.

Cain/god disobeyed Adam and Eve

Cain said to Tamah: why don't you come to visit me? Tamah felt sorry for him and went to sit next to him. He held her and began to kiss her and fondle her. Tamah told god (Cain) to stop. Mother will not like what you are doing to me. She was naked. Cain held her down and said: you are going to give me a god to be like me, and he raped her and she conceived his godly seed of the devil.

Cain fell asleep. Tamah left the hut, crying. While she was on her way home, the devils, who were spying on the hut, rushed and grabbed Tamah. Satan went in the hut and strangled Cain to death. Then Satan took Tamah. She cried: let me go! Satan said: in Hell I'll let you go. From now you will be my hell.

He put her on his horse called Death and all the devils began to ride their horses with great speed to the mountains to get away. (Cain) became a godly spirit with no flesh. He was the first spirit of the seed of Satan to go to Hades after his spirit left his body. **Gen.31:36**

Eve said: my lord, Tamah should be back by now. Let's go and fetch Tamah from Cain. When they went inside the hut, Cain lay on the floor dead with a broken neck, with his tongue hanging out his mouth.

Eve began to cry and roll on the earth bawling, O Lord! O Lord! Where is Tamah? Where is my Tamah? I told you not to let her visit this murderer. First he killed Abel and now my Tamah is nowhere to be seen.This hut stinks of his sweat. O Lord have mercy on me for bringing up this god of the devils on earth to destroy us.

Adam said: let us take his body from this filthy place, and they washed the body clean. There was a big stone near the hut and they placed the body on it.

Adam looked towards Heaven and said: O Eternal Father, I present you the body of god which had a spirit of the seed of devils in my flesh. Have mercy on us for this trespass.

We tried to teach him the right way to live long on earth but god was disobedient and did the opposite and conspired with the devils to destroy us. Give me the spirit Elijah to be my son in the body of god (Cain) in the salvation to be my saviour and king in the kingdom on earth with the word.

Suddenly the cloud began to cover the earth and the Eternal spoke in the cloud: My son, your request is granted according to the testament written in Heaven to create the spirit Elijah by the WORD. If the devils made a god in the world to be your son by the Word to be with the word to remove the devils from the earth, and gods who have no faith in Elijah in the time of salvation.

The creation and sanctification of Elijah in salvation as king in the kingdom of God (Cain)

The sun withdrew its Light and the whole earth was in darkness. Eve said: Lord, speak the Word so Elijah can come in god's body to be a spirit like us in the Light by the Word.

CHRIST in the body of Adam said: Elijah, come and Sanctify in the kingdom of god. Suddenly there was fire all around the stone. Then there was a ball of fire. Elijah entered the kingdom of god, and the perishable body stood up with the immortal spirit Elijah sanctified in the image of god and he said through the mouth of god (Cain): Christ, I'm here as your saviour, full of grace and honour to be the king in the kingdom after the work in salvation is complete in Zion Eve's flesh.

Eve fainted and fell on the earth in fright. Adam looked at Elijah in god's image. Elijah looked at Adam and said: you called for me to take over the kingdom of god. I am before you to help you establish the kingdom on earth to serve you, CHRIST my lord, the kingdoms from your flesh and save your immortal spirits.

Adam and Elijah embraced each other and shook hands. Eve woke up and said: this is my begotten son; my flesh is satisfied with spirit Elijah, our saviour on earth.

Elijah said: I'm here to save your flesh and immortal spirits with you and CHRIST my lord, and to give you the victory on earth in your holy flesh after I cast out the devils from the earth, to a place where there is much fire.

The godly spirit (Cain) cries in Hell without flesh Deut.27:22; Mic.4:8

The godly spirit cried in Hades: O Lord, the devil strangled me, my spirit left my kingdom and now I am in this heat in the earth, dying of thirst without flesh. Curse Satan for raping my mother to conceive me in her womb. O Lord, curse all devils on earth for wanting to destroy you and my mother by making me a god on earth.

Cursed are all gods born and passing on my seed of devils. They will end as a godly spirit like me without flesh of my mother in this heat in the earth.

O Lord, it is better my mother's womb was my grave, instead of being born to suffer in flames dying of thirst.

O Lord, let all the devils hear my cry day and night. I conspired with them to take Tamah in captivity. They encouraged me to rape Tamah to pass on my seed so they can have an inheritance on earth with gods from my seed to bring the world to darkness.

O Lord, I had no faith, and was disobedient and trusted the devils. They are deceitful, same as me in nature. I am ashamed for raping Tamah to make a god to be like me. Now I am suffering for a few moments of joy.

CHRIST the Lord in the body of Adam replied

Though you were no help to me when you lived in my flesh, it was not yours! All flesh is mine. You lived in it with disgrace and was disobedient. Now you have passed on the accursed seed of the devil in Tamah to make a god to multiply your wickedness on earth in my flesh. What you did was disgusting. You were a vagabond in my flesh and deserve to be in fire.

I'll meditate on what you said. I warned you while you lived in my flesh to stop associating with devils. I told you if you did well and had faith in me you could live to be a ripe old age and have exemption to rest in peace on earth if you were obedient, and not suffer in fire after death.

You have disobeyed and have become a godly spirit with no flesh, since you left your kingdom vacant. It is righteous for the spirit Elijah to sanctify your kingdom to bring it back to life to be my son in your kingdom. Now my spirit is satisfied with Elijah in my flesh. He is my son in creation, who knows good and evil. God (Cain), you chose to follow the devils. Elijah is the same as me and your mother – immortal spirits in the Light by the Word.

Elijah is a holy spirit and graceful in your kingdom with everlasting life. Through Him, all kingdoms with spirits from your seed will be cast out from my flesh and return to you when He speaks the Word to me in salvation.

And when Elijah raises your hands to me, I will come to create new spirits in their kingdom and they will give me praise. Spirits from your seed, you will inherit. When Elijah speaks the Word, the spirits that are cast out, he will judge who has no faith like you to be with you in fire.

Every time Elijah raises your right hand and left hand to me in the time of salvation is for me to come and cast out spirits that have passed your seed in Tamah's flesh to be your inheritance till the last spirits of gods leave her flesh to be with you, in fire, for raping Tamah.

I told you cannot have my daughter to make another god on earth. When Elijah speaks the Word to me, you and the devils will have power over your spirit for deceit, you pass your seed in Tamah to make a god for the devils, in my flesh.

Now you are in trouble for having no faith and became a rapist like the devil who made you by raping your mother. You were deceitful, a murderer like him. You had a free choice to do good, to live a long life on earth, but chose to follow the Ten Commandments of the devils and conspire under oath to hold Tamah in captivity to make gods from her flesh.

The godly spirit of god (Cain) cried loudly. The earth quaked with his cry: O Lord; I've heard your punishment in this heat. Ask your Elijah to have mercy on me and guard me against Satan and the other devils. I am afraid of them. If Elijah casts them out and they come to where I am in this place, they will blame me for bringing them in this Hell and I will suffer more punishment for disobedience.

Ask Elijah to bring me back to earth to warn gods from my seed to obey and have faith in him, so they don't come in this chaos in the earth to suffer for their ignorance like me, not wanting to know about the truth of the END of gods when Elijah judges the godly spirits that are cast out of kingdoms in the time of salvation.

Peace in the world is the answer

CHRIST/Adam answered: I've put everything in the hand of Elijah to give me kingdoms that are good in his eyes from my flesh and to give the devils and you spirits from your seed when I remove them from kingdoms on earth. My flesh is righteous for spirits that are of creation through Elijah.

When your spirits multiply kingdoms on earth, Elijah will release you, god (Cain), to do as you say, and spirits of gods from your seed who believe you are speaking the truth and have faith in Elijah, He will save from the flames to rest in peace for eternity.

Christ/Adam said: (Cain) god, Elijah will make what was impossible with you possible in this world for peace and everlasting life. So be patient in this heat, until Elijah releases you before salvation to warn your gods on earth. He is a spirit of peace; it is not Elijah's desire to see spirits suffer if they have faith in Him. He will give every spirit what they desire, a free choice, faith or Hell. Those who have a desire for Hell will go to Hell and those who have a desire for peace will be saved to rest in peace. **Mt.7:17; Ps.63:7–10; Jer.20:13; Rev.13:10; Ps.60:1–7; Jer.30:16 1cor:7.7.15**

Elijah's way is simple. When the hour comes for spirits of gods to vacate the kingdom for new spirits to be created in righteousness in their image, they will continue as immortal spirits and will be accepted above by the Eternal Holy Spirit of Light.

It is only from new spirits created by Christ will the earth produce immortal spirits in the Light to go above to be among angels with everlasting life. Meditate on this testament for eternal life, readers.

Death and Hell Ps.16:10; 1.Cor.15:24; Mt.7:13,26; Ps.63:2–9

CHRIST in Adam prepared his white stallion Faithful and Elijah took the red stallion. They began to look for tracks and they saw a lot of hoof marks from horses and began to ride south in pursuit of the devils for days.

Satan looked back and could see two horses coming at them from far off. The devils split in two directions. Satan accelerated his horses, Death and Hell, and rode towards a cave. He helped Tamah down from the horse named death and put her inside the cave and rolled a stone at the entrance and joined the other devils and went out of sight.

CHRIST and Elijah had looked for Tamah for seven days. Then Elijah said: my lord, go back to Eden to be with Eve. Meanwhile I'll pursue them on my own and will bring her back to you.

Elijah began to search on his own and on the third day, He saw a high wall that was built between the mountains and in the middle there was a gate as high as the wall. He went up to the gate and took a deep breath and blew on the gate and the gate fell. Inside was a palace built, with a lot of devils. Elijah walked towards them, and they became afraid and called for Satan.

Elijah went inside the palace and began to search inside the palace for Tamah. There was a big altar built inside. Elijah looked under the altar and saw a certificate god (Cain) had signed in the conspiracy to kidnap Tamah, saying he was Tamah's husband and sold her to the devils.

Elijah said: what is this contract of marriage you have with the daughter of my lord, with your god (Cain)? What has my lord done to you? You have also killed your god, so you can have Tamah.

You have taken the Lord's daughter unaware of this conspiracy to hold her captive. She left her father and mother's house without knowing of your plans or having knowledge of this plan.

Satan, you have done foolishly. In so doing you took Tamah away after Cain raped her, andyou murdered your god (Cain) to take his sister for yourself. Where is she?

Elijah went on to say: it is in my power to harm you. Take head you do nothing bad to the Lord's daughter.

Satan said: we are devils cast down to earth and we are strangers on this earth. If my god (Cain) fucks Tamah, I have an inheritance from my god, who passed on my seed in her womb, and what is born from her flesh is mine. The flesh of what is born, you can present to the Lord. He delights in flesh.

You are the judge. I have not fucked her, Satan said: what is my trespass? What is my sin that you have pursued after us and searched all over my palace before the other devils and found not the Lord's daughter?

Elijah said: the spirit of her brother Abel above will watch between you and I, when we are absent from each other. Any god born from your seed in her flesh will be yours.

Elijah commanded a pile of stones to fall in the palace ground from the sky and said: every seed that is passed on in her womb, their spirits will come into your mouth like this pile of stones, one on top of each other.

One of the devils said: it's because of Eve we are cast down to earth to live among creatures, and now you come and accuse us of murder and adultery of her god's lust to pass on our seed. You should be glad the poor bastard is suffering for his sin in Hell.

You pursue us like a thief caught in the act to punish us before our time ends on earth. If she conceives seed from Cain, remember Satan passed his seed in Tamah's mother first and if she conceives a god on earth, we will accept her god as one from our seed.

Elijah said to Satan: make sure you and no god passes on your seed in Tamah in my absence, for every godly spirit that comes from her flesh will be returned to you to the last seed from her flesh on earth and this will be the final judgment on all devils in this world, and Elijah departed.

THE OATH Ps.1:2; 19:7; Heb.10:1; Deut.1;11

As soon as Elijah left the palace in the mountains, the devils put back the gate and shut it.

The devils went to the cave and rolled the stone from the entrance and put Tamah on the horse called Death, and Death took off with her on its back with speed. The devils began to chase after Death and Hell. It took one jump to cross over rapid water flowing downwards to a waterfall. Both horse and rider were in the air and landed in a deep pool at the bottom of the mountain.

Tamah held on to a branch because the current of the stream was fierce going downwards. The devils came riding down the mountain looking for Tamah with sniffing dogs and got sight of her and held her captive again. She cried: let me go! They tied her so she wouldn't escape and brought her back to the palace. Satan said: put her in the dungeon.

The devils debated what they should do, fearing trouble now they have Elijah as a threat if they touch her. After the council meeting they brought Tamah out and said: what have you to say?

In fear, Tamah took courage and said to the devils: I know you were thrown down to earth and your god lived with us. My mother fainted when you raped her to make a god; you trespassed in what is holy flesh.

My mother told me when she was naked in the river Jordan praying to the Eternal to have mercy on her for your sin to make a god. You took a deep breath and blew on the water and the water parted, and she was naked before you with god in her womb.

When she told me so, my heart trembled and I had no courage to hear any more of what you did, raping her in the garden with deceit.

Therefore I pray you swear unto me you show kindness to me and my father and mother and whatever brothers and sisters I have on earth.

The devils answered: let us make an oath for life for your people. If we take over the earth we will deal with you kindly and you will be blameless of the death of gods in your flesh.

If you go out of this palace and make a god in your flesh, death shall be on his head if any god go out of this gate and pass on his seed in your flesh. Death shall be on his spirits and you will be guiltless of sin with us and this oath if we are not on earth.

Tamah answered: according unto your words so be it, and she was held in bondage to this oath with the devils. **Lev.24:22; Num.15:16–29**

THE BIRTH OF THE SON OF GOD Rev.12:1

Satan built a small temple in the palace where Tamah could go and cry and pray while she was pregnant for god (Cain). She went to the temple to pray for god her brother to deliver her from hand of the devil to save his god in her womb.

She began to cry, O god, I am now a mother of your god in my womb and the devil is blaming me for making a god from your seed. Satan said he will eat him from birth, if it is a male god.

Elijah appeared in the temple and Tamah said: surely you can help me. She didn't know the devil had killed god (Cain). Elijah was the image of god and she thought she was speaking to Cain (god).

Tamah said: let it not displease thee. I cannot return to give birth to your god in my father and mother's house after what you did to me.

I am ashamed, I am held in captivity by the devils. Because of you

I can't bring this god to my father and mother to destroy my family like you, and to do the same as you to kill and rape women to pass on seed of devils in my flesh.

Tell my father, I'll take the blame for bringing cakes to you. I'll pray to Elijah who is to come in this world to take care of me and my affliction and sorrow for making a god on earth. When salvation comes, Elijah will give me children like sand on the seashore which cannot be numbered. Cain, please go before Satan sees you. He hates you for being born and blames you for being on earth among creatures.

Labour day Rev.12:1 Rev.12:4,6,13

The day came to give birth. Tamah was in much pain; Satan sat with a bowl of salt waiting for the birth to eat it if it's a son for god. Tamah began to cry: O Elijah, save this child. Satan gave her a slap on her face and said: bring forth this fucking god for me to eat. I'm hungry for his flesh. You fucking bitch, bring him on to teach you, mother of gods, not to give birth to a male god for Cain in my palace.

It's because of god/Cain I'm on earth, leaving the good life above, to end with a bitch on earth. Tamah began to tremble. Her legs were shaking in fear and could not bring the birth in case it's a son for god. She was terrified Satan would eat him from birth.

Satan said: bring this god forth or I will pull it out with my hand. Tamah began to cry: it's not my fault! It's not my fault this fucking god is not ready to come into this world to be eaten by you. It is afraid to come out in the world because of sin.

Satan said: go to the temple and pray to your fucking mother and ask her what you have to do. Tamah slipped out of the palace and went to a place where she had prepared to give birth. She opened her legs and the baby god dropped on the ground and was in her blood, yelling.

Tamah cried: O Elijah, save this baby god, and returned to the palace. Satan said angrily: what took you so long. A small cat was curling around his legs. Satan threw it against the wall and killed it. Tamah picked it up and dug a hole outside and put it in the earth.

Tamah returned to the devil. The devil said: now come, make this god.

Tamah said: when I went to bury the cat you killed; I gave birth to it in the field.

Elijah heard Tamah's request and went to the palace where Tamah gave birth to the son of god crying on the ground, still covered in Tamah's blood with its navel uncut, and took it away.

Satan rushed outside the palace and said: Tamah, what did you do to this god of my god? We looked and saw blood on the earth. Tamah said: a lion ate it instead of you.

Satan put his finger in the blood on the earth from this birth and began to lick the blood on his finger and began to feel lust to fuck Tamah.

Satan rushed at her and grabbed her. She began to cry: leave me alone! You want to kill me. Have pity on me. He pulled her towards him while she was crying No! No! Tamah felt weak after this birth. She began to tremble in fear. He pulled her toward him. Tamah cried again, No! No! Satan said: you like it! I'm going to Hell for you. She began to cry Help! Help, Elijah! Satan slapped her and she passed out. Satan called two eunuchs and told them to take Tamah to the dungeon, feed her and prepare her for an offering next full moon.

The full moon offering

The devils had a council meeting to initiate their rite under oath to make gods from Tamah's flesh.

Bazaleel was a devil trained in all manner of skills and he came to take measurements for Tamah. He gave the two eunuchs oil he specially formulated to massage and stimulate her. He fed her to put on weight, and taught her to speak the language of devils.

The other devils made an altar outside for the burnt offering. The altar inside was for initiation purposes in the sanctuary with a joining room with peepholes for devils of lower rank and scribes to see and make a record of events.

Inside the sanctuary were devils trained to keep the fires burning on a brazen altar and assist on the throne.

The day before full moon, the devils brought gifts to Satan and sang songs and gave him praise for bringing them on earth and said: O Satan, be king over us. Satan sat on the throne and they sang songs of their homeland and gave him praise to populate the world with gods. They put a crown on his head as king of the earth and said: godly spirit of Cain, save the king in Hell!

Satan could hear the godly spirit of Cain in flames crying, warning him: if you ever touch the daughter of the Lord you hold in captivity it will be the end of the dark world. CHRIST and Elijah will come to destroy all the gods from your seed, and all devils will come and join me in fire for ever.

The first sign of the full moon a trumpet was blown and all devils gathered around the altar. They killed a bullock and took its blood and sprinkled it around the altar, took the fat and cast it in the fire, took the head of the bull and staked it on the altar in the sanctuary inside, and sprinkled blood around it for the sin offering.

Then they killed a goat and took the blood and cast it around the altar for the burnt offering and took its head and staked it on the altar for Tamah to make gods for Satan.

The devils took a ram and cut its throat and took the blood and sprinkled it around as an offering for Tamah to make a female god, and put its head facing the head of the goat on the altar. The devils outside worshiped the goat and ram. They killed a bull and took the horn and staked its head on the altar inside the synagogue.

Twelve of the high-rank devils came from the feast outside and entered the synagogue with their offering. The trumpeter blew his horn. King Satan came and sat on his throne and they sang songs of praise for King Satan to be the first devil to fuck Tamah. The assistants in the tabernacle were dressed with animal clothing and masks with crocodiles, hawks, leopards, and serpent scarabs on their heads to have power over creatures on earth.

The high priest took incense of musk, cinnamon, calamus, casica, coco oil, jasmine oil, coriander and palm oil, and threw it in the fire. Inside, the tabernacle was filled with a fragrant smell. Then there was silence. The devils were excited to see king Satan fuck Tamah in bondage under the law. **Lev.4:15 ; 4:22**

The two eunuchs brought Tamah in the synagogue dressed in white silk and they lay her on her stomach on the altar. She was afraid to look at the devils; the drummers began to beat their drums. The devils outside began to dance to the beat of the drums.

The twelve high-rank priests cast lots, who should be first. The first six went to the right of the altar, and the other six went to the left. The first six sprinkled blood of the bull over Tamah and they began to lick the blood off her. When they finished the other six priests took blood from the ram and sprinkled it over Tamah and began to lick the blood of ram on Tamah while the king was playing with himself. The eunuchs took the dress off Tamah and she was laid on her back.

Horn on altar. Mic.7:17; Lev.25:10; Gal:5:1; Deut;33:17; Exo.30:10; Num.5:13; 1.Cor.10:20–24

The first six high priests came, one after the other. The first two began to lick the dust under her feet. Another began to suck her toes. One began to lick the palm of her hand while another licked the palm of her other hand. Two high priests came forward and began to suck her breasts and sniffed her body.

When the licking and sucking and sniffing was over, the eunuchs assisted Tamah. She went to the head of the altar and took the cup of libation from the eunuch and she began to drink. This put a lot of libido in Tamah. They began to oil her body. A high priest brought a cupful of blood from the bull to King Satan. He drank and passed the cup to the high priest for the other priests to drink. The devils began to dance in frenzy around the altar to the beat of the drums.

Tamah knelt on her knees and took hold of horns of the bull on the altar to take an oath to make a female god to be a goddess.

The crowd of the devils outside was looking to see when the white smoke would come from the chimney to know the king has fucked Tamah to celebrate. King Satan took his time, scared, hearing the crying of the godly spirit (Cain) in Hell.

The blood of the bull made Satan horny and it stood up like a big cucumber and he went on the altar and fucked Tamah. Tamah fainted and the eunuchs took her away. **Exo.21:20**

The high priests took bread and one cake from the basket and took olive oil and cast it into the fire as an offering for Tamah andKing Satan. The devils that were outside killed a sheep, took the breast and brought it to King Satan to eat on his throne raw with blood. The king got lust for Tamah again and he commanded the eunuchs to take Tamah to his chambers. **Lev.14:20; Mk.5:23; Lev.2:4**

They gave Tamah some liquid to drink and it excited Tamah. They oiled her up but Satan could not satisfy her. She began to cry: O Jesus, I want you non-stop. You are the only one between Elijah and me. Satan wants me to make gods for them.

Satan held her down and said: you want Jesus? I'll give you Jesus, and he began to fuck her wickedly with all malice and hate. She passed out and Satan got up and went to join the other devils.

When the eunuchs came to bring Tamah back to the dungeon, they began to lick the libido on the bed like dogs. No devil was allowed to fuck Tamah but the king.

The high priest proposes Tamah to be their queen

The king sat on his throne and the eunuchs brought Tamah to a meeting with the other kings and the high priest. A high priest said: Tamah, you are committed to make gods under the law. Every god born to the king, we will give you praise. You are more than the goddess in our world if you made female gods for our king. We will worship you and want you to be our queen and we will let your father and mother live in peace.

Your life is more valuable to us. Where is Cain? He is not here to help you or your parents from death. Fear us not but god who raped you. If he returns to earth he will come after you and blame you for suffering in fire, so make gods for us and we will save you from him.

Another high priest said: Tamah, every god you make on earth for our king will love you and worship you for passing on our seed and you will be their mother on the earth under our law to conquer the world, after death. We are sent to hold you in captivity to save you from the seducing spirits after death.

Another high priest said: now you are under oath and our law in bondage. You must do what our king says; give him gods from his seed so he can give us your gods as gifts to populate gods on earth.

Another high priest of the devils said: O King, if we pass on our seed we will give Tamah double from her flesh. When we depart from the earth we will receive our godly spirits and her father and mother will have much flesh on earth.

Another high priest said: Tamah, every god that passes on seed will be a god on earth and they will make a lot of flesh for your father and mother and you will make them happy.

Another high priest said: if gods marry with gods in your flesh your father will have much flesh upon earth and what Christ and Elijah do with it is a secret, which we don't know. We looked in the mystery books, but it is in fine print in the heavens in a language we don't understand, so we can't tell you.

Another high priest said: we know there is a time for salvation in flesh upon the earth, but it is far off, not in your time, and there will be much trouble on earth with deceit and lust and malice and war with much hate for devils on the earth after we leave the earth.

The children your father and mother make are like you and can't live in our world with our king. Only gods are accepted from our seed.

Our king is highly intelligent and the power of his seed will bring much hate and malice by angels above but anyone that trespasses in this world before our time to leave the earth our gods will make war for the earth.

Tamah said: it would be justified, O King, to give the goddess the godly spirits that are from my flesh that come from your seed as her inheritance according to the oath, so I can be free to return to my parents. As you will not be on earth, gods from your seed will satisfy her. You keep saying she is a witch. You must chose who you have lust for. As you can see, there is abundance of flesh on this earth, and when your time is up you will have no flesh to pass on to make gods. O King, you left Heaven for the flesh of creatures on earth. Why don't you go back to Heaven? If you stay on earth, Christ and Elijah will come after you, O King.

I am in bondage on earth. My father said Elijah will save me and I will live for ever in the New World when I depart from my flesh. **Exo.21:7**

A devil said: O King, that is why we are on earth to make gods for the New World. There will be a lot of war and our gods will fight for us from kingdom to kingdom for the earth to death and Tamah and her father will have peace in the New World after this war, for on earth flesh will be everlasting.

Another devil said: King, what about CHRIST and Elijah? What will they do to us when they come to earth? Now we are committed to sin in flesh, under oath, will our gods do battle for us against them for the earth?

It is written in the small print these two can put ten thousand of us to flight. We don't know how it can be done; it is in the mystery books in Heaven. Tamah said: King, you should wait and see when they come to earth, to see what they will do to you and the devils.

A high priest said: the Eternal has much mystery attached to CHRIST and Elijah, which is yet to be seen. We don't know who they are or where they will come from or what direction. That is why we must be strict with our laws and to constantly keep watch for them so they don't come by the back door as thieves to destroy our habitation and plan. We should make it a law that anyone mentioning CHRIST or Elijah on earth should be severely punished so, in time, these two names be forgotten as a mist on this earth.

The high priest said: then let us teach our gods to live in fear of devils and put a mark on them to know who abides by the law, and who don't have a mark are not obedient to devils.

The queen. Is.49:23; Est:2:4; Dan:5:10; Mt.12:42

After the meeting the devils said: King, we want you to make Tamah our queen. The king said to Tamah: kneel and worship me before the devils, and she knelt and she became queen. The king said: now you shall no more be called Tamah but instead Queen Tamuze.

Ammon begot by Elijah

Elijah took the son of god (Cain) Tamah gave birth to in the wilderness, washed the blood off his body, clothed him in badger's skin, fed him sheep milk and honey from the rock, and called him Ammon. He grew up, and called Elijah Father

Elijah taught him all manner of skills and crafts to be a ruler in nations.

He was good with his bow and arrow, and a good herder of oxen, sheep and goats. Elijah told Ammon he would make him great among the families of the earth. If he had faith in him he would have a new spirit sanctified in his body to be his son. **12:3**

Ammon asked Elijah: what is sanctified? Elijah said: I am sanctified in the body of god your father. I am a spirit in his image in glory. Ammon said: Father, show me your glory. Elijah said: if I show you my glory, you will die, but one day when you are old and die, you will see my spirit glory in his kingdom.

I will establish kingdoms that spirits from your seed multiply and the spirits you shall possess in the gate of my enemies. The kingdoms from your seed shall be the blessing on earth.

Ammon grew up and dwelt with Elijah. Elijah gave him knowledge of the kingdom and told him to obey and have faith in Him and he will live long on earth and don't deal falsely with Him and tell lies. Kingdoms from his seed will have an everlasting name with new spirits walking in the kingdoms in their image like himself, in the Light.

Elijah spoke to Ammon like a father speaking to his son: thou shall not profane the name of Elijah. I've raised you up to be a ruler with honour. Your spirit name I will call Israel. **Deut.25:7** This will be a fearful name among gods on earth, when you rule the earth!

Ammon began having dreams of going up a mountain and said: Father, I am drawn to this mountain and must go and see what is up there. Elijah said: your mother is held in captivity up there and you should go and save her from the devils.

Father, he said: if she doesn't want me to save her, what then should I do? Elijah said: I am with thee. Tell her Elijah of her father said that she must depart with you. My Word, which I speak through the mouth of god your father, are living words. Ammon meditated on all what Elijah said.

It didn't make sense who Elijah was, as Ammon knew no one else but Elijah as his father. Ammon was agitated and wanted to know who is in the kingdom of god his father and began to be rude, arrogant, disobedient and argumentative. Elijah was patient with his attitude, and the work to establish the kingdom in salvation from spirits from his seed was far off in the future. Ammon had a free choice to decide his future.

The day came when Ammon decided to depart from Elijah to start life on his own on his horse and bow and arrows without Elijah. He called his father. Ammon felt confident he could save his mother from the devils.

Elijah told Ammon: it is righteous for you to go and save your mother from the devils. I am always available to save her when she calls for my help. At the moment she has not.

Elijah said: Ammon, before we part from each other, I forbid that you should tell anyone I am your father as long as you live. I wish all spirits were of the same nature but I am not like the spirit of god your father, but by the Word. If ever you become spiteful or be rude and arrogant to your mother or me, I'll abandon you.

You shall not lust for your mother or do as god (Cain) your father did to make you a god to be like him with your mother before he died, but you can fornicate with gods born to devils with your mother.

Because when salvation comes, your mother will inherit kingdoms from her flesh, to have new immortal spirits in kingdoms from all seed you pass from god your father. Spirits of gods from the seed of devils are not immortal spirits in her flesh. Spirits of gods will come unto judgment after death in this world. I have given you knowledge of my spirit in the kingdom with eternal life through salvation by the Word, so go and save your mother if you want to be my son by the WORD.

The time came when Elijah and Ammon decided to separate as his begotten god Ammon had to prove he had faith in Elijah to be a prophet. Ammon rounded up his herd, mounted his horse with his bow and arrows and was on his way to the mountain to save his mother Tamah from the devils.

Elijah visited CHRIST in Adam and Zion in Eve. They had many children. Elijah took His rest until CHRIST woke Him up to resurrect Him to His throne in Heaven by the Word, to begin the work from His throne in Heaven to create immortal spirits in kingdoms for salvation

Seed time

Many years later the earth was populated with the people of Adam and Eve. There was much order and discipline. their cities was well built, there was much to eat and drink, cultivated pasture, no sickness, and education with scriptures above. There was much spacc between the people of Adam and Eve and the devils. There seemed to be peace on earth.

Satan, the king of the devils, developed cities and nations. Each nation had its own king with laws and populated with gods. Ammon, with his large herd of cattle, goats and rams was making his way towards the mountain. One of the princes in the palace saw Ammon with his herd and went to tell his devil there was a stranger with a large herd not so far away from the palace.

The fear of CHRIST and Elijah

Satan said: go and keep an eye on him, thinking it was Elijah coming after him and the devils in the palace, and he locked Tamuze in the dungeon. He and the devils went to spy to see who it was. When they saw it was a god that looked like the gods in the palace, the devils threw a net over him on his horse and brought him down in the net. The devils brought him inside the palace, locked him up in chains, and took all his herd.

King Satan called the other kings to have a meeting to discuss the fate of Ammon. He looked wild and fierce when they got together. One of the kings said: certainly he is a god, but where did he come from? CHRIST and Elijah must have sent him to spy on us, one of the kings said. But if CHRIST and Elijah are going to destroy us, why should he send us this god. Another king said: chief, did you kill god (Cain) you made with Eve of the man? Satan said: I'm sure I strangled him in the hut.

A high priest of the temple said: King, why don't we bring him before us and ask him where he is from and who sent him, and why he is here among us.

Centurion

The centurions on watch brought Ammon from the chambers. Satan asked: who are you? Ammon did not understand their language, so Satan called for the devil that studies creatures and he began sign language. Ammon looked outside and saw a lioness feeding her cubs, and pointed at the lioness and put his finger in his mouth and began to suck, pointing at himself.

The kings began to laugh. Satan said: you are a baby lion, and he shook his head, and Ammon started to laugh. Satan began to scratch his head, wondering if he could be the god he wanted to eat that disappeared, standing in front of him.

Satan said to the kings: he is a god. I'll adopt him. Satan called his servants in the palace and told them to teach Ammon how to converse and bring him next full moon, feed him cloth him likc one of his princes in the palace and put a serpent scarab on his forehead.

New moon

Ammon was brought in Satan's chamber and he explained he came from a far country, brought up among creatures, and he was happy to be in this palace. Satan called the high priest to indoctrinate Baby Lion in the commandments and laws, astrology and science of the stars.

Within a short space of time, Ammon could converse and what he learnt with the laws was opposite to Elijah's way. He began to teach the devils and found many faults. The devils began to hate him for being intelligent. Satan put Ammon in charge to teach the princes in the palace.

Satan invited the kings and chief of devils to a banquet with Queen Tamuze and boasted that his Baby Lion was smarter than some devils and asked the high priest to bring him to introduce him to the kings. When he came, Satan said: today you are no more to be called Baby Lion, but Judah.

One of the kings said: if he has to have this name he must accept the covenant of our laws as long as he lives, and if he seeks CHRIST and Elijah he should be put to death like every god on earth.

Satan called Judah and said: you must swear to keep the commandment of the law as long as you live on earth before the kings of the earth. Now worship me and my queen to death. The trumpet was blown loud when Judah swore to worship Satan and Queen Tamuze to death. Satan said: now you shall be like one of my princes in the palace.

Judah rejoiced. He was now a son of the devil in the palace. All godly women in the palace desired him. He was a prince, and he could go in and out of the palace as he pleased.

Satan gave him a chariot and he and the princes would go hunting with their bows and arrows, shooting birds and chasing godly women, drinking, fucking and being arrogant and boastful. He forgot about Elijah. Elijah's way was too straight for him.

Judah trained gods to war and became popular among gods. He built pyramids and palaces for kings in the nations. The devils began to like him as their favourite god of the earth.

Judah became fifth in rank of the devils and a leader of gods on earth and had his own quarters in the palace.

The earth was at peace, and the devils were populating gods. Gods began passing on their seed, making gods much faster than Adam and Eve's people.

Many years later

The devils had a meeting and began to ask questions. We have many gods on earth. Why have CHRIST and Elijah not come to remove them? The devils began to make weapons and teach gods to fight for the earth in case CHRIST and Elijah come to attack them.

The battle for the earth and the world

The secret the devils did not know was that CHRIST was in the body of Adam on earth and Elijah in the body of god, and that CHRIST was not going to leave His kingdom willingly unless He was killed. While He was a spirit in the body of Adam, He had no power. CHRIST had passed on the Word to Elijah, knowing the devils would come after Adam and capture His people. That was the trap and the victory over death.

There was no work for Elijah to do, so he rested until the time came to resurrect Christ to the throne in Heaven. This is where Christ has power to create immortal spirits in the light to establish the kingdom on earth by the WORD. Elijah couldn't do anything, unless there was trouble to speak the Word to resurrect spirits of the people of CHRIST and Zion EVE to be in Heaven, after they Sabbath to be with Christ among angels and to establish the New Testament to create new angels for the world in the Light through Elijah. Meanwhile, Elijah in the body of god, had His rest with the Word.

The world has to be established in the Light in righteousness, truth and justified by the Word to establish the New World in the Light according to the New Testament to remove the devils if they broke the covenant to make a god in the end to dissolve darkness irreversible. This was the purpose of CHRIST of the Eternal – to continue the work in creation by the Word.

PREPARATION 1 Cor;7–9

CHRIST in Adam told His people: I am a living spirit in the body of Adam and every one of your children from my seed shall live for ever, but in order to have eternal life, I must sacrifice my body, for me to create spirits in the Light in the kingdoms on earth.

CHRIST in Adam went on to say: you are immortal living spirits in the Light. No god has a spirit like yours in the kingdom. They are of a different nature from the seed of devils of the dark world. When I sacrifice My body, My spirit shall leave this world and what I leave in this world is My flesh to create immortal spirits with everlasting life in the kingdom. After I cast out the spirits of gods from the seed of the devils from kingdoms, they face judgment by Elijah

Every kingdom on earth Elijah presented to Me will be created. When Elijah speaks the Word it is to create immortal spirits in the Light to continue in the kingdom to populate the earth with spirits of Christ to leave in peace and harmony. After the work in salvation is over there will be no more spirits of gods on the earth in your mother's flesh.

Christ/Adam said: my children, Elijah, do not interfere in human affairs, but you will abide on earth till you Sabbath for your spirit to resurrect to be with Me, where no god or devil can make war on My people.

CHRIST went on to tell His children: the world is between Light and darkness and I can't be the ruler of the world with angels in the Light while I am a spirit in this body. If Elijah is to be the king on earth He must have power over all gods. He must judge every god to rule the earth as king in the kingdom, with immortal spirits in the Light. Through faith, spirits of gods will rest on earth.

When the kingdom of gods is created in salvation, spirits of gods will be cast out for immortal spirits to manifest and will be in their image in righteousness. Therefore the kingdoms will continue with immortal spirits of creation with everlasting life through Elijah after He passes judgment on godly spirits after death, who want to remove us from the earth.

It is only natural, my children, when judgment begins in salvation, the spirits of gods will Passover the kingdom to immortal spirits in the Light manifested in their image to continue in your mother's flesh as you see each other, but the devils can't see you are immortal spirits in the Light, even to this day hey are blind to truth. And see you as a creature with flesh without a spirit.

THE ETERNAL REST OF THE OLD WORLD Lk.6:1

The world of ancient devils will be eliminated for ever, irreversible by the Word. Thus the ruler of the New World will be CHRIST who created Elijah the judge to save you after you Sabbath to be among angels in Heaven.

The Eternal has rested and has faith in His CHRIST to create angels and to put the whole world in the light by the Word.

CHRIST in Adam said: as you can see, my children, Light and darkness has conflict. We live in peace, but the devils outside our gates want to eliminate us from the earth. Peace on earth comes through sacrifice.

THE ULTIMATE LIGHT IS THE PLAN

The work of Elijah is to do with salvation for ultimate Light in the world and to put the devils in captivity with their godly spirits. So the earth can populate in righteousness in kingdoms in the nations, when the battle in the kingdom begins, you will be in Heaven to see the victory over the devil and paradise regained.

The children cried: O Lord, you are wiser than the devils. The elder of CHRIST/Adam's sons asked: my lord, is it possible we can drive out the devils from the earth? CHRIST in Adam said: Son, the devils will be removed from the earth. The kingdoms on earth are occupied with spirits of devils, and they are not accepted in Heaven, my son. There will always be conflict between gods and our people on earth and their end will come in your mother's flesh as the victory over devils with immortal spirits in the Light.

No one can enter a strong man's house and carry off his possessions, unless he first ties up the strong man. Then he can cast out his spirits. It is expedient that My spirit departs from this body to remove the devils to take over the kingdoms on earth from spirits from their seed.

Christ said to his people: the devils will never be forgiven for their sin to make a god in my flesh. They are guilty of an eternal sin to make gods in this world to suffer, for what they do is hidden from gods, but when the spirits of gods are cast out, they will be with no flesh of your mother, to suffer after death through ignorance and deceit, not knowing they had a choice if they had faith.

CHRIST/Adam said: my children, the secret of you being immortal spirits in the kingdom, I have given you to pass on to your children after I have gone but to gods of the devil, it's a parable they can never understand. My children, you can understand because you are holy spirits in the Light in your body, from my seed with your mother, to be with me as the first generation of spirits of the earth.

Elijah is mighty in all secrets of righteousness. He is your saviour who will stand before Me, your Lord, to rule in all generations of the earth. In Him is the spirit of wisdom and understanding to put your immortal spirits to sleep after you Sabbath to resurrect at his good pleasure. Elijah is the judge of the whole earth and only in Elijah must you put your trust to direct your spirits to me to live the eternal life in Heaven.

Christ/Adam said: my children, Elijah is sanctified in the kingdom of god and has the weightier work on earth before me to finish the work in salvation, which I am now testifying, the Eternal Father created me by the WORD and my spirit sanctified in the body Adam in my image to be on the throne in Heaven after My body Sabbath to death.

Now I tell you all this to pass on to your children to have faith in Elijah to save you after I depart from this body, I have enjoyed to be human with you on earth and Elijah My son. Elijah is my first son in creation in salvation in the kingdom from the flesh of your mother. All the people said: Amen.

The preparation of CHRIST

CHRIST in Adam assembled all his people with Zion/Eve and He said: My children, I am harassed by the devils and their gods. They are planning to come in our nation to kill me.

You are all blessed, My children, and bearing children to eternal life. At the moment you live in my presence with your mother, and did not fornicate with gods of the devils.

When your hour comes to depart from your body, you shall be angels ascending to Heaven.

My daughters, CHRIST said: the devils and their gods will find every opportunity to lead you astray to conceive their seed to make gods to do you evil.

The Eternal was wrath with me when your mother conceived god (Cain). We live in peace; the devils and their gods are stealing our sheep, fruit, and corn. Now they are planning to come in our nation to take you in captivity.

Christ/Adam said: I am in distress. I know what I have to do is oblation for Sabbath. Eve began to cry: don't leave me on earth, my lord. Let me Sabbath with you and share this pain with you. The devil raped me to make god (Cain) and want to kill us all because they can't return to Heaven and are jealous of our beautiful children.

Adam said: when the devils come against us you will have rest from this pain, by which I am consumed. Eve made her way to the gates of the city. Satan suddenly came riding on his horse, up to her – Eve said: accursed devil, Elijah is coming after you with the Word. You have no fear of CHRIST and want to come in the holy nation against Adam and our children.

Many generations later, when the earth began to populate **Mt.1:1; Gen.2:4; Heb.3:10; Mt.24:34; Lk.11:31; Ps.33:11; Is.53:8; Ps.14:5; Gen.15:16; Deut.23:2**

In the nation of Adam and Eve and their people there was abundance of food. Their agriculture was fruitful. There was peace and order in their society, with no laws, no need to study sciences. It was built in their nature. There was no disease! Everyone was stable and lived in harmony with each other and was happy with their prosperity. They sang, danced, and praised CHRIST and Elijah their saviour.

The fear of CHRIST and Elijah

The devils were angry to see the prosperity of Adam and Eve in their nation. The devils began to teach their gods how to fight with swords and other weapons of war. Judah taught his battalion how to shoot arrows with the bow, race chariots for war, and taught gods agriculture the way Elijah had showed him, and to raise cattle and other livestock. There was abundance in their nation.

The devils taught gods music, tailoring, and how to make carved images of themselves to worship them as their kings on earth. The devils taught the gods to observe the stars, to heal the sick with herbs and by sorcery, to grow food by watching the full moon, to bring birth in the nation and to bring the first of their female gods to the kings for their harems.

The banquet

Satan invited the kings and commanders of battalions of gods to a banquet, to celebrate his success and the wealth in the nations.

Every king brought his godly queen, princes and princesses to celebrate the king's ball with Queen Tamuze, the mother of gods. Queen Tamuze was dressed in purple and scarlet with a scarab of a jewelled serpent on her head with glittering diamonds, gold amulets with different coloured stones, pearl necklace, perfume that was specially made for Satan to smell on her body, a veil covering her face, handbag, and diamond rings on her finger.

Satan dressed in white linen with a turban on his head, earrings in his ears, a gold ring on every finger, slippers on his feet made from snake skin, and with his crown on his head. All other kings and queens dressed likewise, competing with each other.

The lower ranking devils brought their godly women and their gods. The gods in command brought their godly women given to them as gifts for good work. When they entered the banquet they bowed and worshipped Satan and Queen Tamuze.

Satan gave a speech. He boasted that from the strength of his seed with his queen it has brought much population of gods in the nations, with prosperity, and introduced Judah as his master builder in the nations.

He gave much praise to Judah for teaching gods to shoot arrows for war and helping to set up government and commerce, and being a prophet to gods while they live on earth, to live by the laws of devils.

Satan thanked the other devils for teaching gods the arts to paint, carve images, heal sickness from herbs, sorcery, magic construction and laws of deceit, coveting, sexual immorality, malice, hate, war when they become godly spirits to take the kingdom by force.

The banquet hall was charged with perfume, the devils made for their godly queens. Satan boasted his vision was to turn the world back to darkness and to be the ruler of the world, and all the devils clapped their hands after his speech.

The cooks brought in smoked eels, smoked rats, snake and other smoked creatures as starter, with worms and maggots as a delicacy. Some devils had thirst for blood with a little salt and pepper before the main course after dinner was served.

The commandant of music called the first band to play music for the belly dancers to put on a show for the kings. The band began to play Bangla music and the belly dancers began to compete with each other for a king to take them in a harem to make gods for the king.

The commandant called in the bands to play, one after the other, playing music for dancing. The kings began dancing with their godly queens and everyone began dancing to hot socca music, reggae, soul, with ballad singers singing to the beat of the music. This excited the devils to see the gods make music they never heard in the world. The music of gods was more imaginative than that of the devils, thought Satan, who said to the devil kings: this music will make Elijah and CHRIST jealous and want to come to earth. Satan told Queen Tamuze to dance with Judah.

Satan tempts Judah

Satan said: Judah, the other princes say you are a good dancer among the godly women. Dance with Queen Tamuze. Let me see how both of you dance to the music of gods.

Judah took Tamuze to the floor; the gods began to play his favourite rock music. Judah started to do the twist. Tamuze began to roll and wriggle her buttocks to get Satan jealous, dancing with a god.

Satan said: what is this new dance? Is this to make me jealous? The other princes took hold of the other godly queens to do the rock and roll. This made the other king of devils jealous; they envied Judah for his talent. Judah boasted that he is not afraid of Elijah or CHRIST.

The music was so hot the gods in the street were dancing. They came with banners for war but they threw the banners of war away, and the music of gods made them happy, and they liked the way it was instead of going to war.

While Judah was dancing with Tamuze Satan and the kings decided to set up a meeting to kill Adam next full moon, then said cheers to Satan. Judah was angry every time he saw Queen Tamuze with Satan. **Ex.32:29; 44:18; Ps.78:21**

THE COUNCIL MEETING

The ten kings of devils in the nations sat in council to discuss how to get rid of Adam on earth. One king said: Satan, we are enjoying life with our queens from your seed and populating our nations with gods. If we go and trouble this man created by the Eternal and his people, CHRIST and Elijah are going to come and make war on us and destroy all our gods on earth, and this will be the last we see of daylight if they attack.

Another king said: Satan, after the ball with the mother of gods, I had a chance to think of your vision to bring the world back to darkness. Let us postpone this Sabbath of Adam.

Adam and his WOMAN are not fruitful as we devils, to populate in flesh. We have much choice now with our godly women and, in time, our gods will fuck with the women of Adam and pass on our seed to make gods in his flesh to populate the earth.

Satan replied: I know what you are saying and have thought about it myself, but I am angry and jealous with much hate and malice to kill Adam and fuck his woman, because the god (Cain) I gave her, is now a godly spirit who is fucking our goddess.

Our law for survival is to do evil to rule on earth. Adam threatened me when I tried to take Eve from him with Christ. As you can see, our gods have multiplied more than his people and they will want to fight us for the flesh of Eve.They will say they are born on earth and call us aliens later.

Satan said: we are kings on earth and Judah has authority over our gods to live by our law to death. Though up to this day I don't know where he came from, but he has no fear of death. He is a prophet to our gods. Satan said to the kings: you should be proud of Judah; he has done so much with agriculture for gods to eat.

Another king said: Satan, I am proud of you for making us kings and giving us queens to make our gods, in our nations. Your fearless prince Judah is good at everything, and has no fear. He blasphemes CHRIST and Elijah and hates them like us. Make Judah kill Adam. Adam and Eve and his people are like thorns in our eyes. Some gods have reported when they go and steal fruit in their nation, the people of Adam walk about naked and every time they see their beautiful women they want to rape them.

The devil said: Satan, this excites me and I want to go and steal the woman to make gods. Satan I am sure you feel the same as I do. If we kill Adam there is no reason for the sons of Adam to stay on earth.

Satan said: I am a king with a great problem on earth, burdened with wickedness and hardened in my nature to do much evil to Adam and Eve. Our lust for flesh is out of control and it will consume every devil on earth, now our gods can't stand to see their beautiful naked women and want to rape them. Satan said to the devil: it's just like when we were in Heaven – we could see beautiful angels but according to the covenant we were not allowed to fuck them. We have left Heaven and have the same problem on earth with our gods who see beautiful women and want to fuck them and complain our law is not righteous if they can't do the same as us to make gods with the naked women of Adam.

THE WAY OUT Ps:73.9

One of the kings said: Satan, we have to kill Adam to remove the fear of CHRIST and Elijah attacking us, and take the women captive for our harem so we can bargain with CHRIST and Elijah to leave us alone or we kill all the women of Adam if they attack.

Another king said: Satan, there is a way around it! If we let Judah take the battalion of gods he trained to go and kill Adam, CHRIST and Elijah can't have reason to make war on us, because it's gods of this earth that kill Adam, and not us. Judah's heart is as hard as a creature and has no fear of CHRIST and Elijah. Judah and every god in his battalion has taken the oath according to our law to execute malice, hate, to kill, covet, steal, bear false witness, deceive, and change words in the scriptures to mislead and fight to the end. Satan, you have made Judah a prophet to teach gods everything in your doctrine to fight for the earth with spirits after death.

Let Judah execute judgment on Adam for us with his battalion to be our witness in case CHRIST and Elijah come after us to say it's not devils who killed Adam.

In Zion, I lay a cornerstone Pro.21:14; Ps.73:9; Mt.12:34; P.119 100 Nu.2010:11

All the kings agreed that Judah's faith should be tried with our law and put Adam to death. The high priest called Judah to come and swear by the Ten Commandments to have faith in the law of the kings of devils to death.

Judah has one desire to be a king with the kings of devils on earth. He is angry and envies Satan's power and want a chance to make a name for himself. So far Judah has kept the knowledge of the kingdom Elijah had taught him, as his secret. The devils did not know.

Judah was brought in the chambers for a council meeting with the kings and bowed to the knee before them. Satan said: Judah, you are master in everything you do. There is famine in the nations and our gods are getting agitated with hunger. There is much disease and the gods are fighting each other for food.

There is much food in the nations of Adam and his people. We have a covenant with death and Hell. If we made gods that is why we gave you authority to rule our gods by the ten commandments of our law. **Deut.7:13 Ps.21:19**

You are a prophet to the gods on earth, to live by the law of devils to death. Adam and his people have an abundance of food in their nation, while our gods are hungry and dying. The anger in my heart, I put it into your heart. I'll have no peace until you accomplish my hate and malice. **Ezek.7:3; Nah.3:8**

Take the legion of soldiers you have trained, and go to the nation of Hebrews and kill Adam. Leave the rest of his people for us kings to deal with. After you kill Adam, report to me in the palace.

This is your first mission to prove your hate for CHRIST and Elijah. We expect success from your hand. Judah left the council meeting in haste, put on his coat with many colours, and called a battalion of soldiers with bows and arrows to ride the horses and chariots. **Eph.6:20; Ezek.17:15; Is.47:6**

The battalion left in the night carrying torches to the nations till they got to the nation of Adam.

Use restraint

CHRIST in Adam knew His time had come to put His plan to the world. He kissed Eve and his people goodbye and said: my time has come to do the work I am created to do. My spirit can't do anything while I live in this body and for Elijah to do His work on earth in righteousness. Today is the beginning of judgment on the earth until I return in the kingdom for final judgment.

The people gathered around Adam. CHRIST said: my people, use restraint and give no god a reason to attack you. In peace I live you on earth. The son of god (Cain) has gathered his soldiers to come to our nation.

CHRIST/Adam said: my children, I know you will weep after I'm gone, but the world will rejoice. You will have grief and harassment, but it will turn to joy. I'm leaving the earth as I came. I have made known to you all things before it takes place. Elijah is having His rest. I'll wake Him up after I depart from this body to finish My work on the earth. **1.Pet.2:8; 2:24; Deut.21:22–23; Is.5:19; Jn.9:25–34,39; Jn.10:34; 12;34**

CHRIST in Adam could hear the noise of chariots and horses racing towards His nation. When they arrived they waited for daybreak and rode up to the gate of the nations.

The soldiers shouted: Adam! Come forth to the gate. Adam walked slowly towards the gate and stood before Judah and the battalion of soldiers, naked. Judah looked at Him fiercely with hate. Adam looked at him,

CHRIST in Adam knew He was the son of god (Cain) with His daughter Tamah held in captivity in bondage under oath, who Satan strangled. Judah began calculating: maybe CHRIST is a SPIRIT in Adam, because Adam was not afraid of him and his battalion of soldiers.

Judah drew near and said: where is Adam's house? Show me.

CHRIST in Adam said: why have you come here with your battalion of soldiers, dressed in a coat in many colours to do battle with me? Judah held Adam by his beard and said: I want you to fight me to death. In front my soldiers in your nation. Show me where CHRIST is or else I will fight with you to death if you don't show me where CHRIST is.

CHRIST/Adam said: I am an old man, who you want to do battle with. Judah said: I want you to hand over your nation and all your people to me, willingly, as a gift to the devils. CHRIST/Adam said: I can't do that. All people are from My flesh and are in the hand of Elijah.

Judah said: I command you by the law, to hand over your people in your nation. If you are not willing, I shall cast you into a pit where no one will see you or even hear of this day. I set before you, life or death.

CHRIST/Adam said: it's in your nature to do me harm from the hardness of your heart, and want to cast my body into a pit, a man of peace who has done no evil to you on earth and protected by CHRIST.

Judah said: come follow me up this high ground by the tree and I'll tell you what is in my heart and what I will do to you this day. CHRIST/Adam said: you are arrogant and have no respect, speaking to me this way.

Christ/Adam said: it is the same arrogance god (Cain) your father spoke to me and left Tamah pregnant with you in her womb to be an adopted god like god your father. Now he cries in the heat for what he did to your mother to make a god to be like him. I am an old man with grey hairs before you, naked and you are ordering me by the law of devils to come up to a tree with no fruit.

By the tree CHRIST/Adam said to Judah: whose ox have I slain, or whose daughter have I taken away in captivity to oppress by your law? Who have I defrauded or with which devil have I conspired with, to receive a bribe, or which god is of my seed that is born in my flesh? Tell me!

CHRIST is witness.

Judah said before his soldiers: CHRIST is witness this day. You have not made a god because you are not a devil. Only devils can make gods in flesh, to pass on their seed to make spirits for their world.

CHRIST/Adam said: Judah, Elijah forbids that you should not go against CHRIST. I'll teach you the good way like Elijah, who adopted you. Consider the way he brought you up and what He has done for you to do good on earth for gods, but you have no faith.

If you do wickedly to my people or me, you shall be condemned like the devils. And every god from your seed will be judged in the end of days by CHRIST and Elijah.

When the commander of his soldiers heard he said: Judah, did you hear what this old man said to you? Judah became angry and held Adam by his beard and pushed him and said: where is CHRIST and Elijah?

Adam kept His cool and said: Judah! Why have you come here in a peaceful nation dressed in a coat with many colours with a battalion of gods in uniform with bows and arrows to slay me? Why did Satan and the devils chose you to fight me and not come himself with the devils. If you kill me, you will be a murderer like god your father, and Elijah will abandon you for ever.

CHRIST will prevail against Satan and the devils if you kill me, then Elijah shall serve Him kingdoms from my flesh and not you. Judah, why are you against me? It's the devils you should be against for what they do to your mother.

Go and tell the devils to come and fight me as a man. It's the second time I ask you to go and tell the devils to come and fight me, but you insist to do evil to make a name for yourself. You are a youth and know nothing about battle.

Judah held Adam by his beard, full of hate and felt humiliated and said: you are an old man and inferior to the devils. Who do you think you are? The devils hate Elijah and CHRIST; I took the oath, because I hate CHRIST and Elijah. I do not believe CHRIST or Elijah will come and save you, Adam.

CHRIST/Adam said: Judah, if you kill me CHRIST and Elijah will remove the devils and gods from the earth. Judah shouted with anger and boasted: I am a prince and live in the palace of Satan. There is no one on earth who can remove the devils from the earth. We are gods from the seed of the devils, populating the nations with gods, whereas you are a few; your males have little seed and can't populate fast like us.

CHRIST/Adam said: if you don't stop boasting in front of the soldiers, Elijah will come and remove you. If He speaks the Word from the mouth of god your father, he will throw you in the pit to be with devils and god your father, who is sorrowful and cries for making a god to be wicked like him on earth. All the soldiers began laugh at Judah.

Judah said: Adam, if Elijah speaks the Word and casts out the kings and the devils, I will be the god of the earth and be king. I am sent by Satan to kill you with all the hate in my heart. When I am a godly spirit I'll be king and challenge Elijah for the earth.

CHRIST/Adam said: the commandments in our nation say thou shall not kill. Judah said: you have a law by ONE who is elusive. No one knows who CHRIST is. I'll kill you so I can see him after you are dead.

JUDAH PUT ADAM TO THE TEST Ro.8:20; IS:47.6

Judah said: Adam, why is it you and your people don't put clothes on your bodies? CHRIST/Adam said: I came in this world naked and so are my people, who will leave without flesh after they Sabbath.

Judah said: you and your people live in hope CHRIST will save you from death. CHRIST/Adam said: for the third time, I ask you to go and tell Satan to come and fight me as a man who stands for peace, but you insist to be the first god to cast the first stone on my body.

CHRIST/Adam said: Judah, I warn you not to kill me before the battalion. They will be your witness on earth and will tell all gods on earth and their spirits will blame you after death when they come before the judge of the earth. Judah got angry and said: I am a prince in the palace of Satan and hope to be a king after death.

CHRIST/Adam said: you secretly envy Satan who has your mother in bondage under the law and you are afraid, if you don't kill me, what he will do to you. Secretly you want to be a king in your deceit like god your father, who conspired with the devils to kidnap your mother.

The unleavened bread

Judah said: my soldiers have been riding for days without food and they are hungry. If you have faith in CHRIST, put CHRIST to the test and make him feed my soldiers with bread. CHRIST in Adam said: Judah, make your soldiers sit on the grass and sit with them. The soldiers began to laugh at Adam naked before them. CHRIST/Adam said: you see the small sheep in the field? I'm going to stand near it. Watch, so you can tell gods what you see. The sun began to shine bright on Adam's body. It dazzled the gods. Adam held his hands up towards the sun and suddenly bread began to fall on the grass by the soldiers. The soldiers picked up the bread.

The first Passover of ancient days Mt.4:1

Eve came with an alabaster box with ointment and said: what has my man done to you, Judah? You come to our nation with soldiers to kill Adam. The soldiers began to laugh at this old naked woman and said: go back.

CHRIST/Adam said to the soldiers: leave her alone. She came to anoint my body before it become a sacrifice to death. You will always have Judah with you. Judah, tell Satan your king that Eve anointed my body before you throw it in the pit. It will remind him of god your father he strangled. After he held your mother in captivity, pregnant with his accursed seed of Satan.

Eve returned to her people, crying, saying: Judah's father killed Abel. Now his son wants to kill Adam, bringing a curse on this earth with satanic gods.

Adam said: Judah, it is better you were eaten at birth.

By the devil, Judah said: I won't eat flesh from your body, nor will I drink your blood. Adam said: you are in my flesh and will be out of it and also spirits from your seed will be judged after death if you kill me. Elijah will return the spirits from your seed to you if they don't have faith like you, and you will receive them at the gate after death.

Judah said: today you will not go in the pyramids to sleep, but in the chambers of death and god my father will kill you if you go there for giving Elijah his kingdom on earth. I hate Him in my father's image.

Adam said: you hate Elijah who brought you up, and hate CHRIST who you have not seen, and love Satan, who holds your mother in captivity in bondage under oath. Judah felt humiliated and spat in Adam's face.

Satan sent me to kill you. It is according to the law for gods to live on earth until death. Christ/Adam said: you are in fear of CHRIST like the devils. Judah answered: you put your faith in CHRIST, who you have not seen, to save you from death. I fear no one. Not even Elijah who brought me up.

One of the soldiers took a sword to slay Adam. Judah said: put a hood over his head. Judah smote Adam in his face and asked: who is it that slaps thee? The soldiers began swearing – fucking this and that, tell Christ to come and save you from us.

The ancient Passover. Paradise lost Is.66:3; Hos.4:2; 2.Cor.3:6; Heb.2:14–15

Judah said: Adam, tell me who is the CHRIST and I will let you go.

CHRIST/Adam said: if I told you, you will not believe and if I ask you who Elijah is, you will not answer before your soldiers. I am contented. CHRIST is my hand and my eyes and will sacrifice my body to death of his body, so your king can reign by force and boast about destroying Adam in PARADISE on earth. CHRIST'S throne is in Heaven, where your king of devils can't sit. Elijah will have no mercy on you if you and your king kill any of my people in the nation.

Judah said: where is he? Adam said: Elijah will punish you and every spirit from your seed. The commandant said: Judah, who is this Elijah Adam keeps speaking about?

Judah looked at him with anger. The soldiers brought a colt among their horses and they put Adam to sit on it, took a rope made a noose and put it around Adam's neck, and tied the end to the branch on the tree.

The death of Adam Ro.5:14–15, 18

Judah said: If you don't tell me who CHRIST is, what is your last word? CHRIST/Adam asked Judah: is it lawful to save an innocent man or kill him? You are the prophet with the law, to teach gods to live by the law and have authority over them. I've told you to go and tell Satan to come against me but you want to be a murderer like god (Cain). If you steal and rape any of the woman in my nation to pass on the accursed seed, woe is unto you and all from your seed.

Judah got angry, took the rod in his hand and hit the colt. It jumped and went forward and left the body of Adam hanging on the tree. Judah said: let us wait to see if CHRIST will save him or if Elijah will come and snatch his naked body from us **1.Pet.2:23–24; Jer.1:11; 1:2**

The body yielded to death, and the SPIRIT CHRIST came out of His body. He who hung Adam on a tree, it was written, is of the accursed seed of god. **Deut.21:16; 18:22; Ps.9:13–14; Pro.16:18, 23**

The soldiers took the body of Adam and put it on the colt, removed the rope from his neck, and rode off with the body. When they arrived in the valley, Judah took the body and threw it in a pit. Then he took a big stone and threw it on the body. Judah and his battalion rode back to their nation.

Judah went to the palace of Satan, and said: O King, Adam is dead. **Is.65; Ro.9:18; Rev.16:21**

Satan took a ring off his finger and put it on the finger of Judah. Judah bowed on his knee. Satan removed a gold chain from his neck and put it around Judah's neck, said thanks, and made Judah second ruler after him in the nation.

Judah went to his chamber in the palace, keeping the secret of the kingdom to himself and waited for the opportunity for him to be a king. **Deut.7:9; 13:22**

Satan became afraid of Judah, because he had no fear of CHRIST and knew that secretly Judah cunningly wanted power to be a king to rule gods. Satan told Tamuze: Judah killed your father, so she could hate Judah and keep away from him. **1.Pet.2:8; Gen.49:11**

The death of Adam and the resurrection of CHRIST'S holy spirit

(Zion) Eve went outside the gates and fell on the ground and began to cry for Christ: O my lord, O my lord, take me with you to Heaven.

Elijah came and picked her up and said: CHRIST has come out of the body of Adam. His spirit has gone to war with the ancient devils.

Eve cried: Elijah, the holy work of CHRIST is in your hands. She fell on her knees and said: Elijah, save me from the devils.

Eve was holding her hands over her head and all her children began to weep for her without Adam and the dread of the devils coming after them.

Michael came to take the body of Adam back to the Eternal who created the image of His CHRIST after the Sabbath to death. (The gods must to do the same before they Sabbath to have faith to be saved by Elijah in salvation.) **1.Cor.6:20; 4:7; 9:16; Ps.19:1**

THE ENTRANCE OF THE ANCIENT WORLD

When CHRIST' spirit got to the reception, a goddess opened thc Book of the Dead and asked: who are you? You don't look like a devil! Are you the one who divided our world between Light and darkness?

I am CHRIST, son of the ETERNAL! My visit is to put the world in order for peace. The receptionist said: the king of devils is my father. He is chained to death by Satan and other devils. The king of devils said: only your ETERNAL father can unchain him.

Why did the ETERNAL send you to be among devils? Satan is not here. He went on a mission on earth to destroy you. All the chambers are full of devils; go and see if you find one that is empty and wait till Satan return. He would be delighted to see you in this world.

The goddess is crying for Satan to satisfy her. He left her to fuck the woman on earth to make gods for this world. Now that you are in this world you can't get out of here. Only the goddess has the key to the exit. If she lets you out to return to earth, send Satan to her. She is driving us crazy in here. We have no peace. It's hell since he left her to go and make gods with the woman of flesh.

She boast the Holy Eternal Spirit is the only spirit perfect in the Light, that can unchain the king of the devils of the Ancient World from the covenant to death if he ever made a god with The Eternal's creation or any devil made a god is to dissolve darkness in the world and all devils, and spirits from their seed by the Word.

If you came to unchain the king of devils, the goddess will come after you for unchaining the most wicked devil in this world. The receptionist asked CHRIST: what is your purpose to be here before I let you in the chamber? CHRIST said: my purpose in this world is to put it in order. At the moment it is totally out of order.

The New Testament begin from here to make the Old Covenant obsolete because the Old Covenant with the king of devils is ancient, based on peace and respect, and has now collapsed. Light and darkness can't be in the same world. One must eliminate the other irreversibly.

Also there is division on the earth. One must eliminate the other. The plan for the kingdom is to have immortal spirits in the Light with everlasting life by the Word after all spirits from the seed of devils are removed from the kingdom, and return to the devils spirits who have no faith.

The receptionist asked: if you succeed with this master plan, what will happen to god (Cain)? I heard he is the first god of Satan my father? He is my kindred from the same seed? CHRIST said: he did the same as Satan – killed my son and raped my daughter to make a god. He had no faith and will be with the devils for breaking the covenant for making a god in the flesh of my daughter. All spirits from his seed will be carried away to the gate of the sun if they don't have faith to rest in peace for eternity.

The receptionist at the entrance said: I fear that if you go out, you'll be a danger to our world in darkness. Go see if you can get a chamber that is open and wait until Satan returns to decide your fate.

In the maze

CHRIST began to search in the labyrinth of tunnels until HE saw a door in the first chamber. HE broke the seal and opened the door and many devils inside saw a great Light standing by the door and they began to scream in fear and asked: who are you?

I am CHRIST.

They asked: what do you want? It is not time to stoke the fire. CHRIST closed the door and sealed it with a new combination.

Outside of the chamber, CHRIST took a look around in the tunnel and saw a second chamber. HE opened the door and a devil came towards HIM furiously and hit CHRIST'S head against the wall. CHRIST could see him, but the devil could not see CHRIST, as his light was too bright for his eyes. The devil fled into the dark, and swung a chain at CHRIST. It missed.

CHRIST pulled the devil inside as he was trying to escape, and closed the chamber and sealed it.

CHRIST went deeper into the labyrinth and saw a third chamber. The door was sealed like the previous two. CHRIST broke the seal and entered the chamber. Inside, the king of the darkworld was chained to death, the most deadly killer in the world, and the most feared by every devil. The king of devils.

The king shouted: what do you want? Satan chained me and you divided my world. Last time I saw you was before you resurrected to your world in the Light. All I get from the goddess is insults. You are a holy one, who will do good in the next world. Why did you come back? Is it to take the goddess with you or is it to give me back my entire world, so it can be the way it was? Set me free from this covenant of death. I am in chains. If you have a good heart, set me free.

CHRIST said: I am the son of The Holy Eternal who divided the world between Light and darkness, and I've come to make the covenant obsolete because the devils made a god in my flesh and hanged my body on a tree. Satan declared war on angels in the Light. He has entered paradise on earth and raped (Zion) EVE and made a god in her flesh. It is clear to me that angels in the Light and devils can't co-exist in peace. His god raped my daughter to make him a god in my flesh and now Satan has captured my daughter and hold her in bondage under oath of devils.

Her son has hanged my body on a tree. That is why I'm going to destroy the evil in this world and I'll begin with you, who made Satan and the devils to do your wickedness with war, hate, and jealousy for the Eternal's creation in his part of the world in the Light.

The Battle of Armageddon

CHRIST looked at the king of devils chained to death. Christ commanded the chain to break, and the king of devils was free. With hate he came at Christ with great force. CHRIST fell to the ground. As Christ was getting back on His feet, he came at CHRIST and butted HIM in the head. CHRIST fell back on the ground. He took an iron bar and swung at CHRIST.

CHRIST held on to the bar. The king of the devils and HIM were putting their strength and power to the test. CHRIST overpowered him and took the bar and threw it aside.

The king of devils ran out of the death chamber where he had been chained. He ran into the main chamber, where multitudes of devils were together with the goddess, and closed the door behind him. He shouted breathlessly: CHRIST is here to destroy us! The devils began to scream in fear of CHRIST. **Act.20:8**

The devils that were cast out of Heaven were with the goddess. The king of devils got jealous and held the goddess by her throat: you fucking bitch! You see this bastard Satan of yours has brought CHRIST to destroy us in our world!

First it was the good Eternal, who you divinely praise, divided our world with a covenant of peace between his angels in His world in Light and devils in our world in darkness. Now His CHRIST wants to eliminate us for eternity!

The goddess cried O king, this bastard Satan with his false vision. I warned him to leave the woman alone.

I told him she is pure flesh and trouble will come if he ever made gods in her flesh. Most of the devils cast out of Heaven are here and did not follow Satan to earth said: O King, this CHRIST and His Elijah are like slime in our world. They work together with a new system. They call it in Heaven the New Testament. You can never catch them together. While one sleeps the other is awake. They work in code with a Word that can penetrate anywhere in the universe. They are out to have dominion in every world. Let us hold CHRIST here and chain HIM to death. Let the goddess go out to seduce HIM to see where HE get HIS power from and you can use it to bring the world back to darkness.

The world is the prize

CHRIST found the door to the main chamber and opened it. The devils saw CHRIST standing in the Light. They could not see because HIS Light was too bright for their eyes, and they fell on each other in fear. The goddess ran out crying: have mercy… have mercy on me, holy one, and went to her lunar chamber in fear of the king of devils.

The devils that were in the main chamber went numb with fear when they saw CHRIST hold the king of the devils and throw him on top of the devils for trying to chain Him to death. Christ closed the door to the chamber of death.

Slowly they came forward. The devils had no other choice but to attack to chain CHRIST to death. When they got to the area of the trap which the Eternal had set up before he divided the world, CHRIST said: come forward, all of you. I'll show you my power. He put HIS hands up. They stood trembling in fear. They looked up to His outstretched hands. CHRIST kicked the release control under HIS feet and the devils fell into thc pit, one on top of the other.

THE SWORD OF DEATH WITH FOUR BEASTS Deut.32:25; Rev.4:6

The king of devils managed to escape through a secret door in the main chamber with the four beasts guarding his throne with the sword of death.

The king sat on his throne with four beasts chained to it. CHRIST found the door to the secret chamber to the throne. He sat with the sword in his hand. The room was walled with mirrors to give a false impression of where he was sitting on the throne. **Rev.4:9; 5:6**

The king of devils let loose one beast called War. It had eyes in the front and back and it began coming at CHRIST with fire from its nostrils and smoke from its mouth, roaring. The place trembled with its noise to kill CHRIST, but because of the mirror it didn't know where CHRIST was. The beast was seeing CHRIST everywhere.

CHRIST kicked the dust on the ground and it became flies and they began to go in the eyes of the beast called War and it became useless and couldn't see.

The king of devils let loose the next beast called Hate. It began to growl, making a lot of noise. The king shouted at the beast: kill! Kill! The beast began breathing out smoke and fire as it got close to CHRIST. CHRIST kicked the dust and the flies began to fly on the beast, blocking its eyes and going up its nose.

CHRIST looked at the other two beasts and the chains broke. They looked at HIM and at the king of devils. CHRIST said: Peace and Love, and they began to attack War and Hate. **Jam.7:11; Rev.4:7, 4:9**

The king of devils became angry seeing the two beasts had turned against him, and began attacking, brandishing the sword of death at CHRIST. CHRIST held his hand with the sword. **Rev.5:9, 6:1**

CHRIST held the strain and overpowered him and held the sword of death. The king of the devils began to cry: don't take my part of the world. The two beasts, Peace and Love, picked up the king of devils and followed CHRIST back to the main chamber and cast him in the pit. The two beasts Peace and Love took the two beasts War and Hate, and cast them in the pit upon the devils to wait for final judgment.

The other devils, chained in the other chambers, Love and Peace cast in the pit to wait for final judgment. CHRIST then sealed the pit and left Peace and Love to guard the pit. **Rev.5:6, 6:1, 15:7**

CHRIST closed all escape routes to the earth.

The goddess at the exit from the Ancient World Rev.15:2

After CHRIST finished HIS work in the dark world, CHRIST rested. The goddess came from her lunar chamber and saw CHRIST asleep. She began her enchantment to seduce HIM to deep sleep.

The earth began to shake where Elijah was having His rest and He woke up and said: Wake up, CHRIST my lord. CHRIST came out of HIS sleep. The goddess made herself pretty and attractive, using her seductive charm and said: son of my Eternal, you have won the victory over devils in the pit. CHRIST, there are many kinds of death. You have to conquer before you leave here to be on the throne with victory. I am a goddess because I have given birth to all the death in the world. I am a mother to death and have the key to the exit to death. If anyone lives here, it is to bring death in the world. **Rev.15:2** Come with me to my lunar chamber and stay with me, or take me with you and I will be satisfied.

CHRIST said: if I take you with me, you will contaminate my world with death and disease. The goddess said: your father left me with this bastard. He threw me in the pit when I was pregnant with the Light and the Word. You came here and unchained him. He has been cruel to devils and me. It took many devils to cast him in the pit with all his cruelty, hate and malice and envy for the Eternal with the Word.

You want to leave me here all alone while Satan is fucking your daughter to make gods to pass on his seed to make spirits that can't satisfy me with women on earth. Don't send his spirits to me to cry for your flesh. I let Satan out of this world thinking there would be peace. Now you have come here to destroy death and want to get out by the exit to earth.

CHRIST said: I didn't come here to do you harm, so let me go out in peace. The goddess said: if I let you out, you would not come back, just like your Eternal Father. I suffered so much for Him with the Word. He never came back. I still feel the pain from His birth in the pit.

I was so proud to see my belly in the Light in this dark pit. It was like the full moon. The king of the devils cast me pregnant in the same pit you cast him in and it is justified. I wish I didn't have visions to do good in this world. A good spirit is your father in perfect Light. My king did much evil to me, for doing good in this world.

Don't leave me here, CHRIST, to be torn between good and evil. CHRIST said: this is your problem. You are either evil or you are good. You want both at the same time to satisfy you. You can't have Light and darkness in the same place.

The Eternal has suffered much and took insults by Satan, who tormented you with lust and He sent him back to you. If you didn't let Satan out of the exit, he would not have trespassed and raped my woman created pure, to make this god to destroy paradise.

You cannot have me, no matter how charming you seem to be. I can't commit adultery. It's not in me. I have Eve Zion; she is My queen for ever, who the Eternal created with me. Please let me out in peace, so I can continue My work.

Disease by death

The goddess said no, and became jealous over Zion and spewed death of cancer, death of leprosy, and all the diseases of death the king of devils had given her. She spewed it all over CHRIST, but He was immune. When there was no more disease to come out of her mouth, she collapsed and fell down before CHRIST and passed out. All she had left now was to seduce Christ to do good or evil in the world.

VICTORY OVER DEATH Ro.6:9–13

CHRIST did HIS holy work and shut all exits of the Old World that lead to earth, and took a rest before going to Hades to set a trapdoor for Satan and the devils and godly spirits of gods to wait for final judgment from the earth for ever.

The goddess made herself attractive and came from her lunar chamber and saw CHRIST resting. She tried to use her magic power to seduce HIM to a deep sleep and said: now I have him all to myself. There is no jealous devil left. He can sire me with everything good.

The earth began to tremble where Elijah had His rest and He sprang up from His sleep and said: CHRIST my lord, wake up from this sleep. The words got to CHRIST and He woke up to see the goddess near HIM, doing enchantments over HIM.

She said: you have cast the king of devils to the pit with all the devils I made for him but there are two hundred devils left and they are on earth making gods. CHRIST, It is only you and I left in this Ancient World.

If you want the key, come with me in my lunar chamber to make an angel with me, or take me with you and I'll be satisfied.

CHRIST said: if I took you with me, you will contaminate my flesh on earth with death and disease. The goddess said: your father left me with this brute you threw in the pit along with the devils cast out from Heaven. Now you want to leave me all alone with two beasts, Peace and Love. And later you'll send the godly spirit of Satan who rapes your daughter to fuck with me. They can't satisfy me. They are not strong like devils and will be crying for flesh on earth.

I let Satan and two hundred devils out of the exit, thinking I should be fucking with kings on earth and eating flesh of creatures to satisfy me. Instead they built a tower in Babylon to fall on gods for their spirit to go in everlasting fire. When I saw this vision of what Satan and the other devils make their gods do on earth for flesh, Christ, you have a reason to be angry to send them in the everlasting fire in this world.

CHRIST said: I didn't come to do you harm so let me out in peace. The goddess said: if I let you out, you will do the same like the Eternal. When He spoke the Word there was one big explosion in the world and there was light.

I was so proud to see Light and stars, glittering in the dark. The king of the devils was jealous and also Satan and other devils of the Eternal. He divided the world between Light and dark from the Word that came from his mouth.

The goddess said: I wish I didn't have visions to do good in this world with my enchantment to encourage your father's spirit to come in this world. He created himself perfect with the Word and HE want a good world without evil in it.

I am evil and want good. The Eternal is a good spirit. I asked him to come in the world to make it a better world. I don't know where He came from. The goddess said: Satan deceived me too. CHRIST, don't leave me here to be torn by two beasts Peace and Love.

CHRIST said: this is your problem. You want both. Neither can satisfy you.

The Eternal had restrained Himself from punishing Satan and his devils, suffered much insults from Satan and his devils tormenting angels, created good and pure, and cast him and the devils out of his world back to you.

If you didn't let him out of this exit, he would not rape my woman, created pure, to make this god (Cain). You can't have me. I can't commit adultery, I love Zion. She is my queen. The Eternal created us to be together for ever and if I went with you it would be an abomination.

Let me out, goddess, so I can go about My business in the world. She said no and became jealous of Zion who is the spirit of Eve and spewed death of cancer at CHRIST from her mouth to contaminate Him, but CHRIST was immune to it.

The goddess hands over the key

The goddess spewed out of her mouth leprosy and every disease that causes death on CHRIST, but HE was immune to all the diseases. When she had no more disease to spew out, she collapsed and took dust and threw it over her head and said: now you are holy and pure like the Eternal. Here is the key to lock me up in this Ancient World alone with the two beasts.

The goddess began crying: O CHRIST, have mercy. The cry echoed in the world for all to hear to keep away from doing evil on earth or perish.

Enter through the narrow gate that leads to Hades Mt.7:13

CHRIST said: goddess, salvation is far off. Will you take the job as a receptionist at the entrance at Hades? She said: to do what? HE said: it is not good you are alone here when you can work in Hades to weigh every spirit of gods that enter. Take their names and enter them in the Book of the Dead for the final judgment in the everlasting fire when they leave Hades.

She accepted the job as receptionist in Hades. CHRIST said: I'll let you out at the narrow gate so you can journey to Hades to direct the spirits to the chambers.

This will be the New Testament between you and I. Elijah will be the judge to return every spirit from the seed of gods that comes from the flesh of Zion and Jerusalem that has no faith in Elijah to save will join Satan and the two hundred devils you let out of the Old World. They will stay in the chambers till the final judgment to everlasting fire in the sun.

Elijah will direct images/kingdoms prepared for salvation to have immortal spirits from one end of the earth to the other. After I cast their godly spirits from the kingdom Elijah will send the godly spirits that have no faith in him to you, enter their names in the Book of the Dead and lock them up in the chamber in the fire of Hades with Satan and the devils.

The Eternal only accepts immortal spirits that are created holy by the Word in the flesh of Zion and Jerusalem through Christ. Goddess, you will be satisfied with all the spirits from the seed of Satan and the devils, who have no faith and choose to be in fire in Hades, for doing the work of devils while they were in the kingdom and against the New Testament for peace.

Goddess, you will remain in Hades until the last spirit from the seed of devils departs from the kingdom in the final judgment to everlasting fire in the sun and the earth becomes a paradise. As it was in the beginning with immortal spirits by the WORD.

The goddess said: now I will be satisfied for a good world without devils.

The journey to earth

Michael came on a chariot of black horses to the cloud of the earth and waited. Elijah and Eve went to the pit where Judah had thrown the body of Adam.

Elijah went to the pit and brought up the body of Adam. It had no smell or disease or was going rotten; it was holy pure flesh. Michael came down from the cloud and Elijah gave Michael the body. He put the body inside the chariot. Eve began to cry: O Elijah, the son of god has brought shame on me. Elijah comforted her.

Elijah spoke the Word and the wind came unto the clouds and took Michael and the body to the Eternal in the heaven of heavens.

CHRIST'S journey to the earth Gen.1:9

CHRIST put new shutters to the sea with doors and set new plates to the earth, and the entrance for the spirits that have no faith in Elijah to enter Hades to wait for the final judgment.

HE set up the portals in the north for air to go through the portal in the south to circulate air to make mist and clouds for the battle of the kingdom, when he would return to cast out spirits from the kingdoms on earth to create immortal spirits in the light to continue in their image to populate the earth with immortal spirits through Elijah with the Word.

Christ set the up watercourse to water the earth for vegetation and drinking, water to flow from rivers and streams. HE set up Hades in the bowels of the earth to be on, in fire and vents to release the heat into the sea to rise and make rain upon the earth.

Global heat in the end of days Gen.1:6

CHRIST set up three portholes – north east to south for the wind to blow on the ice, south west and north to bring hail, frost, snow and rain, and north west to south to cool the earth up to the time of salvations after the flood. When the water upon the earth is driven to the north and south it will be frozen till salvation.

Christ created portals north east to south and south west to north for hot air from the sun to blow on the ice to scatter mist and clouds in the nation in the time of salvation.

This holy work is for Elijah to command the wind on the earth for when Christ returns in salvation to create immortal spirits in kingdoms in the nations on earth. After Christ casts out the spirits of gods, Elijah will save who have faith and pass on those who have no faith to the spirit of the sun to remove them from the earth to the gate of the sun, till the end of spirits of god in the kingdoms on earth.

When Elijah speaks the Word immortal spirits that sleep on earth will wake up to resurrect to Christ in the cloud to take them to Heaven. The spirits of gods which are cast out from the kingdom with no faith in Elijah, the spirit of the sun will remove from the earth to the gate of the sun to fall in the fire for eternity.

THE THRONE IS THE PRIZE Gen.1:2–3

The throne in Heaven was prepared before CHRIST was created in the world by the Eternal. He declared when CHRIST come into the world HE would sit on this magnificent throne to dispense justice, righteousness and have authority to rule the world under a New Testament to make the covenant with devils obsolete when his son Elijah speaks the Word.

The Eternal said: he will take His rest from the covenant between Him and the devils of ancient darkness for His CHRIST to establish His testament to create new angels in the light, to put the world in the Light by the Word if the devils made a god with His creation.

The throne in Heaven is the finest in all worlds. When Christ takes over to continue the work in creation HE will sit with sovereign power, dignity, with authority to rule all worlds by the Word.

The throne of the Eternal Holy Father is the highest of Heaven, the place where He will magnify his power and glory and show his majesty and be served by angels.

From the throne in Heaven CHRIST will execute justice and judgment to establish the New Testament in the world, to build unto his foundation, to populate the world with new spirits in the Light from His seed, and by the

Word in salvation through Elijah, for new spirits to have glory, honour and dignity, created by the Word to possess eternal life in the Light, as subjects of CHRIST and Zion among angels from HIS flesh on earth.

The journey to earth

All the angels in Heaven were waiting for CHRIST to come to Heaven from the battle of Armageddon. Eve was with Elijah, waiting to see her CHRIST in the spirit.

Jesus came down with a carriage with white horses, waiting for Christ on the clouds to submerge from the water. Every angel in Heaven was tense, waiting for this victory over devils and to meet CHRIST for the first time.

Suddenly CHRIST emerged from the deep and began walking on the waters. He came to Elijah and Eve and said: Elijah, everything is now in your hands on earth. Save my people's spirits after they Sabbath and resurrect them to me. CHRIST began to walk to the clouds. CHRIST met Jesus and they embraced each other with joy. Jesus was happy to be with his father. They hugged each other, and then they waved to Elijah and Eve and went inside the carriage.

There was thunder and lightning all over the earth and rain and the leaves on the branches of trees on earth clapping vigorously by strong wind. The Eternal said: My son, I love you. Come up on the throne prepared for you to sit in majesty, honour and to have authority to rule the world. When Satan and the devils heard the Eternal's voice they were in fear of their end on earth.

Eve and Elijah were happy to see CHRIST and Jesus together. Elijah spoke the Word and the wind came unto the clouds to take up CHRIST and Jesus to Heaven. CHRIST went in the tabernacle and sat on the throne to take power to rule the world with authority, and to create angels in the Light and remove devils on earth to the final judgment.

There was clapping in Heaven, with shouts of hallelujah Elijah, hallelujah Christ, Lord of the WORLD, from the kingdom of Adam.

The angels blew their trumpets in Heaven, to welcome CHRIST in Heaven. There was much excitement in Heaven, angels singing and dancing for CHRIST to sit on the throne in victory over devils. They began to sing: the kingdom of the world has become the kingdom of CHRIST to reign for ever.

Twenty-four elders, who sat on thrones, came with joy and fell on their knees and bowed to CHRIST with respect and said: praise be to you, CHRIST the Lord of the universe. Reign with power. Rule and have dominion in the worlds.

Hail Elijah, judge the spirits of gods who have no faith in you to death and destroy those devils for raping holy women on the earth.

CHRIST told them his plan for the New World. There came flashes of lightning, and thunder and a loud voice saying: now you can create in salvation through your son Elijah with authority over the gods on the earth. If any god chooses to go into captivity, he will be carried away by the wind to the gate of the sun. If any god has faith in Elijah, he will sleep in peace and escape the fire.

Elijah, king in the kingdom

Great and marvellous are your deeds, true to your CHRIST. worthy to be king of the earth with no fear to bring glory to CHRIST from all nations on earth in righteousness.

In the tabernacle Jesus read the New Testament and declared the battle in the kingdom on earth to remove spirits of devils from Zion's flesh and the elimination of devils and darkness in the world. The creation of immortal spirits in kingdoms through Elijah to establish the kingdom in salvation with immortal spirits created by Christ to continue to populate the earth in righteousness for peace in the world for ever.

After Jesus read the declaration for the new covenant, multitudes of angels that came from other planets shouted: hallelujah! Salvation and power has come for Elijah to judge the spirits from their seed of devils that have no faith in Him, when CHRIST casts out spirits of gods from Zion's flesh. CHRIST reigns.

Passover is coming Mt.10:28–36, Ps.37:8-9; 37:12–25

Eve gathered her people in the tabernacle and said: my children, I've seen CHRIST'S spirit, from Adam (body) and saw Jesus also with him in the clouds.

CHRIST our Lord went to prepare a place for us in Heaven.

When the devils come in our nation, you must use restraint. If any god attacks you, suffer it, so your spirit enters the eternal life, as innocents with no blame.

Remember what CHRIST our Lord said to us while He was in the body of Adam: do not be afraid of those who kill the body and cannot kill your spirit.

Judah dishonoured me before Adam was hanged. When I sit as a queen in Heaven, I will dishonour him and god his father who raped your sister in captivity under the oath in bondage.

Zion/Eve said: my children, if you are killed, your spirit will leave your body and will have rest and sleep until Elijah wake up your spirit by the Word to resurrect to Heaven to the place our Lord has prepared for you.

Do not engage in any fight with gods and the devils. Let yourself be an example to the gods, to be seen as innocent on earth and harming no one and living in peace.

(Zion) Eve said to her daughters: we are like sheep for the slaughter; therefore prepare yourselves for the worst time in your life on earth. CHRIST our Lord has taught you scriptures while HE was in Adam. From birth Christ has prepared you for the time when He will not be with you on earth to be with him in Heaven.

Preparation for salvation to set your spirit free

Zion/Eve said: my children, since our CHRIST is raised to HIS throne in Heaven, set your heart on the life above where HE is seated, and not on the earth with gods and the devils. The gods will always want to fight and be against you till they perish. The word with Elijah will come on them.

Zion/Eve said: my children, let the peace of CHRIST be with your spirit. When/Zion Eve was through speaking, the congregation said: Amen. They returned to their homes confident, knowing Elijah will save their spirit after the death of their bodies to live for eternity. **Ro.8:1–2; 7:24-25 ; 6:3–4 ; Ps.29:11; 9:6-9; Ezek.8:12**

The punishment of Queen Tamuze

Satan invited the kings to his palace. One of the kings said: Satan, there is a rumour going around that gods want Judah to be a king. The soldiers boasted that even Adam and Elijah are in fear of him.

Another king said: Satan, the fear of Judah is like a snare. He is always drunk and becoming wicked and cruel as a fighting cock to death.

Satan said: I hoped when Judah went to kill Adam, that Adam would kill the bastard and we would have reason to say he murdered our god to take revenge, but Adam seemed to be in fear of him. Now one of the princes saw Queen Tamuze leaving his house drunk late in the night.

Another king said: we are kings on this earth. Your queen made an oath to make gods to live under our laws from your seed. If she makes a god for Judah, it's abomination and he will want to be king of gods and there will be a revolt in the nations. What a calamity! First she fucks with god (Cain) and now Judah killed the father of Tamuze.

Satan got vexed and called the eunuchs and said to prepare the queen and bring her to the brazen altar in the sanctuary, and tell the scribe to come and take note.

When Tamuze came she said: King, what do you want with me with the kings? Satan said: strip your clothes off. I'll tell you what I want.

The kings began to blaspheme her with curses: you fucking whore. Just like your mother, you are filled with the abomination and filth of the earth, polluting yourself and giving god (Cain) your virginity, passing the king's seed to make a god for him.

Satan said: Judah is going to kill all your brothers and I'm going to do a new thing on earth to sire giants to kill all gods from your flesh. Then you will see who he fears most.

You committed abomination with a god from your filth in the palace. If I see a teardrop come from your eyes, you will know about abomination in this fucking palace. She began to cry: O King, have mercy. Don't let Judah kill my brothers.

Satan said: Tamuze, my hate, malice and jealousy is toward your people. Tamuze began to cry: O King, have mercy. If you kill my people there will be no one left on the earth. Kill the gods who are always sick, hungry and cheat with malice and tell lies.

One of the kings said: your body is unto us till death according to the oath to make gods from your flesh, and when you die will give your body to the gods to burn.

Tamuze answered: your seed is accursed. Under the oath I make gods for you to perish like god (Cain) with dishonour for raping me in your conspiracy to make a god to make a mockery of my father and mother to pass your seed in their flesh. You want Judah to kill all my brothers to take over the earth with gods from your seed. **Ps.55:11-21; Mk.7:25,27**

My body will never go to Heaven where you came from. It faces death every day in this palace. There is no point to fight death, if death is unto my body. Tamuze went on to say: Satan, you have corrupted Judah. You misled him with false hope with your law to imitate you and kill to bring shame before Elijah and CHRIST. I want to die, so this body can be free of the oath and to be at peace. I'll drink until I'm dead, so I can be with my father. Do what you want. I am bored being a queen with your deceit with much sorrow. I would rather be dead than to continue with this oath and false vision to rule the world.

Another king said: Satan, she is getting too smart. You should not teach her to speak in our tongue. You hear what this bitch says to your face. She has no respect and has no shame. I fear in your vexation and torment. If you put your hand on her Elijah will come after you.

Satan answered: this whore makes me jealous and torments me like a viper with malice to destroy and make war for the earth. I am going to eliminate her brothers from the earth for this abomination with Judah. This creature I've put in my palace is like a cobra in the palace with no fear. I made him a prince, put the law in his hands and now he is fucking my queen. The murderer boasts that no one can touch him. He has a secret no one will know until he becomes a ruler in the nation among gods. The gods want him to be king. **Pro.9:16–17**

Queen Tamuze chastises Satan to kill her to be free

Tamuze said: you can never satisfy my body. It's like a consuming fire that always wants more coals for fire, just like the goddess. You can't satisfy her and have to run away with a vision to bring the world back to darkness to destroy what is holy and pure in your eyes on earth.

Satan said to the kings: she is tormenting me. I have no peace. I know if I put my hand on her I'll kill this whore. Tamuze said: kill me, you coward. This body is no good with all the filth you put in it to destroy what is pure. It looks pretty to you bastards filled with abomination.

Kill me and burn my body to ashes and take the ashes and put it into the pussies of your giants to kill gods with big ones like yours in my flesh, to lust and shed blood. I want to be dead. Kill me or tell the murderer to do it for you.

Satan said to the kings: you have always have lust to commit adultery with my queen; you can fuck, put all your curse with all your abomination in her. The first king came and began to fuck. She was in much pain and sore. Another king came and began to call her bitch, whore and she began to cry and bleed. Another king came. She began to cry: bastards, and she passed out. They gave her water to drink.

Another king came and began to swear at her: fucking this and that, and the pain was more intense. You fucking bitch, repent. Tamuze said: I rather die than repent to you fuckers.

Another king took his turn and started swearing: you motherfucker, repent. She cried: kill my body so I can be free from the oath and your abuse.

Satan came and shamelessly undressed himself in front of the princes and went into her with vengeance and nearly tore her apart and began putting all his weight on her to smother her from crying, saying: you whore, prostituted with the kings of the earth filled with incurable disease and filth of abomination.

She answered: now Elijah has reason to cast your ass out of the earth for your abomination in holy flesh and I'll be free of you for ever according to the oath. Satan became scared at the thought of losing her and told the eunuchs to take her away and look after her.

The scribe wrote: Tamuze, mother of the gods, prostituted herself with the kings of the earth for her abomination with Judah. **Rev.17:2; Esek.20:30; Mk.7:25, 27, 29–30**

After the Meeting of Kings in the Synagogue

The kings plan the decree for war. King Judah will lead the attack to exterminate the sons of Adam so that all males from His seed perish from the earth.

Satan called the eunuchs and told them to show Queen Tamuze the decree to destroy her brothers from the face of the earth, and she should come and make supplications unto him for her brothers.

Tamuze put on her royal clothes of fine linen scarlet purple-pink, amulets, diamond rings on her fingers, gold and diamond tinkle bells on her feet, and put on Satan's favourite perfume made especially for him to smell.

Tamuze came to his room, took the veil of her face and said: what do you want with me, King, since you had the kings abuse my body with lust for holy flesh to make gods.

You have not invited me in your bedchambers since last moon. As you can see, I'm still alive. I know you hate me and want to kill me. Go ahead; treat yourself to my death, so I can be with my brothers you want to exterminate.

Satan said: you fucking bitch, Do you want to know why I've not invited you in my chamber up to this day? Tamuze said: it doesn't really matter. There is no fear in love, neither in death. Satan said: I am your king and you have no respect or fear me to kill you.

Tamuze said: your kings got much pleasure with you, to make me fear you. I am not satisfied until you kill me and I'll have rest from this oath. Satan said: you have become evil and my fear is not in you any more. The snare of the death has come unto thee.

Tamuze said: I was innocent when you took me in captivity and you know the great fear I had of you. Satan said: did you come here to mock me because Judah has no fear of devils or Elijah or CHRIST and want to teach me to fear you? **Pro.20:2; Ps.34:1; Ps.19:9**

You were obedient and trembling in my bed before. Now you boldly speak like Judah. **Phil.1:14**

Don't ever think you shall escape death in this palace.

The harvest has come Gen.8:22; Hos.8:11; Pro.10:5; Joel.3:13; Jer.51:33; Mt.13:39

I want to make it plain in your head. There is going to be an increase of concubines in this palace, with your mother and sisters, when Judah kills all the men from your father. Their wives will come for me to multiply gods on earth.

You shall cry for me to give you gods in these days when they come in the palace as my new maidens under the law. I don't care how you perish. I shall have no sex with you when your sister comes. What is your request, now you are here in my room?

Tamuze put Satan to the test, to set a trap for him and the devils Ro.7:12

Tamuze tried jealousy. She said: O king of nations, with so many new maidens to pleasure your heart, it will faint and tremble and it will make you weak like a woman. You will have no power left in you. If you can't satisfy me, how will you satisfy so many Hebrew women? They are hard to please, as you well know. Satan said: what is that to you, if I take more concubines?

Tamuze looked at him. He looked at her with love and hate, and she said: so you want new maidens to pollute their holy flesh with other bastard devils with their accursed seed to make gods?

Tamuze walked slowly towards Satan lying in the bed. She stood looked at him and began to undress herself slowly, took some perfume and poured some drops in the palm of her hand and blew the perfume in his face, and the scent went up his nostrils. All the hate he felt turned into lust and he said: for one night's pleasure, I give you what you desire. You are my sunshine on earth, my beautiful queen. I hate I have to be like a beggar to have you. I feel to kill you for tormenting me.

She drew near and touched his big cock. Satan said: please, I'll give you anything; half of the earth.

Tamuze said: my flesh is holy; it seems good to me up to this day. My request, O King, my body will please thee if you let me be free from this oath under laws. It's burdensome to me. I hate what I am doing. All I want is peace.

Set me free of this oath to be among my father, mother, brothers and sisters to perish with them from the earth.

O king of nations, I hate what I do and what I do to please you. I feel I am a prisoner to death. My people have caused you no trouble or harm. You want to persecute and exterminate them from the earth.

King, let the oath I made with you to make gods be my loss. I know Elijah will come to save their kingdoms after my death.

I am fed up being in bondage to devils to live under the law to make gods to perish from the earth after they die and to pass on your seed. I have held my peace. Judah is an enemy. I fear he will kill all my people. O King, if I have satisfied thee, stay in bed. I don't want you to see no concubines. I want to prepare a banquet for thee. Satan fell in a deep sleep.

Tamuze locked Satan in his room and secretly went to see Judah .and pleaded with him not to kill her people for the devils.

Tamuze's banquet. The last supper

Tamuze set up the banquet. She made herself beautiful with scented perfume and all the kings and their queens were invited. Tamuze gained confidence of Satan and he said: my queen, whatever you ask me, it is granted thee.

Tamuze said: O King, do me a favour and set me free of this oath, so I can perish from the earth. I've kept my mouth shut. I fear Judah will do me much damage. He is deceitful as much as you, and lies. There is no truth in him and he will want to take the maidens from you.

King, let it be in writing that Judah will not go with you to take my mother and sisters in captivity, and seal it with the ring on your finger, so it is on record in the future.

Satan was full of lust for Tamuze. He called for the scribe and it was written according to the request. Tamuze asked it to be in all languages.

Satan said: my queen, it was in my heart not to bring Judah to fuck your sisters. I am afraid he would want to take some for himself to make gods like us. Tamuze said: O King, he is an enemy to my people, whom I fear most. Do not let him go to make gods with my sisters.

Satan became worried, left the banquet and went outside the palace. In the garden he began walking up and down, meditating on King Judah, who he made king of gods and who wanted more power to rule.

Fear of Judah was like a headache. To hold Eve and her daughters in captivity was in his grasp to make gods, thinking of what Tamuze said: if Judah went for her mother and sisters, he will kill and want to take some of them for himself to make gods in his nation.

Jealousy and fear Pro.20:2

Satan began to be Jealous of Judah taking the beautiful daughters of Eve, and was in fear of Christ. Eve brought back memories of the Garden of Eden; he had to rape Eve to make a god and was cast out of Heaven. Now she has a multitude of maidens, Tamuze wants out. She wants to be free of the oath and is eager to die. A decision has to be made. Satan began speaking to himself and couldn't make a decision.

If I don't go to capture Eve and her daughters I will look like a coward. Elijah and CHRIST – where are they? In great fear, everything he did is coming back to mind. The goddess laughing loud in his head. Leave the woman alone. She is trouble if you make a god with her in the Garden of Eden. Now Eve has a multitude of beautiful maidens to make gods. Tamuze wants me to go fetch her mother and sister. I fear trouble will come.

Tamuze wants death, to be free of this oath. It's only in death we part. CHRIST and Elijah are elusive; they don't fight! They are the invisible enemy.

Satan began talking to himself: I can't handle this problem alone. It's not as simple as I think. I want vengeance. I feel hate and malice on Eve for my downfall. I'm afraid to fall alone. Judah has zapped power from me, and is more wicked than me, and has success on earth. I am like a frog on the earth that keeps jumping and plunging in the water to mate. If I go in, this water is for ever.

Satan went back inside the palace and returned to the banquet. With hate, jealousy, with fright, all the kings thought he had a vision from the goddess. He called for the high priest and told him to fetch Judah and also the scribe. He knew his end had come on earth and Judah would take over to rule gods on earth.

Judah came well dressed in royal uniform in blue and white, with his kingly crown on his head, looking smart and fierce. Judah said: Aba, you called for me. Here I am, as you requested.

Satan took a good look at Judah, thinking back to when Judah came to the palace naked and thinking of what Tamuze said. He can't bear the thought of her to be free. She is afraid of Judah. Satan took the ring from his finger and gave it to Judah to put on his finger, and said: Judah, when I am not in the nation, you are ruler of the palace and over all gods in the nations.

Tamuze came to Satan, fell down on her knees and said: O king of nations.

Satan held out his hand. She stood before him and said: do me a favour, O King; go and bring my people here in the nation to be with the king and let it be written you did not give Judah authority to go to kill my mother and sisters. I can't endure to see the evil that shall come unto my mother and sisters if Judah goes in their nation.

Satan replied: my queen, it was in my heart to eliminate all your brothers so they don't pass on seed of Adam with the gods to add to my sin in holy flesh while I'm king with authority. Let it be recorded, all the sons of Adam that Judah slew was with my authority. Let it be recorded as a remembrance of devils throughout every generation on earth. The judgment on Adam and his sons perish with his seed on earth as a memorial to devils for making gods on earth.

Harem in the palace

The godly women in the harem were the firstborn given to kings as a gift according to the law to Satan, and were guarded by the eunuchs. They were taught how to give pleasure to the king by practising on each other or lying on statues with great members.

The godly women in the harem who were not virgins and pregnant for the king chose their mistress in the harem. Sometimes this caused much jealousy and fighting in the harem.

Maidens who had not been with the king had priority, and were perfumed with oils that stimulate. Those who lost their virginity despised the virgins, who would be next to have the king's pleasure.

There were the fun rooms in the harem. The devils would put on masks to look like dogs, alligators, wolves, falcons, crocodiles, black panthers to fuck like creatures of the earth. The fun room had peepholes with a slanting chair, for priests and commandants to see those for sale. The eunuchs would tilt the chair and the girl's legs would be wide open so those who peeped could see what they were buying.

The walls had mirrors that reflected everything the devils did in the room with the women who were not virgins. To satisfy their lust for flesh like beasts on earth, the devils would whip the women.

The queen had not the slightest idea what went on in the harem but could hear much crying coming from the harem and was in fear if her mother and sisters were brought in the harem, that he devils would whip them to satisfy their beastly lust in flesh to make gods.

The godly women in the harem were abused by the kings until they were replaced and given to gods as gifts and the first female born would belong to Satan.

The kings debate in the synagogue of devils Is.24:5

The kings got in the synagogue to plan the capture Eve and her daughters with Adam to make gods to take over the earth. A king said: Satan, I apologize I was not in the palace to partake in abomination with your queen. According to the law, if Tamuze wanted to enquire about anything she should have spoken to you. It's disgraceful for your queen to be with Judah. If Judah thinks he is spiritually gifted, let him prove himself.

Another king said: Satan, since Adam died, Elijah and CHRIST have not attacked us. The time has come to capture Eve and her daughters, in order to make gods with the holy women of Adam. The gods we have among us are weak and need a boost to improve their intelligence.

Satan said: I intend to do a new thing on earth to populate giants so we can have more protection on earth. I am conscious and hesitant to assault the women. I fear Elijah and CHRIST are up to something.

A king said: Satan, we cannot afford to take any risk. We got away with Queen Tamuze to make gods. If we go and take Eve and her daughters to hold in captivity and we get caught, we will never see daylight again. We will be the laughing stock of the world for breaking the covenant to make gods in holy flesh. This time is judgment on us if we fail on this Passover.

The women are beautiful like the angels in Heaven we were not allowed to fuck, and this temptation to fuck these holy women to make gods is our downfall or our victory for the earth.

Satan: if the sons of Adam perished only Eve and her daughters will be left and no sons of Adam left to give them children except us kings to fuck EVE and her daughters, this temptation is a trap set for us.

Satan said: this is the problem that faces me every day and night. Tamuze has no dreams to warn me like the goddess who sees things before they happen, and if I return to the goddess, she will laugh at me and call me an idiot with false hope. That is why we are gathered here – to make a mutual decision, so I don't get blame alone if this plan fails to take the women in captivity. We got away with Tamuze. So far so good. The earth is within our grasp to take it for ourselves.

I thought if I got rid of Adam, his people would scatter, but they have not. The Hebrews have no fear of death knowing what Judah did to slay all their men. The women are still in their nation and have not left it.

My queen is the same and fear no devil as she says she will see no sorrow, and neither will she shed tears after she dies. We devils are dealing with people as hard as granite that won't split. I've gone down on my knees to please Tamuze. She only laughs at me, saying you kings have godly women who are your queens in your nature. I have a Hebrew queen I hold in captivity under oath and laws by force of our nature.

A king said: Satan, we don't seem to be going forward, and we left the heavens because we could not fuck angels. Now we are on earth, if we capture the women of Adam it's going to bring much trouble on earth. Can't we not postpone this plan?

Satan said: we have all broken the covenant to live among angels created in the Light in peace when we left the our world in darkness. We are all bastards sitting in this synagogue for making gods from the flesh of my queen, we are not happy and live in fear of Christ and Elijah. We can achieve nothing unless we put Christ and Elijah to the test to destroy them on earth to bring the world back the way it was. It can't be done unless we make gods to fight with us for the earth with our godly spirits after death; we chained our father to break the covenant of peace with the Eternal.

A king said: Satan, we have a problem with the covenant of peace that is why we are cast out of Heaven, so CHRIST can come and create angels in the light in the world without devils and gods. At the moment as the world is still between Light and darkness, so let us enjoy our time on earth be content with your Hebrew queen.

Another king said: Satan, it stands to reason your Hebrew queen lives not in accordance with the covenant by making gods for you from the seed of ancient devils in the flesh of Adam on earth. Our godly queens are from your seed and can't have enough of us devils. If you can't satisfy Queen Tamuze, how could we satisfy angels in Heaven where the laws were stricter with us not to fuck them to make gods? We devils are accursed outside our nocturnal world. No matter where we go outside our world, we are not welcome. Now the gods want Judah to be their king. They say he is one of them in the flesh like creatures on earth.

Satan said: you see how ungrateful gods are. They tell lies and gossip, are deceitful, and want this boastful bastard to be their king. If you gave the gods a chance they would fuck their own mother like me with the goddess. That is why I am going to make giants to be our new creation to destroy gods if they don't live by our law to live in flesh until death. It will be survival of the fittest on earth. The giant godly spirits will be our hope for the battle in the kingdom for the earth and hope we can see them multiply in flesh from our seed in the future instead of gods.

Another king said: Satan, if the gods want Judah to be a king, why do you have a problem with that? As far as I can see, he is a god like them, a skilful leader, ruthless and most feared among gods. He envies you and imitates all your wickedness. Why don't you give him a chance to be king of the gods to rule them by our laws?

Another king interrupted and said: Satan, remember, we have the right to make laws for the gods born from our seed on earth by your queen under oath. As long the sons of Adam are on earth they are exempt from our laws and no god can be heir to your throne on the earth. None are born free. They are all born with flesh to live by our law to death to be godly spirits. Neither can gods go to Heaven where we came from, for their godly spirits are not accepted by the ETERNAL. If we go and fuck these Hebrew women and make giants we will be breaking the peace covenant even further.

A young king said: Satan, I have much respect for you making me a king and think there is a way we can go around this problem of fear. Why don't you make Judah a king and tell him to take a few battalions of soldiers and slaughter all the males, so he can really be a king, a ruler of the gods and we can take the women and share them between us kings as concubines to make giants so there can be much war on earth against CHRIST.

SATAN USES GUILE ON JUDAH

Satan told a devil to fetch Judah and tell him to come to the synagogue. Satan said: Judah, the kings have been hearing that the gods want you to be a king to rule them and have agreed and want to put your faith to the test to be a king of kings on earth. What do you have to say about this promotion? Tell us, do you think you can be a king to rule over gods on earth? We are old from the ancient nocturnal world under a covenant of peace. We have given you the laws to govern our gods with authority to rule them when we are not on earth. You came to us like a god of the earth.

No god is as intelligent as you. No fear of Elijah is in you, but with our fear you shall rule gods on earth, according to the law given you, to rule gods on earth to death.

Satan said: Judah, we have no right to make the people of Adam live by our laws, but you are a prince in my palace, born on earth. Would you like to be a king of the gods on earth?

Judah said: I have a desire to be a ruler, but if you make me king of gods; I will carry on doing your evil, as a prophet to gods to live by your laws to death.

Satan said: you cannot be king of the earth while sons of Adam are heir to the earth. You have to eliminate them from the earth, so you can be king of gods.

JUDAH TRICKS SATAN WITH GUILE Ro.8:20-21; Gal.3:11; Ro.1:24–32; Gal.1:11

Judah said: when I hanged Adam he said if I killed any of his people, CHRIST and Elijah would come after me. If I go and eliminate His sons from the earth, what is in it for me? I'll be condemning myself and all who pass on my seed. Why don't you get prince Joakim, your favourite son, to slay them or you yourself? I want to be a ruler but it has a price to pay. Supposing the Hebrews kill me. There is no profit to me. My wickedness might cost me everlasting death and to every god that passes on my seed. Adam warned me that if I touch any of His people Elijah and CHRIST will come after me.

This put fear in Satan and the kings. Satan said: Judah, you are a prince. How else can you be a king if you don't slay the sons of Adam. We made ourselves kings by taking the earth by force. While there are sons of Adam on earth you have to be a king by force. It's by your wickedness you will be king on earth through me.

One of the kings asked Judah: you became prophet of the law to teach our gods with our authority when you took the oath. Tell us, what is the law to our gods on earth before we make you a king?

Judah said: the law is to do every kind of wickedness, covet, adultery, do evil, greed, depravity, envy, murder, deceit, malice, slander, arrogance, boastful, disobey, ruthless, jealousy and hate of Elijah and Christ.

Satan said: Judah, all this is in the law and it is implanted in your nature to be a king on earth like me.

Judah said: King, I am wicked but my wickedness by the law is not justified before Elijah. Who will judge me if I slay all the sons of Adam to please you to inherit godly spirits from my seed after death in the gate?

JUDAH SEES FOR THE FIRST TIME THAT WITHOUT ELIJAH THERE IS NO HOPE FOR PEACE Gal. 3:10

Judah began to meditate to himself: I had no faith in Elijah; the sons of Adam have faith in Adam and CHRIST Elijah to save them after death. I am accursed, a prophet to teach gods the law given by devils who took the earth by force. There was silence. All the devils where looking at Judah thinking.

Judah was thinking and going back to his youth when he was called Ammon. Elijah told him: go and save your mother from the devils. If you need help call me, remembering the Word of Elijah who was good to him but had no faith in salvation for peace, but observed the wickedness of the devil is in his nature. It is war against what is holy and good, and to do what is evil. Judah realizes it is his choice. If he wants to be a king with the devils he has to be evil like the devils against Word of Elijah. Go and save your mother. If you need help, call me. If I am to be a king I must slay all the brothers of my mother on the earth.

The temptation of Satan to make Judah king, Judah must envy Satan's power. He has to be malicious, ruthless, and murder for power by force, no turning back. Satan made him a prince when he hanged Adam. Now Satan wants him to be a king. I must eliminate sons of Adam. A struggle for power, a struggle for peace, is a sacrifice to eliminate everyone you hate in the world, with vengeance and hate for everyone that is good. Judah said: I am not perfect. I want to be a king of kings to pass on my seed in holy flesh. The devils rejoiced and celebrated with Judah the Passover with them. **Is.2:30**

THE KINGS. THE DAY OF DECISION FOR THE FIRST SABBATH OF THE EARTH

The kings got together in the synagogue of Satan and began to celebrate paradise lost. Satan boasted: from the strength of my seed I will bring the victory on earth to devils. A king said: Satan, we have killed Adam and everything going is like it was before. What do you think? Do you still have fear of Elijah and CHRIST? Satan just looked at him.

Another king said: if we go and kill the sons of Adam, you will be condemning us with you. I was told this by my queen, who had a dream and saw all devils receive judgment and was crying to go back to Heaven.

Satan said: you keep thinking of Heaven when you should be thinking of capturing the Hebrew women and eliminate the men of Adam, so they don't to pass on seed of Adam on the earth.

Another king said: Satan, the people of Adam have faith in Elijah to save them. They say they are freeborn and our laws on earth have a lot of errors and any god born on earth is not justified in holy flesh. What do you say, Satan?

Satan said: what is justified to these Hebrews will be justified when they feel my anger and become our slaves to make gods to be sinners with our anger, hate, maliciousness, and deceit like us on earth.

Another king said: Satan, I heard these Hebrews have no fear. They say their love is for CHRIST and Elijah alone and have faith the two will remove us from the earth and we will be punished seriously if we spill their blood on earth. The battalion of gods said they heard Adam say CHRIST will come and justify the covenant if we shed the blood of his people and Elijah will cast us and our gods to a secret place reserved in the earth for us. My godly queen says she had a dream about us being in this gloomy place. Sometimes it's hot and cold and there is much sorrow. No bread or water, it's hot. She had perspirations and jumped from her sleep.

Another king said: my godly queen said she had a vision. This CHRIST appeared to the Hebrews with a book with many names of Hebrews killed and she said it was a two-part dream. Then she saw much snow in one place and another place with howling winds. She began to cry in her sleep. I was in fear when she told me this dream.

Satan said: how can you fuckers think you can have victory if we don't spill blood to establish gods on earth. If we don't cut off the seed of Adam, all our gods will be rubbish on earth. King Judah hanged him on a tree and left his sons on earth. The covenant is a testimony between everlasting life with angels in the Light or everlasting death if we made a god with the Eternal's creation.

King Judah said: O king of nations, do you think CHRIST will be against gods who slay the sons of Adam? Satan said: Christ punishes devils for their sins and punishes gods who have no faith and assault the holy ones because they are not accepted above.

Satan said: King Judah, you have submitted yourself to do evil when you became king of the gods with supreme authority to punish who do good and to silence foolish ones who have faith in Elijah. You honour your elder kings who made you a king and who are not deceitful like you with lust for my queen.

Judah, you have committed adultery and abomination with my Tamuze and hanged Adam. You are like devils who can't go to Heaven. You had a free choice for peace but you took my power to be a king and committed to the law to do the work of devils and to be a sinner to death. You boast and brag you are a devil. You have become a judge of the earth to pass sentence on any god who will disobey the law on earth.

A king said: Judah, king of the gods, this is the opportunity for judgment against innocent men to put order on the earth. Kill the sons of Adam with your battalion. You have authority to judge and eliminate holy men on earth to rule on earth by force like Satan, with hate for what is holy and good.

Satan said: Judah, the men of Adam don't know when you go, that their life will be a mist that will vanish for ever from the earth. The time has come to capture the Hebrew women and to slaughter their men. Holy people don't fight, neither will they oppose you, and we will capture their women after their men Sabbath to death. After you have done this you can boast to your battalion of your judgment.

Satan said: Judah, leave their women to us. If you want to be king with the devils, you must establish the law and have faith with the doctrine of devils to kill the sons of Adam, who call themselves holy men of the earth. Their blood shall be on every god that is born according to the covenant to death. You shall show no favour. Kill them all from the oldest ofmales to babies just born.

We are not law breakers if we love our own godly children and fucking them is not committing adultery. If we pass on seed with holy women they will make us more gods to populate the earth. I say one thing, Judah; you deceitfully want to slay holy people to make a name for yourself as king. If you eliminate them from the earth you will be king of gods and we will be free of judgment, and it will be our victory after death of gods to accept their spirits with no mercy.

Satan said: Judah, Elijah is only interested in the kingdoms of gods for Christ to create with immortal spirits and not interested in laws of devils. He discriminates against us and loves CHRIST. He looks at gods and devils as shit with no right to make gods in the holy flesh of Adam and Eve.

If you want to keep the crown on your head I don't want to see your face until the oldest son to the last suckling with the seed of Adam is dead, so every god that passes on your seed on earth, their spirit will return to you after death.

You are the judge between good and devils on earth. It is in your heart to rule and to be king with us. Leave the women to us devils. Make sure no god in your battalion fuck with the woman when you enter their nation.

The final discussion on the Sabbath

The kings in the synagogue said: Satan, Judah must swear by the oath that he shall not slay the women or fuck any of them. Neither shall his battalion of gods pass our seed in the women to make gods to add to our sin.

If Judah fuck the women you can't make him a king on earth for devils to get punished for his sin to fuck holy women to make gods to death.

A king said: Satan, we will see if Elijah and CHRIST will come and save the sons of Adam and we will know if Elijah will save Eve because she made a god (Cain) for you who you strangled for fucking Tamuze.

Satan, now is your chance to capture Eve to live under the law of sinner on earth.

Satan said: King Judah, take as many gods that are trained for battle and kill every male to cut off the head of the sons of Adam, so the earth can be populated with gods without the people from the seed of Adam.

The Sabbath of the sons of CHRIST Ex.24:8; Ex.30:10; Zech.9:11; Heb.13:20

Every family of the holy people of CHRIST/Adam was inside their houses singing and eating and in control, well prepared for the hour when they will die to have everlasting life. They knew their bodies were to be sacrificed to death. The devils called it the Sabbath to kill the body to rest for ever. **2.Cor.3:6; Pro.21:22–25**

King Judah set out with his battalion of soldiers on horses, on a seven-day journey to holy land of Adam. Every soldier had his bow and arrow and sharpened spear and cutlass to cut off the heads of the sons of Adam.

As they got close to the Hebrews, so as they are called by devils, the people could hear the noise of galloping horses getting closer and closer to their holy land.

When they got to the holy land with villages, Judah and his soldiers surrounded the nation with no walls. They saw no one and the soldiers began to shout for the elder to come outside his home.

The elder son of Adam came out and said: King Judah, what do you want? You come in our holy land, with a battalion of soldiers with bows and arrows and sharp cutlasses and spears.

We have not coveted gods and nor have we stolen anything or done anything wrong. Why are you here? If it's bread and water you want, we will be happy to give you.

King Judah looked at the elder. Their eyes locked, Judah said to himself: if I don't kill I can't be a king and Satan will kill me.

The elder said: did you come to shed innocent blood of peaceful people? Elijah will not be pleased with you.

Judah asked: where is He? Call Elijah and tell him to come and save you. **Pro.21:24**

The elder said: I don't know where He is. He could be anywhere, even looking at us as we speak. I know when I see Him again it is to send us to a place where you can't come with your soldiers. King Judah, go and tell the devils that sent you, we have no war with you and your battalion. We are not afraid of devils. Why did they send you in our nation to pollute it with shit from your horses with your arrogance?

We are peaceful people from birth. We live in peace and harmony in our nation. Why are you here? What have my people ever done to you to come to remind us of the sin of god (Cain) your father with our sister to make a god like you, to come and mock us with your soldiers?

You come with arrogance and hate for people who are innocent. You were also rude to Elijah, a man that brought you up as though He was your father. The last time He was here, He said you turned against Him when Satan gave you the law. **Mt.5:21**

Satan has taken our sister in captivity when she was pregnant with you in her womb, and oppressed her with laws under oath and now you are here as king with the law of devils. We have no war with you or your soldiers. Please leave our holy land in peace. **Mk.3:36**

No peace. Danger of judgment

The elder said: Judah, if you came here with the intention to slay holy people, you shall be in danger of judgment by shedding blood of innocent people. Judah, leave our nation in peace before you and your soldiers bring condemnation on gods if you spill one drop of blood on holy people in this nation.

Thou shall not kill 2.Pet.2:24; 1.Pet.2:23 Dan.2:47 Eph.4:24; Rev.2:26-27; IKi11.45–47

We are against killing anyone. If any god sheds one drop of blood in this holy land, Elijah will remove you and the devils from the earth.

Judah asked: are you the elder son of Adam? The elder son said: yes. Judah said: if I say one word you will be the first to perish from the earth like Adam, your father. Adam had hoped Elijah would save him. I've listen to you. I hate Elijah in my father's kingdom.

Tell all your brothers in their homes to come out with their sons, even those that suck. I am a king of gods in all nations and they obey me, so tell your brothers to obey you and come out from their homes.

Is it lawful to kill? 1.Pet.3:9

The elder said: Judah, we are people holy and pure and free from laws of devils on earth. We do not obey foreign laws. Go tell Satan what I told you, to tell all his devils. We are prepared for a Sabbath. If he wants to shed blood on earth, tell him to come, but if you shed blood on any one of my people, you and your battalion and gods from their seed and yours will perish from earth. When salvation comes CHRIST will come and cast them out from kingdoms. A cock crowed in the nation.

The cock crowed a second time near his feet Ro.8:20–21

Judah said: Elder, I am a king and you have no respect for the king of gods and his battalion. If I open my mouth the battalion of gods will go inside your homes and cast out all holy men, from the oldest to the youngest, and the gods will slay them.

Judah called the soldiers and they came forward. The elder said: Judah, you are threatening us. If you spill one drop of blood in the nation you will be condemning yourself and every god will be against you in every generation to salvation.

The elder said: Judah, where Elijah will put you and gods from your seed in the time of salvation, there is no bread or water, only fire for ever, if you slay any brother of mine.

The cock crowed a third time

Judah said: Elder, for the third time I'm commanding you to tell your brothers in the nation to come outside with their sons. If not, you will be the first to be slain. The elder said: if Elijah speaks through the mouth of your father you will be in the chambers under the ice where there are howling winds and freezing cold to cool down your temper. You will have no hope in life if you slay me and shed holy blood. CHRIST says vengeance belongs to HIM, and hates anyone who spills the blood of his people. Judah shuddered at the thought of chambers of ice in freezing conditions.

Gods must not sin with holy women Ro.1:29-30

The elder said: Judah, did you come with soldiers to practice sexual immorality with your battalion on holy women to make gods like your father (Cain) to end in the pit for raping your mother?

Their spirits from your seed will blame you and the soldiers for making them to pass on your accursed seed with malice, deceit, and hate for holy people that live in peace.

Any god that fornicates with my sisters to make godly children will perish in the time of salvation. CHRIST will come and cast out your spirits from their flesh and they will hate you if pass judgment on my people this day.

Faith in Elijah. The worker on earth Gal.3:11; Ro2 1–2

The kingdom is an everlasting kingdom and will be established with holy spirits of creation when Elijah speaks the Word to CHRIST. I am sure you know the scripture Elijah taught you before you became a prophet of the law of devils, now you are a king of gods. Did not Elijah tell you to save your mother, held in captivity? You and your battalion of soldiers should be fighting devils, for holding your mother in captivity. I am ashamed to say you are naturally wicked.

Abomination Is.14:29–30

The promise Elijah gave you was to give you back every spirit from your seed of god (Cain) your father if you commit abomination with your mother, and multitudes will cry for the flesh of your mother, if you pass on the accursed seed of (Cain) to make gods with your mother like the devils. Judah, you have allowed Satan to deceive you, just as he deceived your father (Cain) who is crying in the heat for rape and murder. You put your hope in the devils; you hanged my father and want to kill his sons to make a name for yourself on earth. When Elijah gave you this promise, it was not by the law of devils. He promised to let your spirit rest in peace if you had faith in him. You are a god in the kingdom from the seed of god (Cain) and think if you fornicate with my sisters you will make multitudes of gods. You have no faith and put your hope in devils. Because you are not of holy seed, you hate us. Like Elijah promised, if you had faith HE could create a SPIRIT in your kingdom to be accepted as his son and your spirit would have rest. Judah, if you or any god rapes holy women, you won't be a king. The devil will kill you just as he killed your father and took your mother while she was pregnant with you in captivity to make gods.

Satan will surely do the same to you if you to pass on seed of god your father, whom he hated and blamed him for being among creatures on earth. He will say you are corrupt like your father (Cain) who was eager to take your mother's virginity to make a god like him. Now you want to do the same to be the first with my sisters to pass god your father's seed before the devils capture the women in the nation. It will be a testament against you and also the battalions of soldiers and generations of gods on earth to everlasting death in fire.

The commander next to Judah got afraid he would lose his rank and said: King, we were sent by Satan, king of nations, to kill the men and he and the kings will deal with the women. A Hebrew inside said: our women are innocent;. Go away and leave us in peace. **1.Ki.1:45–57; Is.5:22–23**

The kingdom is everlasting

The elder said: Judah, you are angry because Elijah will not give you eternal life in Heaven and promised to give you back spirits from your seed. The kingdoms from the flesh of your mother are holy for everlasting immortal spirits in the Light. When you perish from the earth it will be there in abundance to give her new children by the Word of Elijah to be on earth with her and him. You have knowledge of this, Judah.

Jealousy and hate for Elijah, who loved you and adopted you from birth

You do not want to accept who you are from the accursed seed of god (Cain) your father and jealous Elijah will give your mother a new son that is accepted in the kingdom by the Word with eternal life. Because you are not accepted above, you hate Elijah who loves you. It's Satan who killed god your father you love, that was born in sin like you in holy flesh. If you shed blood of innocent people you will break the covenant of peace like the devils on earth. And spirits from your seed will come in condemnation, and will come under judgment.

Adam's body you hanged on the tree to death will be remembered on earth in all generations of the earth, even after your soldiers are dead. Judah spat in his face. Judah took his sword and sliced off the elder's ear and said: you have insulted the king of gods of the earth.

The elder said: violence is in your nature and the gods in your battalion can't stand the truth. You know you are a tainted king, presumptuous and hateful, and became a prophet to kill holiness with Satan's authority.

The soldiers began to kick the elder on the ground and began swearing – fucking this and that – spitting in the elder's face, he staggered and said: you soldiers come like thieves to steal and kill. It's in your nature from birth to hate holy people and shed their blood to Passover the earth to devils.

Judah is struggling with the truth Ro.1:24–32; Gal.1:10–11; Ro.8:20–21

Judah blocked his ears and shouted: shut up, and spat in the elder's face. The elder said: you have dishonoured my father and have no respect for sons in his flesh on earth. If Elijah was your father, you would love me. You belong to god your father of the seed of Satan now in the heat for rape and murder. He was the first murderer on the earth. He killed my brother Abel, whose spirit name is Jesus, who you don't know for you were not born when he slew him.

Your desire is to murder holy men to make a name for yourself like Satan who raped my mother to make god your father who raped my sister to make you a wicked god like him on earth.

Judah was in fear the soldiers would know the truth about his birth he tried to conceal, and he said: now you are going to be a dead man. The elder said: I'm not afraid to be dead. You are determined to do as your father, who killed Abel and conspired with the devils to take your mother in captivity. You came with soldiers to kill me and her brothers in the sight of my mother and sisters to make a mockery of her for making god your father with Satan. He has deceived you as he did to your father to death.

God (Cain) your father was a liar and a conspirator with the devils in your mother's captivity to become a sinner. You were born possessed and blinded like him to the truth. You are a postulant dedicated to carry on your father's wickedness to my family on earth for the devils.

Satan is a coward

Satan and the devils are cowards. They deceived you and sent you with a battalion to kill my father (Adam). You did what the devils fear most, so they could say it's you who killed Adam and not them. Now they will say it's you who disturbed the peace on earth, and put the blame on gods on earth for killing holy people of Adam on earth. Judah, you are a foolish king. If you shed blood you will have no peace when you leave this world.

The commander to the king

The soldier next to Judah said: king of gods, our law says any god who loves Elijah and CHRIST to make gods wise kill them. King, what is your judgment? He wants to open our eyes to truth. You are a prophet of the law and not this elder, who hates our devils and calls them strangers on earth.

King, you boasted Satan gave you the law with authority to decide the future of gods on earth. Elijah opened your eyes to have wisdom and knowledge of good and evil. You said you did not know where Elijah came from, but you chose to be wicked instead of doing good like Hebrews. So let's slay the elder and the men so I can return to my godly woman Satan gave me as a gift.

The hour before the Sabbath

Judah began to be in fear for the first time of Elijah, who he thought was an ordinary man who loved him like a son, taught him scriptures and the good way. The commander looked at him as though he was in a trance.

Judah heard voices. Satan telling him: kill, Judah, kill! Lift up your sword! Kill the elder. The sword was like a heavy weight in his hand and he could not lift it up. He blocked his head from the noises of Satan. The soldiers were looking at him for the order to strike but words could not come out of his mouth. He was hearing the voice of Satan: kill, Judah, kill! Making drilling noises in his head, and he began to cry, burying his head in his hands, tormented by spirits. Kill, Judah, kill, to be our king.

The soldiers began to throw insults at the elder. What have you done to the king with your witchcraft? You put a spell on him. They began shouting: King, are you all right? The commander said: give us a sign to kill. Judah tried to lift the sword to give the OK, but it was a struggle to lift the sword for soldiers to kill the sons of Adam on the earth.

Judah picked himself up, got angry, and with hate said: Elder, is there any more you want to say before you are dead? The elder said: peace on earth and all my people who have faith in Elijah, sleep in peace until Elijah say the WORD to wake up to be with CHRIST in Heaven.

Faith in Elijah Is.26:8; Mal.3:16; Mk.11:21; Mt.27:63

Judah said: when you get there; you will remember it's through me killing you that got you there for ever. Judah took his sword in his hand and pierced it in the elder's heart. The elder looked upward and said: Elijah, save my spirit so I can be with CHRIST my father, then he collapsed dead.

Sabbath over death. The blood of CHRIST Ro.4:20–25; Heb.10:23; Heb.10:26–29

The rebellion

Immediately as the elder fell and died, the soldiers drew their swords and rushed inside the houses, searching for the men, old or young, even suckling baby boys, and threw them outside to be slain in the street. From house to house and village to village they threw the men outside and they took their cutlasses and cut off the heads of the sons of Adam, down to the last suckling baby boy.

There was blood everywhere and the women rushed outside their homes holding the dead bodies of their beloved men and children in their arms, crying, beating their breasts, taking the blood of their beloved and washing their faces in the blood of their men and baby boys. Judah and his battalion of soldiers killed them all without mercy.

Faith in Elijah

Everywhere there were dead bodies of men and children. No man attempted to escape the brutality and barbarity. They had put their entire lives in the hands of Elijah to save their spirits, to resurrect to eternal life.

Salvation

The gods, with sharpened cutlasses, looked at the women, but the women had no fear of them. The women looked at them in shock and said: the same judgment will be done to you and your children in salvation and it will be justified.

The soldiers just laughed and went inside their homes and began to steal food, sandals, and whatever they saw, they took. Then they went back outside and told the women to bury their dead. **Jer.48:15; Essek.9:2; 21:10–28; Zech.11:35; 1.Pet.1:2; Mt.26:55**

The kingdom is taken by force Ro.8:5–7

Judah and his battalion were getting ready to leave on their horses and chariots. Eve went up and stood in front of the battalion and looked at Judah and the soldiers. Judah said: what do you want? Go bury the dead you love.

Thou shalt not kill. You have come against us Ro.8:31–32

Eve stood before Judah and said: I am ashamed at your anger and taunts by your soldiers. You have become an enemy sent to take revenge because you are not a CHRIST.

My sons have never done anything wrong to you. You have power and authority. You have paved the way for the devils to come after my daughter. Because of your wickedness we face death, like sheep for slaughter.

Eve said: Judah, you have passed judgment on my sons, and sad for god (Cain) your father, for making a murderer like him to come and kill innocent people on earth for the devils.

The end of paradise is not lost today, but when salvation comes, Elijah will judge you and will utterly destroy you and every spirit from your seed when He speaks the Word to CHRIST to put an end to your seed and your law on earth.

The justified kingdom

My sons you have killed is like a famine on earth without seed to continue on earth. Today you have made a mockery of me in front of your battalions. They are a witness for every generation for kingdoms of gods from my flesh when CHRIST casts out spirits from your seed from my flesh back to you and the devils. It will be justified to remove gods from the earth.

Wickedness of spirits without flesh Ro.12:12; 1.Pet.5:9

Zion/Eve said: Judah, Elijah will establish kingdoms from my flesh and spirits from your seed will join you till there is none left to do wickedness on earth in my flesh.

Judah, the pain, which I'm suffering for my sons, I can bear, but when spirits from your seed are cast out, they will be without my flesh. The pain they will feel will be unbearable for exterminating my sons from the earth. When CHRIST removes the spirits from your seed in kingdoms from my flesh on earth, only then I'll be satisfied with righteous justice.

The gathering of the bodies of the dead Rev.14:1

The women gathered the bodies of their dead men and sons and counted them and those women who were pregnant and it was written in a book a total of 144.000. They buried the bodies of their men and sons.

The sleep of CHRIST Is.26:11; 1Cor.5:7–8; Heb.5:1–2

Three days after the men were buried, there were rushing winds and the leaves on the trees began clapping. All the women rushed outside their homes. Elijah spoke the Word, and said: spirits of CHRIST that sleep in the earth WAKE up from your sleep and rise.

The spirits of the Hebrews (Christ) and their sons started to come out of the graves. The spirits of Christs were holding their baby boys in their arms and began walking on air. They were in the same image of their bodies in the earth, walking upwards and waving their hands at the women, going towards the pillar of cloud over the holy land. Jesus was waiting in the clouds to meet his brothers raised from the earth, waving to his mother and sisters.

When all the spirits of CHRIST got to the pillar of clouds, Elijah commanded the winds to go unto the clouds with multitudes of spirits of CHRIST with Jesus. The clouds vanished, taking the sons of CHRIST to HIS throne in Heaven to celebrate their victory over death. There was loud clapping in the heavens and joy on earth with the women praising and saying: Hallelujah Elijah.

These were the first spirits of CHRIST with Eve. They did not kill, commit adultery, steal or covet. Elijah established the promise to save spirits of CHRIST after the Sabbath of their bodies.

The women returned to their homes, feeling uncomfortable with strangers entering their homes. They felt sad, gloomy, knowing the devils are coming.

The declaration to Eve

I am Elijah declaring the end from the beginning of ancient times the things that are not yet done.

My Word shall stand even to your old age when I speak unto CHRIST on HIS throne is for HIM to come and cast out spirits from the seed of gods in kingdoms in every nation on earth and to execute judgment on spirits cast out from the kingdom that have no faith in me in fire.

Eve said: Elijah, in the time of salvation will spirits of gods care to know the truth.

Elijah said: When you Sabbath you will be on the earth to observe these things, but when you will be in Heaven, you will be seeing the work of CHRST creating immortal spirits in kingdoms from your flesh.

Eve said: when the time comes for me to depart from this body my spirit will be in your hand to resurrect me to be with CHRIST by the word.

Elijah said: Zion/Eve, you will continue on earth in your image until you Sabbath and resurrect to CHRIST to see justice in your flesh from HIS throne in Heaven when I speak the Word.

WHAT IS THE SABBATH? Mk.2:27; Lk.6:9; Heb.2:14

Eve said: Elijah, is there any other way to go to Heaven without the Sabbath? Eve Elijah said: this Sabbath of the body is a sacrifice to death so your spirit can depart from it, was not necessary but the Eternal, knowing everything before it happens, knowing the devils in the world want to bring the world back to darkness and would come after you and Adam so He manifest His CHRIST and you as the spirits in Adam, this was His secret.

THE SABBATH WAS FOR ADAM Mk.1:44; Mk.2:27

In order for His CHRIST to be the ruler in the world, Adam "the body" had to be the sacrifice "Sabbath" to devils on the earth to make the covenant between the devils obsolete if the devils made a god with his creation, so CHRIST can replace it with a New Testament. The devils don't know you are Zion's immortal spirit in the Light, in the body of Eve

THE SECRET OF THE ETERNAL Job11:7; Is.55:9; 1.Cor.15:43; Ja.2:26

Elijah said: Zion/Eve, as long as you manifest in the flesh you are in your image until your spirit departs. Satan raped you to make a god in holy flesh. He broke the covenant of peace to make a god on earth. Satan knew that when CHRIST comes in the world he would have power to cast him out of the world with all devils, if they made gods from their seed in flesh.

The fear of CHRIST and Elijah Ro.8:2021

The devils sent Judah as a jackass with laws and his vanity made him a king in his deceit so he could come and capture you and your daughters to make gods to put the blame on you as the sinner for making them to fall and not knowing Satan is a rapist to make a god in the flesh of CHRIST.

If you had kept close to Adam you would not have been raped by Satan. By making a god the covenant of peace with devils is broken and has opened way to salvation to save you and your flesh.

Spirits of gods live in your flesh until the time of salvation on earth, to establish the New Testament with immortal spirits of creation by CHRIST to continue in the kingdom to resurrect.

Vengeance is mine, says CHRIST

When CHRIST returns, it is in the time of salvation to create, manifest and sanctify kingdoms worthy for new spirits to be by the Word.

Eve said: Elijah, it is terrible to bring a god in the world to perish from my flesh, and only spirits that have faith will rest in peace. Elijah said: Zion/Eve, that is why CHRIST in Adam spoke the Word for me to manifest and take the kingdom of god who was not righteous to save you and do the work for you in your flesh. **1.Pet.2:9; Ps.95:1-2; 1.Cor.3:6; 2.Tim.1:12**

Eve's epitaph after the Sabbath

Eve said: Elijah, how long do I have to live on earth? Tell me, Elijah, before the devils come after me and my daughters. You are the only holy one left on earth. Elijah, I know your purpose is to save spirits of CHRIST, after Sabbath.

Eve said: Elijah, save kingdoms from my flesh, and present what is worthy in your eyes to CHRIST to be like you in creation by the Word, to continue in kingdoms graciously by your Word to CHRIST on HIS throne in Heaven. **Hos.14:2; Gen.37:5**

Zion/Eve said: Elijah, I am a woman in distress. Make your plan for me clear, so I can tell my daughters before they Sabbath on earth to be with CHRIST and their brothers. There is no saviour except you on earth to turn to.

Sin

Elijah said: Eve, this sin of the devil has brought me into this world to save you from the devils and to remove them from the earth. It is not a hard thing to do. I have to catch them all in the act of trespass to take action if you need my help.

You are suffering. CHRIST is suffering. You both are created to live the eternal life together. CHRIST is on HIS throne in Heaven and you are on earth in distress and want to take your place on the highest throne in the world. You want to know how I can put you there.

It is not through sin you will get there. You have no saviour on earth, beside me to regain paradise in peace and to make you take your righteous place in the world as queen.

You have asked me to save you and to save kingdoms from your flesh from spirits of gods.

Elijah said: Zion/Eve, do you understand the pain spirits of gods born in your flesh will suffer when they are cast out of it? It is you they will blame and not the devils for making a god. Never will the spirits of gods blame the devils for passing their accused seed to them through rape.

They will preach Eve is the one who sinned, not the devil. They will even say it's Adam who was disobedient to god, and not god conspired with the devils to hold your daughter in captivity to make gods. They will even be afraid to mention the devil or be afraid to say it's Judah who killed your sons and hanged Adam on a tree. **Gen.3:5**

While you are on earth, you will be deprived of heavenly privileges and live among the accursed on trial of faith, if you want to sit on your throne in dignity and honour.

Gods shall spring upon the face of the earth and you will see kingdoms from your flesh in multitudes, rooted in sin, bearing kingdoms abundantly and grow to no end burdened with sin. Your spirit shall be put to sleep in peace on earth and will wake up to ask gods to forgive you, when I return to baptize you myself in the Jordan.

Salvation

Elijah said: Zion/Eve, before the spirits of gods are cast out from your flesh;

you have to ask gods to forgive you for making a god in holy flesh created to have immortal everlasting SPIRITS in the light.

Salvation is not possible for kingdoms from your flesh unless you repent before gods on earth and ask for mercy so I can grant you forgiveness to be accepted as a righteous queen of the universe.

Salvation is the only righteous way for CHRIST to return to cast out spirits of gods for slaying your sons from the earth, to manifest new spirits in your flesh and to continue to multiply in images on earth.

Salvation is the righteous way to save your holy flesh from ruin with spirits of gods, in their images on earth.

Elijah said: Zion/Eve, you have put your spirit in my hands to save you from spirits of gods after death. CHRIST has made me judge on earth with authority with the Word. All spirits He cast out from kingdoms from your flesh will naturally return to the devils without flesh for their ignorance and disbelief for not having faith in Elijah to save them from the heat for eternity.

Zion/Eve, you have asked me to tell you my plan. How you can join your CHRIST on HIS throne, while you are still in your image. That is a good question, which concerns your happiness and CHRIST'S my lord on HIS throne in Heaven.

My way is righteous. You lost your virginity by the devil through rape. You were not an angel in Heaven but an immortal spirit manifest in flesh and must have faith to be a queen of the universe to sit on the throne in Heaven

According to the Testament salvation should be put to the test by faith in me to remove the devils and gods in your flesh for ever.

The battle in the kingdom is to cast out spirits of the seed of the devils from your flesh to create new spirits in the Light through CHRIST by the Word to be as it was in the beginning in the kingdom with immortal spirits by the WORD.

Elijah said: Zion/Eve, you have experienced many things since CHRIST was resurrected and seeing your sons eliminated from the planet earth for ever. It is plain to see there is conflict between devils in the world and spirits created in the light and your children in the flesh in the light.

Peace in the world comes through sacrifice and patience to populate one kind from another. The devils destroyed the hope of every god by letting Judah and his battalion shed holy blood on earth. That has made the spirits from their seed not accepted above. First hanging the image of CHRIST and shedding the blood of HIS sons with you on earth.

Salvation comes to CHRIST

The kingdoms of gods from your flesh will be salvaged to be created with immortal spirits sanctified in righteousness, when the Word is spoken is for CHRIST to come and give you children in the Light in multitudes.

So it is natural CHRIST will return to cast out all spirits of devils from his flesh to be the father off all spirits He creates by the Word to continue in his flesh on earth to be among angels in the Light, to live in peace. **Lk.6.1**

Eve, I'm telling you the end before it comes. Your future is ahead of you, and so are your daughters' spirits in your flesh, There will be no peace on earth until CHRIST returns and removes spirits of gods from your flesh to the last seed of the devils.

Elijah said: Zion/Eve, CHRIST said Vengeance Is MINE and I'm saying to you before it takes place, a body well prepared, worthy to be created I will be putting before CHRIST on HIS throne in Heaven. CHRIST will not come to create immortal spirits unless it is though me.

CHRIST will give you children with no labour pains by the Word, with immortal spirits to continue to be productive to make spirits to populate the earth and spirits created in salvation to live in peace and harmony while you are in Heaven.

Zion/Eve said: O Elijah, I have given you and CHRIST a lot of work on earth to rebreach kingdoms worthy for salvation. I will inherit kingdoms as my gift to CHRIST through you.

Elijah said: this is the purpose why I am created to do the work in salvation and to save you and all spirits of Christ after death. and to make the Old Covenant obsolete to live by the New Testament.

Elijah, I was afraid I could never see CHRIST again. Forgive me sincerely for this hard work to create angels in the world in the Light through CHRIST for peace.

Elijah said: Zion/Eve, salvation is a long way off. You have to be patient. When the earth is populated, there will be multitudes of kingdoms for CHRIST to create immortal spirits, in all nations on earth regardless of skin colour to live for ever, world without end.

Trial of faith

Eve, After you Sabbath you will be a spirit living among gods and godly spirits of the dead, so choose a body to sanctify. Live a quiet life after you wake from sleep.

When you get captured tell Tamah not to be be afraid of Judah but to be in control.If he slap her she should turn the other cheek and suffer the grief and have faith in me to save her.

Your daughters will be in harems. When you are held in captivity you must understand you are on trial of faith among gods on earth in your flesh. When you return from sleep, you have to repent before gods and ask for forgiveness and ask for their mercy before you resurrect and sit as a queen of the universe at the appointed time for eternity.

Who can be saved?

Eve said: Elijah, what will happen to spirits cast out? It's a fearful thing for them.

Elijah said: Zion/Eve, those who have faith in me will be saved from Hades, and rest in peace in the earth. Any spirit from Judah's seed that has no faith in me to save them from Hades is not worthy to be saved from Hades; they will have to ask Judah to save them when they don't have flesh for being disobedient and live by the law of the devils. Any god who offers their kingdom to Elijah as a gift to CHRIST to manifest a new spirit to have eternal life, his spirit will rest in peace in the earth when CHRIST comes in salvation.

Zion/Eve said: Elijah, is there any chance for a spirit of god of the devil to resurrect? Elijah replied: the New World is going to be in the Light and every spirit will be in the Light just like your children with CHRIST in Adam are natural angels in the Light in holy flesh. Spirits of gods are not in the Light, regardless of skin colour.

When salvation comes there will be global warming with immortal spirits manifest by the Word all over the earth in the Light in kingdoms. It's the beginning of the end of spirits in your flesh, with the immortal spirits created walking freely on earth and living a long life till their appointed time comes to leave the earth to go to Heaven to be with you and CHRIST and other angels in other worlds. This is the plan given you, with promises before it takes place at the end to begin the New World without the Word in nature of Light for eternity according to the New Testament which the devils did not know.

Elijah said: Zion/Evc, you and CHRIST are created to resurrect to Heaven to sit on the throne as conquers of death in the world, and for CHRIST to make everything new in the world by the Word as in the beginning with the Eternal with the Word.

Elijah said: Zion/Eve, every spirit of gods of the devils has a free choice. They must have faith in Elijah and no one else for their peace. If they are ignorant of this choice and don't believe, they will fall. It's their choice to fall like the devils that had a choice to obey the covenant not to fornicate with the Eternal's creation to make a god.

Zion/Eve said: Elijah, spirits of gods are born with sin of devils. If they have faith in you would you let their spirits rest in peace?

Zion/Eve, every god is born burdened with sin of devils – deceitful, malicious, hateful, jealous, eager to make war and shed blood. If any god has faith in Elijah, they will know how strict judgment is after death and will prepare their body for salvation as their priority to be created with an immortal spirit for their spirit to rest in peace.

Faith in Elijah is to do good for kingdoms through CHRIST. Zion/Eve, I am merciful to those who put their spirits in my hands for peace in the world. Any god who has faith in me will not allow anyone to tempt them to fall. The fear after death in Hades will make them think of their end on earth.

Sabbath for peace

Zion/Eve said: Elijah, what about if spirits of gods Sabbath and they have no faith or for instance if they are ignorant and commit suicide, will they fall after death to Hades?

Zion/Eve, every god is born to live to death. Before they commit suicide they should have faith and put their life in my hands. They would know the judge of the earth is there to save their spirits to die with dignity. Faith in Elijah is to do good for their spirit, and not suffer after death in fire but to rest in peace. But to commit suicide is having no faith; it is self-murder. No hope for peace. Faith, patience, observation and sacrifice bear peace by having a relationship with your saviour to save your spirit after death.

Questions asked

Eve said: Elijah, am I worthy to be with CHRIST my lord as HIS queen? We are so far apart now spiritually. My lord is holy, free and I am suffering on earth because of this sin to make a god with seed of Satan.

Elijah said: Zion/Eve, you must be patient and suffer this rape by Satan to make a god and Judah his son that hanged Adam with hate. You must look towards the wider world. While gods are passing on seed in your flesh, you cannot be a queen to receive imperfection in the world, but when salva tion comes you will have multitudes of spirits in perfection in the Light who will call you Mother of the Universe and not only the earth, so be patient. Your grief will Passover to joy and laughter. Already you have 144,000 perfect spirits from the seed of CHRIST and this is just an example of this everlasting joy and laughter of your children that will be waiting for you in Heaven, justified with mercy andforgiveness after you tell Satan and god and his son Judah to repent for their sins before the gods of the earth by the Jordan.

Elijah said: Zion/Eve, you can't go to Heaven now until the appointed time. There is a time for everything. A time to cry, a time to laugh, a time to build, a time to break down, a time to go upward, a time to go downwards, a time to destroy and a time for peace.

If you die , you will live after death. If you are lost, you will be found to put the crown on your head in Heaven with laughter and not in sadness but in joy.

Zion/Eve, you shall not be ashamed for the god (Cain) you conceived in your youth to remind of the past any more. God (Cain) born in your flesh was not a righteous spirit in your flesh. Satan took your virginity to dishonour you in the world, You are the most excellent mother in the world and by the Word you will have angels populating the world from your flesh with excellent beauty for majesty.

Kingdoms on the earth will be like pearls lost and found in the net and cleaned spotless before you and CHRIST on HIS throne in Heaven.

Elijah said: like the sound of shaking leaves when the wind comes, the devils and godly spirits will be carried away and fall one on top of each other as when the leaves fell in paradise and covered you. When the devils and godly spirits go through the gates of the sun, they shall have no power to put out the flames. They shall cry for eternity and blame each other for rape.

Zion/Eve, blessed are you women in your image. Your flesh shall bear immortal spirits in kingdoms in glory, when you leave the earth, you will receive angels in righteousness, in peace and joy and singing. All the leaves on the trees shall clap for you for justice in salvation. Fear not Zion, neither be dismayed. I will save your spirits. I'll remove all the devils from the earth. Judah has become your enemy. I'll chastise him for his cruelty.

Zion/Eve, why do you cry? You shall be built upwards with immortal spirits through CHRIST like stars without number. Judah condemned himself and spirits from his seed. My way was too straight for him.

Zion/Eve said: O Elijah, thou art my battleaxe and weapons of war to destroy the devils in this world. Let the tempest chase them all to fall like a spinning wheel and gather kingdoms from my flesh for CHRIST to do HIS holy work in manifestation and sanctification. Elijah said: when you sit on your throne in Heaven you shall rejoice when you see salvation in multitudes and the final judgment on multitudes that has no faith.

Any god who preaches against you shall not prosper. Every god that says Eve sinned, is against you in judgment and they shall fall for lack of respect for the queen of the universe for leading others astray to fall.

The warning to gods who are preachers

My thoughts are not your thoughts, neither are my ways your ways. For as Heaven is higher than the earth, so is my way higher than your thoughts. If any god has no respect for the judge of the earth and has no mercy for the queen of the universe, they shall fall for ignorance. The New Testament is by CHRIST and Zion HIS q,ueen and every god must have respect. Spirits from the seed of gods in the kingdom are warned to repent. Tell seducing spirits that want you to fall to go away.

Zion/Eve returned to her daughters in the holy land knowing the plan of Elijah for her and salvation for her flesh, for CHRIST to give her children by the Word.

Her daughters said: mother, what did Elijah say to you?

Eve said: my children, I am crushed by a burden of trouble I've brought on you on this earth. When the hour comes, be strong and put your faith in Elijah to save your spirits. Be strong and have no fear of devils. You will ascend as angels. They can't kill your spirit Eve began to cry: there is nothing I can do for you. O CHRIST, hand over their pain to me. Have mercy when they start to make gods.

My daughters, Elijah promised he will baptize me in the Jordan before I resurrect to be with you before CHRIST starts creating immortal spirits in the generation before salvation.

These are the words Elijah spoke to me before He parted, my daughters. A great plague will upon you after you give birth to gods. You will be dead. I wish you well have much faith.

Elijah said he was sorry for you and me, my daughters. Elijah said he would not like us to be ignorant of what the devils will do, and we should be prepared.

My daughters, the devils are coming to take you in captivity to make gods. Use restraint, so you are blameless when judgment comes on them and their gods.

Judah returns from shedding the blood of CHRIST

Judah returned with his battalion and reported to Satan that all the sons of Adam were dead, perished from the earth, and only the women were left.

Satan called the chamberlain and told him to tell Tamuze that Judah has slain all her brothers and only her mother and sisters are left in the holy land and she must come to Satan to make her petition to save them.

Tamuze came to Satan's bedroom and said: King, what is your bribe this time? You have to cheat and deceitfully ask me to come and satisfy your lust to save my mother and sisters as if it's a favour you are doing us. I feel like a whore in this palace doing you a favour to make gods under oath. I was in fear of you when I signed this shit you call laws of the devils.

Satan, you are coward

Tamuze said: Satan, Judah slew all my brothers and hanged my father, and you ask me to come in your chamber to tell me my mother and all my sisters are now about to perish from the earth or to hold them in captivity to live under your law. Satan, you are a coward and fear punishment by CHRIST. You had to send Judah and gods to kill my people for you.

Satan said: Tamuze, it was in Judah's heart to do so like god (Cain) from my seed. Remember it is Cain who took your virginity and wanted to be the first to pass on my seed to make a god worse than him to live with him on earth. Cain looked at your people as inferior to us devils. He hated Abel and wanted to make a name for himself and then stoned Abel to death. That is why I broke his neck – to save you from him.

The sealed letter to the gods

Satan said: Tamuze, Judah is a king of gods; it is he you should fear. His way is forceful to do evil in the nations. I fear he will cause much disturbance on earth and all from his seed will want to be cruel like him. I fear for the gods on the earth if he ever rules the earth. I will have to send him away very far away if it will please thee, so he doesn't corrupt our gods with violence.

Tamuze said: Satan, I fear he will say it's because of me you put him far away, and he will devise evil against me. Please don't send Judah far away, and put it in writing and seal it with the ring on your finger so if he comes after me while you are away he will see I asked you to save his life.

Tamuze said: I'll satisfy your lust if you put it in writing. Satan asked: what is your request? with shaking hands. She said: write, this letter is for Tamuze to keep for all gods in future generations to know it is Tamuze who asked Elijah to save the son of god and let no god reverse it to dog. Satan sealed the letter with his ring and handed it to Tamuze

Satan said: now, my queen, take off your clothes. Tamuze said: Satan, I have one more request – get rid of all the women in the harem. They have no respect for the queen mother who made gods under the oath. They sin in my flesh. Give them away as gifts to the commandants and soldiers. When I go outside the palace they laugh at me. They all have many faults and are not perfect like me.

O King, you spend too much time in the harem with these maids. You can't satisfy these hungry bitches.

Satan said: they fight over me. You are never satisfied, never like what I do to you. You think it is disgusting. My lust for you is like the consuming fire in Hell and you find fault with everything I do.

Tamuze said: you left the holy life above knowing what is good, but you behave like creatures of the earth, even like a dog, in the harem that worships godly women on your knees, with lust for them.

The false king

Judah became popular among gods in all the provinces and began to get respect and made the princes jealous. The devils also began to hate his popularity in their provinces and his boasting saying he is the chosen god to rule, and that even Elijah approves of and fears him.

God has killed one holy but Judah has slain thousands of holy men from Adam. This brought some fear and unease of revolt by gods to follow Judah instead of the devils.

He would boast whatever devils do, Judah can do, and build and manage governments by the law. He would drink and get drunk and would want to fight anyone who didn't like him.

The celebration after the Sabbath

Satan invited kings, queens, commanders, princes, high priests, and soldiers in the battalion of gods to celebrate the victory of the first Sabbath to death on earth. Judah was drunk and didn't come.

Hope

Satan knew he had to prove to Tamuze he was not a coward. To go and capture the women was a gamble, hoping Elijah and CHRIST had lost interest in Eve and her daughters.

Sometimes Satan felt uneasy like a rat nibbling around the cheese before the trap set off. He scratched his head and was in a dilemma to think straight. His sin brought back memories of his deceit in the Garden of Eden and because of his sin he was cast out of Heaven for raping Eve to make a god (Cain).

Satan began to hate every holy woman. Now Tamuze is dictating what he should do and calling him a coward. The words of Tamuze were in his head. You are a coward! This he can't take. He has to prove himself to her, and he is a king of nations.

Satan felt his time has come to make way. He can't do it alone; every devil must fall if he falls. He can't bear to fall alone. This temptation to hold Eve and her daughters is risky. If he fails he can't return to Heaven and will be in fear of Christ and Elijah.

All his guests are happy and drinking and dancing. He called the chamberlain and said: go and fetch Queen Tamuze and tell her to put her crown on her head to show the gods her beauty.

Tamuze was sorrowful and not in any mood for partying with gods. She was sad about what had happened to her brothers and now her mother and sisters are alone with uncertain future and in fear of Judah and what he will do.

The chamberlain said: Queen, the king wants you to come and meet his guests to show your face. Tamuze said: go and tell the king that when he goes to Hell, there he will see my beauty for killing innocent people of the earth.

The chamberlain told Satan what Tamuze said. Satan got angry and rushed to her room and said: it is Judah who shed blood. I'm not your enemy. Sometimes I'd like to put my hands around your neck and break it like I did with god (Cain).

Tamuze said: do it; take away my grief.

Satan said: will you come out or do I have to drag your ass out of the room to meet the guests and celebrate the Sabbath.

Tamuze said: you can do what you want. I'd be happy to be free of you and your deceit and laws.

Satan said: you fucking bitch, when the new maidens come you will be in the harem and a virgin will take your place.

Tamuze let loose what was bothering inside her and said: I am glad I did not give my virginity to you. Cain passed his seed in my womb to make a god before you held me in captivity and you can't bear the thought he took it before you and you are not the first to fornicate with me to make a god.

Tamuze torments Satan to prove he has power

Satan said: Tamuze, I will break your neck like him if it's the last thing I do on the earth for tormenting me like the angels I left in Heaven.

Tamuze said: that is all devils are. You are a tormentor on earth. You like to feel you have power over women, and like the stupid bitches in the harem who fight over you. You like to feel important. You lust for human flesh. You think we are like creatures on earth – inferior to you and ignorant. When you can show your power over CHRIST and Elijah, I'll give you respect, but to me you are a coward, a snake that runs away when you hear the sound of an eagle.

Satan felt humiliated by Tamuze and went back to the celebration with his head bursting with pain, feeling for the first time he is defeated and all eyes in the world are on him to see what he is going to do.

Satan began feeling isolated. He has nothing to boast about like Judah who is like a cobra sapping his energy and wanting to rule. Satan said to the kings: where is Judah?

They said: the fucker did not turn up. He may be somewhere, boasting he is the chosen god and drunk, screwing some bitch. Satan looked worried and felt on the run and can't see his pursuers. My power is sleeping away now. This bitch wants me to show my power over CHRIST and Elijah. I'll give you respect if you have power over CHRIST and Elijah is tormenting him to put his power to the test.

Tamuze said: you are a snake that crawls. Satan can't take the insults by Tamuze. He wants to break her neck. She is like a silent enemy, like CHRIST and Elijah, and they are elusive. I've become transparent in her eyes. She can see hate, malice and deceit. I am worthless to her. She is not afraid of me any more. She is pressing me like the wind that comes and disappears. She is tormenting me to death.

Satan said: I've become a slave to this bitch. I have to prove myself now to please her, and get rid of my godly women in the harem where I get my joy and fuck them like creatures with my inflamed passion for flesh.

Satan stopped the music and made a speech. He thanked everyone and told the commanders and soldiers to go in the harem and take any godly woman they liked, from the oldest to the youngest, as his gift to celebrate the victory of the Passover. The soldiers said thanks and left with their new mates from the king.

Satan called the scribe and told the chamberlain to fetch King Judah. Judah arrived drunk and Satan gave him a province and said all gods from his seed shall have his name. The scribe proclaimed that Satan gave Judah his province to rule, and Satan sealed it with the ring on his finger and felt deflated.

Babylon

Satan toasted with Judah for his province and asked Judah: what you will call it?

Judah said: I will call it Babylon. They both laughed when Judah said to him he was brought up by a lion.

The celebration after the Sabbath

The kings got together in the synagogue and began to debate how they were going to share the women of Adam when they are captured.

A king said: Satan, everything is going in our favour, I don't think Elijah and CHRIST will come and save Eve and her daughters, because she made a god in sin and death. Christ and Elijah lost interest with the woman on the earth and are enjoying the good life in Heaven.

Another king said: Satan, my queen had a dream. She saw a god come out of a god. It came from nowhere, and it came with a woman and she made many gods and the father of the gods came from nowhere and the two gods began to fight over the woman.

The mother of the first god disappeared and began to cry for her husband to save him, and a holy one Elijah came to calm her down. From that time she cried no more and she joined her husband. He gave her many children. They all look like the holy one and the earth was populated with his children in multitudes.

She started to cry in her dream because there were no gods on earth. She began to see spirits descending to the abyss and the people of the man and woman were with Elijah with our queen mother on earth. Satan, I don't think we should go after these women. My queen is crying, thinking if I come with you I won't come back to her.

Another king said: Satan, my queen had a dream and she was crying in her sleep. She said she saw giants fornicating with the strange women and they began to cry in pain.

Then she saw a spirit in the Light. It looked like a man and he said to my queen, you will see what befalls the devils in this generation of gods, and he took Aba and all the devils and they were carried away and they began to fall into a mouth of a monster in the sea to the deep and the gate was closed. My queen began to tremble with fright and she collapsed in my arms. The kings began to look at Satan and were frightened.

Satan said: All gods are born to have dreams to do good and evil and that is why we have to focus on doing evil, so any prophet that speaks the truth, they will believe them. Stop telling your queens about when you were in Heaven. You can't go back there, and neither is any god from our seed accepted in Heaven. If you give them a good fuck before they went to sleep they would not dream.

I have given each of you kings the best of my daughters to be your queen from the power of my seed to propagate gods of your kind. We should concentrate on organising our gods to have dominion in the kingdom after death for their godly spirits to control kingdoms to seduce and tempt spirits in the kingdom.

When the spirits of our gods take root in the kingdom, CHRIST and Elijah will not know that's where we have our power to bring the world to darkness. There will be no flesh left for CHRIST to create angels. Elijah thinks He can cast us out of this world but he is yet to be seen.

We have destroyed the hope CHRIST had in Adam to populate holiness on earth. The earth is not divided any more. All the good seed is perished. That leaves us to increase with gods passing on our seed to make gods with our evil way, so we can bring darkness back as it was in the beginning for devils to rule the world.

Gods have no understanding of our plan until after death, when they are godly spirits with no flesh to carry out the work to destroy CHRIST in kingdoms. The godly spirits of gods from our seed will hold sinners in bondage under the oath and control governments and do-gooders who have faith in Elijah. Godly spirits will propagate propaganda in religion in tongues so they will misinterpret true doctrine to mislead in tampering holy books to lead astray.

The godly spirits of gods will be doing wickedly in war and destruction of flesh and disease on believers in CHRIST and Elijah to lose faith and become sinners. Godly spirits will seduce to preach it's Adam who sins and Eve is a sinner. They are guilty to make a god to be born in sin.

So when godly spirits make war for the earth there won't be any flesh left to establish kingdoms by the Word. Darkness will return with devils as it was in the beginning without Light. When Satan explained his plan to take over the world, they said: hail Caesar of the world.

The captivity of holy women

Satan called every devil in the provinces to report in the synagogue for a meeting. When they gathered together Satan said: the time has come to go and fuck the women of Adam.

Some of you devils are backsliders and forget what we came to earth to do and I am afraid I will be the one to get punished for going after holy women. We have come to earth on a mission to bring the world to darkness.

So before we go and capture the women let us bind ourselves to an oath to capture all the women to make gods and giants with the daughters of Eve to increase godly spirits on earth so we don't diminish because of lack of seed.

When our godly spirits after death take root in kingdoms, the gods will not know that is where we have power to destroy CHRIST and Elijah to death on earth.

Satan commanded Asbi the chief commander of giant devils to come forward to sign the oath, along with Naphilim, Raphaim, Emmim, Nuiguel, Tiemel, Rami, Basa, Bati, Yetari, Baraguiv, Niplim, Jamsi, Basham and Amaros. After all the giant devils signed the oath, Satan said to the giants: I have put you in reservations to bring you on this mission because I fear trouble, so we don't fall in a trap. Your time on earth has come for you to implant your giant seed in holy women to make giants on earth.

When we go in the nations, fuck as many women as possible to make giants and slay every suckling male so the holy seed perishes and the seed of giants increases on earth to take over the gods on earth.

The chief of eunuchs was brought forward. Satan said: you have signed the oath to capture holy women for the nations. Your work will cease in working in harems. Your work will be decided after the victory in the holy nation.

Satan stripped the ten kings of their crowns and made them commanders of twenty devils each. All the devils signed to the oath to have a share of the women they capture.

They had their horses prepared to go to the holy nation of Adam to capture the women to take them as concubines to make gods and giants on earth.

Satan said to the devils: I know the price of peace, righteousness and justice is to eliminate us in the world. Let no suckling male live to deceive your giants to take over the nations on earth.

The gods came to wish the devils good luck. The scribe took count to see no devils were missing on this mission. The devils kissed their godly women and children and mounted their horses. Judah was with them and Satan saw Tamuze standing by the gate and rode up to her and said: Queen Tamuze, what is your petition before I go and gather your people? It be granted thee.

Make your request now and it shall be given thee even half of the earth. Tamuze answered: if it pleases thee, I don't want Judah to go with you to murder my mother and sisters. Let him stay while you are gone. I can't endure to think what he will do; he is wicked enough to kill them all.

Satan said: Queen, this mission is for devils. I'll let Judah stay in the castle to guard you so you don't run away.

Tamuze said: how long are you going to be away? Satan just looked at her and rode off.

The kings and devils rode out from the nation on horseback to the holy land. The women could hear galloping horses getting closer and closer. When they arrived they surrounded the nation. Satan commanded the women to come outside their homes.

Eve came outside and said: What is it you want? Did you come to slay the women?

Satan said: Evc, it's because of you we are here on earth, for my sin with you! Now you have a multitude of holy women in this nation I can pick and choose, so tell the women to come outside to commit more sin on earth. Adam is not here to help you.

Eve said: as you can see, we don't live in walled cities. I am not afraid of you. If you touch any of my daughters Elijah will come after you.

Satan said: Elijah will not save you. He has lost interest in your people on earth so we come to take you and your daughters to make gods for us. You have no men to give them holy children, and we will turn your sorrow into joy.

Eve said: you stole my daughter and put her in bondage to feast on her holy flesh. Your wickedness will return on your head for killing my man, who is better than you and all devils. You degenerates and are a bunch of cowards who attack women when their men are dead to commit sin.

Satan said: Eve, your god (Cain) with me wanted to make a name for himself to be the first in your daughter, by passing on my seed in her. I told Judah not to kill the women. Now come back with us to our nation.

Eve said: to do what? Gods cannot go to the heavens where you came from, and nor will they be on earth when CHRIST comes to establish the kingdom with spirits in the Light through Elijah. They will make everything new on earth. Satan, if your devils touch my daughters or me it will be your last day on the earth. You devils are barbarian and false. There is no truth in your mouth. Why did you come to disturb the peace in this holy land. Satan said: Elijah is not going to save you and your daughter in my palace, neither your daughters in this nation. Elijah did not save Adam, who did not sin. Why would He come and save you and your daughter burdened with sin. Tell your daughters in the nation to come outside so we can take them to the land flowing with milk and honey and it will go well with thee under the law.

If I say one word the devils will go in the houses and rape the women and there will be all kind of sin in your flesh, and their seed will make multitudes of gods on earth to live under the law.

Eve said: You and your devils came on earth to defile yourselves like the creatures on the earth that devour flesh. **Mt.12:19**

Satan said: Eve, your man has died and I've come to take you and your daughters to raise offspring for your sons that are dead.

Eve said: I am of creation and my daughters are freeborn and not under the laws of devils. You are strangers on the earth. You are misinformed and do not know the power of CHRIST and Elijah. In regards to god (Cain) whose neck you broke to take Tamah away, Elijah raised his son from the bush who is your chief prophet of your law. You are much deceived by him who will rule and imitate you. He did not love his neighbour, but came here like you with hate, deceit, malice, jealousy to kill my sons to be a king like you to commit abomination.

He is the son of god (Cain) you killed, and shall receive severe sentence for making me a widow and shedding blood of innocent holy men to death. Satan, if you rape any of the women in this holy place you and every devil will fall like stones, one on top of the other by Elijah.

Satan said: Eve, CHRIST is not coming to save you and your daughters. You have no sons to give you children. When I take you back, you will have many gods to testify it's Judah who slew all your sons and hanged Adam so I can put him on trial before you and your daughters so we don't get blame for this death of your men.

Satan went on to say the gods in the nations shall hate you and all gods from Tamuze will rise against you and your god (Cain) for raping Tamuze to make Judah. Eve said: it is you who will be punished more, for your rape to make him a murderer and a rapist like you to pass on your accursed seed to Judah. Gods from your seed will suffer and die a miserable death, and live to hate each other.

Eve went on to say to Satan: CHRIST and Elijah will shorten your time on earth. If you or any devil rapes any of the women you will be carried to a place where there is no moon and stars, by the four winds to be with your god (Cain) in captivity.

Satan, if you rape any of my daughters to make a god in this world to suffer in my flesh in this generation to Passover the earth to gods, everyone will come to an end. You came here like a thief with other devils to feast on flesh for the Passover.

I assure you when the whole world knows the truth, every god from your seed will hate you for bringing them into this world to be in fire after death.

The kingdom will be free from your gods for an everlasting testament to create children by the Word without your seed, after Elijah removes all devils from the earth for rape.

Satan said: where is Elijah? Tell Him to come and I'll believe.

Eve said: he is slippery like soap. He appears and disappears and never stays in one place. He has eyes that see what you don't see and ears that hear what you can't hear and whereever He is, He can speak the Word that can be heard in the bottom of the earth to the roof of the heaven. If I open my mouth, He will come to remove all devils from the earth.

Satan said: Eve, there is no holy man on earth; Elijah will not save you for making god.

Eve said: you raped me to make god (Cain) and he was not righteous in my flesh. Elijah will speak through the mouth of him who you strangled to death, if you rape any woman in their house to make gods to Passover by force. You devils will have to take our bodies by force. Our life is in the hands of Elijah.

Satan said: Elijah has told you many lies. Until I see Elijah with my two eyes I will not believe He exists. Tell your women to come out so we can fuck before CHRIST in Heaven.

Eve said: Satan, you are an idiot and a coward. Repent for your sins. You hold my daughter in captivity in your palace. You can't satisfy Hebrew women. We are frigid to strangers and only CHRIST satisfies us. When we are dead we will live holy with HIM for ever so we have no fear of you, devils on earth with deceit, hate and jealousy for what is holy and beautiful.

Satan, go away from the earth in peace. You have not the Word to do anything good on earth for us. Forgive me, you knew it is forbidden to make a god in this world. I didn't enjoy you. I felt dirty with your god in my womb from your accursed seed.

Have mercy on my daughters and me before you make any more mistakes on this earth. CHRIST, who we all love, is better than you.

Satan got angry. A devil said: she is insulting you and asks you to repent and have mercy. Say the word so we can go in their houses for the women to ask us for mercy. Let us teach them to respect devils and gods.

Mumbo jumbo parable

A devil said: Satan, this woman wants to lead us astray with scriptures with mumbo jumbo parables from snakes and apples and mystery spirits to put the fear in us.

All eyes were on Satan. He felt he had to make a decision. The law of devils on earth is not valid. It has hope, but no promise for every god who is born on earth.

Eve said: Satan, don't you see how stupid you were when you raped me? My flesh is created to be everlasting and when you leave the earth there will be much flesh to produce spirits for eternal life in perfection, justified in peace through CHRIST when Elijah speaks the Word.

Repent, Satan, for your sins

Adam knew scriptures. If your god had any intelligence he would not have conspired with you and lost his kingdom to death. He is waiting for you to accuse you for your fault and deceit in giving him hope in his flesh to make him perfect. Instead you made him the first murderer to kill my Abel so you can take his sister to make gods. Now I am a widow because of the god of your god (Cain) with hate and wickedness in your nature.

Are you not ashamed to make gods suffer after death in fire? Elijah will judge between you and I if you don't repent for raping me to make a god to suffer in Hades. Repent and leave the nation in peace.

Satan said: fuck you, Eve, I will not repent. Satan got angry and put his thumb down and all the devils rushed inside the homes of the women to rape them.

Satan said: Eve, now every kingdom will be filled with drunks and sinners to death.

Eve said: Elijah will not spare any devil or have any pity on any god. When CHRIST casts them out from my flesh, they will be carried away by the whirlwind out of the earth to the secret place for your arrogance and vanity.

CHRIST will give me children in my flesh and they will be justified through Elijah with thc Word and you will not be there to see it happen. You will be in a place reserved for you and all your gods.

Satan said: I know the thought of CHRIST and Elijah for peace is to give us an unexpected surprise. We will let no prophet of peace to be among you to deceive our gods with dreams. You can't run away! We will capture you and your daughters in the nation and hold you as a ransom to death. **Is.24:8, 24:19; Pro.25:30**

Eve said: Satan, you have made an error by making gods on earth so go back where you came from in peace. You come here like a thief, to steal women to satisfy your lust like creatures on earth. Satan, don't defile my daughters to conceive your accursed seed to make gods to slay each other for you. It's a waste of holy flesh.

Satan said: I will not repent to you or CHRIST or Elijah who I do not know. I am in the world before them. They should bow to me for making gods to inherit the earth from my seed in this generation. Where is Elijah? Where is CHRIST? They have not saved your sons. No one knows where Elijah abides. His activity to do holy work is hid in the scriptures in Heaven. Don't put your faith in Him. I am here to take you and your daughters back to make godly women for me to give to these barbarians who came with me to make giants.

Eve said: Satan, a severe sentence will come to remove you and the barbarian devils. They will be condemned for ever for making giants with my daughters to fight with gods. When they die they will curse you for making them suffer in Hades.

Satan said: if I give a sign to these giant devils, they will go and rape the women in their houses. Eve said: Satan, you are an idiot leaving the good life above to come to earth to lust with women who menstruate.

All the devils began looking at Satan. In his head he heard Tamuze saying to him you are a coward. I have to teach her a lesson for making Judah. He is with her, imagining Judah is going to rule if he doesn't capture the women. The goddess saying you will be back in his mind, imagining much dread, his thoughts going backward and forward. Eyes looking at him and voices everywhere at him to see what he is going to do. He said: to Hell, put his thumb down, and the devils rushed inside the houses and began to rape the women.

The giant devils began to eat the suckling baby boys, blood coming out of their mouths, going from house to house. The women were crying in pain. The giants committed all kind of abomination and threw the women out when they had enough. They chained them together and set their houses on fire. Then they brought them out of the nation.

The devils mounted their horses and chained the women to each other like slaves, and began following them by foot. Some cried for rest. They were beaten with rods to move on. They were thirsty on this journey. They were staggering, one after another. Finally the devils gave them rest, and went to water their horses.

Eve fell upon her knees and spread out her hands and said: Elijah, I am ashamed to even lift up my face to thee. The devils raped my daughters to make giants and gods to bring shame on me in Heaven. The devils are taking us in captivity. Elijah, give me a place to escape from this bondage by the devils. The earth has become unclean with filth in this abomination. There will be no peace in my flesh.

The women wept for their babies that were slain and eaten, and were yoked with giant devils.

Sea monsters Cam.4:3

Suddenly Elijah spoke the Word and a mist covered where the women were, and where the devils were came an earthquake. The devils fell. Then came a tornado and the devils were caught in the whirlwind and picked up and carried away. They began to fall one after the other in the mouth of the sea monsters and they journeyed to the bottom of the deep to Hades. When they got there, the doors of Hades were opened and the monster spat them into the trapdoor and the door was automatically locked. There they met the goddess, who took count of how many devils returned from the earth.

The goddess said: Satan, I told you to leave the women alone or you would be back. She put all the devils in the chamber and kicked the switch and they fell in. The fire was ignited in the earth with the devils to await final judgment. The end of devils on earth.

King Judah in the palace of Satan

In sin my mother conceived me. **Ps.51:5**

Satan gave Judah authority to rule from his palace and look after Queen Tamuze while he went away. Judah was in this chamber, meditating on himself, going back to his youth with Elijah.

Elijah predicted he will be a ruler and his seed would be all over the earth. He had knowledge who Elijah was and CHRIST in Adam and his mother, Queen Tamuze. A few doors away he was supposed to save from the devils and with a strict warning by Elijah he should not have sex with his mother.

What Elijah offered Ammon-Judah was far off Heb.11:13; Act.2:39

Elijah taught him scriptures. He knew the good way but his nature was evil. He had an affinity with Satan. Both driven by a hungry power to be rulers of the world.

They both had the same grief and hate. Judah, the only son of god (Cain) of the seed of Satan is not accepted in Heaven. Elijah offers him spirits from his seed in salvation and the kingdoms from his mother's flesh will be for creation, to have perfect spirits in her flesh. He blames his mother and god his father for not being perfect.

The offering to be saved is far off by faith

Elijah told Judah that if he had faith and believed, he would rest in peace and be saved from Hell and his image will have a new spirit to be his son in his body. Judah hated the way he is, because of god his father, not perfect, who raped his mother with the accursed seed and could not humble himself to accept the peace offer Elijah offered him, which was righteous, and hate festered and grew worse and worse. Now he is in the palace as a king with a warning by Elijah not to have sex with his mother. To do so is abomination. Elijah's way is too straight for him. Judah found himself struggling with the way he is born, like his father, not perfect, and with lust for his mother.

Satan offers false hope not seen by his word

Satan offered Judah hope that he will live after death and he will rule on earth and in his world when he destroys CHRIST and Elijah.

Satan said: if you want to be a ruler you must be wicked like me and the devils with the law. Judah realized his wickedness was consuming him more and more at the very atom of wickedness. He realized he was more wicked than Satan, who fears CHRIST.

Faith in Elijah, hope in Satan

Satan knew Judah was superior to him with knowledge and his wickedness by having no fear of CHRIST and Elijah, who he feared most. Satan became the student in wickedness and Judah was now the master, with knowledge and understanding in things of the future. Satan did not understand how Judah had knowledge of secret things and was deceitful as much as him to be a ruler of spirits from his seed after death. He told Judah there is life after death on earth, but did not tell him where they would end. Judah abandoned faith and went for hope with hunger for power to rule the earth spirits instead of peace, and did not want to sacrifice his kingdom to have a new spirit in the Light. This situation is with every godly spirit in the kingdom, who does not want peace today.

Babylon Gen.11:4; Ps.147:2; Num.32:24

Judah was meditating on setting up his province Babylon, to make his province the commercial city for trade and to conquer nations to be the absolute ruler on earth, to build cities and disperse gods all over the to rule the earth spirits.

The difference between Satan and Judah

Satan hated righteousness and was hungry for power and wanted to bring the world back to darkness at all costs to be a ruler of the dark world by breaking the covenant of peace between the Eternal Spirit of Light and king of devils of ancient darkness. Satan wanted to prove to himself he can bring back the world to darkness by force without the Word.

The wider world plan Jer.14:18; Essek.17:5; 2.Pet.1:9

Judah has no experience of that world of darkness; he is still a spirit in the kingdom from his mother's flesh. He hoped he will live after death. He was born in sin and not an immortal in the kingdom. Elijah gave him the choice of faith to rest in peace after death. He is ignorant of death; he has no experience of death because he is still a spirit in the flesh he was born.

Judah's hunger for power is to rule on earth in the nations with his laws in governments in corruption to control gods on earth and control spirits in the kingdom to do wickedness to those who don't obey his law on earth. This is the plan of Judah.

The power of CHRIST and Elijah

Judah meditated. To rule the world he will have to declare war against Elijah and CHRIST, the two most elusive spirits Elijah and CHRIST, who had a bigger plan to bring the whole universe in the Light to eliminate darkness totally from the universe for it to be populated with angels in the light living in perfect harmony in the world in peace.

The righteous peace begins in salvation

The covenant between the devils of Ancient World of Darkness was broken when Satan raped Eve to make a god (Cain) and then murdered god (Cain) his son, Judah hanging the body of CHRIST on a tree, shedding blood and eliminating the sons of CHRIST from the earth to death, abomination with his mother and capturing daughters of CHRIST to sin and propagate gods on the earth, to be their ruler as their mighty god.

The final judgment is by righteous justice for peace in the world to eliminate all evil in it for ever by the Word, for godly spirits to be carried away by the whirlwind to the gate of the sun to fall in everlasting flames.

CHRIST has chosen the time for judgment is salvation to do HIS holy work to create immortal spirits in kingdoms in salvation to continue on the earth to populate spirits in His flesh to be angels in Heaven.

The queen and the king in Satan's palace

For the first time Tamuze had the opportunity to be alone in the palace with Judah and she began to feel restless. She anticipated Judah would come after her in her bedroom and rape her like a barbarian.

Faith in Elijah

She was puzzled he kept away from her. She did not know Judah was her son with her god (Cain) she gave birth to in the bushes and covered her first god with straw. She had faith in Elijah she had not seen, to save him from Satan, who warned her if it was a boy he would eat him from birth and if it was a girl he would save it to make gods.

Tamuze became restless and asked the two servants to massage her with the stimulating oils, thinking it would relax her, but this had the opposite effect to removing the fear of Judah. She became restless and curious why Judah kept away from her.

Curious and wanted to know why Judah killed her father and brothers, Tamuze told the servants to go and tell Judah she wanted to speak with him. She remained naked on the couch.

The godly servants went to Judah and told him Queen Tamuze desired his company. Judah followed them and went inside the queen's room. The servants closed the door behind them and kept watch outside.

The nakedness of your mother Lev.18:7

Judah stood by the door with his hands folded and looked at his mother's nakedness and her well-shaped breasts. Tamuze looked at him, observing, and curiously looked at his features, studying him closely and remembering the feeling of her first god kicking inside her body, when she was held in captivity by Satan and held in the dungeon, pregnant by god (Cain).

Tamuze was in a trance, thinking of her youth, and now this strange man, much feared for his cruelty, was standing and looking at her.

Bone of my bone, flesh of my flesh **Gen.2:25; 29:14**
She began thinking: here I am with a barbarian in my bedroom. Instead of doing like the devils and fucking me by force, he is only looking at my nakedness.

Judah said: what do you want? She tempted him and opened her legs and said: Judah, you know what I want. Judah stood looking at her. Still puzzled, she started to tempt him. She got up from the couch and went on her knees on the carpet and began crawling slowly towards him.

She looked up at him and said: Judah, can I touch you? I've wanted to do this since the first time you came in the palace. She put her hands around his legs. **Col.2:21** Judah felt a rush of blood all over his body; she felt the same feeling of a close contact which had disappeared suddenly when she gave birth to her first god in the bushes. **Rev.12:2** She began to cry.

Judah kept silent and did not tell her that he was her god. Judah is tempted by Tamuze and remembering what Elijah said: don't fornicate with your mother, for the day you do you will die and all from your seed will be your inheritance at the gate. Her warmth and innocence in this contact and her bounding, holding his legs, crying. The sweat on his body excited her.

Tamuze said: You are the only one between Elijah and me in my bed-chamber. Why are you standing there like a greedy dog lusting for flesh? Don't you have any feeling? Kill me, or fuck me.

Abomination 1.Cor7:1; Isa.48:8

Bone of my bone, flesh of my flesh Ps.91:1–8

Judah picked up his mother in his arms, and did not tell her who he is. She held on to him. The smell of musk, cocoa butter and smell of goat like Cain was on him. They held on to each other, remembering her rapist brother saying bone of my bone, flesh of my flesh, and crying stop it. Judah began to fuck like (Cain) his father in abomination with his mother and not telling her he was her first god. She slept in his arms.

The dream of Tamuze

Tamuze had a dream of wrath. All her people gathered together with their faces covered and in this dream she asked for Judah to live for ever.

She was told a final judgment has been decreed against Judah. He will not ascend to Heaven for all eternity for killing Adam. He will be bound in the chambers in the snow for a time. His spirit is not accepted. Judah will have multitudes of gods from your flesh and their spirits will be removed and fall.

In the dream Tamuze saw clouds and she could see Elijah speaking to a holy one like her father and could see spirits coming out of images from gods in multitudes and children in the Light were coming towards her and suddenly a strong wind came and lifted her to Heaven and Judah disappeared in the dream.

The devils thirst for water at the wells Mk.14:25; 22:18

Elijah spoke the Word and there was a great noise of thunder, and zigzag lightning in the sky followed by stormy winds. The devils got back on their horses and began to run away in fear that it was a sign of CHRIST and Elijah coming to do battle.

The harvest, the tornado and the earthquake Ps.83:15; Rev:3:5; Is.29:5–8; Job.9:16; Heb.12:18–28

Elijah was patient, waiting to catch the devils all together. The women were exhausted from walking and needed rest. When they got to the valley between mountains, the devils gave them rest and went a distance to drink water from the wells and to give drink to their horses. **2 Pet.2:17**

Eve began to cry and said: O Elijah, the devils are taking us to the nations to destroy us. My daughters have conceived with seed of giant devils, to bring more corruption upon the earth in my flesh. We are here in this dreadful place, taken away from our nation and in captivity exhausted. Elijah, take action for us by the Word.

Tornado Ps 83:13; Is.29:5

Call a tornado for me, Elijah, and let it carry all the devils in a whirlwind from where they are and let them fall into the consuming flames of fire in the sun for bringing shame on us upon the earth. Let them perish (17) in disgrace. Thou alone, Elijah, is upon the earth before CHRIST in Heaven. (18)

Elijah spoke in the ears of Eve and the daughters to stick close together and see action as requested.

When the devils got to a little distance from the women, there was a mighty earthquake. The devils fell off their horses. The earthquake was followed by a tornado with flames of fire devouring upon the earth in a whirlwind coming towards the devils, and all the devils were hoovered in the whirlwind of smoke and fire and it took them away from the earth. They fell in the mouth of sea monsters to journey down to Hades, where CHRIST prepared for them before He went to Heaven. The women were frightened and distressed. Elijah saved the women. **2.Pet.2:17**

Eve said: Elijah has answered me with tempest for their sin to make gods to multiply their spirits in kingdoms from my flesh. I am filled with their (24) bitterness and hate on earth. I am sorrowful for my daughters yoked with seed of devils gone from the earth with swift judgment (25) to the gloom and darkness of the deep waters to receive spirits from their seed. **2.Pet.2:17**

The kingdom is saved from the devils, as an example Heb.12:23–26

The women were the hearers of the Word of Elijah. They prepared themselves to be saved. (23) The devils did not expect this swift judgment by the Word.

Whirlwind and stormy winds in the nations on earth Amos 1:14

For many days there was rain, thunder and zigzag lightning in the nations. Dogs were barking and creatures of the earth were howling and crying. There was no sunshine or clouds over the whole earth, and there was no sight of stars in the sky for days. **Act.27:20**

Fear on the earth

The gods and their queens and their princes were scared and started to cry for the devils. They put their hope in King Judah to save them before they die from these storms and hailstones falling on the earth. (24) They said: the devils disturb the peace on earth.

Disturbance and judgment

The princes called on the palace. Judah was with Queen Tamuze. They said: the devils have disturbed the earth for going after holy women and they have not returned. Something has happened on earth since the devils left the nations. One of the princes said: my mother is crying for her king and she can't stop. Judah, come with us to look for our devils.

King Judah tells Queen Tamuze: now you are my queen Rev.17:17; Mk.19:24

Judah got on his horse and the princes began to ride to the holy nation. When they got to the place where Eve and her daughters were gathered, when the women saw Judah riding towards them they cried: now Judah is coming to kill us. Eve said: have faith.

The earth was split between where the women were. Judah and the princes had to ride around to get at the women. The women screamed: the devils have gone from the earth! What do you want with us?

Judah asked: where did they go? He got no answer. One of the princes said: our mother is crying for her devil king. Where did he go? Eve stood in front of Judah and said: if you want to know where the devils have gone you will have to go to Hades to find them. They are waiting for you there.

Another prince asked: where is the road to Hades, so we can ride to meet them? Eve said: Judah knows the way. According to the law you have to be dead first and you will be a spirit, taken by the whirlwind to them. There is no water to drink there, so drink much water before you go to Hades.

A place prepared for the wicked by CHRIST

Another prince asked: what does a whirlwind do after death? Eve said: ask Judah; he has the laws of death. When spirits have no flesh they cry for water. You see, the devils were thirsty for death and they drank the waters by the well and were taken to a place prepared for them for their sin, and the earth quaked with violence. Then a tornado came to take them to a place swiftly, so tell your mother to stop crying on the earth. Her devil king has disappeared from the face of the earth and to put her hope in Judah to show her the way, when her spirit leaves her kingdom.

The princes looked at Judah for an answer. The women were looking at him to see what he was going to say or do, since he murdered their men. Now the devils had disappeared he looked, and saw a man standing at a distance and perceived it was Elijah.

Elijah and Judah

Judah rode up to Elijah. Elijah looked at him. Judah said: what are you doing here? Elijah said: Do you want bread to fall from the sky for you to eat with the princes of devils, or do you want wine to celebrate the devils' harvest to fuck women with your lust?

Judah said: I will not take even a shoelace from your shoes or any women, lest you say you have made me rich with the women the devils raped. So was his arrogance towards Elijah with hate, because Elijah only offered him peace after death. Elijah said: you disobeyed and committed murder killing the innocent brothers of your mother, hanged her father, and now you are committing abomination with your mother, doing the same as god (Cain) your father and the devils.

The warning to Judah, restraint by Elijah

Elijah said: Judah, if you fornicate with any of the women to make gods their spirits shall enter the gates of my enemies in Hades. The kingdom from the flesh of the women shall be the blessing in the nations on earth and not spirits from your accursed seed.

Elijah said: make this known to all gods born from your seed they are from the seed of god (Cain) of the devils. If they pass on your seed of god your father while they live in kingdoms on earth, it is up to the final judgment when salvation begins in kingdoms on earth, and after their spirits depart from the flesh of your mother it will be to a place where there is fire and no water for ever.

Judah began to feel anger, hate and fear for Elijah. He asked: where are the devils?

Elijah said: I removed them from the earth for ever for raping your mother, her mother and her sisters to make gods and giants to destroy you and other gods on earth.

Elijah said: Judah, I will release Satan for one hour before salvation begin for both of you to repent before gods on the earth for your abomination with Queen Tamuze to make them, Judah, you did a lot of wickedness to my people to provoke me with your anger. I have restrained from all sorts to kill you and have my arms open for peace before CHRIST comes in salvation. Judah bowed his head in shame, for he knew the scriptures Elijah had thought him was the right way, but could not humble himself to Elijah.

Pity for the wicked spirit for the son of god (Cain)

Elijah had pity on Judah. Elijah said: I will punish thee if you harm or do wickedness to Eve and her daughters, so you may know my Word stands against all wicked spirits of gods on the earth that have no faith in me to save them. Judah could not look at Elijah in the eye and returned to the women.

The secret Judah kept to himself Dan 2.47

The princes came up to him and asked: who is this old god? They knew not Elijah was in the image of god his father and in the kingdom. Judah did not answer and kept the secret of Elijah from them.

Judah asked Eve: did Elijah save all your daughters from the devils? Eve replied: what meanest thou to ask if Elijah saved my daughters? The devils brought those you see in this dreary place.

The devils raped my daughters and burnt all our houses and brought us here in this wilderness. My daughters are shivering and trembling with grief for their suckling babies eaten by the giants who defiled them afterwards.

Now they are before a murderer and princes of devils saying their queens are crying for these barbarians Elijah removed from the earth.

The debate

Judah got the princes of the devils to one side and they began to debate what they should do with so many Hebrew women that looked like Queen Tamuze. Judah said: I fear if we leave them here, we will perish from the earth like the devils.

Fear of Elijah

Judah said to one of the princes: go back to the nations and tell the chief of my battalion to come with their chariots and bring as many carts from farms to take the women in the nation. Meanwhile they will walk and follow us slowly toward the nation, till you return to us.

Some women fell and died of exhaustion. When they finally got to the nations, gods were staring at them shouting, Hebrews, Hebrews, witches. They removed the devils from us and disturb the earth with windstorms and hail and no sunshine. don't bring them here. As they passed among the crowds on carts, the gods spat at them and had stones in their hands, wanting to stone the women.

Judah divided the women among the princes and they ended up in harems in their palaces. Satan had emptied the harems in the palace before he went to capture the women so it was easy for the women who were Judah's portion to stay temporarily in the houses as his concubines till he built his palace in Babylon.

The word will set you free Rev.18:8; Jn.8:32

Judah went inside the palace and saw Queen Tamuze and said: Satan and the devils have perished from the earth by Elijah.

Queen Tamuze began to dance and sing: now I sit as queen on the throne free from the oath of devils, I am no widow of Satan and will no more have grief and sorrow. I am free today. Tamuze went on to say: one day, Judah, death shall come unto my flesh with multitudes of spirits crying. They will curse me for making them while I was held in captivity under oath, by the devils.

Marriage in the flesh, not in spirit

Tamuze said: Judah, Satan was a coward. He had you to kill my father and brothers so he could go after helpless women to make one of my sisters his queen. He said that I'm never satisfied. Now he shall cry for my flesh for eternity. Elijah has judged between him and I for marriage in my flesh while he held me in captivity to make gods. Now I'm free from the oath.

My father told me Elijah would save me, and I have faith that one day I'll see my god I gave birth in the bush before I Sabbath. I asked Elijah to save him when I gave birth to him in the wilderness.

Judah could not humble himself to tell Queen Tamuze that he was her first god with (Cain) Elijah brought up. He was in fear Eve and her daughters would tell her that he is her first god. Judah put a guard with strict orders. Tamuze must not see any of the women or even talk with them. Tamuze said: now you want me to be like a lizard in the palace, trying to dominate me?

The dragon Rev.12:7–12

Tamuze went on to say: Satan feared you like a dragon for flesh You devoured his strength. He lost his place in Heaven and led you astray with his laws to blaspheme Elijah and CHRIST.

Judah, rejoice with me. The devils have gone to the bottom of the sea. Satan tried to please me. He thought I was ignorant and like a creature with flesh that lives to die and all I was good for was to make gods in my flesh. I had to endure all his deceit for peace, which is to your gain, to do good for gods in eyes of Elijah for peace.

You are a king of the earth. Make a covenant of peace with Elijah and don't be a fool, Judah. Let us rejoice. No more devils to disturb us in this palace. You have authority over every god as a king of nations. I sit, as a queen, in peace and any god who disturbs my peace will go in captivity by Elijah if I ask for help. **Mt.16:26**

Queen Tamuze said: Judah, you can live in this palace in peace. Use this opportunity to do good as a king. What profit is it, if you should gain the whole earth as a king and all spirits from your seed perish after death by these laws? If you should fornicate with my sisters, Elijah will not like it.

Judah reveals his plan for the earth after death

Judah said: Tamuze! I don't know where Satan came from, but my plan is to take over the earth after my death with spirits from my seed to enter kingdoms with the spirits of gods to fight with me for the earth and persecute the spirits that have faith until there is no blessed flesh left on earth from you and your mother, so the earth will have spirits without flesh.

My wickedness, Tamuze, is to destroy your flesh, and to be king of the earth spirits from my seed without your flesh. I am not accepted above from where the devils came from, even if I do good on earth. This peace Elijah offered me is for my spirit to sleep for ever. I am not like you, who have faith in Elijah. Your spirit is accepted to above and will live for ever.

Without flesh you are rubbish Mk.4:8; Lk.12:32; Mt.25:34

Tamuze said: Judah, without my flesh your spirits will be like rubbish on earth and will have no desire to live by your laws. When they have no flesh they will want to tempt spirits in my flesh to do wickedly like you to kill, make war and lead others astray from the truth and will join the devils in captivity to suffer pain and misery for eternity.

Tamuze asked: Judah, have you seen where Satan and the devils came from? You live in hope that Satan will make you live as a king among devils in his world. Satan is deceitful. He will do the same to you as he did to god (Cain). He conspired with Cain before he held me in captivity, pregnant with his god under oath. Satan will chain you to death as he did to the king of devils, who is his father, and all devils will laugh at you with their laws and you will have no one to save you when you cry for help.

Salvation is the end of spirits of gods and the law

Tamuze said: Judah, when my Sabbath comes, I will live and when salvation comes, Elijah will put your law to an end, when CHRIST cast out spirits of gods from my flesh, so there will be much flesh for eternity after salvation on earth. My father taught me scriptures and to have faith in Elijah to save me.

Judah, let us rejoice inmy freedom. I am free from this oath. The devils are no more on earth and have left you on earth as king to make peace. Elijah is for peace in the world. Why do you want to make spirits of gods to make war against Elijah to make him angry to eliminate you and spirits of gods who will want to destroy flesh on earth like a dragon.

Tamuze said: Judah, you are the only king of the kings of devils left on earth. While you live in the flesh, try to do good and not evil. Elijah is patient with everyone who obeys and will punish you if you keep being wicked. One Word from His mouth and you will Join the devils so stop being angry and accept you are a god and have faith, so peace be with your spirit.

The Ten Commandments

Judah held Tamuze in his arms after speaking and carried her to her bed. Tamuze cried: no! don't force me to have sex with you. I'm free from the oath and you will make Elijah angry with me.

Judah said: it is lawful for me to have you. I'm your king and from now on you are my queen, bone of my bone, flesh of my flesh. Tamuze cried: stop! You behave like the devils who are forced to have sex with hate.

Judah was inflamed with lust, strong emotion exploding in him. He kissed her eagerly. She slapped his face. He grinned at her: I am your king. I'll commit abomination with you. As long as I'm in your flesh, I'll be angry and fuck you until I depart from it.

Tamuze began to cry: your vanity and boasting will consume you if you force me to have sex with you. Your bones will stick out, and you will see me no more. Satan thought he could abuse my body for ever while he was on earth with his stupid oath. One Word by Elijah had him flying like a kite. My flesh is like poison that will kill multitudes of spirits from his seed. If you force me to make a god for you, death is to the spirit.

The princes and queens of the nations come to the palace of Satan

The servants came knocking on the bedroom. The queen asked: what do you want? They said: the queens of the other nations want to see Judah.

Tamuze woke him up and said: you have guests in the palace.

Judah came out. A queen began to cry: O King, will the devils come back? Life is unbearable without my king's lust. I can't sleep and I have had bad dreams since my devil left. Judah said: it will be more unbearable after death when you will be spirits without flesh of my queen. Your kings have perished and put me in charge of you to live under the law to death.

The false promise under the law Rev.12:9, 17; Rev.13:12–14; Rev.13:2-6; Rev.20:7–8

There is no hope for you if you have no faith. The peace is for spirits of gods who live in flesh who has faith to rest in peace on the earth. The law says gods must honour their fathers. Your mother is free in this palace to bless you while you are alive. Your father has put a curse on you to death. There is no peace for you after death, so we will fight for the earth after death. That is your hope, or perish, according to the law. I am your king and the devils have left me in charge of gods on earth.

Judah boasted of his power. There is no king on earth like me and my queen. He boasted: Tamuze no longer belonged to Satan and the devils. By my power I set her free from the oath and now she lives under the law as my queen of gods on earth in life and after death.

The queens began to cry: O king of nations, if the devils don't return there is no hope and we will perish like them. The law is with you. We put our hope in you. O king of gods, we will fight with you after we die to live on earth.

O king of gods, we will do as you say. The queens of the devils and their princes returned to their nations and the elder princes made themselves kings with their mothers to pass seed to make gods on earth.

Judah, king of Babylon Rev.18:2

Judah concentrated to build Babylon to be the city of the earth as the commerce centre. His nation was populating more and more. He built a new palace for his queen in Babylon and harems in the far end of the palace with high walls. Every street in Babylon had watchtowers. He set up schools for pharisees to observe the law and teach the law to the gods. He built a temple for worship. The pharisees would be like his secret police that would punish anyone who spoke of Elijah or CHRIST for the gods to be in fear of them.

King Judah looked upon himself as the chosen god with knowledge of arts and crafts and culture of a higher civilization among the gods of the earth. He linked himself as lord of the storms and winds, earthquakes, lightning and thunder. The only king that did not perish from earth with the devils and all gods began to worship him as the mighty god even up to this generation.

THE BEGINNING OF MANKIND Connection Gen:1:12

Greed set in and the queens began to get jealous of the new kings paying much attention to the pregnant Hebrew women in captivity. The new kings began to sell some Hebrew women to rulers of gods of other tribes in the nations, so when the children were born, they could sell them. The rulers made marriage with women in their harem in bondage.

KING JUDAH'S MARRIAGE TO QUEEN TAMUZE TO MAKE ISRAELITES

Judah said: Queen Tamuze, Satan is not returning. I am king of nations and you are free born. I am going to make marriage with you in the flesh to make children to look like your brothers. Tamuze said: what would you call them? Judah said: I will call them Israelites. Maybe Elijah will accept them to go above. There is no one like your brothers on earth with pure seed to make Hebrews.

Queen Tamuze, you make children with my seed and I'll make children with your sisters and I will mingle them with your children till we make Israelites.

REMEMBRANCE OF GOD

Tamuze said: you speak like god (Cain). He raped me to make a god to look like him. Now you want to make children in the palace of Satan to look like my brothers you killed.

I was pregnant with his godly seed in my womb, while I was held in captivity by the devils in bondage under oath in this palace. I am now a free woman from this oath and you want me to be a mother of Israelites to be wicked like you with your laws to take over the earth to make Elijah angry with me.

Nimrod against Elijah

Judah got angry. He held the rod he hit the horse Adam sat on before he was hanged and said: I call this rod Nimrod and it will do the same to you if you don't worship me as your god. From now on, you will no longer be called Queen Tamuze but Queen Babylon with your king, to rule your mother and sisters and all on earth.

Violence, cursing, deceit, grief

Like a tyrant and fierce with the rod in his hand, he said: now kneel down and worship your king, Queen Babylon. Tamuze began to cry: have mercy on me; you are only doing this to provoke Elijah to anger. Judah slapped her on her face and said: I command you to worship your king. Tamuze was in fear of him and began to tremble in shock. You are like a devil, she cried. You are no damn good forcing me to be your queen. You are deceitful. You are a destroyer of holy people. Elijah will cast you out for me from this palace, so I can be free from your law. **Pro.10:6; 11:9; Ps.10:7; Rev.13:6; 1Pet.4:13**

The whole world will laugh at you for not accepting peace with Elijah. You put your trust in your seed to multiply in abundance on earth. I am pregnant for you. Is this the way you treat me with your god in the name of Israel in my womb to add to my shame to make a god in my flesh to be wicked like you to be against CHRIST and Elijah, to war with you for the earth?

Captive Tamuze under laws of marriage in the flesh

You are a fool like the devils and corrupt and boastful in your imagination, wicked and abominable like a devil. You want to destroy my flesh and my sisters you have in captivity with my mother and want to put us to shame with marriage in our flesh. Instead you rejoice with me for my freedom. You are violent and want to hold me still in captivity under laws of devils. Elijah will be our judge. You are so disgusting, Elijah doesn't want to look at you.

Silent in submission 1.Tim.2:11–12

Judah held her by her throat and said: I'll kill you. No one can satisfy you. You are like a whore in Babylon, who can never have enough. Every time you mention Elijah, you will be punished by your king, until you learn submission and silence under my authority. According to the law, women in my harem keep their mouths shut.

Queen Babylon shouted: you fucking bastard, wanting to take over the palace with your laws and rules. Kill me with this Israelite in my stomach to shut me up. You hate my people and killed their men who were innocent, holy and righteous on earth and took advantage of their women you hold in captivity. **1Tim.1:7**

Rage, malice, lust, jealousy, hate Gen.15:13-14; Lk.24:49

Judah was furious she answered back and said: the object of my hate and malice and anger and jealousy is directed to you and god (Cain) of your mother, who yoked his seed in you to make a god like me to destroy the holy on earth because he feared Satan would kill him. He wanted to make a name for himself on earth to be the first to fuck you to make a god.

Judah said: you are a whore and burdened with sin with the devils to make gods to live until death from your flesh. Babylon shouted: it is my flesh you lust for, isn't it? And it is like perfume upon the earth in the flesh of every god from birth. You cannot have enough of this perfumed flesh. The devils are crying for it; now you are enjoying it. You will die in it and not glory in your abomination after Elijah casts your ass out of the earth to cry with the devils without it, and all your bastards that live in it to pass your seed will see CHRIST for hanging his body.

Judah hit her a slap on her face. Babylon fell on the ground, dizzy. She cried: go away from me. You are wicked. Even Satan was better than you. Judah got excited and tore her clothes off and took her by force and began swearing – fucking this and that. It is my wickedness in your flesh that made me king to enjoy you more than devils and to rule you as king of the earth until death.

Judah said: I command you to worship me as your king. Elijah does not care for sinners. Babylon cried: I don't want to be your queen or worship you. You are vain, and wickedness is in your nature with deceit and want to take over the palace of Satan and the devils to make Israelites to pass on your seed in my flesh to live by the law to death.

You know you are trespassing in what is holy and forbidden to make gods, so stop forcing me to have sex. I have to endure this shame until I'm dead, but I will live to see you cry and beg Elijah for mercy before gods. Tamuze went in her room, slammed the door and began to cry: O Elijah, have pity on me; save me from this tyrant.

Elijah spoke in her ear: when you Sabbath you will be free when you are a spirit. I myself will baptize you in the body you chose, before this wicked reprobate and all spirits from his seed in the Jordan. Be patient and don't lose faith in me.

THE PROMISE TO BABYLON Heb.Ro.9:8-9; Ro.4:20; Gal.3:14

Jesus, the spirit of Abel will come in that generation to tell spirits of his seed the truth about him and to prepare their kingdom from your flesh for recreation to be holy spirits with eternal life. Then they will be my beloved sons from your flesh in the Light by the Word.

If the spirits from the seed of Judah refuse to accept peace like him, they will return to him by the power of the Word for being stubborn, disobedient and ignorant. **Gal.3:19**

I promised Judah before he took the law of Satan, the spirits from his seed shall be his inheritance when they depart from kingdoms from your flesh. Their kingdom is your inheritance to have new spirits created in salvation by my Word to CHRIST in Heaven. He put his hope in Satan to make him a king on earth. Tamah, you will see judgment on the devils and Judah and all spirits that have no faith when you are in Heaven. Knowing Elijah's plan for her in the future, Tamuze queen of Babylon, fell asleep.

Faith in Elijah Gal.3:22

Judah, in his anger seeing Queen Babylon his mother would rather die than give up her faith in Elijah, told her all that was in his heart with anger, called her a whore, choked her to near death, slapped her and fucked her. He could not shake of her faith in Elijah. To make Elijah angry, Judah went in the harem, took Eve in captivity and dashed her head on the wall and blamed her for making god (Cain) his father, and separated her from her daughters and said to her daughters: you motherfuckers, I'll kill every baby born in the harem that looks like god (Cain) of your mother with Satan. He went on his chariot, hit the horses with his rod, and sped out of the palace to Babylon city.

Beyond reproach

Judah felt he was beyond reproach. He made his mother his queen. If he was violent to her it was no one's business. He felt his mother was his. She brought him in this world and she should obey him and not have anything to do with Elijah. He disobeyed Elijah and it made him hate Elijah even more to see Elijah had a hold on his mother and she couldn't get him out of her life with this faith, and wanted to punish her with cruelty to submission to share his dream to be king of the planet earth and Tamuze as his queen.

Observance of Judah

Babylon observed him well, not knowing he is her son. She observed that since he took the law of Satan and the devils he became conceited and was falling more and more in the trap of the devils, imitating the devils for power to take over the earth. He had to prove he could be more wicked than the devils and had to kill innocent Adam to make a name for himself to be a king on the earth.

The words of Elijah to Judah, you will be a ruler of nations, is stuck in his head. He did not understand that the reason why Elijah wanted him to be a ruler was to set an example to do good in the eyes of the devils. To become a ruler he has to earn it in deed. That was his guarantee for his peace on earth after death if the devils had attacked him when he went to save his mother. All he had to do is call for help, and Elijah would cast them out and it would be justified to save his mother and himself and sanctify a new spirit in his image in due time to be his son in righteousness for his spirit to rest in peace.

The stumbling block – Elijah and Christ offer peace for kingdoms

Judah did not think much of the peace offering while he was a spirit in the kingdom from birth for his spirit to rest in peace for ever so his kingdom could have a spirit by the Word to be Elijah son in his image in salvation to live in the New World in the Light. He had no faith. Judah did not know the power of Elijah until Elijah removed the devils from the earth. He understood now why the devils were in fear of CHRIST and Elijah and thought he could declare war and fight against them with godly spirits for the earth.

Elijah takes a review

Elijah is patient with the behaviour of his begotten god Ammon. Judah has brought problems to CHRIST and His family. His spirit is of the accursed seed, subject to violence, conspiracy and deceit.

Judah doesn't realize how lucky he is to still be alive in the kingdom. Judah has wearied Elijah with his anger and abomination with his mother and murdering of innocent sons of CHRIST in the presence of their women. Now he has them in captivity with no mercy. The plan for world peace has to be justified according to the scriptures.

The kingdom has become polluted

Elijah's work is to save the kingdom to have everlasting life in salvation and save spirits of Christ in the Light. He gave Judah the choice for his kingdom to be created with a new spirit to be his son in creation, for his spirit to have everlasting sleep. Judah had no faith. Elijah and Judah separated. He was now grown up and had knowledge of everlasting life Elijah taught him from youth.

THE TRIAL OF FAITH, PATIENCE BEFORE ACTION IS TAKEN Heb.6:15; 11:9,33

Elijah took a break. No one knew where He was. His people did not know where he abode or what became of Him. Fear and trembling seized the women with this murderer of their men. All they had is faith in Elijah to save them after death.

THE MASTER BUILDER Nah.4:5; Ps.118:22; Mt.27:1; Essek.27:4; Heb.11:10

Elijah is the master builder with the plan of CHRIST. He is not the one who made the plan. CHRIST created Him to establish the plan for CHRIST to have dominion in all worlds according to the scriptures for world peace with angels in the Light by the Word, and with everlasting spirits in the Light in the kingdoms. **Heb.19:15; Hag.2:22**

VENGEANCE IN THE KINGDOM TO ELIMINATE ALL SPIRITS NOT IN THE LIGHT FOR WORLD PERFECTION Ps.24:8

The battle in the kingdom is directed by Elijah for CHRIST to come and cast out spirits of gods from the kingdom from the flesh of Zion and Jerusalem and create immortal spirits in salvation. The spirits cast out come on to final judgment by Elijah to save the spirits that have faith in him and to pass those that have no faith to the spirit of the sun to remove them from the earth to the gate of the sun. Every spirit has a choice to choose their fate.

THE TEMPLE

In anger Judah took his chariot with his commandant and a few soldiers and they raced to Babylon city. When they arrived, he began to boast: Queen Tamuze is pregnant by me and I'm going to build a temple for her to have my child in the centre of Babylon for everyone in the city to come and worship my mother and child in my temple. It will be a new foundation to start Mankind for the queen of the earth.

The commandant asked: what kind of child will it be, since you are king of nations? Satan was king of nations and he called us gods with your queen. Judah said: every seed I pass of god and is fertilized with my queen and those she gives birth to will be called Israelites. The spirits will be my inheritance after death to fight with me for the earth. The commandant said: what about spirits from my seed? Since you are a god like me, will they fight with my spirits after death? We have to share the earth else there will be much war by gods in the flesh of Queen Tamuze, spilling our blood on earth to death.

The commandant said: King Judah, since we killed the sons of Adam, I have dreams and see much blood on the earth and Queen Tamuze is always laughing and drunk with much blood on her hands and saw Satan crying in howling flames for Tamuze our queen mother.

Judah said: I am the chosen king and I am alive on earth to take his place because he was a coward and had you and I to go and kill innocent men so he could take their women for himself. That is why he is crying because I have what he wants on earth – our queen mother to fuck.

That is why you see the queen is always laughing and rejoicing with her god on the earth. I would not like you to be ignorant, Commandant. Just stop living in hope. The devils will not return. Do like me and call your children by the new name.

The Hebrew women I have in my harem are pregnant with gods and giants. I'll give you a baby girl to pass on your seed with her. The commandant said: King Judah, what name shall I call the girl you give me? Judah said: call her Mankind so your children can pass on your godly seed to make Mankind like Israelites to populate the earth in multitudes from our seed.

Your Mankind and my Israelites shall take over the earth through our Hebrew queen mother and the baby girl I give you from Tamuze's sisters in captivity and make multitudes on the earth. That is how the devils made gods to pass on their seed on earth through our mother's flesh.

It is lawful for us to do the same as the devils

The devils did not come to earth with their goddess to make gods with her. They use our Hebrew queen mother to make gods for their goddess, so it is lawful we make Mankind and Israelites for our Hebrew queen and make her the goddess of the earth. The devils are finished on earth like cowards of the world in sin, crying for the flesh of my queen.

The commandant said: King, now I know you are wise. You are wiser than the devils and took over the throne of Satan for us to yoke our seed and make our kind. But, King Judah, we are gods. How will I know what is my kind to inherit on the earth from your kind?

Judah said: all gods that have different features from Israelites, I will call Mankind, and they will be yours; and those that look like our mother's brothers who we slew will be my Israelites. The commandant said: King, but our other brothers will be jealous and will want to hate Queen Tamuze for not giving them children from her sisters in captivity, and will say you and I want to control Hebrew women to interbreed them on earth, to make gods jealous on earth with our creation since the devils left the earth.

Judah said: all the children born by Hebrew women in the harems that are Mankind, I'll sell in the market, which will give our brothers a chance to make Mankind for their tribe so Mankind can mingle with one another on earth so they don't have to be jealous.

Commandant, Judah said: to make my Israelites it needs mingling, interbreeding and much propagation to make unicorns to look like our queen's brothers we killed. The commandant and Judah shook hands on the future of the earth.

The foundation of Mankind and Israelites

Judah and the commandant started to measure the sight to build the temple in Babylon together with the help of soldiers,

The building was erected as the foundation for all mankind on earth to worship the mother of Israelites and Mankind. Judah dedicated the temple to Babylon to begin the process to change the features of gods he blamed the devils for not being perfect.

The statue of Mother And Child

A statue of mother and a child on her arm hewn out of a large stone was in the most artful manner to portray their beautiful Queen Tamuze to be admired and worshipped by gods, Mankind and Israelites. The statue was inside the centre of the temple. So worshippers could come and sit in the temple, buy candles and burn incense outside after they worshipped, and would ask for favours from the statue. pharisees were trained to help the people who would come to the temple with problems in the nations after she gave birth.

Queen Babylon was in the fullness of her pregnancy with her first child with Judah as the god of Israelites to make spirits to war for the earth after death.

The gods in the temple waited to celebrate the birth; they began in their excitement to call Tamuze Ishtar, goddess of stars make Mankind for the king of nations.

They called Judah God of the world for life and death and swore by the temple of Babylon to kill any god that do not worship King Judah as the God who made Mankind on earth.

The pharisees were trained to police the gate night and day to protect the temple and to ask for gifts to enter to worship the statue of queen and child.

The pharisees were trained to indoctrinate worshipers to pray to the statue with child. If they made a mockery of the queen of Babylon, they would frighten them that she would send spirits from death to attack them. They were trained to execute the law from birth of the first Israelite.

The birth of Israel was the beginning of change of name from first god with Queen Tamuze to Israel

When Queen Tamuze was ready to give birth she was brought inside the temple from the palace. Special incense was made to send up a signal of white smoke for the crowd outside the temple in Babylon to know it was a boy to spread the news in the nations.

The gods gathered outside in multitudes and began singing and dancing with timbrels. Others were blowing their trumpets, harp players were playing, and god's hands were clapping: hail mother of gods. Give our king a god in the name of Israel. This was a new thing Queen Tamuze making a god with King Judah king of gods. With great excitement they began calling Tamuze goddess of the earth. Others were shouting: Hail queen of storm. Make us new children to look like you, and they began to clap, their hand mother of gods don't suffer in silence, for this birth let us hear you cry in this world for children born from the seed of Judah in your flesh.

The gods were shouting outside the temple: O Queen Tamuze, give birth to our Israelite to pass on the seed of our king to multiply like gods on the earth. O mother of spirits, don't be silent. Make our king his first Israelite to rejoice with you on earth.

Fear in birth

Queen Tamuze pushed and pushed but the baby wouldn't come. Weak and tired, she had rest. She drank water. Her legs were trembling and nervous of what Elijah would do if the Israelite did not have faith like Judah, sweating, remembering when she gave birth to her first god. Satan threatened her he would eat it from birth, because he blamed god (Cain) for being on earth. Clap, clap, the crowd began: mother of nations, and don't be afraid to make our Israelite in Babylon.

Judah began to get angry shouting at Tamuze: what is the matter with you? She cried: it is afraid if it come out. You will make it do wickedness on earth. Go take your bow and shoot an arrow in the sky for Elijah to see you or kill some badgers to make coats of skin for the birth. I thirst for honey; go get some for me.

Tamuze said: Judah, it's I who is going to suffer when this baby Israelite is born to have peace on earth. If you don't go I'll die in this childbirth and you will cry like the devils with no peace. Go away, Judah, from me if you want your Israelite to come out. Judah shouted: it is Elijah who is making you suffer, not me. Judah told everyone in the temple to go outside except the midwife. The midwife began to say: mother of Israel, now take a deep breath, and she started chanting: O spirits of mumbo jumbo in abomination. Tamuze began to cry loudly in pain: O Lord have mercy, and slowly Israel came out and he began to cry aloud in the temple. Judah rushed inside with the others. The incense of white smoke went up. It's a boy, the outside shouted with joy, he will be our pope. Others shouted: no, he will be our prophet of war and thunder. There was much jubilation. Israel is born in Babylon. Many brought gifts for mother and child in the temple.

The offering outside the temple

After the birth, they brought a big black bullock among the other bulls and had it to yoke with a white heifer. Then they killed the heifer and burnt it in flames of fire and took the ashes of the heifer and put them in a jar for future generations to remember the birth of the first Israelite in the temple of Babylon. Then they killed the bulls for burnt offerings for sin to make Mankind with Tamuze's sisters in captivity and share their flesh among gods on earth.

The birth of giants Hos.10:13–14

Judah was in bed with his mother, Queen Tamuze of Babylon and there was much cock crowing and howling of wolves crying in the night. Tamuze said to Judah: your Israelite is crying at me. I thirst and I hunger for bread. Judah got angry and said: Is it Elijah you thirst for, or is it bread from Heaven? You are never satisfied. She said: it is your Israelite that is thirsty and wants bread from Heaven so it can be satisfied to sleep in peace.

There was much crying coming from the harems and in the palace. Tamuze said: what is this noise? I can hear babies crying. Judah, go and see. The daughters of Eve were giving birth all at the same time. The babies were huge and the birth was difficult and painful. All the daughters of Eve held in captivity died in the harems giving birth. The guards rushed in the palace to say: the Hebrews are dead in childbirth.

Some mysteries hid Lk.8:10–14

Judah made haste to the harem and saw Eve crying: all my daughters are dead after giving birth to giants. Babies need midwives to assist them. Judah went back to the palace and said: Tamuze, my queen, your sisters have given birth. She kept her silence, looked at him to say some more, and said: can I go and see my sisters and their babies? He said: no, all your sisters are dead.

Tamuze said: what are you afraid of? Why can't I see my sisters and help them in this death? You want me to be an alien to my people even in death. First you kill my father, then my brothers, and now my sisters are dead in your harem. Even your Israelite is kicking me in my stomach. What do you want from me? she shouted and went out and slammed the door behind her.

Judah the dragon of the earth Rev.12:4–6

Judah rushed inside after her with hate and anger, held her by her throat and said: I'll kill you if it's the last thing I do on this earth. She said: Don't say it, just fucking do it and you know who will come after you. I'm filled like a cow with your bitterness. You are like a dragon and want to devour my flesh with hate and lust. Kill me, so I can join my sisters in death.

Sister of god my father 1.Chr.28:3–4

Judah knew in his anger he would kill her. He ran out of the palace holding his head wanting to cry, but tears won't come. His hate for god (god) his father in the heat for raping his mother with hate and deceit and can't humble himself to tell Tamuze he is her first god with god (Cain) brother in the flesh of Eve and doing the same abusing his own mother shamelessly Now the babies were crying, with the dead bodies of their mothers on his hands.

He will hold his mother as ransom for his wickedness Job.33:24–27; Pro.6:2–3

Judah said to Eve: I am inflamed with malice, hate, jealousy, deceit, lust, greed and hunger for power. I'm like a consuming fire that's eating my insides to destroy what is good, and bringing tears in my mother's eyes. She wants me to kill her for Elijah to come after me. The same she did to the devils, Tamuze wants to do the same to me. She warned me she will see my bones sticking out of my flesh. **Job.33:21**

She is like a witch with her words, yet I hate it when she doesn't speak and keeps silent. I want she and I to taste death together, to be king and queen of spirits on earth.

Judah, father of the fatherless

Tamuze was in much grief and sorrow hearing all her sisters are dead. Eve Told Judah to go quickly in the nations and bring mothers with suckling babies to breastfeed the godly giant babies. Judah said: now I am a father of giants of the seed of devils who are no more on earth.

Eve said: did not Elijah adopt you? What is the big deal? Hurry to save the godly children to make Mankind with them. Judah took his battalion of soldiers and went from house to house to capture the women with babies and brought them in the palace harem for the babies to suck milk. Eve said: what a calamity on earth.

The soldiers took the bodies of the daughters of Eve and buried them in a field outside the nations. Judah locked himself in a room, afraid Elijah would be coming after him.

The other harems that had the daughters of Eve died giving birth to giant babies

The new kings in the other nations with their godly queens of the devils who were their mother came in haste to see Judah and Tamuze, queen of Babylon. They were in fear, trembling and breathless. The servant went to Queen Tamuze and said: you have guests. She said: I don't want to see any one. Go and tell the king to see his guests. I'm not in the mood to see anyone.

Judah rushed in haste to see the kings of gods and said: what you want with me? The godly queens began to cry: O King Judah, all the Hebrew women are dead giving birth and their babies are crying and we don't know what to do. Also the rulers in the other tribes say the Hebrews we sold to them are dead giving birth to huge baby gods.

Judah began to shout at them: why did you sell them? The queens began to cry: the Hebrews did not like our food and did not have the strength to give birth. Judah, don't be angry with us. The Hebrew women complained every day they didn't like to be living in harems. They said they are freeborn and not used to be in captivity under our kings. Now we have many speckled babies to adopt, crying to be saved.

Judah didn't want to upset Tamuze with this death of all her sisters. Tamuze is the only daughter of Eve left on earth to make his Israelites. Her mother is old, past bearing.

Judah told the godly kings and godly queens he will take some of the babies and the rest they can have. They must hurry back to their nations quickly and get their soldiers to enter the houses of gods and take the women with suckling babies and bring them to their harem to breastfeed the children and bury the dead women in the fields before their spirits attack us. The king and queen rushed back quickly to their nations to do as Judah suggested to save the godly babies.

The spirits of the daughters of Eve sleep in the earth after death

Three days after the death of the daughters of Eve there was thunder and lightning in the sky. Every god was afraid the devils coming to take revenge. Judah ran in his room and hid under the bed trembling, afraid what Satan would do to him. Eve and Tamuze heard Elijah commanding the clouds to cover the earth, and said: spirits of CHRIST, awake and rise from the earth. There was an earth tremor. The spirits of the daughters of Eve began to come out of the earth and began walking on air, going upwards to the clouds to meet Jesus, to show them the way to Heaven.

Eve rushed outside the harem. Tamuze rushed to the window in the palace and they began to see the spirits of the women that gave birth to giants walking on air, going upwards, waving goodbye to Eve and Tamuze in the clouds. No god could see this because are not immortal spirits in the light but Eve and Tamuze were the only two immortal women of CHRIST left on earth. When all spirits went in the clouds. There was a flash of lightning in the clouds and a sudden wind came unto the clouds and took the spirits of the daughters of Eve to the heavens to, join CHRIST and their brothers. Eve and Tamuze kept this a secret from Judah. **Esek16:44; 1Cor 15.21–22**

Eve and Daughter Tamuze immortal spirits Is.51:6 The only two immortal holy women left on earth in their humanity Essek.16:44, Mic.7:6, Zech.2:7, Jer.50:42, Ps.137:8, Essek.23:2, Is.52:2

Eve was barren and old, and became a nursemaid to the godly children in the harem and brought them up for Judah. Tamuze was held in captivity now betrothed to Judah under the law (**Lev.19:20, 25:44–46**) to make Israelites (**Gal.4:25, 5:2–4**) for war for the earth against Elijah. **Heb.2:14-15)** to destroy the kingdom to death **Ro.8:12-13, Heb.39:11, Ro.8:18-23**

JUDAH, THOU HAS CORRUPT MORE THAN DEVILS Essek.16:47
EVE IS HUMILIATED IN THE HAREM Is.119:23

The making of Mankind and Israelites. **Joel.3:8, 2.Cro.31:5–6**

Judah went to the palace of the other godly kings and began selecting the female baby gods of the dead daughters of Eve to make Israelites to have features like thc people of Adam he killed, and took them with him to the harem in his palace.

Eve was clothed in sackcloth, supervising the feeding of giant babies of her dead daughters raped by devils now in captivity by Elijah while Tamuze brought up her Israelites in the luxury of the palace. **Essek.16:47**

THE NEW KINGS SELL GIANT BABIES Gal.4:23-27, 5:20–21

The princes of the devils made themselves the new kings with their queen mother and kept some girls from the Hebrew women that died in their harem giving birth to giant babies to propagate Mankind with gods. They sold some of their giant baby gods to merchants, rulers and tribal chiefs in other provinces.

KING JUDAH, THE FATHER OF THE FATHERLESS Is.22:21

Judah became the God father of babies of the Hebrew women that were raped by devils. He brought up the babies and began to mix and mingle the children with different features – children with children with his mother to look like Hebrews to be his creation of Israelites. The giant baby boys he set apart to train as his new warriors to for war, and to protect his Israelites. The babies he didn't select, he sold or gave them as gifts to his commanders of his battalions and soldiers to mix and propagate, to make Mankind.

Babylon city began to populate. The city began to be active with commerce of all kinds of trade. Judah felt confident, boastful of his power, feeling the earth is his. Everywhere he went; the people bowed and worshipped him as God who created Mankind and Israelites. No one spoke about the devils anymore.

Many generations later Pro.29:16; Essek.10:10; 2.Cro.27:23; Job.39:16

The giant children of Anak devils Judah brought up, he trained to do battle with shield and armour and sword and taught them to shoot the arrows with bows to fight against any uprising.

The other kings imitated Judah and began to train their giants to protect them and Mankind. Giants began populating in the provinces with Ogs and they began to make Golieth giants.

Mankind and Israelites began to take root with different features, size, and height and were everywhere on earth. There was great demand for Mankind. Tribal chiefs came from other nations to buy or sell Mankind for their harems to mix and mingle with gods.

Life in the palace

Tamuze, queen of Babylon, wore embroidered clothes, make-up, gold rings and necklaces. She was always pregnant with Israelite children running after her with tinkling bells on their feet in the palace or playing with Siamese cats and rabbits.

In the palace garden there was a variety of exotic birds, singing and making noise; peacocks showing off their plumage when the cats came around in their territory; and fishponds with all kinds of coloured freshwater fish. The palace had all sorts of rest rooms. When Judah and Queen Tamuze and children were together, servants would bring fresh fruit to them.

When King Judah and Queen Tamuze of Babylon were resting together from the heat of the sun, servants would fan them,and harp players would play soothing music for the king to fall asleep. The servants would wash the dirt from under his feet, clip his toenails and massage his feet with herbal oils. The king would fall asleep on Tamuze's breast like a little boy. Those were rare moments when there was peace in the palace between king and his queen mother. While he was asleep he dreamt.

O NING OF NATIONS, HEAR THE WORD OF CHRIST Hos.1:1; 1.K.14:22; Jn.3.16

CHRIST loves the world so much, that HE gave Elijah, HIS begotten son, authority to save those who had faith in HIM to save the kingdom to have spirits of creation with everlasting life. Spirits from the seed of gods who had faith in Elijah, He will save in salvation from falling to everlasting fire after death.

ELIMINATING THE SPIRITS OF GODS Gen.3:15

Elijah told Judah that the final judgment will be when CHRIST comes to remove spirits of gods in the kingdom, and if spirits from his seed had no faith in Elijah to save them, they would not rest in peace on earth, and would be joining him in the gate of the sun.

JESUS SPIRIT TOLD MANKIND AND ISRAELITES WHO THEIR FATHER IS Jn.8:38–44

You are the son of god of the devil? Your wish is to do the desire of god your father. He who carries on sinning was king with the devils in the beginning. For this purpose Jesus and Elijah will manifest to destroy the work of Israel's spirit in Cephas, whose godly spirit was in the same body with the spirit Jerusalem in the body she called Mary.

THE PROPHET WITH THE LAW SHALL BE IN THE SAME BODY WITH JERUSALEM, AND JESUS SHALL CAST HIM OUT Zech.14:4; Essek.16:2

Judah, after death, is a godly spirit and can't carry on doing as he did with Tamuze queen of Babylon when she was human with him as King Judah. Jerusalem is a holy spirit Jn.3:8-10. For this purpose Jesus came to cast out King Judah of Babylon. His godly spirit name is Israel and went from the same body with the spirit Jerusalem into the body of Cephas.

Mankind and Israelites did not know what was going on in the spiritual world and the purpose of Jesus and Elijah in John was to save Zion and Jerusalem from the godly spirit (Cain) and his son Judah also a godly spirit (Israel), returned from captivity blaming their mother for not making them perfect to be accepted above after death.

Babylon city

Babylon was populated with Mankind, Israelites, giants and gods. Judah captured more provinces to set up the first empire on earth.

Elijah said: Judah, the fear of you and the terror of you will be upon the spirits of gods in the kingdom living on earth when you return from captivity; every spirit from your seed in the kingdoms on the earth will be in fear of the name Israel after you depart from your mother's flesh. All spirits from the seed of gods who have no faith in Elijah will return to you after death. The kingdom from your mother's flesh shall abide upon the earth and shall be for creating immortal spirits as myself to be my people.

Mankind and Israelite. First king on earth Hab.2:1; Rev.17:5–8; 1.Cor.1:10

King Judah, the builder of Babylon, warrior, huntsman and presumptuous, became the first tyrant on earth. He shed blood and eliminated the holy sons of Adam-CHRIST and Eve, and made Mankind and Israelites with the children of the daughters of Adam and Eve who were in his captivity.

King Judah wanted to make a name for himself among the inhabitants on earth. As the ruler of the earth Judah, king of gods, caused confusion on earth. He boasted he made Mankind to get praise. The gods began to complain. They said: Judah did the same as god (Cain) his father in Hades, who killed his brother man Abel to make a god with his sister. Now he is doing the same with his mother and queen of the earth. He wants us to worship him as God of the earth. Others said: he is the only king of kings left on earth.

The Tower of Babel Jer.50:14,24,31-32, Gen.9:1–7

Judah built a pyramidal building that towered over the city of Babylon, with a temple at the top where he and Queen Babylon could sit. The second tier was with many rooms where his Israelites would occupy on ceremonies, and the other tiers were for Mankind and rulers of the provinces.

The base of the pyramidal was in the centre of the square where all the people would gather to postulate and worship the king and queen. Around the structure of the building were steps to each tier of the building to go up and down the building with ease.

The statue and altar Jer.17:1, Ex.17:15, Ps.90:3, Dan.3:7

Inside the tower in Babylon was a statue in the image of god (Cain) in Hades. In front of the statue was an altar for gods to sacrifice every new moon to god his father in heat to confuse Mankind with his authority over them and to make Elijah angry in god his father's image that they are sacrificing their life to god (Cain) and not him.

Tamuze and Eve knew who was CHRIST. Judah knew Elijah was a spirit in the image of god (Cain) and wanted to provoke Elijah. He had kept this secret from Satan and the devils and wanted Mankind to believe he created himself and the world, to lead them astray from truth of who is his father, to sacrifice their lives to the spirit of the other world, to deny Mankind faith in Elijah to fall to Cain after death to destroy the kingdom so they become godly spirits to fight with him for the earth against CHRIST and Elijah. That was Judah's plan.

Judah wanted all Mankind of the earth to put their faith in him and worship him as God almighty and his mother Queen Tamuze of Babylon to death by the law and for their spirits after death to go in the kingdom on earth to have power on earth. Judah knew the devils were captured in Hades and could not bring the world back to darkness. Judah wanted spirits from his seed to be godly spirits to be earthbound to enter the kingdom to seduce and destroy it with disease, lust, and immorality on any who has faith in CHRIST and ELIJAH.

The wicked multiply 29:16

The truth of the scriptures is hidden from the people on earth, so spirits from the seed of god can multiply on earth from the accursed seed to prevent the kingdoms from being created with spirits in the Light in salvation to continue in perfection to resurrect to the heavens to be among angels. Creation is through FAITH in ELIJAH so the spirits of gods can rest in peace and not fall like Judah with no faith to be with devils after death in the fire.

Peace in the world hidden in the Bible

For the inhabitants in the world to live in peace every spirit in the kingdom must be of creation in the Light in the name of Christ according to the New Testament to be accepted in Heaven. The devils broke the covenant of peace by making a god with the Eternal's creation. The devils made war in Heaven and transgressed in holy flesh. Judah the son of god (Cain) shed blood and exterminated holy men of the earth and hanged Adam. **Mt.21:2; Gen.49:11** In the bibles, death of Adam was by the godly spirit Israel that returned in the body of Moses, in Exodus and so is the godly spirit (Cain) in the body of Aaron, principal of godly spirits after death to possess a body. The truth of CHRIST and Elijah is hid from all Mankind. Pharaoh sent to call the godly spirit (Cain) in Aaron and godly spirit Israel in the body of Moses. They said to Pharaoh: it is because we have sinned we will tell you the TRUTH. Lord Elijah is righteous. The godly spirit Israel in the body of Moses said: I and my Israelites are wicked. **Ex.9:27** Pharaoh said: tell Elijah I'll let his people, the Hebrews of Isaac with Jerusalem in the body of Miriam go. They shall no longer stay in Egypt. Tthe godly spirit Israel in the body of Moses said through the mouth of Moses: now you may know the earth belongs to Elijah. Pharaoh said: don't you fear ELIJAH?

According to the bibles (**Gen.3:14–15**) Judah has caused confusion upon the earth among Mankind and Israelites. Elijah told him: I shall put enmity between you and your mother and your accursed seed she conceived in her womb.

CHRIST shall remove your spirits from the kingdoms from her flesh and you will be cast out before the end generation.

Contempt for Elijah

Judah had contempt for Elijah in the kingdom of god (Cain) his father. He was a boaster, vain, deceitful, and used his power as a prophet of the law of devils and became the first tyrant on earth in the nations. Multitudes began to be in fear of him, making Mankind to submit to him by the law to rule over them with authority subject to him until death. The Israelites cried to Israel in the body of Moses, and said: you want to take us to the wilderness to die. You have deceived us to take us out of Egypt .The godly spirit Israel said through the mouth of Moses: fear not. Elijah will show you what salvation is about if you have faith. Elijah said to the godly spirit Israel in the body of Moses: why criest thou unto me to save your Israelites? Tell them to go forward. Stretch out the hand of Moses to separate my people and your Israelites so my people can go first in the clouds. And your Israelites can follow you through the sea if they have faith in me.

QUEEN BABYLON AND EVE HAD FAITH IN ELIJAH

King Judah built the Tower of Babel to show Queen Tamuze the power of his strength to destroy her faith in Elijah. She had no part in his rebellion. She made Israelites for peace to shut him up for her peace, but her faith he could not shake off.

WOE TO HIM Eccl.3:10

Judah was presumptuous. He wanted praise and wanted Mankind to worship him as the god who created them, to be their ruler, but Queen Babylon knew he would stumble and fall and would have no one to help him when he died. He would be among the devils for supplanting them with guile, not telling them CHRIST was in Adam and Elijah was in the body of god (Cain) who they feared would destroy them.

Elijah's mandate is to save the kingdom and the spirits of CHRIST and Zion in Eve and Tamuze, queen of Babylon, an immortal spirit in the Light who has faith in Elijah to save her when she Sabbaths her body to death.

THE FIRST TYRANT OF THE EARTH 1.Jn.3:8

Judah knew Elijah is patient and merciful. Judah has tried everything to make Elijah angry. He blasphemes against Elijah, sovereign spirit in the kingdom of god his father.

All or nothing attitude Lk.14:13

Elijah brought him up to do good but he turned against Him in doing wickedness to gain power to have a foundation by imitating the devils to make Mankind and Israelites with his mother's flesh, to look like the people of Adam.

Elijah is merciful and takes no pleasure in Judah's death. He took the oath of the devils to be a prophet to carry out their law to death. Judahwould rather be a rebel than his spirit sleep in peace for eternity in the earth. It's either all spirits from his seed perish with him. He is angry and jealous because Elijah won't accept him because he is a god. CHRIST doesn't accept spirits of gods above. but gives gods up to the time of salvation to live in the kingdom and must have faith to rest in peace or face final judgment in the sun.

All spirits of the seed of gods suffer because the devils broke the covenant of peace to make a god in the world with the Eternal's creation Heb.7:18; Heb.5:11–13; He8.13

Judah is a jealous god. Regardless of all the sin his mother committed under oath, her SPIRIT will be saved and not him. He will enter the gates of Hell but not her. He has hate and wants to destroy the kingdom as his victory to rule with godly spirits on earth. The hate of the devils is rooted in his nature for everyone who is holy and good.

Torment and suffering Deut.27:22

Every spirit of gods suffers the same torment as Judah and hate the way they are born and ignore the peace while they live in the kingdom. They pass on seed to others to make a god like them to live in the kingdom until they depart from the kingdom not knowing while they lived in the kingdom they had a choice to prepare their kingdom for salvation to rest in peace if they have faith in the only saviour, Elijah.

The Covenant is broken by rape to make a god and eliminating the sons of Christ on earth. The devils deceived Judah, made him king ff he killed Adam

Judah imitated the devils and thought that if he is to be a king on earth, he must have authority over all the multitudes of godly spirits in all nations on earth, after the kingdom is destroyed.

Peace on earth Ro.16:17–20

Elijah is for peace and love and for a perfect world in the Light, where there is no death for eternity, and every immortal spirit created in the kingdoms of Mankind to continue in their image in perfection to populate the earth in righteousness to live a long life and resurrect to be among angels in Heaven created by the word. The New Testament by CHRIST gives every spirit a choice to worship their god to death or rest in peace through faith in ELIJAH. Spirits who have no faith in ELIJAH expect god to save them after they depart from the kingdom. Salvation is for the kingdoms ministered to CHRIST by Elijah for Christ to create immortal spirits in the light in kingdoms. Salvation is the only way kingdoms of Mankind can have immortal spirits with eternal life through judge Elijah by the Word.

Faith in Elijah is to have peace. Elijah doesn't like to be called god the lord. Lord god respect his holy name Elijah. Jesus called him Elijah with respect, as the holy son of Christ by the WORD

Elijah gave every spirit of god in the kingdom a choice to choose peace or face the baptism in fire in the sun in the final judgment. The spirits decide their fate for eternity. No religion can save a spirit if the spirit denies ELIJAH, the judge of the earth.

Who hanged Adam? Ro.12:21, Ro.13:1–5
Death of Adam was by the godly spirit Israel in the body of Moses Essek.22:25, Jer.11:9, Act.22:13

The truth about Elijah's holy name is hidden in religion since Babylon from generation to generation. The bibles say a body well prepared, Elijah seeks. The body is the kingdom. It is the sacrifice, the offering to death. The kingdoms that are worthy for creation, Elijah directs to CHRIST.

Every spirit that is not in the Light is a trespasser in the kingdom, waiting for salvation. To have peace, it must have faith in Elijah indeed.

The only consideration Job.15:11, 2.Cor.1:5–7

The only saviour is Elijah, it is written in the New Testament. The greater work, Elijah will do to save spirits after death and to rest in peace for eternity. The kingdom is established with a righteous spirit in the Light, with knowledge of life, which was hidden from the spirit of god. **Ph.12:1, 1.Ki.2:25**

No exemption from punishment 1.Cor.5:11–13, 1.Cor.6:13–14; 2.Cor.12:14,21; 2.Cor.13:2,4

Judah knew he is not exempt from punishment for his abomination with his mother and the error of god his father raping her to make him. Judah did the same like god his father passing the accursed seed. Judah blamed Tamuze his mother, hated god (Cain) his father, and hated the world, tormented with anger of devils to destroy CHRIST'S flesh because he is not accepted above, shedding blood of CHRIST.

Judah began to think to put Satan's plan to action to eliminate the gods if they had no faith in him. The gods began to blame Mankind and Israelites for taking over the earth and were missing the devils. Judah invited all the people to come and worship the statue in the image of god (Cain) within the Tower of Babel to show Elijah that all the people worship god his father's image and not Him, to get Elijah angry.

All the altars were set up with wood to light in flames before the statue of god (Cain). The people were invited to come and worship. The first sign of the new moon the gods were to bring their sons and daughters to sacrifice to the god (Cain) in Hades for their spirits to live after death.

In the day of the new moon it shall be opened Essek.46:1; Ps.81:3

The new moon appeared and the trumpeter blew his trumpet at the tower and the procession began. The people began to fill in the square. The rulers and Mankind and Israelites began to take their places on the tower. King Judah and Tamuze, queen of Babylon, sat at the tower.

The horn was blown and everyone began to prostate on the ground and worship King Judah and Tamuze, queen of Babylon. Then they stood up and began to say: O mighty God and goddess of the earth, from you came all the people on earth. We worship you and our God. Fill the earth like stars in the sky from his seed. Make Mankind and Israelites mingle with gods and giants to live for ever.

They prostated and stood and said: O mighty God of nations, we fear you and our faith is in you to death. Let there always be bread to eat and water to drink before we die. They went back on their knees until the trumpeter blew his horn at the Tower of Babel.

The pharisee began to talk and give praise for the entire work King Judah did in Babylon to make Mankind wise to live on earth in prosperity. The only wise king left with our queen mother of the earth. O queen of Babylon, live for ever.

The ancient devils came, and committed adultery to make gods. They raped Hebrew women to make giants and were cowards to kill Adam and His sons. The devils gave our God the law to rule on earth. O mighty God, you are a king of kings, worthy to rule over us with our queen for ever.

The sacrifice of gods on earth Deut.32:17, Ro.14:9–10

The people stood in silence and looked up at the tower with King Judah and Tamuze queen of Babylon and said: Hail Caesar, and Judah put his thumb down, and the fires were set on the altars before the image of god (Cain). Then the gods began to sacrifice their sons and daughters and threw them in the fire on the altars to god and devils in Hades who made them on earth.

This went on from new moon to new moon for gods to sacrifice as a burnt offering to be spirits on earth to go in kingdoms to prevent Elijah from saving Queen Babylon's spirit. Ro.14:22-23, Ro.8:10, Ro.8:6-8

The waste of flesh Is.1:13-14; Hos.2:11; Essek.21:21; Lev.20:14

Tamuze told Judah: too much of my flesh is going to waste. I have no desire to participate in Sabbaths/feast of new moons to kill gods of devils. You should be the first to sacrifice for the peace covenant on earth. You have forgotten who you are and destroy kingdoms with the spirits to death with your law with your plan to rule. I want no part in these Sabbaths while Israelites and Mankind abide in the same nature as you in my flesh.

Judah got angry and held her by her throat: you always complain. You are never satisfied with me. The Israelites princes in the palace rushed at Judah: don't kill our mother! There was much struggle and a young prince grabbed the rod and hit him on his head. Judah fell and passed out. Babylon ran in the harem to hide from Judah. When she found Eve she said: Mother, Judah tried to kill me. I don't want to go back in the palace.

This perished body must put on immortality 1.Cor.15:54; Essek.16:44–45

Eve said: this is my punishment for making god (Cain) and this is your punishment for making a god to pass on his seed. We have to suffer humiliation and torment by gods, Israelites and Mankind until we Passover from death. Elijah will save our spirits to be like Him and CHRIST your father in Heaven.

Eve said: while you live under the law, have faith, my daughter, and your labour will not be in vain. The kingdoms from your flesh will have new spirits by the Word. Judah can't inherit your flesh no matter how much seed he passes to make gods. Have faith for peace in the world. **1Cor 15:43–44**

The Sabbath will set you free 1.Pet.4:15, 1.Pet.2:21

Tamuze said: Mother, I wish I knew what happened to god (Cain). Since he killed my brother Abel nothing seems to go well for me. I go from one problem to another on earth since the devils held me in captivity to make gods.

Now I am betrothed to a murderer under the law who exterminated our people on earth. He imitates the devils (**1.Cor.14:18-22**) and wants me to keep silent. Every time he opens his mouth I get angry when he speaks to me. I am ashamed when he forces himself on me. He shed the blood of my brothers. **1.Cro.1:10**

Eve said: my daughter, I would not like you to be ignorant. Judah is your son with god (Cain) who is in Hades. The devils strangled him when they took you away from us and held you in captivity. It is Elijah who brought Judah up to do good, but he has become wicked and even turned against Elijah and CHRIST your father.

Now Judah has yoked his seed in the daughters of your dead sisters in the harem. They are in fear of him. Everyone is pregnant. Tamuze said: I asked him what he was doing in the harem. He said he is making Mankind to mix with his Israelite children in the palace to make Israelites to look like us and my father's children to Passover the kingdom to them.

Tamuze said: Mother, what do you mean, Judah is my god? Yes, my daughter, Eve said: Judah is your first god of god (Cain) who you gave birth and left in the bush. Elijah heard him crying, and brought him up. Now he is your king.

Mother, so Judah knew I was his mother and committed abomination with me to add to my shame? I fear my father be wrath with us for making gods. I made a god to know good and became evil. Your god (god) is in Hades. Judah is the evil one I fear. If the devil had eaten him at birth I would be free from the law. Now the earth is populated with gods, Mankind and Israelites in my flesh. Mother, now I fear for my life.

Eve said: my daughter, now that you know Judah is your god; you must have faith in Elijah to save you after you Sabbath. Elijah is disappointed in him. He had no faith and did even worse than god his father who killed Abel. We are the only two left from our family on earth and you have to suffer for your sin for making this tyrant on earth. I fear if you stayed in the harem, Judah will take out his anger and kill the pregnant women here. I think it's best you return for peace.

Tamuze said: come to the palace with me and speak to Judah. All I want is peace in my life from all this deceit, hate, envy and wickedness on earth and hope he can get some other women. I'm ashamed.

Eve said: he likes Hadassah, his daughter with your dead sister's children that survived the plague in this harem and she can't have enough of him.

They went to the palace and Eve confronted Judah. You have shed blood of my people on earth. Now you want to kill your mother who saved your life from devils, and have no love for her. Elijah brought you up to do good but instead you commit abomination with your mother and blaspheme Elijah.

Judah answered: it is not against you, Eve my malice is directed. She is the object of my rage and has yoked with the seed of your god (god) to make me unholy pure like him. Now I pass on his seed in her flesh to make Israelites and Mankind better than him who is your god. Tamuze is to blame for me being born and not accepted to go above.

Eve said: Elijah gave you a choice for peace so He could create in your body a holy son to be like him in creation by the word. We are the only two holy women left on earth and you want to take revenge on your mother who is innocent and being held in captivity with your law after the devils departed from the earth.

Judah shouted: Tamuze is a whore burdened in sin. Death will come to all you holy people until there are none of you left on earth, I am your king and have more power than the devil who held Tamuze in captivity to make gods and you are now in captivity as a nursemaid to Mankind with my seed.

Eve said: you are wicked. Fear ye not Elijah or CHRIST whose body you hanged on a tree? **(Mt.21:2)** Elijah will take revenge for us. You hold me in captivity and Tamuze to make Mankind and Israelites to pass on your father's seed. Their spirits will hate you for not being perfect. You killed my people and now you want to make Israelites to look like my people you hate. Judah, I am a witness to what you did – killing my sons.

Eve said: Judah, you are a transgressor and your sin is grievous to my daughter. Stop fornicating with her. She only endures what you do because she is in fear of you and you make her cry. I am sorry for you and all born from the accursed seed you pass on to the children of my dead daughters. Their godly spirits will have no peace. And Eve walked back to the harem to be among her daughter's children in captivity.

Judah looked down and could not watch Eve in the eye. Tamuze began to cry: Judah, why have you done this to me to give me children in abomination to bring shame on me? Elijah told you I was your mother. god (Cain) is your father. He raped me because he wanted to make a god to be like him. He is not from the seed of my father, but from the flesh of my mother. You came in my room and saw your mother's nakedness and fucked me to shame me.

Tamuze said: as soon after you fuck me, I fell asleep. I had a dream. I saw multitudes of spirits from your seed leaving their bodies, descending, and children in the Light running towards me from the same body and the spirits from your seed perished with you.

Judah, you have brought shame on yourself. You kept all what Elijah taught you as your great secret from the devils and me. Judah said: now you know I am your god, you will worship me for ever. I had no fear of devils that made me your king. I'll seduce you and see your nakedness for making me and leaving me in the bush naked in your blood on the earth and denying me the pleasure to suck milk from your breast at birth.

Judah said: Tamuze, I'll destroy your holy flesh to the last drop of blood in the nations on earth with godly spirits from my seed. You put your faith in Elijah to save you to establish kingdoms in salvation from your flesh. You will have to wait a long time for salvation and you will know who you fear most when I return with godly spirits from my seed to Passover the kingdoms to death. I hate all you hypocrites who make gods on earth to make kingdoms for spirits to perish.

Tamuze cried: Elijah was good to you. It is the devils that made you a king to deceive you with their oath and laws. You made me your queen to shame my people to pass on the accursed seed for gods to make gods on the earth. The devil deceived you to be a killer of innocent people who did you no harm while they were on earth.

Tamuze said: Judah, your spirits shall make Mankind and Israelites in multitudes to take root in my flesh but they shall have no peace after death if they have no faith like you they will join god (Cain) your father in the fire. Cain had the same hope as you. Before he raped me he conspired with the devils to take me in captivity. You are ignorant, doing the same mistake as god (Cain) with the devils. You have done like all the devils to make gods suffer in the end .Your father was ignorant of the truth and filled with hate, Abel my brother is the first son of my father with my mother.

Judah, since you came to the palace, you saw all what the devils did to me with much trembling giving birth to gods. You will lose your life and end with devils for the sorrow and shame I've suffered by you.

It is you who have no faith in Elijah who I've never seen. Elijah brought you up and told you to come and save me from the devils. When you came to the palace in the mountain, you did not try to save me.

Temptation

When you saw me you were in temptation and lusted for me instead, like god your father and all the devils to make gods in my flesh to make spirits for their world.

Think not I came to destroy your law Essek.25:15, Mt.7:6

Instead of love for your mother you turn to hating me. You hate CHRIST you have not seen and Elijah who you knew before the devils gave you the law. You humiliate me under oath to make gods. You saw me trembling in fear. I had to endure all what Satan did to my body for peace, so the devils didn't attack my people. You thought of satisfying your lust and failed to save me from devils.

Elijah did not spare the devils 2.Pet.2: 4

Judah you… Imitating the devils. I am sorrowful with grief. I've suffered much under oath before your face. You are no help to me. Instead you add to my sorrow.

From the body of Babylon, King Judah Jer.26:29

Judah, I'm ashamed to say, you can't save me. You have committed abomination and have become a hateful enemy yoking your accursed seed in my womb to provoke Elijah. You have deceived me with your lies and supplanted the devils to be a king. To take the throne you had to shed the blood of my brothers to be a king. I feel unclean with you with the blood of my brothers on your hands.

The device against Babylon to kill her Jer.51:11

If you were a wise son, you would have considered the opportunity for peace, and not become the prophet of the law of devils, but you gave up your peace to satisfy your lust for my flesh to be with the devils in the world. You have no hope with CHRIST and Elijah for what you did to me.

Judah could not stand to hear the truth. He stood there in shock. He blocked his ears, stunned as though bitten by a snake and its venom working its way in his body. Stung by truth, staring at Babylon and couldn't move in self-shock of what his mother knew about him.

Tamuze went on to say: you tried to prevent me from heavenly entry. My spirit will go above after I depart from my body to be with Elijah. You know scriptures and the Testament was made known to you about salvation.

Suddenly, as if awake with hate and anger like a thief caught in the act, he slapped Tamuze on her face. She fell on the floor and cried: I don't need your mercy. Kill me so I don't have to suffer in this body burdened with your abomination to make Israelites to pass on your seed to suffer after death by your law.

He dragged her from the floor and threw her on the bed like a rag doll and began to fuck her while telling her: you will have children for me till you die and you will see who is your master builder in salvation. It is I who furnish the heavens from my seed in kingdoms from your flesh on earth.

I am your firstborn from the accursed seed to be your king and I'll fuck you to death in this body till you are dead like your sisters, giving birth to Israelites.

Babylon cried: you fucking bastard. Kill me if you hate me so much. I don't want to see your face another day. Judah held Tamuze and began shaking her, saying: I'm your king and you will see my face even when my spirit leaves this body without your flesh.

The serpent and his rod Num.21:19; 1Sam.4:2

Tamuze began to cry in humiliation, kill me. Don't slap me around; kill me you bastard born with wickedness. You, Satan with your rod, you will meet your match in wickedness. Judah held her by her throat and spat in her face with anger for calling him Satan of the earth and threw her on the floor and shouted: I've taken the oath against thee, against Elijah, against CHRIST and all your people to death. He put his feet on her throat.

Elijah appeared in the room and saw Judah pressing his feet to her throat. Judah looked and was in fear and said: what do you want? Tamuze cried: he wants to kill me… Save me from him. Elijah said to Tamuze: rise, fear not me. Behold! Because of your faith in me you are in the presence of Elijah. **Lk.7:47**

Woe Jer23:1, Mk.14:58

I've come to warn this Satan and supplanter the throne of the devils with malice, deceit, hate, and jealousy while living in your flesh; a destroyer of innocent people who have done him no harm, beginning from you and all your mother's children that were on earth. Rev.11:18

First and last warning 2.Pet.2:4

Elijah said: Judah, in front of your mother, this is my first and last warning. If you harm Tamuze, you will be in the chambers prepared for the wicked and you will be doomed with the devils that are waiting for you for sitting on their throne with Tamuze, and your arrogance and presumptuousness in wanting to be a king on earth with your mother. Judah began to tremble in front of Elijah.

Elijah said: Ammon is your name Essek.16:3
To express distinction, Ammon + Judah

Elijah said: Ammon I called you by name, when you walked with me. The devils call you Judah. This is my final warning to you. If Tamuze or Eve shed one tear by you I'll be back and this time it will be you who will be crying to me to save you from the devils who you place your hope in after death.

AMMON, THOU HAST MULTIPLIED FORNICATION Essek.16:29

Elijah said: Ammon, I've restrained myself from punishing you. I've held my peace. I am slow to take action because of your anger for the way you were born, which is no fault of yours. You were brought up to know the scripture and the Choice given thee (**Gal.3:18**) between peace or perish before you took the oath to serve the gods of devils with the law to death.

I'VE BROUGHT UP A DESTROYER OF FLESH, WHO HAS NO FAITH Is.54:16

The next time you see my face, it will be to pass judgment on you while you are in your mother's flesh. Judah said: would thou destroy the righteous with the wicked? (**Gen.18:23**) Elijah did not answer Judah's question and vanished before Tamuze, now called the Queen of Babylon and Judah her king.

They both stood there watching each other. For Tamuze (Babylon) it was the first time she saw Elijah. Her faith saved her.

DON'T TOUCH WHAT IS HOLY, LOVER OF PLEASURE 2.Tim.3:4

Judah tried to touch Tamuze. She said: don't touch me else I cry to Elijah for help. One teardrop and you are finished. You heard what your master said to you, and she went to the harem to meet Eve to tell her the good news.

FAITH FOR PEACE IS THE WEAPON TO KEEP EVIL AWAY

Judah thought Tamuze, queen of Babylon, had no wisdom and understanding of scriptures and was indoctrinated under the oath of the devils and now he was betrothed to her under the law and felt he could abuse her by his strength and power to destroy her faith in Elijah.

Tamuze kept her secret of faith in Elijah and suffered in silence. She endured all her grief in silence for peace so the devils didn't attack her people when they were on earth. Her heart was not with the gods she made, and she looked at them as though they were not hers. She had no fear when she gave birth to Judah though she was threatened by the devils to eat him from birth; she made gods for the devils. Making Israelites for Judah under the law was no big deal.

Tamuze knows every spirit from Judah's seed on earth will end up in fire if they don't have faith in Elijah to save them from falling in the sun for ever. So she rejoiced in seeing Elijah and her faith was strengthened and she had no doubt Elijah will save her after death.

Babylon uses her faith as a weapon to be free from Judah. To be with Eve without his threats. They both put their spirits in the hands of Elijah. This made Judah angrier. He had lost control over Tamuze (Babylon) and Zion Eve.

Rejoice in your faith and not iniquity, but in reality for peace 1.Pet.1:26; 1.Cor.13:6

Tamuze went to the harem and found her mother Eve nursing Mankind children. She said: Mother, Judah is constantly forcing himself on me in the palace, to make his Israelites. Mother, since I've been held in captivity by the devils to make gods under oath I did it for peace for the devils to keep away from you and my father. Judah has committed abomination with me under the law to add to my shame. Now he is yoking his accursed seed with the daughters of my dead sisters to interbreed with his Israelites in the palace.

Eve said: my daughter, your father and I brought you up the good way. Your affliction has taught you what is good and what is evil on earth. Your goodness is better than thousands of gods and Israelites.

Your sisters died giving birth to giant babies and gods in this harem from these giant rapist devils, then died. I am in much sorrow for the death of your sisters. Eve hugged Tamuze and went on to say: Elijah will save our holy spirits. He is merciful. (**1.Cor.7:25**) Elijah will put Judah to shame for his arrogance to commit you to abomination with his deceit.

Elijah will put enmity between kingdoms from your flesh and him and his seed Gen.3:15

Mother, Tamuze said: the devils forced me to take this oath to make gods for them. They said if I took the oath they would leave you and my father in peace. I was pregnant at the time with Judah of your god (Cain). He raped me and I conceived his accursed seed in my womb. I agreed to this oath because the devils said you and my father would be free from them though it seemed stupid to me. All I wanted was for them to leave you in peace even if they abused me. Father said to me, have faith in Elijah.

The man's religion is vain Jam.1:26, Jn.8:38-44

Mother, Judah tried to strangle me. He had his feet on my throat and pressing on it. As I was about to pass out Elijah appeared and saved me and warned Judah, if ever you and I shed one tear, he will join the devils. Elijah said, my faith has saved me and He vanished. Now we can have some peace from this tyrant who uses me to make Elijah angry.

Devil worship

So far Judah was lucky Elijah was slow to anger and restrained from speaking the Word on him, for rebelling against CHRIST in Heaven and hanging His body on a tree to death to be a king with the devils. Judah wanted me to worship him. He said he is my king, and wanted to take over the earth with laws of devils to destroy the kingdom, with spirits of gods after death.

Weak in faith Ro.12:12–14

Mother, when Elijah warned Judah if he laid his hand on me to make me cry it is the end of his humanity in my flesh. And his spirit would be with the devils in Hades.

The fear of the devils in the deep blue sea

In anger Judah took his chariot in haste and rode the horses to his chosen Anakin giants from the Anak devils he had adopted to be his warriors and began putting his energy in training them to fight with spears and shields until they became his elite fighters.

With cruelty to rule over nations Essek.34:4

Judah trained Mankind with his battalion of gods who were with him when they killed all the sons of Adam-CHRIST from the face of the earth. Mankind joined forces with the gods in training and became his new soldiers for war to rule the earth.

O KING OF NATIONS, WHO WOULD NOT FEAR THEE? Jer.10:7; Rev.19:19; Lk.14:13

Judah set up the battle formation with his Anakin giants, Mankind and gods with chariots and bows to attack and conquer the nations and eliminate the new kings, gods of the devils in the nations.

THE FIRST EMPIRE ON EARTH Rev.3:4

This battle was a trial strategy of Judah's secret plan for the earth. The battalion of gods on horses was in the front formation. The battalion of Mankind on horses was followed by the warrior giants on carts with Judah in command with his chariot marching forwards to the nations to the sound of the war drums loudly beaten by the drummers.

WAR OR PEACE Eccl.3:8

The people in the nations could hear this drumming. When they saw the battalions of soldiers marching toward them they began to fear for their lives and ran inside their homes and closed their doors.

The army of soldiers surrounded every exit. Judah and his battalions, followed by the commandant and some Anakin giants stopped at the headquarters of the nation. The war drummers stopped and there was silence. The commandant of the soldiers of Mankind shouted to the king and chief rulers: come out and surrender your nation to us in peace or we will take it by force.

The people looked through the shutters of their homes in fear. The king came outside, outraged, with other officials and said: why comest thou in our nation to battle against our people with swords and spears and arrows? Judah pulled out his sword from its sheaf and cut off the head off the king.

HE MADE THEM CEASE BY FORCE AND POWER Esra.4:23

The other rulers came out and began to shout and were outraged. Who gave you right to come in our nation? The gods rushed at them and they were hanged. The other rulers objected for the hanging. The Anakins picked them up and said: don't you have any respect for the king of all nations? And began to squeeze them in their hands and blood came out of their mouths and they went limp in the hands of the Anakin giants.

The other leaders stood there trembling, and cried: have mercy, O King, had a taste of the rod to make an example, and were escorted to the exit of the nation and told to leave and never return to the nation.

The spoils

The battalion of gods went from house to house and threw the men outside. Mankind rounded up the men and the Anakin giants went in to rape the women to make giants for the nation. Then Mankind would take their turn to have intercourse to populate Mankind for the nation. The gods would take what was valuable.

The men that were captured were held to build the nation with a city with watchtowers and temples for the people to worship the queen of Babylon and her king. Pulpits were built in the inside of the temples for priests to gather information about troublemakers, who later would be put in fire as a sacrifice to god in Hades at new moons.

This strategy of surprise attack Judah pursued with anger and hate went according to his plan and he went on to conquer nation after nation and became king of the earth. This is what he wanted to achieve after his death in the spiritual world, to be king of the spirits on earth.

The peculiar people. Judah zealous to make Israelites Num.9:3

The Israelites steadily increased in the nations and were not allowed to mix in order to keep their peculiar features. They sent the birth of their children to record their genealogy in Babylon city for future generations as the chosen people of King Judah, their creator and God of the earth to live by the law to death.

Judah had a dream that Elijah said to him: enmity between thee and your daughter. She will eliminate the Israelites Ps.22:23

Fear her all ye from Judah's seed. She is his inheritance to make spirits to war for the earth to prove her power to rule as his queen on the earth.

(Ex.20:20; Jer.10:7; 1.Cro.1:10; 2.Tim.2:19) He marries his daughter and she multiplied in her flesh from his seed. He has inherited her by the law. The spirit of Tamuze in Babylon is free after his death. **1.Cor.7:38–39**

Elijah's purpose is to establish kingdoms from the flesh of the spirit of Tamuze in Babylon. Judah is concerned about his inheritance of spirits from his seed. **Jn.8:38–44**

Cursed is he that lies with a daughter of his mother's sisters Deut.27:22; Ro.8:9; Eph.2:3; Num.9:1

Mankind and Israelites are his people with the daughters of his mother's sisters, to make spirits in humanity to pass on his seed to take root all over the earth to be their king of the spirits with his daughter as queen after death according to his secret plan.

The deceiver imitates Elijah to destroy mankind Jn.1:19-27; Jn.1:12-14; My.24:22

Judah held to his plan after death as his secret to be ruler in the kingdom like Elijah. His motive was to destroy all flesh with spirits of gods in the kingdoms in the nations on earth to rule the earth as king with godly spirits after death.

Judah knows the scripture and wants to attack first in the nations before Elijah starts his work in salvation with CHRIST to create immortal spirits in the kingdom to eternal life.by the Word

WHEN Christ come to earth is to cast out spirits of gods in the kingdom from nation to nation, for final judgment by Elijah with the Word to establish salvation in kingdoms for creating immortal spirits Mt.16:17; Jn.1:12; Ro.7:5; 8:8–10; 7:8–19

The battle in the kingdom is a spiritual war. Mankind with spirits of gods in their humanity will not be able to see until they are spirits without flesh. Judah's war plan is for his spirits after death to enter kingdoms to destroy the kingdoms in the nations on earth with latest weapons of war, so there is no flesh on earth. to rule with the earth spirits.

THE SPIRITS THAT HAVE NO FAITH IN THE BATTLE IN THE KINGDOM WILL FALL

In the days of salvation CHRIST on the throne in Heaven and Elijah with the Word, the spirits of gods in the kingdom will come against the Word. After CHRIST casts them out from the kingdoms they will come unto the final judgment for ever for peace in the New World, with immortal spirits created in kingdoms to continue to populate spirits in the Light in the kingdoms. Elijah has given Judah years months, days, hours, minutes, times and seasons to put his plan in order to challenge him for the earth. The battle in the kingdom has begun as Mankind can see in the nations and hear in the news of wars on earth, and global warming. Melting of the ice is a sign of salvation in the kingdoms.

JUDAH SHALL FIGHT AT JERUSALEM Zech.14:4 ps.19:4
THE RULER WILL GO THROUGH ALL NATIONS IN THE KINGDOM Mt.11:12

Judah said: my spirits will be in the kingdoms of the rulers in governments and preachers of the earth to lead astray in religion to destroy the kingdoms on earth. In the sight of CHRIST and Elijah, I'll destroy and put the Light out of the world, and devour the flesh of Jerusalem like a violent dragon filled with lust, for not accepting me as the king of the earth. Judah in the body of Cephas Jesus said to him: the desire of god (Cain) your father you will do, to destroy the kingdom. **Jn.8.34, 44**

THE SECRET PLAN OF JUDAH: EVERYONE THAT IS OF THE DEVILS HATES SPIRITS IN THE LIGHT Jn.3:20
JUDAH HAS DECEIVED SPIRITS OF GODS IN THE KINGDOMS ON EARTH

Judah's secret plan is for when he is a godly spirit to rule the earth spirits as king of the earth with Haddasah as his queen.

JUDAH HATES HIS MOTHER. HE IS A MURDERER 1.Jn.2:9, 30:15

Judah knows the scripture and will attack first in the nations to prevent Elijah from doing the work in salvation through CHRIST to create immortal spirits in the kingdom to have eternal life to be with angels above.

A time to lust. A time to hate. A time for war Eccl.3:8

Spirits of gods in the kingdoms in their humanity that have faith, the godly spirits will declare war on their brothers because of jealousy, anger and malice for having faith in Elijah and CHRIST to save them. Godly spirits will declare war on the people of Elijah with Jerusalem through Isaac on earth. They will use their advantage to tempt spirits to fall to fight after death for the earth. The godly spirits are jealous because Elijah's people are immortal spirits accepted above and can't fall like them in the everlasting fire in the sun.

The coming of CHRIST

On the days of salvation CHRIST will come to create immortal spirits in kingdoms with spirits of gods presented to Him by Elijah from all nations. Christ will cast out spirits from kingdoms that are worthy for creation in the flesh of Eve and her daughters, for Elijah to judge the spirits and save the spirits that have faith in him and pass on the unfaithful spirits of gods to the spirit of the sun to remove them from the earth to the gate of the sun to everlasting fire for ever.

The godly spirits of Judah shall fight against the people of Jerusalem Zech.14:4, Ps.19:4

The godly spirits will make war on Mankind in all nations Mt.11:12 Ps.49:9

Judah said: I'll be king of the earth with my godly spirits. We will be in the kingdom of the rulers in governments and preachers in the nations to lead astray in religion in the sight of CHRIST and Elijah. Godly spirits will tempt spirits of gods in the kingdom in the nations. They will seduce them to make war on the people of Jerusalem with Elijah with violence. Godly spirits will be like dragons for flesh of her people in the nations on earth.

SPIRITS OF GODS IN THE KINGDOM ON EARTH Jn.8:34,44; Mt.24:6; Essek.32:27; 2.Cor.10:3; Ps.46:9

Jesus said to Mankind: it is the desire of the godly spirit (Israel) your father to destroy the kingdom. He is the murderer who eliminated innocent sons of CHRIST from the earth in the first civilization. All Mankind must be aware of these wars on earth in the nations. There is no purgatory once a spirit of god departs with no flesh, no mediator if you don't have faith in Elijah to save you. You shall fall. If you are a spirit of creation by CHRIST, in the kingdom, you shall not fall but sleep in peace after death till the time to resurrect.

ONE HOUR FROM EARTH TO HELL Rev1810:17 1Cor4.11 Dan3.6

The godly spirit (Cain) entered the body of Judas after he returned from captivity. The godly spirit of Israel entered the body of Cephas after he returned from captivity. Jesus and Elijah cast them out from the same body as Zion and Jerusalem. To tell Mankind the truth about them: if you have no faith you will perish. Jesus knew his enemy… you don't. Peace be with you.

QUEEN TAMUZE AND MOTHER IN SACKCLOTH Is.49:23

After Judah fought all his battles to rule as king on earth Judah returned to the palace in haste and saw all his servants wearing the dresses of Tamuze. He asked them: why are you dressed in the queen's clothes? They answered: she gave them to us as a gift. He got angry. Where is Queen Tamuze? he said.

The servants said: she is in the harem wearing sackcloth, living with her mother. Judah said: so they are making a fool of the king of the earth in my palace!

JUDAH ASKS EVE AND BABYLON TO COME AND SPEAK TO HIM IN THE PALACE, BECAUSE HE IS UNHAPPY

Judah was angry, hurt, and had come from fighting in the nations, returning to the palace full of lust for his mother. It was more than he could bear to know she had left the palace for life in the harem with her mother and the women. He told the servants: if I go in the harem, I'll kill her. Fetch me a drink. And he began to think, if I go in the harem and Tamuze or Eve shed one tear, Elijah will come after me.

She called me a serpent

Judah went inside the harem. Tamuze and Eve looked at him, then they asked him: what do you want? Judah had an apple in his hand and said: I brought it from a far country especially for you, Eve. I want your advice. Could you come and talk to me in the palace? Eve followed him to the palace. When they were there, Judah locked Eve in a cell in total darkness.

Judah incarcerates Babylon Jer.31:40

Judah went back to the harem and asked Tamuze and Hadassah his daughter with one of the dead daughters of Eve who he liked, to come and join him and Eve in the palace. When they got there, Tamuze asked: where is my mother? Come. Follow me. I'll show you, Judah said. And he locked all of them in the cell with Eve and said to the women: you will not come out until you worship the king of the earth.

He went back to the harem and threatened the pregnant women and said: if any of you give birth to males I will sacrifice them as burnt offerings for god (Cain) and the devils in the bowels of the earth. Some of the women fainted. Others pleaded: O King, have mercy on Mankind children.

Rejoice not against Me, Satan , my spirit shall be my Light **Mic.7:8**

A few days went by. Judah thought the women would be hungry and would submit, and go on their knees to worship him as their king. Little did he know the women enjoyed the peace so much. They fell asleep.

Judah became curious, and went to the cell. He unlocked the door and had a peep inside. He saw the women fast asleep, but the bodies of Eve and Tamuze were full of Light, lighting up the cell. Judah ran outside, thinking it's a trap. Elijah and CHRIST had come to punish him. Terrified, he left the cell door open.

After he had a drink, he called the guards to check the women in the cell. They returned and said: the women wanted water to drink and bread to eat. Judah said: give them what they ask and tell Eve I want to speak with her.

Tamuze couldn't be bothered and stayed with Hadassah in the cell.

Eve came with the guard. Judah offered her an apple to obtain a favour from her. They looked at each other, eye to eye, and Eve looked at him and said: my daughter's children are pregnant with your Mankind, and they will be giving birth anytime soon. They need us to assist with giving birth. Then she looked at Judah and said: Judah, are you not ashamed to lock up your mother in a cell in this palace? The devil held her in captivity and locked her up with you in her womb in his palace, and now you are doing the same as the devils, locking her up in your palace with your daughter Haddassah.

Tamuze has withheld tears, so you can be humble and ask Elijah to have mercy on you for blasphemy, and for hanging the body of her father. Elijah has no pleasure in your wickedness and your hate for holy people. Your mother and I are the only two holy women left on the earth. Though you hate us, we would rejoice if you repent and have faith in Elijah for your peace.

Exhortation from Eve to Judah

Judah, you have resorted to doing evil of every sort in excess against the patience of Elijah. He has restrained Himself from punishing you. Now you are king, use your power to do good while you are still human like us, so your spirit can have peace, Elijah will give Tamuze a son to go above. Ask Elijah to have mercy on you, and teach the Israelites and Mankind to do the same, so they can have peace on the earth and not suffer like god (Cain) your father in Hades.

The Lilies Parable and the Salomon Parable

Eve said: Judah, every spirit from your seed will hate you for passing on your seed to them to be born to hate their mother because they are not perfect, just like you hate your mother living in her flesh. There is only one consolation for all spirits from your seed; they must have faith in Elijah to save them from falling to the devils. If you are a wise king, you should know there are many faults with the doctrine of the law, which you took under oath.

The devils are no more on the earth and left you with their law to populate spirits to fall to them. They did not destroy the kingdom. Before you had the law, Elijah prophesied you would be a king of nations. It was for you to do good and not to do like the devils in His sight.

Deceit of the Devils

You supplanted the devils because they did not know CHRIST was in Adam and Elijah in your father's kingdom. You allowed the devils to tempt you up to take the oath and their false doctrine to live by their law to death to claim all spirits from the flesh of your mother. Spirits from your seed will hate you when they fall for you knowing the truth and not telling them about faith for peace.

Judah said: Eve, I hate to give up my spirit that lusts while in the flesh and loves pleasure, for peace to sleep for ever. If Elijah had created a spirit in my body it will enjoy life with Him for ever. It is not right to me.

The covenant of peace 1.Cor.7:7–9

Eve said: you're are either a spirit of creation in the Light or a spirit of the devils of Ancient World of Darkness. The covenant of peace was between the Eternal Spirit in the Light and the ancient devils of darkness to respect each other's nature and to live in peace in the world because spirits of creation are not the same as devils. **1Cor 7.7:8–9 Heb.13:4**

Violation of the peace covenant

The devils violated the covenant of peace by declaring war in the heavens against angels in the Light and had you to shed blood of CHRIST in Adam on earth. This law is against the covenant of peace, killing my sons and shedding their blood. It will go against spirits of your seed as well. Salvation is the time to eliminate spirits of gods to death in this world for ever for going against the peace covenant and for not respecting the nature of CHRIST and HIS people.

There is no purgatory for spirits of gods from the accursed seed. Neither can any spirit from the accursed seed be born again. There is no mediator in the world between Christ and devils, once a spirit of god is removed from kingdom is to face judgment.

Elijah is the judge to save your spirits from falling and no one else in the world. CHRIST has put HIS faith in Elijah to save the kingdom by the Word and all spirits of CHRIST on earth. CHRIST and Elijah are the two spirits created. One to serve the other. Can you fight the Word? Judah bowed his head.

The problem with this life on earth

Eve said: Judah, do you understand the problem you have caused in shedding blood of innocent people with your battalion of gods? My sons did you no harm, nor put any trouble in your way. We lived in peace in holiness in our nation.

What do righteous people have in common with gods of the devils that are wicked and lawless and shed blood on earth?

I'm speaking to you frankly now, Judah, for peace. What association can your mother's spirit after death have in common with your spirit after death? You married Tamuze in her flesh, not in the spirit. You are passing the seed of god (Cain) your father from the devils of the Ancient World of Darkness.

What harmony had the spirit in Adam had with you before you hanged HIS body on the tree to death? Did not CHRIST speak to you through the mouth of Adam to go and tell the devils to come and do the hanging? Is it not your lust for power to be a king that made you do the hanging?

Eve said: Judah, you knew the relationship between CHRIST and Elijah before you became an unbeliever, a hater, a blasphemer, a prophet to gods to live by the law under oath to death. You are presumptuous thinking you will inherit spirits from your seed to make war against Elijah for the earth.

Eve said: Judah, Elijah had no agreement with god (Cain)to be in his kingdom. It was not his flesh. All spirits from your seed live in kingdoms from your mother's flesh who came from my flesh.

Judah, you know the scripture. Elijah dwelled in kingdoms from our flesh and walked among us. We are His people, and want to live in peace in the world.

Before you became a prophet to gods with the law of devils, Elijah promised you would inherit all spirits from your seed if you had no faith. It's only spirits who have faith in Elijah, He will save from falling in fire. In the time of salvation kingdoms will be created with immortal spirits in the light by the Word. Judah bowed his head in shame and put his fingers in his ears so he couldn't hear what Eve was saying to him.

Change your attitude

Eve said: Judah, the only wrong I have done is to give birth to god (Cain) your father in this world. You know he yoked his seed in your mother by force for you to be a god like him. He ruins his chance for peace after death, by passing on the accursed seed to you. His kingdom became the first in salvation to continue with spirit Elijah by the Word to live for eternity so spirits of gods may rest in peace through faith in Elijah.

The truth of Eve: I knew nothing of devils in the beginning

Eve said: Judah, I'm not ordering you but telling you the way it is. I was like you in the beginning and innocent of what is a devil, and so was your mother before you were born. I was ignorant. The deceitful devil raped me and I conceived and gave birth to god (Cain). At all times, to bring a god in the world is forbidden in flesh.

No faith, no peace. (I knew scriptures after the devil committed adultery)

Eve said: Judah, spirits from your seed will have no peace unless they have faith while they live in the kingdom. Every spirit from your seed is born to trouble, just like you hold us in captivity and lock us up in a cell in your palace. Your spirits will end up in the gates after they depart from my flesh for trespassing in the kingdom and will never return to earth again.

The law is a religious doctrine against the Word

Eve said: Judah, If you pursue your doctrine with your laws of devils, there will be much sorrow in captivity and much grief by devils and it will be you alone against multitudes that will pluck out your eyes for making them to suffer. I'm telling you so to warn you of the consequences facing you if you make war to shed blood on earth of innocent people, to destroy the kingdom. If this is your desire, I'm sorry for you, if you want to fight against the Word by Elijah.

True religion is to save spirits from falling

Eve said to Judah: let your gods know before they will be godly spirits after death, if they provoke Elijah he will not save them from falling through the gate in everlasting fire. They will be severely punished for ignorance of the truth. Make this plain to them before you start the battle in the kingdom to shed blood on earth with your godly spirits The Tower of Babel you built in Babylon city will fall on all who have no faith like you, as a warning, to all who follow religion.

Judah did not think much of Elijah or CHRIST Deut.32:18

Eve said: Judah, if god (Cain) your father had faith you you would not be born to be boasting of your wickedness. Adam offered god (Cain) the same peace, but instead he chose to follow the devils and looked at Adam as inferior, same as you because you were a king with the devils and thought the same of Elijah. You have exchanged the promise of Elijah for false hope of the devils after death with your spirits to declare war for the earth.

A time to live and a time to die

Eve went on to tell Judah: I'm telling you all this so gods don't blame me for not telling you then say Eve is the sinner for making a god. It's not the fault of gods to be born. I tell you before you depart from the kingdom I don't want another god to pass on your seed to give birth to another god to blame me and call me a sinner because they are afraid of the devils who rape to make gods.

You are having intercourse with the women from my daughters who died in your harem to make Mankind in multitudes. You will receive multitudes of spirits when they depart from your mother's flesh. When Elijah speaks the Word in salvation is for CHRIST to come and cast out spirits of gods out from My flesh.

PRAISE ELIJAH, WHO DOES THE WORK IN SALVATION THROUGH CHRIST Mt.5:7

Eve said: Judah, Christ will create immortal spirits and they will multiply on the earth to resurrect and live in all worlds. You should give praise to Elijah for teaching you so much in order for your body to have an immortal spirit like Him to be His son. But you have become a foolish king like the devils Elijah removed from the earth.

TAMUZE, QUEEN OF BABYLON, AND HADASSAH CAME OUT OF THE CELL AFTER EVE'S SPEECH

Tamuze said to Hadassah: Behold Judah, your mighty God. Tamuze said: Judah, did the devil have peace on earth for fucking me to make gods on earth? How can I have peace, with you? You who are like a devil and wanted to strangle me to death. I will acquaint myself with my mother and my sister's children who are pregnant by you in the harem for peace. I rather be a handmaid unto the women who are making Mankind babies.

Judah looked at Tamuze with anger and hate. Hearing her arrogance he said: all of you, get out of my sight before I shed blood in this palace. As the women began to walk away, Judah asked Hadassah to stop. She was young and beautiful, and she could never have enough of Judah in the harem. She answered: what you want with me, O King? Judah said: if you kneel down and worship me, you can stay in the palace. Hadassah said: O King, I worship you to death. Make me your mistress under the law, and she stayed in the palace. **Nah.3:4; Mic.7:6**

HADASSAH. A MAN HAS TWO WIVES: ONE LOVED, ONE HATED Deut.21:15

Tamuze took a good look at Judah and Hadassah, then said: Judah, teach Hadassah the scriptures so she doesn't fall and cry after death. Eve held Tamuze by her hand and said: come, my daughter. Now you have found Elijah your saviour who you can trust. Come to be a handmaid to your sisters' children with Judah in the harem.

Darkness in the world will end when Elijah speaks the Word to CHRIST to put it into the Light Mt.24:29

Judah looked glum, seeing all his effort and energy achieving so much success had been in vain without Tamuze, who will go above in peace, I am a god by nature and can't be born again. He said: if I want peace, I'll sleep for ever and can't perish. If I want death I can't have peace.

Judah had a dream about Elijah speaking to him. I shall put enmity between you and your mother. I will remove you in the kingdom from her flesh for your abomination.

Secret message Judah wrote

Mankind, cleanse yourselves. Don't defile yourself in my mother's flesh. Prepare your body for Elijah in salvation. Humble your heart for change. I have wronged you; let no spirit after death enter your body to ruin your chance for peace on earth.

The mistress in the palace of Babylon Nah.3:4

Judah took Hadassah on his chariot and went with her to Babylon city to get her fitted with clothes and jewellery and perfume and everything he could think of to make Tamuze jealous.

Hadassah, the mystery woman of Babylon Ps.45.7:11 Black and beautiful Cant.1:5

For the first ten months Judah took Hadassah everywhere and introduced her to his military officials in the nation and merchants. She was elegantly dressed with precious stones and armbands in gold. She went with Judah to new moon offerings and the fights at the olympiad with giants fighting each other to death.

This brought much excitement to the king to show his mistress his giants were the strongest on earth with skill to fight for him to death.

Judah and Hadassah were compatible in everything to do with wickedness. He committed incest with her. She became famous in the nations.

Hadassah encouraged Judah to bring her sisters from the harem to the palace to make the queen jealous and her sisters began to be corrupt with his excessive lust more than her.

Judah invited rulers and horsemen and princes to increase the making of Israelites and Mankind for him. They would go in the room with a statue of god (Cain) his father in Hades to defile the women in front of the statue.

Hadassah made love to the men who came to the palace and became a whore and did what they wanted as she was still in fear of Judah and if she didn't do as the men wanted, Judah would take the rod and spank her.

The sisters of Hadassah began to multiply in the palace. The children who didn't look like Israelites, Judah would cast in the fire as a burnt offering. He would say to the women, I will make you stop whoring to make gods to go in the fire. Hadassah said: O my king, your excessive lust for whores will be discovered one day for making my sister whore for you.

Judah got angry and said: you are a whore because your mother whores with the devils and you are polluted from my seed that made you. I'll give you the same cup your mother drank my…. To contaminate you.

Till you get giddy like a drunken woman in the palace and I'll pluck out your breast which gods suck. I'm god your father who will do all this wickedness to you.

My abomination with you is little compared with the giant devils who fuck your mother's mother with big ones like horses.

Hadassah said: you make me your mistress. I made Mankind with you, and now you warn me if I gave birth to gods you will cast them in fire in new moons as an offering to the devil in Hades who raped my mother's mother to make gods and giants! Hadassah said to Judah: my father, don't you like to look like a god?

Judah said: Hadassah, I made you with the daughter of the daughter Eve that was raped and gave birth to your mother in my harem. You are my favourite daughter.

The giants you went with in the palace are your cousins. Their mothers and your mother were sisters from the women who Sabbathed in the harem giving birth to giants and gods, and their future is in my hands.

I took you from the harem. Brought you to the palace and made you my mistress, You wash yourself, paint your eyes and dress yourself in elegant clothes with jewellery. You lie in my bed and want me to fuck you with incense burning in my room like a whore. When your spirit departs from the kingdom you will see the devil who raped your mother's mother before you were born. Now is it I who make you a whore in Babylon? You are naturally wicked. It's in your nature.

Fear of Elijah. Warning

Judah began to stay in the palace more and more and became passive – a recluse in fear and depressed and submissive to the appetite of Hadassah's excessive lust for sex.

Hadassah took over the running of the palace in the heat of their passion. They feasted, got drunk and rejoiced. Anything Hadassah wanted, Judah gave her.

The whole earth was surprised and astonished at the tyrant that became a pussycat in the hands of Hadassah his mistress, while his Queen Tamuze lived a solitary life away from the people. Tamuze, the mother of gods, was great and beautiful, become a tributary and sad, wanting to die, to be free from living in captivity.

Well-favoured mistress turns to witchcraft Nah.3:3–4; Deut.27:22

Hadassah became as wicked as Judah. She became popular with the merchants. They would give her jewellery for favours with the king. She got apartments in the city and took all her sisters from the palace and made them whore for her, and use the place to entertain her lovers. She began to involve herself in witchcraft and cast a spell on Judah. She was now the lioness in the palace in Babylon with everyone chasing after her.

Her beauty went to her head and she wanted to be their queen. She became the joy of Babylon. She took the same cup Judah made her mother to drink his piss and did the same and gave it to him to drink. This made Judah mad in the palace. Judah held her by her throat and began strangling her. She used some witchcraft on him and he loosened his grip and she spat in his face like a serpent and he fell wriggling on the floor.

Hadassah went to the harem to Eve, who had brought her up from birth. The children from her sisters were glad to see her but when they came up to her she shouted at them: don't touch my clothes. You are not clean. Go away. She thought she would make Queen Tamuze jealous with her elegant clothes and jewellery.

Queen Tamuze said: well-favoured mistress who sells her sisters for whoredom and do witchcraft, the same shame, which Judah has brought unto me, will be upon thee, Hadassah. When I fall I will rise and you will sit in the dark. When Elijah destroys Babylon you will be in the rubble in the streets. I will endure my shame until Elijah executes judgment for me.

Daughter in law against mother in law

Tamuze said: don't forget, you were born in this harem and became Judah's favourite in the harem. Judah took your children with him to mix with Israelites in the palace with his mother in abomination. Now you don't want your children to touch your clothes. Elijah will judge between you and Judah and I. You are Judah's mistress to do thee as he pleases.

Hadassah became cruel and slapped Queen Tamuze on her face and said: who the fuck do you think you are? Tamuze fled from the harem. Eve said: Hadassah, you slapped my daughter. You have no right to lay your hands on her. You are cruel and wicked as Judah who made you in this harem. Tamuze is a handmaid to your sister's children. Your sin with Judah is upon the children of Mankind with your jealousy. Rejoice not because you live with Judah. I will endure my shame against your father who made you his mistress and sells your children. The shame Judah your king brought on to me will cover you with rubble for passing his seed to make thee in my flesh. Hadassah pushed Eve and hurried outside.

Hadassah went to the horseman and asked him to take her to Babylon city. She went to the captain of the military she doted as her lover among many others.

Hadassah was quick to go to bed with whom she liked to fuck her. She was wicked. Her mind was one track. She liked the giants with big ones. They excited her and she excited them.

Judah was sulking, crying and became unattractive with a long beard, always complaining about her never being in the palace and was afraid to be alone. Judah was not enough to satisfy Hadassah's sexuality. Now he loved Tamuze who he hates, and Hadassah hated who Judah loves. Judah heard the horseman pulled up outside the palace.

As Hadassah got inside Judah was standing there. He said: what is this, my well-favoured mistress? It is late. Hadassah looked at him and said: what is it you want of me? You nearly choked me to death. I live by your law to death. At least you could allow me to prepare for it. I did to you the same you did to my mother with the same cup with my libation to drink to god in Hades as an offering, and you went mad. I am not any more like the little maid you brought up in the harem who was stupid about your religion.

THE MYSTERY HIDDEN FROM YOUR EYES GIVEN TO YOU Col.1:26; Mt.19:3, 7–10; Rev.17:1–2; Deut.27:22

Hadassah said: you are my father. You are a mighty God. I did everything you wanted in the harem to please you. You yoked your seed and bore many children for you to mix with children of your queen in this palace to make Israelites. Your queen chose to live in the harem to be a maid and now I'm in the palace with you as your daughter, maid and mistress and made me whore in your palace with many men in your bed.

Your queen is over the wall. Why don't you ask her to come back and I'll stay in Babylon city with my sisters to liberate you from this dotage.

Your queen said to me: you have brought shame unto her. Elijah will judge between her and me and you. Who is this Elijah that is more powerful than you to destroy the Babylon you build by your wisdom? Tamuze said: when she falls she will rise and I'll be in the rubble in the street. Judah said: don't pay attention to what she said. She is only jealous of you and I in the palace. Hadassah said: I know you are deceitful. The future will tell. If Babylon falls to cover me, Mankind and Israelites will know you were not honest with me.

Judah began to tremble with fear. Hadassah, you are my favourite daughter, I don't want you to leave me. I'll give you whatever you want. Stay with me. Her youth and beauty excited him like when he corrupted her in the harem with his lust. Now she was overpowering him and sapping all his energy. He needs her more than she needs him. She is the lioness of Babylon, chasing her lovers. Being a mistress for a mighty hunter in the palace of Babylon is not enough. She's got a taste for cruelty and wants power like her father to rule Babylon.

Hadassah said: my king, you said I could do what I want. I want us to have a banquet in the palace to celebrate the Passover for my mother who gave birth to me from your seed. I am in the palace with you to death.

Judah said: Hadassah, it is an excellent way to celebrate the Passover for the kingdom, my beautiful daughter. I'll make a law for all generations on earth to commemorate our Passover when we are spirits after death, to celebrate our victory for the earth together.

Hadassah said: my king, let us celebrate this victory to death with a banquet. If it pleases my king, to make your queen jealous before we perish together. Hadassah invited all her lovers: rulers, kings, merchants, and captains in the military, witches, magicians, astrologers and those who wanted her to be queen of Babylon. She began to hate Judah for doting on her and yet feared him at the same time. Judah began to have bad dreams and would cry in his sleep, and it frightened her.

Since Hadassah moved into the palace with him, he became pensive and pessimistic and intransigent towards the queen and lost control and interest in government. She is the one in control, using her charms and her wickedness to run the palace in this scenario. The mighty hunter and his well-favoured mistress turned to witchcraft to be the ruler of Babylon.

Tamuze fled from the harem after Hadassah slapped her face and was walking in the wilderness. She stopped to have a break to meditate. Elijah appeared to her and asked: where are you going? She said: O Elijah, I am fed up. I fled from this mistress of Judah's. She came to the harem and was cruel to the children and abusive to shame me. All I want is peace. I am free from the oath and this tyrant, and now his mistress under the law insults me.

Elijah said: return! You must suffer your shame and be strong with your faith in me. How else can you receive forgiveness if you don't submit to your shame. If she slaps you, offer the other cheek. The time will come when I will multiply kingdoms from your flesh exceedingly for your affliction.

THE PROMISED SON BY ELIJAH Deut. 1:10; Gal 421–22, 26, 28; Ro.9:9; Eph 1.11 6.2–3

Elijah said to Queen Tamuze: I will give you a son that will multiply as angels in Heaven in the name of CHRIST and they will bless you. Tamuze said: the son you will give me – will it be between us by the Word to CHRIST? Elijah said: it is not a hard thing for me. Be patient and our son will be born when you are a spirit by the Word after you Sabbath. It will be the promised son. And He vanished and Tamuze returned to be with Eve. Tamuze told her Elijah promised her a son. Eve said: have faith, my daughter, in our saviour and you will have a son that is accepted by Christ.

WORLD WAR I. THE FEAST OF KINGS

King Judah, conqueror of nations on earth, invited the new Israelite kings in the nations, government officials, pharisees, scribes, commandants of his army, astrologers, magicians and merchants to feast with him and his mistress in the palace in Babylon.

When everyone was through eating and drinking, Judah introduced Hadassah as his mistress in the palace. She was young and beautiful, dressed in purple and scarlet glittering, diamonds and gold necklaces with precious stones, painted eye shadow and makeup and with the disk of the moon between horns on her head. She was much admired and everyone congratulated the king on his new mistress.

THE SPEECH

King Judah stood to give his speech and there was silence. He opened his hands wide and said: behold, and pointed his hand at each of his Israelite kings and princes. Then he pointed his hand at the rulers of Mankind and his commandants of gods. Then he pointed his finger at the direction where Tamuze Queen Babylon was with Eve in the harem, then pointed his finger towards Heaven.

And he began boasting: I have excelled of the flesh of Queen Tamuze of Babylon. All of you are my creation, not like what the devils made with my queen.

By my strength and wisdom I have removed the devils from the earth and taken the Hebrew women they raped to make gods and giants from them to create all of you to be my creation from my seed. The kings and princess and Mankind began to clap their hands for he is a jolly good king, much whistling and cheers.

Then he began: I have removed the devil kings from the nations to replace Israelite kings in the nations to rule Mankind giants and gods by my wisdom. I've captured the Hebrews that were raped by devils and cast the devils out of the earth.

The Hebrew women were bound in captivity by devils and I gathered the women like eggs from hens. No god opened their mouth to save the women.

I brought them to my harem and yoked my seed and made you kings and princes and Mankind in fertile eggs, so you can multiply spirits on earth to live under the law with my authority. The guests stood and said: praise the king of all nations. Mankind said: cheers. The Israelites said: we honour you, father and our mother, while we are in her flesh as a mighty god of Israelites.

King Judah went on to say: my abomination to make Israelites with Queen Tamuze of Babylon and Mankind with Hadassah will establish my foundation to stretch the flesh of Queen Tamuze of Babylon and Hadassah from the earth to the heavens.

Judah said: let it be written, through me I will multiply Mankind and Israelites with knowledge. I will make images for the brute in my father's image (Elijah) to create spirits in the Light to ascend to the heavens. If CHRIST or any of his sons visit the earth from Heaven, they will be punished.

All the guests stood up and said: god in Hades, save the king. Judah sat with Hadassah and she gave him a kiss.

The elder Israelite king stood to worship his father King Judah. All eyes were on him. He said: behold my father, the mighty God of the earth. A giant stood and said: our king has the knowledge of all secrets hidden by spirits of the other world. He beat Adam with the rod and holds his daughters captive as his inheritance on the earth, who died giving birth to us giants to do battle for the earth with you, O King.

Another Israeli king stood and said: brothers, all flesh on earth be the spoil to death so we can be one flock of spirits on earth from the seed of our king of nations with our Queen Tamuze and mother. The kings and princes said: cheers! Mankind said: woe if we lose the battle without flesh of our queen, when CHRIST comes for her flesh.

Another Israelite king stood and said: brothers. All eyes were on him. Peace be with you. let us worship our king of kings. Behold our father King Judah. The conqueror of nations has changed the course of history. The guests said: cheers and began a clapping ovation: he is our king for ever, conqueror of the earth. Let us rejoice with our king's achievement. Some kings said: carry on, brother king. He went on to say: brothers… He stopped and looked at them, and then there was silence.

Then he said: this battle to conquer nations was a prototype of the real battle for the earth. Our mighty king has proved it can be done with our spirits after death. As godly spirits we will go in the body of rulers in the nations on earth with the latest technology and destroy the kingdom from nation to nation as our king has done in the sight of the spirit of Adam and the spirit of the brute (Elijah) in god (Cain's) image to rule the earth for ever. There was much fear to fight against the spirits that cast the devils from the earth.

Another Israelite king stood and said: behold our king of nations, I worship you with your mistress Hadassah who worships you to death. Let us use this feast as an occasion to celebrate our father's Passover. He has created us to be his people to pass on his immutable seed from god (Cain) who made our king from the flesh of Queen Babylon, our mother.

Everyone looked at the king revealing a secret of Judah and was nervous and said: I give way for our father, the king of kings, to finish his strategy and plan for our future. The guests began to whistle. Others said: hear; hear O mighty God and hunter with world power. Let us hear your plan. King Judah stood and opened his arms wide, then pointed his finger upwards and everyone looked to the ceiling as if they saw a ghost and were in fear.

Judah said: I shall devour flesh like a dragon with my mistress. If my spirit is cast out from my mother's flesh, I warn this brute in my father's image, my spirits will do the same with violence to the inhabitants on earth who have faith in Him (Elijah) and His CHRIST.

With thee, Hadassah, after death we will destroy them in the battle in the kingdom when we are godly spirits. (Jer.51:20)

The warning by Jesus to mankind in later generations Mt.13:11

King Judah said: I know the mystery of the kingdom and what is hid. When we are godly spirits we will go in the kingdoms to fight against spirits in their humanity from nation to nation to destroy the kingdom to prevent salvation in kingdoms with immortal spirits by the Word to take over the earth with godly spirits from my seed.

Hadassah stood and said: O mighty king, I'll praise thee thou whilst you comfort me with joy. I'll be with you as your queen of the spirits without the flesh of Queen Tamuze of Babylon, whom you hate. and you will have peace on earth and not go in fire.

King Judah said: Hadassah, from now you are my star. Queen Tamuze of Babylon is a burden to me on earth and will never have another seed of your king in the palace. When the time comes for Babylon to fall I'll be in captivity. Woe to me in the chambers in a violent place where the winds howl.

Hadassah said: O King, you will be among the ancient devils and there will be no one on earth to save you. Before you leave me on earth I'll lick the dust from your feet, for our spirits to have the same passion and desire to do battle for the earth together as king and queen of godly spirits for ever.

The Beginning of religion in Babylon and the end of religion in salvation

The law is a spiritual doctrine to death contrary to the scriptures based on eternal life, peace and love and justice. Judah became the high priest of the spiritual law to death. The pharisees were handpicked to enforce the religion by the law to death. They exploited their power and position and were like secret police in Babylon city.

The pharisees liked to be seen in market places, collecting taxes for

King Judah and to see the citizens observe the law and go to the temple to worship the statue of Queen Tamuze of Babylon with an Israelite child on her arm to death.

The people lived in fear of Judah as he was wicked and punished anyone who did not worship him as the mighty God. Those who died for rebellion were buried with a jar of water in the grave for their spirit to drink before it left the earth.

THE KINGDOM IS A SACRIFICE Ro.8:24

(31) Judah kept to his plan to declare war for the earth with godly spirits to rule as king, which the devils failed to establish on earth with spirits from their seed and not knowing who is CHRIST and Elijah. Judah murdered Adam and His sons to be a king on earth with Satan and the other kings to share the world with them.

(33) The bibles say **Jn 8.7** (Judah) threw stones on the body of Adam and His spirit (CHRIST) will come and cast out spirits from the seed of Judah in the kingdoms. The spirits of gods that have faith in Elijah, ELIJAH will save in salvation and they will rest in peace. The godly spirit (Cain) said through the mouth of Paul: say to the Roman spirits of gods who don't have faith in Elijah is onto fire after death. (**Ro.10:15**) They will have to ask the godly spirit Israel to save them (**Ro.10:14**) because they worship Israel as God (Israel). They know not the godly spirit of Judah's name is Israel, who rebelled against Elijah and slew the sons of CHRIST, when he was King Judah with the devils (19).

The godly spirit(Cain) returned from captivity and said through the mouth of Paul: to the Romans, Elijah is not a god or God. If Elijah did not spare Judah who he brought up, neither will Elijah spare you if you don't have faith in Him to save you from falling in fire. **Ro.11:22**

OBSERVATION OF CHANGE IN THE END GENERATION Ro.13:11; Ro.12:2

What the bibles failed to say! Who is the godly spirit (Cain) after he returned from captivity? And what was his mission? godly spirit (Cain) told the Romans through the mouth of Paul: Elijah accepts a body well prepared as a sacrifice for creation to have a spirit with everlasting life by the Word to CHRIST. Observe the change in your generation. In one hour CHRIST can cast out multitudes in the kingdom for salvation to create immortal spirits to continue in their image.

Darkness Ro.13:12; Ro.14:17–18

The godly spirit (Cain) said through the mouth of Paul: the end is coming to spirits of gods in the kingdom, and immortal spirits will be created in the kingdom to continue to live everlasting life for eternity. Every spirit of god is accountable for his action and if he falls in fire should not blame Elijah. This is what the godly spirit (Cain) said to the Romans as a warning to the spirits of gods in the kingdom: the godly spirit (Cain) said through the mouth of Paul to the Romans, the devils broke the covenant of peace by having Judah to hang the body of Adam/CHRIST. It's Elijah who cast the devils out the earth, justified for peace. (**Ro.15:4**) Peace be with spirits of gods who have faith after death.

The secret Ro.16:25; 1.Cor.1:4–6

The godly spirit (Cain) from captivity said to the Romans through the mouth of Paul: Elijah is able to make their kingdom have an immortal spirit through CHRIST. The mystery of the ages is revealed to you. That which was hidden by God Israel, it is made known to Romans. This secret concealed for many generations is to be made known to all spirits of gods in the kingdoms on earth to have faith only in Elijah the saviour so through him Christ will come to create their kingdom with an immortal spirit with knowledge to have relationship with CHRIST.

The challenge for the earth is at hand 1.Cor.1:21

The godly spirit (Cain) said through the mouth of Paul to the Corinthians: where is the godly spirit Israel, the prophet of the law, who wants to make war in this generation? Has not Elijah shown him how stupid he is to challenge Him for the earth? Jesus warned the godly spirit Israel in the body of Cephas the New Testament is not for him and his godly spirits (**1.Cor.1:18**) but for all Mankind. The godly spirit (Cain) said through the mouth of Paul to the Corinthians: Jesus is a spirit with power over all godly spirits that returned from captivity to tell the spirits of gods/Mankind in the kingdom the way to be saved after death. They must have faith in Elijah to rest in peace for eternity.

The mystery of Jesus 1.Cor.2:6.8

The godly spirit (Cain) in the body of Paul said to the Corinthians: Jesus manifested his spirit in the flesh so Mankind could see him as a human being. The godly spirits released from captivity could not manifest in flesh to be seen because they were not a spirit of creation in the Light. The godly spirit (Cain) said through the mouth of Paul to the Corinthians: Jesus is an immortal spirit with knowledge and wisdom in the world. The spirits of gods/Mankind in the kingdom will perish if they follow human doctrine contrary to the New Testament. The godly spirit (Cain) said through the mouth of Paul: no spirit while they were human saw Jesus's spirit, but in order to tell what is hid Jesus had to sanctify and manifest in the flesh for spirits in their humanity to see him in his image. Jesus sacrificed his body to death. His spirit was resurrected to Heaven by Elijah

The godly spirit (Cain) confirmed to the Corinthians through the mouth of Paul: the devils had no understanding of the mystery of CHRIST'S spirit in the body Adam and Elijah in his kingdom.

Elijah revealed to Judah he is in the kingdom of god (Cain) of the devil. Judah did not accept Elijah, divine spirit in the image of god his father in Hades. Judah rebelled against Elijah (14) who is the judge over all spirits of gods. Judah knew CHRIST created Elijah by the Word and that Elijah is the first spirit in salvation (**Ps.76**) Elijah created to judge spirits of gods after they depart from the kingdom.

Sabbath celebration

The Sabbath was celebrated by the devils after King Judah eliminated all the sons of Adam from the earth.

The first Passover

The first Passover: The devils captured Eve and all her daughters in their nations and raped the daughters of Eve with CHRIST in Adam to make giants and gods. The holy women died giving birth to giants and gods. Elijah captured the devils and cast them out of the earth for eternity for rape to make gods is a sin

The Passover

King Judah brought up the babies in his harem. When the giants were of age he selected them and began to make Mankind. He began to mix, mingle and interbreed to change the features of gods and called them Mankind with the children with Queen Tamuze of Babylon to make Israelites with the women from the flesh of CHRIST in captivity.

Pentecost

All the people in the nations spoke a different language and celebrated to give thanks and praise and worship to King Judah for making them on earth. In fear and respect he was called God of Mankind, God of Israel and God of all the people on earth after the devils were captured. **Lev.23:10; Acts:1**

Judah distinguished himself from gods because he was the only king left He was called a mighty God for respect.

The godly spirit of Judah (Israel) was in the body of Cephas and hasted not to be in the city of Jupta to celebrate the day of Pentecost. The name Judah gave his spirit when he was in the king of Babylon was to be called after his death is Israel the God of Israelites

The earth spirits are short of glory

The population of the earth began to multiply and spread out with gods, giants, Mankind and Israelites. The Israelites were made kings in the nations and spoke Hebrew among themselves. They were not allowed to mix, so they could be established on earth as Israelites. Their children were registered in Babylon for genealogy for future generations.

Babylon city was the capital of his empire, built on the blood of CHRIST and on his foundation (**Hab.2:12**). This is how Mankind began with his daughters and his mistress Hadassah. **Rev.17:5–6**

THOU SHALL NOT KILL Gen 9.5–6

For slaying and shedding blood of Adam-CHRIST on earth and the elimination of His sons in the kingdoms from the face of the earth, Judah will have to explain to all spirits from his seed in the kingdom why he killed the sons of CHRIST to establish his Israelites on earth to look like the people of creation who he slew and who did not harm anyone on earth.

THE WARNING

In the beginning Elijah told Ammon (Judah): your mother is held captive by the devils in the mountains. Go and save her.

If you have faith in me and need help call me to send them back where they came from, for holding your mother in captivity to make gods for them under oath.

Ammon (Judah), every god the devil makes with your mother is your brother. If the devils harm you I will punish every devil and for holding your mother in captivity.

Ammon (Judah), you must not fornicate with your mother; she is the daughter of the man Adam. His spirit has a right to every kingdom from her flesh. If any god fornicates with your mother he will be cut off to be with the devils for making gods with the man's (Adam) daughter in captivity. **Rev.17:13–14**

Judah became notorious for his skill, imitated the devils and was told by Satan and the devils if he wanted to be a king he must kill Adam. He got excited and hanged Adam and went against Elijah and CHRIST in Adam.

This is how the devils set him up with the law to fall. The devils gave him a province he called Babylon. That is where he began to make Mankind with his daughter Hadassah and Israelites with his mother held in captivity under the law to death. **Rev.17:5–6**

PROVOCATION REV.13:13

Judah kept killing and became a rebel, and against Elijah and CHRIST with his religion to live to death. He opened schools for pharisees to teach the law to gods, and set up his military. He built the Tower of Babel as a symbol of his power and strength on earth, and sacrificed gods to death every new moon.

Judah built his palace in Babylon and made Tamuze his mother his queen though she never played any part in building his empire, Tamuze had faith in Elijah to save her from sin under oath and under Judah's law to be free after death for ever.

Judah was presumptions, committed abomination with his mother to excite himself and to provoke Elijah to get Him angry. Elijah said: his day will come. The time I speak the Word his presumptuousness will certainly stumble and fall. **Jer.50:14-32**

From Babylon the family of Mankind, gods, giants and Israelites spread about the earth.

Religion

Wherever people went on earth they carried their religion with them and in later times due to people speaking different languages, interpreted the religion differently. The religion by the law was contained by the Israelites who preserved the law of Judah their king and God of the earth with his mistress Hadassah of Babylon. **Rev.13:14; Rev.14:8–11**

Statues were sold for Mankind to worship mother and child on her arm at their homes. This was integrated in religion all over the earth. This can even be testified in excavation around the earth and some places of worship with mother and child.

Mankind made statues of Judah and his daughter Hadassah with moon disk in horns painted in black. They gave these statues names like Madonna with child, Isis and Osiris. The history of these Judah and Hadassah statues was well known in Babylon but out of fear of Judah everyone whispered about Judah and Hadassah. They gave them alias names to hide their true identity. **Rev.14:8,10**

More honour was given to the queen of Babylon than the mistress Hadassah, second queen of Judah. He promised Hadassah she will be be queen of the godly spirits when they are spirits without his mother's flesh.

Worship Rev.13:8; Jn.8:38–44; Dan.2:46–47:44; Hos.4:6; Eph 6.12

Judah kept all what Elijah had taught him as his secret. He deceived everyone to believe he is the almighty God who created the world. They called him Nimrod, serpent, dragon, beast. Jesus called him Beelzebub. Godly spirit (Israel) Judah put fear in the people on earth with his godly spirits. Jesus cast them out of Mankind, who was following him/Jesus to know the truth. The fear of Judah (Israel) was on every spirit from his seed in the kingdom thinking if they have faith in Elijah or in any other god he will attack them, if they don't worship him as God almighty even in this generation of Israelites, and all Mankind from his seed. They worship him as the creator of the world. Multitudes will fall like him because they don't have faith in the saviour Elijah or pay attention to the choice they have to rest in peace. Judah even deceived the devils and they were in of fear him after he killed Adam.

Jesus and Elijah were sent by CHRIST Rev.11:1–5; 1.JN.3:8,10; Rev.13:8–10

For this purpose Jesus's spirit sanctified and manifested in flesh and cast Israel out from the same body Jerusalem (the spirit of Babylon) was in for making her cry. He entered the body of Peter.

Judah (Israel) thought he could do as he wanted like when he was her king in Babylon to enter the same body with Jerusalem who is free from the law and bondage, Jerusalem is a holy spirit, the daughter of CHRIST who awakes from sleep to tell god (Cain) and Israel to repent before all Mankind and Israelites for their sin to make them before she goes above to see the final judgment in the kingdoms on earth.

After Judah's death

Mankind made a statue of him. They called it Shamah the dog (god), and his mistresses statue next to him, they called Ishtar, Madonna with child. They made a statue of Eve and called it Anu, and Queen Tamuze of Babylon with her Israelite son in her arms, they call Mary, mother of god.

Religious statues and names of

Tamah, Queen Tamuze, Queen Tamuze of Babylon mother and son of Judah statues, Eve Anu statues, Hadassah mother and son Belhadassah of Judah statues. Judah Shamah the dog (god) with Hadassah called Ishtar mother of Mankind, whore of Babylon called mystery woman (Rev.18:3;19:1-2) the abomination of her father, called the beast, serpent, dragon, Beelzebub, high priest, pharisee, God of Israel, Judah and Israel, Israel and Jerusalem, Nimrod, Lion king, Enoch walked with God, lord God, god of god, king of kings.

Spirits of the dead in Babylon

The godly spirits from captivity with no flesh began to enter bodies of Mankind. They seduced them commit rape, murder, violence, war, epileptic fits, jealousy with hate. Mankind was in fear, thinking it is the devils that came back to earth and were against them and started incantation, magic, sorcery, taking herbal bath s and blood baths to keep away godly spirits. This began as spiritual religion, and everyone began to indulge in witchcraft with godly spirits of the dead possessing their bodies and speak through their mouth, to lead astray and frighten their neighbour who has faith in Elijah and CHRIST to save them.

The blessing and curse. The mystery of God Rev.10:7; Deut.11:26

Two godly spirits returned from captivity. The godly spirit Israel entered the body of Moses, prince of Pharaoh and the godly spirit (Cain) entered the body of Aaron. Jerusalem was in the body of Miriam as a prophetess to her people called Hebrews. Moses is not a prophet; he is an Egyptian possessed by the godly spirit Israel in his body speaking through his mouth. (**Num.12:3**) Elijah said to Jerusalem and godly spirit (Cain) in the body of Aaron: hear now my WORD. If there is a prophet among you I will make myself known unto him in a vision and speak to him in a dream. The godly spirit Israel in the body of Moses is a prophet with the law to death so don't be afraid to speak against him.

The godly spirit (Cain) in the body of Aaron said to Pharaoh: Elijah said to let his people go. (**Ex10.3**) Pharaoh said I will let the Hebrews go but the Israelites stay. The godly spirit Israel in the body of Moses said through the mouth of Moses to Pharaoh: my Israelites must go to serve Elijah. Pharaoh replied to Israel in Moses: their spirits are from your seed. You are their god that is evil and much evil is before them. (**Ex10.10**) The Israelites cried to Israel in the body of Moses: you have deceived us and want us to die in the wilderness. Elijah said to Israel in Moses: why criest thou unto me to save your Israelites? Tell them to go forward. You have made my people (Hebrews) slaves in Egypt (**Ex.9:17**) and wanted to rule my people (**Ex.9:18**). Israel in the body of Moses said: their kingdom is the blessing to created immortal spirits in the flesh of Jerusalem in the time of salvation. Israelites and Mankind worship him as their God and fear him in life and after death. Even writers are in fear to write about him thinking his spirit will come attack them so they call him all kinds of names. Jesus came to tell you the truth and he was crucified. Jesus with his godly spirits.

The godly spirit Israel in the body of Peter lied; he did not want Mankind to know Jesus cast him out from the same body as Jerusalem in Mary. Jesus showed Israel he could walk on water, Israel, thinking he was returning in captivity, cried for Jesus to save him. Israel in the body of Peter called Jesus king of the Jews with multitudes of godly spirits in the body of Mankind. Israel was the king of Babylon, who had returned from captivity. Jesus knew he was the deceitful enemy of Mankind to destroy all kingdoms on earth with his godly spirits in the bodies of Mankind. Judah's plan was hid from Mankind in that generation. Jesus cast out a few godly spirits, so Mankind could believe. Jesus said he did not come to destroy the law of devils but to tell Mankind the way to everlasting life and be aware of the prophet with the law to death. Jesus told Mankind in that generation the way to eternal life is through faith in Elijah. On the cross Jesus called for Elijah to take over to finish the work by the Word for CHRIST to create immortal spirits in the time of salvation.

THE NATURE OF THE SPIRITS OF GODS IS IMMUTABLE Ps.5:15; Ja.1:13; Ja.1:13–14; Heb.6:4; 1.Jn.3:7; Jn.8:7

A devil or a god cannot make an immortal spirit in the Light. CHRIST cannot make a god and vice versa. Spirits in the Light are of creation and not like spirits of gods of the seed of devils. You are natured in the way you came into this world. Spirits of gods have a choice for peace according to the New Testament if they have faith in Elijah, because it is the spirits of gods are born in this world in sin from the seed of devils from the Ancient World of Darkness.

All kingdoms are righteous regardless of colour and belong to CHRIST, for CHRIST to create immortal spirits in salvation through Elijah to continue on earth in their image to make immortal spirits to populate the earth with spirits in the Light, world without end. Born again is false hope and temptation to be lead astray in religion contrary to the New Testament by Christ. Multitudes are called to rest in peace but few accept the offer until they have no flesh in fire. To know the TRUTH they had a choice for peace while they had flesh.

Know the history of the kingdom and its beginning Mt.13:11; Gen.10:10; Mt.11:12–24; Num.9:1

The Eternal created the body Adam in the image with the spirit CHRIST and his Zion, sanctified in his flesh to manifest in her image called Eve as His new creation on earth. CHRIST was the secret of the Eternal – His CHRIST to come in the world, to sit on the throne in Heaven to create new angels in the Light and rule all worlds and to make the Old Covenant obsolete by a New Testament if the devils made a god with the Eternal's creation. His CHRIST would create his Elijah with the Word to cast out the devils and their gods in the fire for breaking the covenant of peace in the world

An accursed seed of devils cannot make holy spirits in the Light

The kingdom suffered violence and was taken by force by the devils. They raped the draughters of CHRIST-Adam with Zion-Eve and killed all the sons of CHRIST on earth. The devils were captured by Elijah and were cast out of the earth for ever. The spirits of the seed of devils are not accepted in

Heaven and can only rest in peace if they have faith in Elijah.

THE BLESSING AND THE CURSE Mal.2:2; Deut.11:26; Ro.8:19

All the kingdoms belong to CHRIST and are sacrificed to death. The spirits of the sons and daughters of CHRIST were resurrected by Elijah. And so will be the immortal spirits created by CHRIST through Elijah in the days of salvation. All spirits of CHRIST that sleep on earth will awake on the days of salvation and will resurrect with CHRIST to the heavens. The spirits from the seed of gods that have no faith come unto final judgment and have no exemption to rest on earth after death and will be with no flesh in fire with the devils.

FAITH IN ELIJAH IS TO SAVE A SPIRIT TO REST IN PEACE FOR EVER

The earth has become populated with spirits of gods in the kingdom that is different from spirits of creation through Elijah with Jerusalem by their son Isaac by the WORD. When CHRIST comes in the days of salvation is to remove spirits of gods in the kingdom to create immortal spirits when Elijah speaks the Word. If a god calls himself a pastor, a bishop, evangelist, doctor in religion, witch doctor, father or cardinal etc. if a preacher is of the seed of gods and doesn't have faith in Elijah he will fall. Just use your common sense and meditate on five letters: F A I T H. No god can save another, much less himself. Jesus said: Close your door and meditate on it. Faith in Elijah!

IF YOU ARE NOT OF THE SEED OF Isaac Ps.25:13; Gen.17:19; Jer.22:28

Elijah presents kingdoms of gods that are prepared for salvation to CHRIST on his throne in Heaven. When Elijah speaks the Word CHRIST will come to cast out spirits of gods and create immortal spirits in their image to continue in perfection in their kingdom. The spirits that have faith will sleep for ever. It is a simple judgment. No one has to be educated or have to pay preachers to have faith. Save your money, and use your little common sense. It's a free choice for peace or Hell. Elijah says if you have faith you will prepare your body for salvation. The choice is yours to decide your fate. Jesus said: close your door and communicate with the saviour Elijah.

Religion of Babylon continues in this generation, worshiping statues

The religion the devils left is to live by the law to death or be punished in fire after death. This death put fear in the spirits of gods in their humanity to worship Judah as God, and live in hope that God can save them after death from fire. The law of devils is contrary to The New Testament by Christ for gods to rest in peace for eternity if they have faith in Elijah and not suffer in fire for eternity.

God. Who is he? Ps.53:1; 13:3

King Judah wanted to define himself from gods and wanted respect. Israelites and Mankind called him Mighty God because he was the only king left on the earth after Elijah removed the devils from the earth for ever and ended as a godly spirit in the name of Israel in captivity with multitudes of godly spirits.

Worship of God Ps.14:1–3

The worship of God is religious indoctrination chiefly to worship Judah as a king of Babylon. He made his mother his Queen Tamuze of Babylon who called him a serpent, and a dragon who wants to devour her flesh. Tamuze did not worship Judah. The gods called him Maduk, a rebel. Hadassah, his daughter and mistress, worshipped him and licked the dust from under his feet. He called Hadassah his star. Other writers called her Ishtar, which was her new name after she fell in the rubble in the tower in Babylon. Where was God when Babylon fell?

Jesus showed Mankind where the godly spirit of God was hiding

Jesus washed the dust from under Peter's feet to point out the tyrant of the earth as a godly spirit hiding with no flesh of his own in the body of Peter. Jesus manifested his spirit. He showed himself to humanity in this world while the deceiver was stalking Jesus as a godly spirit in Peter's humanity, wanting to be a king again as in the days of Babylon with his godly spirits from captivity. Jesus is not a king or an Israelite. Jesus is the son of CHRIST, the heir of CHRIST on HIS throne in Heaven. Neither did Jesus cry for God Israel to save him on the cross. Jesus called for his brother Elijah, created by the Word in salvation to take over and continue the work in the kingdom when salvation begins for kingdoms of gods and for final judgment on spirits of gods in the kingdoms on the earth.

Giants

The Anak devils were tall compared to the other devils. After the captivity, the giant babies were called Anakin. They became warriors of Judah and protected the Israelites. Nephelim giants, Captorin giants and Zuzumsim giants were all giants were from the seed of tall devils. The giant's children they left on earth began to mix and interbreed and took the names of ancient devils in captivity.

Giants began to take root and populate the earth with gods and Mankind.

The giants, though they were famous for their strength, had a violent nature of their ancestors. Their intelligence was like gods who like to be led. The Israelites and Mankind were superior in intelligence and personality in various shades and sizes and their kingdoms vary with different features as seen to date with all nationalities on earth.

Though Mankind and Israelites lack the strength of giants, their spiritual nature is the same and our brothers and sisters from the seed of devils and not immortal spirits by creation.

Gods

Gods began from the seed of the devil with the captive daughter of Adam and Eve under oath of the devils and for peace Tamah made gods on earth for the devils so they leave her parents in peace. A young girl going with devils for peace on earth. Give her praise because she had faith in Elijah to save her, who she had not met.

When the earth began to populate gods, they began to run away to distant lands to keep to their kind, and religion was about spirits and everyone interpreted religion in different languages. The devils left the gods to battle for their survival. That's why the devils made giants to destroy the kingdoms, as they did not trust Judah. They plotted to kill Judah after they brought the daughters of Eve into captivity to make gods. The devils began to mistrust Judah and fear he was too intelligent. Satan called him a serpent. Judah used this as his symbol while he was human and Hadassah had a moon disk between horns on her head as his star and queen.

The plan

Judah realized Elijah and CHRIST are spirits and knew he would not go above. Elijah made him wise in scripture and he thought he was wiser than Elijah and challenged him for the earth. **1.Cor.1:21**

This challenge, Elijah took seriously and gave Judah a lot of years to pass on his seed to make spirits for war in the kingdom. CHRIST set the timing clock for salvation to create immortal spirits in kingdoms of gods which is to HIS benefit to create spirits on earth by the Word of Elijah. According to the New Testament, by justice for peace in the world with immortal spirits in kingdoms by the WORD, is to be as it was in the beginning in the Garden of Eden.

This is the history of Mankind and the way of peace is through faith for kingdoms of Mankind to be created with immortal spirits. The way to eternal life is by the Word to CHRIST. Peace be with your spirit. As Jesus says: peace I leave this earth after I Sabbath. Elijah! Elijah! Don't pray in vain; think of the price for change. If you don't have a desire to change for your peace, go on sinning and cry for ever later. Then you will have no one to blame but yourself. If you want to read more, go on reading to have faith in the free choice.

Chapter 2

Hadassah had a dream before the fall of Babylon

Hadassah began whispering to her God Judah: I had a dream! Judah said: what is it, my favoured queen? Hadassah said: I saw two spirits and they were dazzling me in the Light. Then one went in the body of your queen mother who made your Israelites. Your spirit was hiding in the same body as hers and the spirit in the Light entered her body and cast you out of her body and you were angry and crying because you were naked with no flesh, and you ran in the body of an Israelite.

Then I looked and saw the other spirit in the Light went in the body of my grandmother Eve and He cast out the spirit of god your father, who was hiding in her body, making her cry, wanting her flesh so he could be human again and his spirit ran unto an Israelite.

The spirit that went in the body of my grandmother became human and began speaking words to Mankind to repent. They asked him where he came from and he said he is a witness of one he brought up crying in the wilderness.

Then I looked and saw the other spirit that went in the body of your queen mother and he was looking like an Israelite and your mother was asking him for forgiveness for her sins in front of multitudes of spirits and the spirits began shouting No! No! No! It's because of her we suffered in flames of fire.

Then the spirit that looked like Mankind stood and said repent now in front of the spirits, and great fear came on the spirits and the two sinners went on their knees. And multitudes of spirits were in great fear of this spirit and said, we forgive you O queen of the earth, and they all began to run in the water before he could speak another word.

Suddenly there were no more spirits on earth except your mother and my grandmother with the two spirits, and they went in the river, laughing and splashing water on each other and your mother was singing and dancing by the river.

Then I looked and in the dream you came above the water with multitudes of spirits, angry and afraid, and the spirits began to enter the bodies of Mankind and Israelites and began following these two spirits who were telling the world of your adultery and abomination and the ten commands of the law and destruction and I could see great fear in your face with shame.

Woe to him that is alone when he falleth Eccl.4:10

What can this dream mean, my God? Multitudes in that generation will know the truth of our wickedness to make Mankind with me and Israelites with your mother and will know you can't save them after death. **Genesis.6:4**

Judah said: Hadassah, I'm your God by nature. I repent for making Mankind on earth to mix and mingle to make Israelites. The devils will give them grief after death if they don't have faith, I can see Mankind from us will continue with our wickedness on earth, making gods in our nature to do like us to do evil against each other.

The fear of you, O King, is like a roaring lion Pre.20:2

Judah said when I fucked the daughters of the children of daughters of Adam I hanged, they conceived. You were the one I loved the most and said: I'll make Mankind with you to make all kinds of people beautiful like you, and you will be my queen to rule the earth with the law.

The snare of the pit is upon thee Is.24:17

God/Judah said: Hadassah, we have corrupted all flesh with our incest. All spirits from my seed are corrupt. Our nature is of ancient devils. **Jer.11:5; 23:11; Essk.25:8**

CHRIST spoke through the mouth of Adam, and warned me not to Sabbath Adam and asked me to tell the devils to come and do it, but I wanted to make a name for myself as king. CHRIST warned me that if I Sabbathed Adam His spirit will come and cast out every spirit that trespasses in the flesh of his daughters with Eve. All flesh on earth is holy and Elijah will present kingdoms to him by the Word and only spirits from my seed that have faith in him will rest in peace.

The whore from the seed of the adulterer Is.57:3

God/Judah said: in truth, my daughter, your mother's mother is my mother's sister and god my father in Hades is my mother's brother. You are my queen. Now swear to me thou will not deal falsely with me with our son Belhadassah, who you say is your prophet. **Mt.24:45; 21:33**

Olive branch in the house of God Ps.52:8 Ps5.4

Hadassah said: O my God, I am your olive queen. I'm under your spell from my youth (1.Pet.4:7). If Elijah comes, you will not abide in the kingdom from the flesh of your mother. I will join you. Have not your maiden pleases thee to be your queen to death?

You have chastened me to give you pleasure and to me what pleases thee my God. You are a God that has pleasure in wickedness.

The promise is by faith Ps.51:5; Josh.7:11; Rev.18:4; Ps.56:9; Jer.50:20–1; Jn.1:10; Pet.2:24

God/Judah said: Hadassah, this dream you had is to make Mankind know to live by faith for their kingdom to be created with a new spirit.

My mother conceived me from the seed of god (Cain) of devils and we live according to the law of the nature of the devils by force. Hadassah, your God (Judah) who you worship to death is of god (Cain) seed. We will not live in the kingdom for ever like the spirit Elijah with the Word to CHRIST.

The sinner shall surely be put to death Deut.4:5; Lev.20:10; Gal.3:10; Lev.6:15; Ro.50:12–20

Judah said: Hadassah, this dream is to testify God made you to make Mankind to serve him and worship him to death.

The law is a religion to indoctrinate all Israelites and Mankind to worship your God to death. They are under no obligation to observe the

New Testament to save the kingdom from our mother's flesh. This is why Elijah was created, to save the kingdom and his people by the Word.

The spirit you saw is Elijah, who is the judge to establish the kingdom through CHRIST in salvation to cast out our spirits and replace the kingdom with His spirits. I've broken the covenant of peace with Him. I had no faith. The law is curse on spirits of gods.

Judah said: Hadassah! The covenant of peace was broken by your father, when I committed abomination with my mother and fucked with you to pass on the accursed seed of god my father, who raped my mother and she conceived me from his accursed seed.

Salvation is the victory by the Word through faith Ps.89:28; Eph 1.34:21

Salvation will come to the kingdom in the flesh of CHRIST on earth and our spirits will fall because we are not perfect. Elijah gave me the choice for a covenant of peace so my kingdom could be created to be His son in perfection and if I didn't take the consolation prize all spirits from my seed would be my portion on earth in the gates of the sun.

What shall your children do to have eternal life?

Hadassah said: my God, what is this covenant for everlasting life with blessings in the kingdom? Could not Mankind from us have this blessing to live for ever? Judah replied: no, my daughter, you are from my seed and our spirits are of the same nature and we are trespassing in the holy flesh of CHRIST. Only the body of Mankind that is righteous can have an everlasting spirit by the Word of Elijah according to the scripture.

If our children have faith in Elijah, He will save their spirits to have peace. All our children are born under the law to sin and make gods. The promise is for our children's kingdom to have a new spirit of creation.

Lk.10:23. A certain man of the law asked Jesus: what should I do to inherit Eternal life? Jesus answered: you know the scripture and the law

Judah said: Hadassah! Elijah explained this Testament to me. before I took the law of devils under oath I did not think much of the promise.

I had no faith. We have committed abomination. Our spirits are against living in the flesh, which is holy and righteous, and CHRIST will only accept spirits of creation by the Word.

Hadassah said: what about the Israelites with your queen mother? I did much whoring to mix and mingle my children with hers to look like the Hebrews you killed. Much blood was spilled on earth from my grandfather's sons. Will they have preference over Mankind?

God (Judah) said: no, my daughter, they are from my seed with this curse. Only their kingdom is righteous, just like our children. Elijah is very strict when it comes to the flesh of my mother and your mother's mother, and will accept kingdoms from their flesh that is well prepared for salvation. It is peace or destruction for our children's spirits if their desire is to fornicate in holy flesh and pass on seed.

Eph.15:6; Heb.8:6–8

The promise to Eve and Tamuze is for kingdoms of Mankind and Israelites to have everlasting spirits in creation by the Word to be as it was in the beginning with our grandfather and mother who we hold in captivity. All kingdoms are in the hands of Elijah to judge all spirits of gods after CHRIST casts them out from the kingdoms on earth.

So, my God (Judah), Hadassah said: all this incestuous fucking to make children to populate the earth in sin is for Elijah to pick and choose kingdoms for salvation from our sweat? Judah said: Hadassah, Elijah gave me the choice. It's either having faith in Him, or fire. And the same choice he gives our children's spirits – to have faith in him and prepare their bodies for salvation for CHRIST to create immortal spirits to be accepted above.

The spirits of our children will be our inheritance after CHRIST casts them out, and those that have no faith will join us in battle for the earth. The only consolation left is for our spirits to have faith to rest in peace so they don't come crying to us and say it's our fault for being born.

Fear of death Co.l1:26; Is.52:7–8

My God, Hadassah said: is this the mystery Elijah revealed to you, which the devils didn't know? You kept it to yourself all this time. Why do you still want to destroy the kingdom then to be punished by devils if we lose the battle for the earth? God said: it is this fear of what the devils will do to me for going with my mother that makes me wicked and hope the spirits after death will fight for the earth with me. I don't know where the devils came from, and they lie a lot and behave like creatures.

The godly spirit of my father is in the bowels of the earth in fire, being punished for raping my mother to make me wicked like him. He conspired with the devils to take my mother in captivity, who is for peace on earth and has faith in Elijah.

Elijah doesn't accept me the way I am, and also you, because we are not of the good seed like my mother to go above. Our desire is to live to death like god my father. He had no faith; else you or I would not be born. Neither can we be born again. We can't change the nature of our spirit. Elijah is determined to give CHRIST the victory.

Hadassah said: all this religion, my father, is only to worship you to death?

Hadassah, Judah said: my mother didn't worship me. She called me a maduk, a rebel, a serpent. I chose you from youth to be the mother of all the people from my seed on earth. When you licked the dust from under my feet you became my Ishtar in the palace.

This dream you had, Hadassah, is to let you know Elijah will give the kingdom of our children eternal life from the poorest of Mankind and to let you know CHRIST is the ruler of the world and give kingdoms eternal life to who has faith in Elijah to speak the Word to Him.

Elijah will present kingdoms from our children from all nations to CHRIST on His throne in Heaven to come and create immortal spirits in their kingdoms to be his people without discrimination to continue in their resemblance to populate the earth with immortal spirits. The spirits from our children at birth will be saved and have peace. When Elijah directs kingdoms in the nations, the spirits created will take residence on earth in the name of CHRIST to be His people on earth.

Mankind and Israelites will know the truth in the time of salvation about Elijah and CHRIST, who you saw in your dream. When Israelites and Mankind hear the good news that they must have faith in Elijah for their spirits to rest in peace so their kingdom be created with new spirits in the Light by CHRIST to go above in perfection, they will give Elijah praise for saving them.

If our spirits are wise they will have faith in Elijah to save them from fire after CHRIST casts them out from the kingdoms in the nations to rest in peace so spirits who have no faith like me, we will accept as our inheritance of spirits after death for the battle in the kingdom.

Hadassah said: my father, all this inbreeding to change the feature of gods to populate the earth with Israelites and Mankind is accounted for nothing. The more the people fuck, the more kingdoms they make for Elijah. Elijah will take the best of our daughters' kingdoms for himself and Christ.

Hadassah said: my God, if you had faith, all this evil would not come unto spirits from your seed on earth. Judah said: it is because I had no faith you are my daughter and queen. God (Cain) my father had no faith and did the same as I with my mother before I was born and lost his kingdom in salvation to Elijah, which is why we are angry – because we are not perfect like Tamuze and Eve. Our spirits are different under the laws of our nature. We cannot be born again to change our nature. It is death to gods in the world, if they have no faith to rest in peace after death.

Hadassah said: my God, this death makes me sick. You know all this scripture and you and I made Mankind on earth to suffer death. This is a sin. When our children get to know the truth they will want to pluck my eyes out for incest with you. They will call me a whore, a motherfucker with the son of god (Cain) in Hades, that can't save them after death.

While Tamuze and my grandmother Eve escape after death, for making you and god (Cain) they should suffer death to Passover the kingdom on earth to us. **Jn.18:28**

Elijah is the saviour of his people in the world Mt.1:21

Judah said: Hadassah, Tamuze's spirits and Eve spirits are righteous in the kingdom. We are trespassing in their flesh. It is true they are among us. If they Passover and sacrifice their bodies and spill blood it will be on us and all of Mankind. All the people on earth will curse us even more for making them not perfect to suffer in this international damnation.

It is the devils who sinned and violated the peace Jam.1:14–15

Hadassah said: my God, Queen Tamuze of Babylon and Eve ought to suffer for making god (Cain) your father with the devils to pass the accursed seed to you in deceit and rape to make Israelites and Mankind not perfect like us. My God, let this Passover feast be in remembrance for rape to make gods for all generations to celebrate the Passover of the kingdom, so their children's children may know these two who have faith in Elijah were held in captivity under your law. It will be a testimony for our children to know the kingdom is no more divided between you and the devils and to worship you as the mighty God who made all equal on earth.

We are deceived Jam.1:16; Ja1.16:17

Hadassah said: my God! If Eve and Queen Tamuze of Babylon die it will be hidden. There will be no Hebrews left on earth to tell Mankind you committed incest with your daughters and made them whore like me to be Queen Hadassah of Babylon who took over the palace from your Hebrew queen mother in captivity under the law in bondage to make gods.

Mankind, don't be angry with us if you know the truth! Jam.1:19–21

Hadassah said: my God, as long as Mankind walks on earth under the sun it will be a testimony they are sinners like us, not perfect, and to teach their children not to deceive themselves and to accept the way they were born. If they want peace the choice is theirs to have faith in Elijah and not us.

Elijah will save his people. He is their saviour Hos.13:4; Mt.1:21

Judah said: but Hadassah, Elijah said to me, one teardrop from my mother or Eve and He will come after me and I'll leave the earth like the devils in a whirlwind and the people on earth will be fatherless, so worshiping your mighty God is useless if I can't save them after death..

There is no saviour besides Elijah Hos.13:4
Hadassah, your God is a god of god

Judah said: Hadassah, while I live in my mother's flesh I'm in fear that when I Sabbath the devils will get hold of me for taking over the throne of Satan to make Israelites with my mother, and making Mankind with the daughter of a devil who is your mother. I will be alone fighting the devils in Hades. My mother will laugh at me for not having faith in Elijah for peace.

O my God, Hadassah cried: when you die, call Elijah to save you. Tell him you have faith now and want peace. **Is.45:15**

Put faith to the test Jam.1:2–3,13,15; Jam.2:20

Hadassah said: My God, before you die, let us put this faith to the test and see if Elijah will save Tamuze and Eve, who have faith in Him. If Elijah doesn't save them, this faith is useless indeed after death.

Judah's dream of a spirit going to Heaven

Judah had a dream that made him afraid and it troubled him much. Hadassah heard him crying in the bed and said: O King, you are dreaming again. What is it this time? Judah said: I saw a man on earth hanging on a tree and I saw his spirit going up to Heaven and in the end of the dream I saw him coming after me with a sickle in his hand and I began running. Then all spirits in the kingdoms on earth started running away from Elijah, and children were in the Light in the kingdom met in multitudes and the spirits of Mankind in your flesh descended to the devils in the bowels of the earth with devouring flames, and the devils began cry to me, if you are a mighty God, save us all from this fire and we will worship you as the king of kings to take Queen Tamuze from us. Satan held me by my throat, shouting mother fucker, I knew you would join us. Are you in fear of CHRIST and Elijah now?

Then I saw in a dream CHRIST'S spirit was on HIS throne in Heaven, watching for Elijah to speak the Word to come down from Heaven to capture me for hanging Adam on a tree, and I woke up after. He said vengeance is His and will repay, eye for eye, tooth for tooth to the last seed of gods in the flesh of Tamah/Tamuze.

Hadassah said: O God my king, what can this mean? You are scaring me! For fucking with you to make Mankind! Judah said: I also saw in the dream CHRIST left Elijah on earth to save Tamuze and Eve. I saw their spirits come out of their bodies and they were pointing their fingers at me, saying the devils are waiting for me after I leave their flesh.

O Hadassah, Judah cried, on earth CHRIST is after me and in fire the devils are waiting for me to terrorize me with fear after death and Elijah is waiting for me to depart from the flesh of Tamuze to open his mouth to say the WORD to take vengeance for abomination to cast out spirits that have no faith like me to the devils in devouring fire.

22. Hadassah began to cry: treason! You have become like a vulture for flesh from birth. O my king, thou has become rich from our sin. It has reached into the heavens and angels are clapping their hands for our spirits to be out of the world together, without their flesh, wanting Elijah to speak the Word to judge us. O King, what will Elijah do to my mother, who is from one of CHRIST'S daughters who died in this plague in the harem?

O Hadassah, Judah cried, I've sinned with my mother in abomination. You are my queen in adultery, cruel, just like me. All Mankind is not perfect. It is too late to stop this wickedness on earth in our adultery and abomination. Our fucking has brought much trouble on earth. Mankind bore children like wild flowers and like grass choking a tree to death. I fear if we stop Mankind from passing my seed, they will want to kill us for stopping their joy to fornicate to death and will say it's we who made them that way.

Hadassah became afraid and said: O my king, this spirit CHRIST you saw in Heaven. Could you not tell Him to have mercy on us and we will set HIS daughter and her mother free? Judah said: Hadassah, CHRIST in Adam warned me not to hang his body on a tree and can't bring back his body. Michael took it to the ETERNAL to be a testament after death is life of HIS CHRIST the devils did not know and tempted me, and said: if I wanted to be king I must hang Adam. Elijah I fear more with the Word. I have no faith. Only you I have after death.

Hadassah said: you have seduced me from my youth and I did whatever you wanted to give you pleasure. O King, it's just dreams. I will see our son Belhadassah, he interprets my dreams. Have rest, my king. I have to prepare the Passover feast and want it to be remembered from generation to generation.

THE STUMP OF THE TREE

Judah woke up crying from his sleep. Hadassah, I've had another dream! Wake up and get me some water. I thirst.

What is it now, O King?

I saw the stump of the tree I hanged the body of Adam and it was surrounded with the spirit of CHRIST'S on earth clearing the grass around the stump, and the stump started to have branches.

Then I saw his son Jesus, face to face in the flesh of Tamuze, and he said to me, I should know who is the ruler in the flesh of his sister, and he cast me out and my spirit was in the body of one of my high priests. Hadassah, please hurry get Belhadassah to interpret this dream for you.

Hadassah said: O King, I saw Bel and he explained this interpretation is unto thee. Have mercy on your mother and her mother you hold in captivity for peace.

All the wickedness you have done to your queen has come unto me since I am your queen in the palace of Babylon. King Judah said: have I not made you a mother of Mankind and queen of Babylon, great by my power and majesty over Tamuze and Eve and the women in the harem?

Hadassah said: O King, a spirit spoke through the mouth of Belhadassah to me and said the kingdom is departing from thee and your spirit shall be driven away by the tempest after you depart from the kingdom from your mother's flesh to celebrate the Passover with devils, and you will have to tell the devils the spirit of CHRIST rules in kingdoms. When Elijah speaks the Word multitudes of immortal spirits will be created perfect in salvation of kingdoms.

Hadassah said: O King, your end is coming to leave me among Mankind on earth. The spirit spoke through the mouth of Belhadassah's to me, my father. you wanted to know your future, you had knowledge and understanding of eternal life before you took the oath to live by the law and you chose to do evil and spill blood on earth for the devils.

You wanted to dishonour CHRIST and deny Him from having dominion in all worlds for ever. All this work in adultery with your lust is looked upon as nothing. You can't save any spirit of Mankind and Israelites from your seed.

Mt.1:21 Elijah will save Tamuze's and Eve's spirits with eternal life. He is their saviour. You are a God of god and without Elijah there is no salvation or deliverance or hope for everlasting life. **Hos.13:4** Hadassah cried: O my God and king, when you die, I'll call for your godly spirit Israel to come and save me from the spirit Elijah.

Judah woke up frightened and cried: Hadassah, wake up! I had another dream and it made me afraid. Hadassah said: what is it, my king? Tell me the dream so I can have Belhadassah interpret for you when I visit him.

Judah said: I saw in the dream the tree I hanged Adam and His spirit went up to Heaven and returned at the end to destroy all spirits on the earth that were in the kingdom. Then I saw multitudes of spirits go in a whirlwind and they fell in the mouth of the water. And I saw spirits in the water in multitudes, like fishes swimming, to the trapdoor in the bowels of the earth, and I saw fire in the water and smoking bubbles.

Then I saw children in the Light in multitudes in the kingdom from the spirits that were sent to the devils pointing their hands at me saying, murderer, murderer. Then I saw a spirit sitting on his throne looking like Adam I hanged, watching Elijah on earth.

Then I saw Elijah begin speaking words and the spirit came down from Heaven again and He said to Elijah: I'll destroy the son of god who hanged Adam on a tree and all spirits from his father's seed that are passed on from god to god all over earth that branch in my flesh.

Then I looked at Him in the clouds with multitudes of spirits in the Light going up in the wind when they departed from the kingdom on earth.

Hadassah said: O my God, these dreams frighten me!

Hadassah said: my God, this spirit hates thee for hanging his body on a tree. His spirit can see what you are doing with me. He is angry; you hold your mother and Eve in captivity with hate for holy people.

O my king, thou have grown to be a mighty God with your wickedness. You shall have power with our spirits all over the earth. Don't let this dream frighten you.

Belhadassah told me to tell you, my father, when the Great Spirit comes it will be to drive you out of the world with all your spirits who have no faith, to the gate of the sun.

Belhadassah said the kingdom can continue with spirits of creation, to have everlasting spirit by CHRIST through Elijah.

All these dreams you are having, my king, are because you killed all his sons on earth because you are not accepted above.

King Judah said: O my beautiful queen, you are my olive. All women on earth will hate thee and will think twice before they fuck to make Mankind from generation to generation in the kingdom with our hate. I am a jealous god. Their spirits will join us after CHRIST casts them out, to fight against Elijah for the earth. .

The dreams of Judah

Judah had a dream that made him afraid and he began crying in his sleep and it awoke Hadassah. She said: My king, you are crying in your sleep. You woke me up! Judah said: I had a dream. Hadassah said: what is it this time?

Judah said: I saw a man on earth. I saw his spirit going up to Heaven and the end of the dream I saw His spirit coming after me and our spirits on earth.

Then I saw multitudes of spirits cast outside kingdoms all over the earth and they were crying and pointing their fingers to me and were flying in the air and falling in a mouth of devils. Then I saw children in the Light in multitudes in kingdoms, pointing their fingers at me and laughing at me.

Then I saw in another dream the spirit of the man I hanged, sitting on a throne in Heaven, looking at me when Elijah began speaking words. His spirit came down to earth and I was running and many spirits were in fear and began running after me, blaming me for passing on my seed to them to fall in the flames of fire.

Hadassah said: O King, what can this mean? You are scaring me! Judah said: I also saw in another dream the spirit CHRIST left Elijah on earth to save my queen mother in the harem and her mother and to save the kingdom. The spirits from my seed were crying, salvation is come. We are naked. Then I saw the devils crying, saying it is not they who made Mankind and Israelites. I sinned and god my father in Hell was crying in the other chamber, crying for Tamuze to send him water. He was thirsty.

Judah said: this spirit CHRIST, He watches all what goes on on earth from His throne in Heaven. When Elijah opens his mouth to speak, He leaves the throne to take vengeance in his daughter's flesh, with spirits of gods

GOD CAME IN THE DAUGHTERS AND BORE CHILDREN Gen.6:4

Hadassah said: O King, all this lust to make Mankind for you and my mother's sister is for nothing. You are God of the earth now, who made Mankind, and was mighty with the ancient's devils on earth. Can't you use their fear to scare Elijah to leave the earth?

ALL FLESH BECAME CORRUPT Gen.6:11–12; Dan 47:2

Judah said: O my queen, I was brought up by Elijah long ago before I became king! He was a spirit in a kingdom. He told me not to commit abomination with my mother in the palace. If I did it, it would corrupt flesh. I had no faith in Him and was tempted by the devil to take the law to death and hope for the best. Now I have no peace with these dreams because I hold Eve and my queen mother in captivity in the harem.

Hadassah said: O King, I will go to Belhadassah. He is my prophet and wise and he will interpret these dreams for me. Hadassah dressed and took the horseman and went to her Bel and told him: your father is having bad dreams continuously and it frightens him often. After interpreting the dreams Hadassah returned to the palace.

Judah said: Hadassah, did you see Bel? She answered: my father, we shall be out of the world together without the flesh of your mother and my mother as godly spirits when we depart from the kingdom.

CHRIST will send Jesus his first son to cast you out from the same body with the spirit of Tamuze for making her cry to make Israelites with his sister and holding her sisters in captivity before the plague of death in your harem. Bel said the kingdoms on earth are corrupt and filled with your sin, lust, anger, hate, malice and violence and jealousy for what is and was holy and pure in your harem.

THOU SHALL NOT COMMIT ADULTERY Gen 6:17:12

Judah said: O Hadassah, we are committed sinners through the fault of ours to be born to be cruel to holy people. All Mankind is passing on godly seed in holy flesh. It's too late to stop this wickedness on earth.

All spirits of gods in the flesh shall suffer after death. Our life is corrupt and much adultery in marriage in flesh will bring multitudes of spirits in kingdoms on earth. When Mankind marries in the flesh to bear children it will take root in holy flesh like wild flowers. Their spirits will want to pluck out our eyes for making them to live to death.

Hadassah said: My father, could you not tell this spirit Elijah to have mercy on us and let his Hebrews go? You hold Eve and Tamuze in captivity we are not accepted above because we are not of the holy seed by the WORD.

Judah said: Elijah I fear more with the Word. With Elijah it is either you have faith in Him or, after death, there is no peace if you don't have faith in Him.

A MAN'S ENEMIES ARE THE PEOPLE IN HIS OWN HOME Mic.7:6

Judah said: Hadassah, you have taken all my strength. I have no peace to death. Hadassah said: I have full measure of your wickedness and will be your queen even after death. Have a rest. My king, I have to prepare the

Passover feast and want it to be remembered from generation to generation with your children with me in Babylon.

The dream of the stump of the tree

Judah had another dream and he began to shout in his dream: go away, go away. Hadassah, he cried, wake up! Hadassah said: what is it? Another dream, my king? He could hardly speak. She rushed to get him some water to drink.

He said: Hadassah, I saw a stump of a tree I hanged Adam and it was surrounded by grass and saw Elijah cleaning around the stump and the stump started to have branches.

And His spirit came to my face and said: I shall know who is the ruler in the flesh of my mother, and He vanished. Hadassah, please, I am trembling and frightened of Elijah while I live in the flesh of Tamuze. Get Bel to interpret for me.

Hadassah said: O my king, I saw Bel and he explained this interpretation. He said the dream is unto thee. Have mercy on your mother you hold in captivity.

The kingdom is an everlasting kingdom Gen.49:10; Ps.110:1; Esck.21:27

Hadassah said: Bel interpreted the dream for you. He said the spirit you saw removing the grass around the stump, that is to say you have to prepare your body to make a clean break. The spirit you saw is the life of the tree.

The grass was choking the stump. By removing the grass there was hope for the stump to come back to life. When a spirit is removed from the kingdom it is for a new spirit with seed to continue to bear new spirits with seed.

Hadassah said: all your wickedness, you passed on to me to be your wicked queen in the palace of Babylon. Judah said: my daughter, have I not made you a mother of Mankind and now you are my queen in Babylon from my seed with honour over all women on earth?

Hadassah said: my king, Belhadassah said your spirit will depart from the kingdom and your mother's flesh. You will Passover to me to make beautiful children like me (31).

When your spirit enters Hades, you will have to tell the devils the spirit CHRIST was in Adam. When Elijah spoke the Word CHRIST went to Heaven to return in time of salvation to create multitudes of spirits in beautiful images of my creation by the WORD.

Hadassah said: O King, your end is coming to leave Mankind who you made on earth. Bel said you wanted to know your future. You had knowledge and understanding of eternal life before you took the oath to live by the law of the devils. Now I have knowledge from you to make beautiful people on earth to be their queen after death with you, my king.

You wanted to dishonour CHRIST and deny Him from having dominion in all worlds for ever. All this hard work and screwing is looked upon as nothing.

You made yourself king who can't save a spirit from your seed on earth, and can't save Mankind and Israelites either. Where can you hide if you go to Hell? The devils are waiting for you. If you stay on earth Mankind will find out you are a deceiving God who wants them to fall to devils.

Mt.1:21; Hos.13:4

Belhadassah said Elijah will save Eve's spirit and Tamuze's spirit. After they Sabbath hey will have eternal life. He is the saviour. Without Elijah there is no salvation or deliverance or hope for everlasting life. Hadassah said: when you die, hide your spirit in the body of an Israelite to escape the WORD by Elijah.

Hadassah said: This spirit hates thee, my God, for hanging Adam on the tree and can see you and I when we fornicate. All Mankind will do the same as us and will call me a whore queen that made them in Babylon with you, not perfect. **Gen.6.4**

O my God. there will be much adultery in his flesh with spirits of gods in the kingdoms on earth before CHRIST come in salvation. We can't fight Him. Just give him back His flesh, and we will have our spirits without flesh. You will be king of the spirits and I'll be queen of the spirits with no flesh.

Judah said: Hadassah, the earth is His and I fear judge Elijah will send us in fire when we depart from the earth and will have much misery instead of joy.

Hadassah began to be afraid of a place with only fire, without flesh, and no water. This knowledge of this truth is hid in Babylon (**Hos.4:1**) and all spirits of God in the kingdom will be removed from kingdoms on earth for exterminating the pure race of CHRIST in Adam. **Gen.6:17**

Hadassah said: Bel said the tree trunk represents the kingdom with the spirit of CHRIST to live in the world with no more interference with spirits of gods of ancient devils to pollute the kingdoms with venereal diseases of devils.

CHRIST will establish the world in the Light by the WORD as the ETERNAL did to separate the world between darkness and Light. The world will be in the Light with angels in the light with the New Testament of peace, without devils and spirits of gods on earth. **Gen.49:10; Ps.110:1; Esek.21:27**

The queens of Israel dream of the end. Dream of 2000 million spirits released from Hell

One of the queens said to her Israelite king: O King, I had a dream of the Passover. The king said: What is it my love? She said: I saw a woman taken by the tempest and she fell in a furnace and she was crying for our God to save her.

Then I saw in another dream 2000 million spirits were released from the furnace and they began to swim till they came above the sea and they were all over the earth and began to kill Mankind and were doing battle with our God for the earth. **Rev.9:15-19**

Then I saw the godly spirits released began to enter the body of Mankind and one began to speak to me through the mouth, trying to seduce me and I woke up frightened to death.

Another queen said to her Israelite king: O King, I had a dream. The king said: what is it my love?

I saw a big furnace with a lot of flames in the bowels of the earth with spirits of magicians, murderers, thieves and those who commit adultery and abomination crying for our God to save them when they saw the devils. Great fear fell on the spirits. They had no flesh and the devils were vexed because they had no flesh to fornicate and began to curse our God for sending spirits from his seed to them while he is enjoying the flesh of their mother.

Dream of repentance

Another queen said to her Israelite king: O King, I had a dream. He said: what is it my love? We are late for the Passover. She said: It will take a minute. I saw spirits falling from the sky in the mouth of the waters and I saw a spirit in the Light and it said to me it is because they pass on seed of our God and refuse to repent for their sins, they fall.

Then I saw the spirits that repented began to fall asleep and they were no more to be seen. Then I saw spirits standing in the Light in the body of those who slept and they began waving at me with flags saying have faith for peace and they didn't worship God our father. What do you think, my king?

The king said: they must have prepared their bodies for Elijah. Then she said: O yes, I saw this great spirit standing on earth, full of Light, speaking words, and a great spirit full of Light came in a pillar of clouds and those he liked on earth with a twinkle of an eye began to walk on earth in the Light among Mankind, and the Great Spirit went back to Heaven. I heard a loud noise in the heaven – hallelujah Elijah. He judged the children of the whore.

Dream of Adultery and abomination

Another queen said to her Israelite king: O King, I had a dream. This one frightened me. He said: We are going to be late. You know father will be angry if we are late for the Passover feast.

I saw the mystery of a great spirit. He brought up God our father. He looks angry because he committed adultery and abomination with our mother to make Israelites and committing adultery for making Mankind not perfect. He said no spirits from our father's seed will have peace on earth. If they have faith in him they will not fall in the furnace.

I went looking for our children quickly to tell them this mystery to have faith, but God our father took them. He said he wanted them for war on earth against this spirit in the Light.

Dream of forgiveness

Another queen told her Israelite king: I had a dream of our mother and our grandmother. They were standing in front of a multitude of spirits on earth and they were asking the spirits to forgive them for making God our father and god his father. I could hear god crying in the earth to spirits to forgive their mother and grandmother so they don't come to Hades.

Then I saw this Great Spirit Elijah saying to God our father to repent and he began to run away from him so he doesn't speak the Word to return in the pit. Then I saw a great spirit come and join our mother and grandmother and Elijah and they began to swim in the water laughing, and I heard a voice saying, I am well pleased with my people on earth.

Fire and water dream

Another queen said to her Israelite king: O King, I had a dream, and in this dream I was crying. I saw fire and water and there was no earth, only fire, and I saw God our father coming from the bowels of the earth. When he got up he began to swim between fire and water and other spirits came up and got caught in the flames of fire in the water, swimming very fast against strong currents. They had nothing to hold on to stay in this world and a whirlwind came over the water and God our father and the spirits vanished. I was floating above earth, looking.

Then the earth appeared with a lot of people and everything was new with our mother as the queen of the earth and when I looked I saw our grandmother sitting on a throne in Heaven next to the Great Spirit CHRIST, as His queen.

Then I heard a voice saying to me, don't delay. The mystery of God will be known to thee and Mankind who worships God to death. Go to the Passover and my prophet will tell you the truth about what your God is hiding from Mankind about himself.

Sanctification dream

Another queen said: O King, I had a terrible dream and it made me cry. This one was worse than the last one. I saw two great spirits in the Light. One went in the body of our mother and the other went in the body of our grandmother.

Then suddenly our father's spirit and his father's spirit were cast out of the bodies of our mother and grandmother and they were crying because they had no flesh and went into the bodies of our brothers.

Then the two spirits that went in our mother and grandmother became human and began walking and talking among Mankind and Israelites.

One was speaking great words and shouting, All you vagabonds and prostitutes in the kingdom; repent! Then the other spirit began telling Mankind things hidden about God (Judah) our father and Hadassah to multitudes that were following him and he was casting out spirits from Mankind and they began to cry through the mouth of Mankind, Jesus, have mercy. Leave us alone. Then I had another dream.

My king, the Israelite queen said: you were a spirit with the other Israelite kings' spirits with God our father the godly spirits call Israel, and his father (Cain), also a godly spirit, was among many godly spirits speaking through the mouth of Mankind saying crucify the spirit Jesus, I said, why? the spirits shouted, he cast Israel from the same body with the spirit of our queen mother. The other spirit Elijah said to Israel, you cannot have her. You are a godly spirit of god (Cain) of the devil. God (Cain) got angry and cut off the head of the spirit that said our father can't have our mother. Then I saw much blood all over the earth and many women began beating on their breasts, crying, you killed my saviour. The spirits began to shout through the mouths of people, Jesus cast out our spirit from Mankind. Crucify Him. I began to cry, don't kill him! He is innocent. His blood will be on my children.

My king, I don't feel good. Go to the Passover feast. The Israelite king said: my queen, you know how strict God/Judah our father is if we don't support him in this Passover. I fear him and his anger. While we are alive we live under his law and even after death. **Ro.14:12; Act.3:9**

The ten Israelite kings celebrate the Passover feast

The ten Israeli kings met before the feast and they began discussing the dreams of their queens. The Israelite kings had fucked Hadassah and kept it as their own secret from each other and were in fear of what God/Judah their father would do to them if he found out.

Hadassah sat next to God, dressed in scarlet and gold with precious stones and pearls around her neck. In her hand was a gold cup with blood inside. She was happy seeing all her lovers under the same roof to celebrate the Passover feast.

Judah ruleth as God almighty Jer.11–12

The commander of the battalion of soldiers who witnessed the Sabbath of the hanging of CHRIST in Adam and the slaying of all His sons from the earth, stood to give a speech.

King Judah, we praise thee as a mighty God with beautiful Hadassah for making Mankind with our gods to mix and mingle to make Israelites with our mother's children

Every spirit from the seed of God/Judah is his inheritance Ro.14:12

The Israelite kings hated Hadassah sitting next to God their father while their mother was in the harem in sackclothes. **Jer.23:10; Jn.8:41–42**

God is a God of god Dan.2:47; Ps.89:7; Ps74:12; Mt.22:21

An Israelite king stood up and said: Hail, king of kings and God of god (Cain) in Hades. Your greatness on earth has gone from the bowels of the earth to the heavens. You are a mighty God for passing on his seed. Live for ever as ruler of the earth with all from your seed.

The beauty and the beast

Hadassah, the most beautiful daughter of Judah, was born in the harem. He separated her from all her sisters from her youth to make her mother of Mankind. She conceived and her first child born was a son. Judah called him Belhadassah. She loved her son and paid more attention to him than to Judah and this made him angry.

Judah took Belhadassah and gave him to his commandant so he could pass on his seed with his daughters to make gentiles. Hadassah felt bitter and was annoyed her son was given away. Judah said: O Hadassah, my well-favoured daughter, he will come back to you one day. Make me daughters to go with my princes in the palace to mix and mingle and make Israelites to be beautiful like you for my queen.

Hadassah grew up with contempt for Eve and Queen Tamuze seeing all her daughters were going in the palace to make Israelites and was determined she would get her own back to make Belhadassah her king.

Belhadassah grew up to be a prophet and wise and could predict the future and became popular with those who practice witchcraft and sorcery. He could read teacups and make a tied rope untie itself, and became popular in Babylon as a magician and interpreter of dreams.

When Hadassah became mistress of the palace, she became free and found out where Belhadassah was. She used her charm and became involved in witchcraft to have power over Judah.

The Passover feast. The kings of Judah sat on their thrones 1.Ki.22:10

All the guests arrived at the palace to celebrate the Passover. There was music, eating and drinking, and everyone was merry drinking the best of vintage wine which the devils had left in a cellar before they were captured by Elijah.

King Judah sat with Hadassah on the throne and said: Hadassah, what is your petition? It be granted thee and it shall be performed. Hadassah said: I am fed up of being your mistress. If I am beautiful in your eyes, make me your queen of Babylon.

Judah said: worship me as your God to death. Hadassah fell down at his feet, took her hair, and wiped the dust from under his feet and licked under his feet in tears and said: O my father, this is how you have to complete the Passover on earth to be ruler on the earth as God with your queen. He took the horn with the moon disk and put it on her head. She stood and sat next to him on the throne as his queen.

An Israelite king stood up and said: let us render praise to our God and his queen who sits next to him and for all on earth from his seed, small and great, to serve him and worship our God and his goddess to death.

The ten Israelite kings in the nations came and fell prostrate before God and his goddess Hadassah, and worshiped her for making Mankind to be free of the mark of the devils and making beautiful daughters for God to make Israelites his peculiar people on earth.

Then they began to sing the song 'By the River of Babylon' to God and his goddess. When they were through singing God stood up and thanked everyone for their praise and worship and said: my goddess is a beautiful star for all on earth to worship as long as there is Light and darkness in the world.

The guests began to whistle and shout with joy: Ishstar, Ishstar, live for ever between Light and darkness in the world. We worship you to death. Make children beautiful like you.

Judah said: I made you my handmaid and mistress and queen. Now they idolize you and make you their goddess on earth. What is your next petition? It be granted thee.

Hadassah said: if I'm beautiful and a goddess, you should have one queen on earth. You are God in wickedness and hate, and I am goddess of jealousy who does not shed tears like the Tamuze your ex-queen in the harem.

Let the last two Hebrews the queen and Eve with my sister's children come and worship you as the God who made Mankind to complete the Passover on earth. Wipe them off the face of the earth like the dust licked clean from under your feet so the memory of holy people perish and not be remembered on earth as long as there is Light and darkness in the world.

Judah whispered in Hadassah's ear

Judah said: if they don't worship, what is your next wish? These Hebrews are difficult people. They have no fear of death. Hadassah said: let the two Hebrews with my sisters' children be eaten by the hungry lions in the den. They put their faith in Elijah, so let us see if Elijah will save them from the lions. Judah said: if you send them there, Elijah will come and tear out your heart before our guests.

Hadassah said: if you make them Passover you will be conqueror of the earth and it will be written that God is more powerful than Elijah after the lions eat them.

If you don't have this victory in the den everyone on earth will say you are not God who made the world and say you are a liar and deceitful and pass on your seed in my mother with your anger to make me to make Mankind and Israelites to pass on your seed with your lust to death.

Judah began to tremble. If I cast them in the den of lions and they die, their spirits will come after us, like the spirit I have seen in my dream, to destroy us in the palace in Babylon.

Hadassah said: you are God with authority over spirits of Mankind. They will fear your wickedness according to the law; no spirits of the dead can come after us.

I will be a bitch with the spirits of the dead. They will do what I say. We must not be afraid if they attack us. Let the Hebrews come and worship you as God of the world before our guests and if they don't, cast them in the den of lions.

Judah called the guard and said: bring Eve and Tamuze and the children in the harem to worship your God and goddess before our guests to witness the Passover.

The guards brought Eve and Tamuze and the children and they stood before Judah and Hadassah, who sat on the throne. The guard said: don't stand there, kneel down and worship our God and his goddess Hadassah.

Eve said to the guard: we will not worship your God of god or his queen who is your goddess. It is they who should worship us. They are not blessed and holy We don't worship anyone on earth but have respect for everyone who is not born pure and holy in the kingdom through no fault of his or her own, but should have faith in Elijah to save them from the beast who puts fear in you as your God, and his jealous goddess.

We are perfect and have no fear of any one who is celebrating the Passover to do us wickedness. My shame to make a god. I will endure, and her shame to make one sit on the throne with his daughter, she will endure, and my advice to every one of you while you are still in the kingdom is that you should be eager to seek peace before it's too late.

Eve said: we put our lives in the hand of Elijah and have faith in Him. When the hour comes to Sabbath our kingdom to death, we shall have everlasting life in the spirit. There was silence in the banquet hall. Eve went on to say: your God is a god of god (Cain) who passed on his seed to you with hate and jealousy to lead you astray with false doctrine to make you fall and have no peace. The guests were laughing and gasping for air, looking at the old Hebrew mother and daughter in amazement, and laughing.

Eve stood there, bent in old age, and stopped talking. She and her daughter Tamuze were standing there in sackcloth. Judah said: Silence! Then all eyes were on them. Eve said before the guests: Your God is guilty for shedding the blood of CHRIST on earth.

You drink blood of bulls to pollute your bodies to your damnation in the kingdom of CHRIST to provoke Elijah. He will bring wrath against you for bringing all kinds of death in the kingdom to establish a foundation under the law on earth.

Eve said to Judah: we know your father, who sinned with my daughter. I made him with much indignation. You want to know if Elijah will save us? We have faith in Him. **Ps.98:13**

You have made Judah your king and God of the earth who has kept the understanding of scriptures to himself so you don't know the truth and the way to eternal life. **Ps.98:8–9**

God can't reign over holy angels of creation in Heaven, nor can he sit on the throne of CHRIST in Heaven, and he will use you to fight for the earth with him.

Your God who you idolize and worship has blinded your eyes, has no faith, and doesn't want you to have the choice to have peace in the world so your bodies can have a spirit in the Light with everlasting life by the Word. **2.Cor.4:1**

King Judah is deceitful and boasts of his craftiness, to make Mankind and Israelites. Elijah taught Judah scriptures so don't let him deceive you in the world through ignorance.

If you are content to live in the kingdom you must have faith in Elijah to save you after death to rest in peace as you are not accepted to go above.

The guests began to cough and were scared. Eve looked at Hadassah and said: the prophet of the law of devils you idolize from youth and who made you his queen and the star of Babylon for making Mankind and Israelites, with his mother's children, he eliminated my people to on earth, I have one judge who has power to save and destroy. If my daughter or I shed one tear in this Passover feast, no spirit from the seed of God your father will be established on earth and you will fall to meet god his father in Hades.

Hadassah rushed at Eve and slapped her in the face and said: how dare you talk to my father this way in front of our guests. With hate and jealousy for his queen, she pushed Eve.

She fell on her back on the floor. Hadassah screamed at the ex-queen Tamuze: you fucking bitch, making children with my children. Hadassah pushed Tamuze and she fell and put her feet on Tamuze's stomach, took the gold cup with blood and spilled it on top of Tamuze to humiliate her and stamped heavily on her stomach. **Ps.137:7; Obad.11:4**

Hadassah's time to take revenge on Tamuze had come. The Israelite kings were at her mercy, and knew if they did anything to help their mother Hadassah would tell Judah she fucked with them.

Hadassah looked at Judah and said: now let us celebrate the Passover, my God. Send them to the den of lions.

All the guests' eyes were on their God. He had a gold cup in his hand, trembling and said: woe is unto me, Hadassah, when the lions feast on their flesh for hating who I hate. I Have no one else but you, my queen, in our world when my time comes.

The guards took Eve and her daughter and the children to the lion's den. They rolled the stone so the lions could come in the den. When they entered the den the lions looked at the guards and began to roar at them and the guards ran away.

EVE AND DAUGHTER AND CHILDREN AMONG LIONS THROUGH FAITH Ps.57:4

The lions came walking up to Eve and Tamuze and they began to stroke the lions on their backs. The lions stood on their hind legs and put their paws on the shoulders of Eve and began licking her face. Tamuze went on the back of another lion and it started running around the den in circles. The children took turns riding the lions. Then the lions lay in the den and fell asleep. **Heb.11:33; Essek.19:2**

Hadassah excelled herself with her charm and beauty with the kings and merchants and other special guests in the banquet she fucked with, and they were in fear of her as much as Judah. She was determined that Belhadassah will be her king and prove himself to be her prophet and wise. Judah was determined for his Israelites to carry on with his religious doctrine according to his plan to fight for the earth to death.

The guards returned from the den of lions and said: O God, the lions have eaten the women! Judah felt sad and said: all my mother wanted is peace. Hadassah said: you will have no peace with me, now I'm your queen in life and after death to rule the earth with you.

Hadassah went to change her dress and returned dressed in an elegant scarlet-and-purple coloured gown and her moon disk in the horn with precious stones on her head. She also had gold disks Judah had given her on each of her hands, and wore Judah's favourite perfume. She sat down next to Judah among the other kings and their queens, rulers in government, merchants and captains. The belly dancers were dancing to the music and were celebrating and singing: there is no God like our God in this world.

Hadassah asked Judah: why didn't you let the devils hang the body of my grandfather to see his reaction? Now you killed Eve and your mother. You inbred my daughters with you with your Israelite princes with your mother who are kings with us today while Belhadassah my first son with you is somewhere in Babylon among gentiles and not here to give you praise for this Passover.

Judah said: Hadassah, did I not choose you from all my daughters? All the women on earth are jealous of you and want to be like you to pass on my seed from generation to generation to make gentiles in the kingdom like us.

Belhadassah's time will come. Let us celebrate. As he said cheers he saw a hand writing words on the wall. The glass in Judah's hand began shaking and Judah looked frightful. His legs began to tremble, knocking against each other. He couldn't speak. Hadassah said: what is wrong. my father?

Judah cried out loud: Hadassah, look! Elijah is here. Look; he wrote on the wall. Tell the kings to come and read the writing on the wall. The ten kings came one after the other and could not interpret the writing.

Hadassah said: do not let this writing frighten you. I'll send for Belhadassah and he will interpret it. He has the wisdom of the spirits of the other world. I'll call him for you. Hadassah called for the horseman, and he took some runners and they went looking all over the city to find Belhadassah.

When they found him the horseman said: the new queen wants you to come to the palace. Belhadassah said: is there a plague? What is the matter? The horseman explained: it is very urgent. We must hurry.

The horseman started to race the horses to the palace. When Hadassah saw her son she said: I am now your queen mother and your father is God of the earth.

Who is God? Is.43:10, 12; Hos.13:4; Mt.1:21

Belhadassah said: my mother, I had a vision and Elijah has made it clear to me the secret of God and his father before we were born from his seed. No God is created on earth or is in Heaven. Elijah is a holy spirit created in the body of god (Cain) in Hades, who passed on his seed to God our father before he died.

And besides Elijah, no god can save Israelites or Mankind on earth. You are my witness. Elijah can save us if we have faith. Elijah will save his people our father holds in captivity. Without Elijah there is no salvation, or hope for peace after our spirits depart from kingdoms on earth.

A CERTAIN MAN DRESSED IN PURPLE Lk.16:19

Hadassah said: Bel, this is your chance to be a king, my son. Go and wash yourself. I'll get some clothing for you to present you to God. Hadassah went through Judah's clothes and found a robe in purple, and sandals, and gave them to Belhadassah and told the guard to bring him to the banquet hall when he was dressed.

HADASSAH AND BELHADASSAH

Hadassah changed her clothing and put on a gown with gold woven in to it, a necklace with precious stones, well-groomed hair, and sat next to Judah and waited for her Bel.

The trumpeter blew his horn and presented Belhadassah. Belhadassah came and stood before his mother and father. Judah said: Bel, I see you are clothed with my clothes by your mother. I am honoured by my majesty; you are her prophet and wise son among gentiles in the nation.

Judah said: Belhadassah! There is something written on the wall and I've asked my ten Israelite kings to interpret to me what is written and they have no idea what is the meaning of this writing on the wall. Anyone who can interpret it will be my successor on the throne and will be the third ruler after me and my queen on earth.

THE WRITING ON THE WALL: BETTER IS A WISE CHILD THAN A FOOLISH KING Ecc.l:4, 13

Belhadassah looked at God his father and his queen mother on the throne. All eyes were on him and he began interpreting the writing on the wall.

Belhadassah said: my father, your subjects have made you a mighty God. you have become king because they fear you will kill them if they don't worship you as the king of the earth. You made your mother your queen. Because you were not accepted above you killed her brothers and keep Tamuze and her mother in captivity.

You made your daughters whore with giants and gods to interbreed with your mother's children. **Hos.4:13**

You know Elijah is created by CHRIST to rule in the kingdoms on earth. You imitated the devils and made Mankind and Israelites. They have no respect for Christ and Elijah your master.

You have not humbled your heart on your son Belhadassah from his youth. Although you know the scripture, I taught you to do good, you hanged the body of Adam and blasphemed His spirit and His throne in Heaven while you were king with the devils.

You made Mankind with the women you captured with your mother's sister who is now your queen on your throne and passed on the accursed seed of god your father. With presumptuousness you destroy holy people on earth to rule the earth as king.

The promise I made with you was before you became a prophet of the law of devils under oath to destroy the kingdom to death. You did the same as god your father who followed devils now in Hades. I gave you a free choice to rest in peace.

Sin is unto death

But you chose to follow your desire to do evil and pollute the kingdom. You did the same like god your father to pass on the accursed seed in your mother to make Mankind and Israelites to fight with you against me and CHRIST for the earth.

CHRIST accepts no spirits of gods in the kingdom. Elijah is their judge Isa.2:11; Gen.18:25; Ps.7:8

CHRIST has no favouritism with gods from the seed of devils. Judah, you have no faith. You followed the devils with many faults, and want to deceive many to have no faith to fight with you for the earth.

The spirits CHRIST accepts are holy, from his seed with Zion (Eve) and immortal spirits HE creates in kingdoms for salvation with spirits through Elijah.

The promised son is by the Word

Elijah wrote on the wall: Judah, all spirits from your seed in the kingdom will be your inheritance. The kingdoms from your mother's flesh are for salvation after CHRIST casts out spirits of gods from the flesh of your mother and Eve from Me.

I taught you the scripture and know the only way for you is peace. You are not my son; my SON has to be created through CHRIST with everlasting life like myself to be accepted by the ETERNAL by the WORD.

The power of the Word Heb.8:7; Ja.5:6; Jude.24; Isa.27:11

Judah, you have challenged me for the earth. Not by all your power or violence and hate and murder and bloodshed with multitudes of godly spirits can you fight my spirit with the Word.

You have imitated ancient devils with many faults that despise holy angels of creation and rape holy women on earth. They were removed from the earth by the Word to Hades to await final judgment for breaking the covenant to make a god to suffer after death.

You are worthless to me. You have no faith. and all spirits from your seed will be ashamed to know you passed on the accursed seed of god (Cain) in your mother to make them be the scum of the earth to be carried away to Hades. You eliminated your mother's holy people from the face of the earth because you wanted to be a king with devils.

Belhadassah looked at his father King Judah and mother Hadassah on the throne and all the guests were in fear. Belhadassah said: O King, this is the interpretation on the wall. My father the spirit Elijah was able to present your kingdom faultless to be his son in creation by the Word so all forms of his seed would be perfect to be his people on earth.

King Judah Dan.2:47; Dan.8.16:23–26; Dan.9.7–8, 24; Mt.18:15

Judah knew the scriptures had been revealed to Bel by Elijah, which he kept a secret to himself. Hadassah said: my father, did you not say Belhadassah's time would come? He has revealed your secret. It's your fault to make Mankind and Israelites with me with all your faults from this accursed seed.

Judah called Bel to him. He prostrated, took the ring from his finger Satan had given him when he became the prophet of the law, and put it on Bel's finger. Judah took the gold chain from around his neck and declared Belhadassah third ruler on earth after him and Queen Hadassah, with authority over his battalion.

The ten Israelite kings came forward and lay their crowns at Belhadassah's feet and wept because Belhadassah became the third ruler after his mother and Judah (God) their father as their king on earth.

Hadassah said: Bel, my king, I've passed the sin of our father on to thee. Judah said: Bel, you shall rule my way and be in charge with your mother in my palace and rule among the kings that bent before thee, my son.

If you have no faith in the Great Spirit, your spirit will have no peace and will descend. I give you power to rule the families of Mankind to the end of the earth.

I will be with thee until I depart from the earth and go to the chambers prepared for me for my wickedness. Bel said: My father and mother, I will rule with thee.

All the guests rejoiced in their new king with authority on earth and (God) Judah said: now all is in your hands to do good for Mankind.

Judah gave a speech

King Judah said: this Passover is to let all on earth know Mankind is mixed, that I made with Queen Hadassah to rule the earth with King Bel. If he does wickedly he will be removed from the throne.

I made thee, Bel, with strength of my seed with your mother Hadassah, now queen of Babylon. The time has come for Israelites to know the truth before the Great Spirit comes and saves His people's spirits and destroys Babylon. Who has faith will be saved to make his promise come true.

Belhadassah your king, who you call your God, is a Maduk, a rebel like Queen Hadassah, second in command over all on earth with her new king.

From now you shall no more be termed forsaken, my son, and give you Beulah to be your queen of the gentiles to pass on my seed to go far off and make many different kinds like God your father to make royal children in the nations to do good before salvation comes for peace.

King Judah said: observe what is going on in the world, my children, before your spirits come to an END in the kingdom and the accursed seed of god (Cain) my father, who made us all not perfect in this generation till salvation begins in kingdoms to create immortal spirits in the Light to take over the kingdom in the world.

Be prepared. Who has no faith like me will fall. Everyone is responsible for his fate, and don't be led astray by seducing spirits.

Hadassah will pay you back what you did Ps.137:8; Rev.17:2; 18:9

The ten Israelite kings came and bowed to Belhadassah and lay their crowns before Judah and said: God my father, Belhadassah is worthy to be ruler. He has the wisdom of a great spirit who will save Mankind who has faith. Belhadassah called seven of his brothers who Judah gave away in their youth, and made them kings of the gentiles in the nations.

Wanted to imitate Elijah

Judah wants to imitate Elijah to conquer the earth. He wants to be a godly spirit so no one can see him and can fight against Elijah with his godly spirits.

Thou Judah, wicked god, profaned against holy people and made Israelites to look like them Esssek.21:25; Dan.2:47; Mal.2.11 2

Judah realized that all his hard work in breeding gods, Mankind and Israelites was presumptuous and vain. Spirits from his seed are not accepted above. Judah whispered to Belhadassah: in truth, Elijah is the king of the earth and his way is justified to humiliate me. I am a foolish king with the useless laws of devils

Hadassah said: O King, what are you going to do? The writing on the wall has made everyone know I gave you a wise prophet, and you made him a king to rule the nations. Judah said: give him a palace in the provinces.

After all the guests left the banquet, the horseman drove King Belhadassah and his mother Queen Hadassah to the palace Judah had given him. Judah remained in his palace in Babylon. He lay on the couch and called for the harpist to play for him to go to sleep.

When Judah awoke he hurried to the lion's den and saw the lions fast asleep and Eve, Tamuze and his children were sleeping among the lions. He was afraid that if he went into the den the lions would attack him.

He ran and called for the guard to let the women and the children out and bring them back to the harem and come back to him.

When the guards returned, Judah said: how come the women are alive? Let us go to the den of the lions, and he threw the guards in the den and the lions sprang on them and feasted on their flesh.

Gossip

King Bel and Queen Hadassah began going out together. When the people saw her with King Bel they waved their hands and said: O Queen, you are beautiful. Make beautiful children for Bel.

Others would say: O Queen, you left the beast for Bel. Others were surprised she moved out of the palace to live with King Belhadassah and left the beast for destroying the Hebrews.

In the crowd to see King Belhadassah, a gentile shouted: O Queen, your God is going mad and crying for his mother to come back, blaming you. He threw all the guards in the den of lions and everyone is afraid to go to the palace. If you don't go back he will kill you and Bel.

Hadassah said to Bel: if I don't go back he will come and kill you. Father can't do without me. It's best you hide at your brothers'.

Hadassah told the horseman to hurry and bring her to the palace. When she entered Judah held her by her throat. She was gasping for air and he threw her on the floor.

Judah said: what is this? You are making an ass out of me. Did I make your son a king to be your lover! I knew from birth the bastard would do the same as me and commit abomination with you.

Hadassah began to cry: you beast! You fuck me like a devil. Judah got angry and tore the clothes of her and put her on his lap and started spanking her. You have forsaken the law of your God, and commit incest more than the hairs on your head, and gave her two more slaps on her arse.

Hadassah cried: O God, have mercy. Thou shall not kill. She started kicking, crying O God! O God, I'll do whatever you say. Don't kill me, please, my father.

Judah shouted: this pain, Hadassah, I'm suffering for incest with you. I can't bear for Bel to have you. I am a jealous God.

I'm going mad. Your absence is unbearable. You are adding on to my condemnation for making you to fuck with Bel to add to my sin with you.

This fuckery is worse than death. I feel like strangling you for making me so jealous.

Hadassah cried: thou shall not kill. Have mercy, O God. I am under your spell. Kill me. I'm no good. I am cruel like you and can't help this wickedness you pass on to me. It is like a wild fire burning inside of me.

Judah shouted: I am your God. I made Bel king to rule. Now both of you plan to make all kind of features to populate the earth from my seed. I regret I made thee. You are cruel and will add more problems upon the earth with your wickedness.

I thought that in my old age I would have peace with you, but you make my life hell. Every time you leave the palace I think you are not coming back, plus all these dreams for shedding blood on earth are terrorising me when I close my eyes. Hadassah cried: my father, I can't sleep with you. You cry and roar like a hungry lion in your sleep and it scares me you want to have control over me with your power.

I tried to be good but your wickedness to rebel is in my nature. This lust is like death. We are under its spell to destroy. Now you hate me.

I seduce Bel to fuck me as my king. You did the same to your mother as her king. My son is my brother and you are our father. We are all corrupt. Let me burn some incense to god your father in Hades. It is he who passed seed of devils to you.

Judah shouted in anger: I repent I made Mankind with thee, and they will do the same as me to make Mankind like me. No matter how much incense you burn, there is no peace for me. I made children for the gates of Hell with this accursed seed.

Your whoring has yielded much unto me from my seed and I will be punished more for knowing scripture and having no faith, when the whirlwind takes my spirit from the earth is more that I can bear for slaying holy men from the earth to be with the vagabond for rape

Hadassah said: O, my God, what is the object of the law? Judah answered: it is to rule by fear so all on earth worship your God with fear. Now I fear for my life, so comfort me. Bel has reveaed the way to everlasting life I kept as a secret.

Hadassah said: you chastise me and got much pleasure when I conceived Bel. I was in much pain and you sent him away from me to live among gentiles after he was born. Now Bel is my wise king. He reads the writing on the wall what was your secret from Mankind and Israelites. He will give me all manner of children to populate the earth with your seed till judgment day.

Ps.52:8; Pro.31:21; Pro.7:25; 1.Pet.4:17; 2.Pet.2:14

Hadassah said: my God, I know judgment will be on us after death. I hope Elijah sends us together in the chamber in Hades.

Judah said: in the chamber in Hades I will pardon thee, my daughter, for incest with Bel. Hadassah cried: My God, My God, have mercy on Bel. He is our son and he didn't ask to be born. He is a prophet with pleasant words. He fucks me sweet as honey, not like you with hate.

You gave me a body that pleases Bel to give thee all manner of gentiles from your seed. O, my father, we are all messed up. This faith is a big commitment if we have to give up our pleasure on earth. Hadassah said: let us go to sleep; I am tired of all these arguments with my Bel and your death. It's not my fault you have no faith. If you had faith Elijah would give your spirit peace and you and I would not be here to be king and queen.

The dream

Judah began to snore like a lion and began to dream and cry in his sleep and then began to shout: Hadassah, wake up! I had a dream. A strong wind came and broke the tree I hanged Adam on and carried the tree with all its branches with fruit, and the fruit turned into people and they were falling in my mouth. Then I looked and saw the spirit CHRIST with a sharp sickle coming after me, and there was no place to hide. I began running towards the stump of the tree and saw Elijah removing the weed from the stump of the tree and it began to shoot new branches with a lot of fruit and it turned to people going up to Heaven and they were pointing their hands at me, saying to Elijah, he is the one from the fire. Send him back! As Elijah was about to speak the Word I woke up.

Hadassah said: my God, you look frightened. She rushed to get him some water. After a few sips of water Judah said: Hadassah, the lions didn't eat Eve, my mother, and the children. They had faith in Elijah to save them.

Hadassah said: not even the hungry lions want your mother's flesh but you are like a hungry beast that can't have enough of me and go mad if I am not here with you.

You can't have a queen who is going to Hell and one going to Heaven. The Passover is not complete

This spirit Elijah saved your mother and my grandmother; let us see if he will save our children in the harem. Let us cast them in the fire as a peace offering. If Elijah saves them we will know He will save our children from the fire and I stay in the palace with you too.

The death of Judah

Judah went in the harem and he took the last of his children born with Hadassah's sisters to sacrifice them as burnt offerings to god his father in Hades. The women began to cry to Eve and Tamuze: King Judah is going to sacrifice our children.

Eve ran out and tried to take the children from him. Judah shouted in anger: move away from me! Eve said: why are you so cruel? What have the children done to you? They are Mankind born from your seed in this harem by your daughters.

Judah shouted: they are mine and not from god (Cain) you made with Satan. He passed on his seed to me. They are not perfect like you. god (Cain) was a useless god, because he had no power. Satan strangled him.

So I am going to sacrifice the children to Cain in Hades for not making me perfect. Ex-queen Babylon Tamuze shouted: Judah! Stop this! Why are you so cruel? You are hateful even to Hadassah's children to make Elijah angry.

As Judah was going to throw the children in flames, Elijah appeared in the flames and said: Ammon, I know you by name. He looked in the flames and recognized the voice, and said: what do you want? Elijah said: I see that you have walked in the ways of the devils and god (Cain) your father in Hades, killing and shedding blood on earth and committing abomination with your mother and your daughter.

Now you want to kill the last of your children with the menstruating woman in the palace with you. Behold, a great plague will come and smite the women you have made in the palace and also those you made in the palace with Tamuze in Babylon.

A cancerous disease shall come unto your bowels and you shall waste away, day after day, until your spirit has no desire to live in the kingdom from your mother's flesh you want to destroy with your immutable spirits of ancient devils.

Your queen in the palace has no desire for you any more. When your spirit departs from the flesh of your mother, I will be waiting to send your spirit to join the devils and god your father in Hades according to your law. I am Elijah even to your old age, who executes judgment on spirits who depart from the kingdom that have no faith in me, and Elijah vanished from the flames.

The end has come

Judah cried: O Eve, pray for me. My end has come. Eve said: did not your mother and I tell you to repent and turn to Elijah for your peace? Now Elijah has spoken the Word on you He can't reverse the Word as it's active.

Judah was denied peace

Ex-queen Babylon Tamuze said: why should Elijah reward you? You loved what the devil did to me to make gods under the oath with much stress. You became Elijah's enemy; you have abused my body **(Lev.18:13)** and want to destroy the kingdom. Because you are not perfect and not accepted above you refuse His peace offering to rest in peace.

The message

When you get to Hades give god your father a kick in his ass for me for raping me to make you suffer in flames for his sin and your abomination with me. Tell the devils I am free from their oath under the law and they will suffer for holding me in captivity.

Your queen a nursing mother Deut.21:23; Is.119:23

Judah cried: what about me, my queen? Don't I get a blessing? Tamuze said: you are a curse unto me, not a blessing. Your time will come and you will have Hadassah to cry with you for slapping me. She will bless you and curse you for making her a whore (Tim.5:2). You were rude to Elijah and killed all my brothers innocently and hanged my father's body on a tree, and blasphemed Elijah and CHRIST with your boasting.

Belhadassah, first son of Judah with Hadassah

Judah returned to the palace. Hadassah rushed to him. My God, did you sacrifice the children to god your father? Judah began to tremble and words could hardly come from his mouth. She rushed for some water to give him. He pushed her aside. Hadassah said: what have the witches in the harem done to you? She got the horseman to go to the city to get Belhadassah. When they returned Judah said: Bel, you are her prophet and wise. Tell me what is going to happen to me. Belhadassah said: O King, you have annoyed a great spirit. He is disappointed with you for not doing good in the world. You have made the Great Spirit angry.

Hadassah said: O my God, can't you fight this spirit and send him out of the earth? Bel said: my mother, this one is stronger than any witch-doctor and can fight with every spirit and send them in flames of fire. Hadassah said: you are a witchdoctor. What can we do if He is so strong? He said: let's live in hope the devils will save him from this spirit. Judah was exhausted and fell asleep. She returned to his palace.

The cancer began to take effect in Judah's bowels. He couldn't eat or drink and became thinner and thinner every day. His bones were protruding through his flesh, and he was lying in bed like a skeleton, crying in pain, feeling hot and cold. Hadassah got a handmaid to lay in the bed with him to keep him warm while she was in Babylon with her lovers. **Job.24:10-12**

THE FOOL HAS SPOKEN. THERE IS NO GOD Ps.53:1; Ps.14:1–3; Ps.35:11-15; Ps.10:7; Rev.13:6

Judah began to cry: O Hadassah, don't leave me alone with this handmaid. She makes me hot when I'm hot and when I'm cold I can't get hot. It's terrible, this cold. Hadassah said: but you are God of the world. Make this cold go away from you. You can't make this cold go away, because you are deceitful.

THROUGH FEAR OF DEATH MEN WORSHIP ME ON EARTH Rev13:13

Judah said: I am a king. It is the people who idolize me and make me God, because I know the scriptures. They fear me. It is Elijah I fear because I have no faith and it is he I have to face when I leave this body. Hadassah said: but you said to me your queen mother was jealous and you don't know Elijah. Why are you so deceitful to me? I gave you the best of my youth. Should I give up my lovers to look after you? **Job.24:14–20**

WOE TO ISRAEL THAT IS ALONE. WHEN HIS SPIRIT FALLETH HE HAS NO ONE TO HELP HIM Eccl.3:10; Job.24:23–24

Now you admit that you are a king and not God. What is the name of your spirit so I can do witchcraft to contact you? My spirit name is Israel, he said (**Ps.76:1**) and when I go in the other world I'll prepare a place for you and I, so we can be king and queen of the spirits of the earth and we will do more wickedness in the kingdom than what we do now in the flesh when we are spirits. When I die, embalm my body and take it to the sepulchre I made in the Tower of Babel so people can worship their God to death, every new moon.

THE SPIRIT NAME OF JUDAH IS ISRAEL. HE HAS KNOWLEDGE OF ELIJAH Ps.76:1–2; Ps.102

After this testament Judah said: Hadassah, now I want peace, I will have Hell. How stupid it is to live like a king and leave the good life to suffer to go to Hades like god my father. Hadassah left him alone to suffer for his wickedness. The cancer was making him mad. He began to cry: Elijah! Let my cry come to you!

I am distressed. Do not hide your face before my days vanish. My bones are sticking out. My heart is failing me. I can't eat my food. I am reduced to skin and bones. My eyes close to death. I am alone like a cursed spirit, now your wrath has come to remove me out of the earth. I wither away.

Judah shouted for the scribes. They rushed towards him and he said: let it be written for the future generations, that people not created may praise Elijah and have faith in Him for CHRIST to come down from Heaven to create spirits in the kingdoms on earth, so spirits from my seed don't go into captivity to be condemned to death. Tell the Israelites to tell their children to tell their children the truth so when salvation comes, their kingdoms be established by Elijah through CHRIST.

Great men are not wise. Not even in old age do they understand judgment Job.39:9

God began to cry: O Elijah, add time to my life. Don't send me away to be in the midst of devils. Have mercy. Your years continue from generation to generation on earth to direct the kingdom to CHRIST. The spirits from my seed will perish without flesh of my mother if they don't have faith, like me. Judah cried: I thirst! The maid rushed inside and gave him vinegar and wiped his face. Judah cried: Elijah! Elijah! Prophesy my future. A voice came through the mouth of the maid: you will be in captivity for a thousand years and you will return as a godly spirit with no flesh. Judah died, and his spirit left his body. It was too late to be saved.

He that hangeth Adam is the son of god Deut.21:23

The whirlwind came and took his spirit away to a chamber prepared for him in the south for a thousand years to cool his anger and hate of CHRIST on earth.

You can't serve two masters 1.Jn.2:1–3; Mk.8:36: 1.Jn.2:8–10

What good did it do for god to pass on his seed to make a god in the world (**Ro.5:12**) with his sister to be called God of Mankind and Israelites to worship him (**2.Tim.1:17**) through ignorance of truth? **Am.3:15**

Elijah said to God: if I am your master, where is your respect? **Mal.1:6**

No one can serve two masters. It's either you have faith to be saved or live in hope of the devils to save you from Hell. Either you hate devils or love your master who brought you up to do good. Judah's desire was to imitate the devils to rule the earth as king, and became a murderer to be king (**Jn.3:5**) to death. The spirit CHRIST in Adam came to power, conquered death and resurrected to sit on the throne of the world.

Fear of Elijah and CHRIST

Babylonians idolized Judah in fear. They worshipped King Judah and made him the God of Israelites and Mankind and put his hope in devils. The devils made him a king to rebel with their law against Elijah and CHRIST, to destroy the kingdoms on earth. The devils failed. They had no power against the Word by Elijah the son of CHRIST by the Word with the Word.

Spirits (gods) of Mankind Ps.25:10
(REFERENCE TO KING JUDAH AS WRITTEN)

Mankind be merciful unto my sin, for it is great.

Judah is known as God, spirit name Israel. **Ps.76:1**

Do you believe in God? Even godly spirits believe and they are in fear. **James 2:19**

Faith not accompanied by action is death. **Jn.2:17**

The fool king wanted evidence of faith and became a useless king with the scripture so it can't be fulfilled. **Jn.2:20; 2:23**. He wanted to be king again and crucified Jesus, the son of CHRIST.

Judah, the lawgiver against judge Elijah, who has power to save and destroy. **Heb.4:12; Pro.26:16**

Elijah: Judah had no faith, and repays me evil for doing good. His kingdom had no hope for salvation and peace (**Ps.53:1-3; 14:1–3; 35:12**) as he declared war for the earth.

The vision of the Sabbath in Babylon by King Belhadassah

King Bel saw the spirit Elijah saving the spirits of His people in Babylon, which had never been seen.

He saw the spirits of Eve and Queen Babylon on a log of fire and they were in the Light and were saved by Elijah. then he heard voices praise Elijah for saving Zion and Jerusalem. Their spirits were in the Light. An angel with a book and a pen was writing, and there was much clapping and praising for Elijah and His holy work.

I saw this Great Spirit CHRIST in a bright Light on his throne watching me and I heard a voice say, I've put a seal to the end. Let the spirits in the kingdom that have knowledge and faith go to the people and put the plan of faith to his people for peace.

But if spirits in Mankind continue to be wicked and commit abomination and adultery in holy flesh proceed by the Word… Then I saw multitudes gathered in the tower, celebrating Pentecost, washing the body of God in Babel tower for the Passover of the kingdom.

Then the spirit said: Bel, you are living in troubled times in Babylon. Go and tell the people about this peace plan before I make an example of the tower in Babylon.

The end vision

Belhadassah saw the vision of the END! Spirits were let out of captivity and they began going in the bodies of Mankind. There was much noise like thunder and battle from nation to nation. There was smoke and blood on earth.

Mankind began to tremble, crying to God for help. No one seemed to understand why there is so much war, famine, draught and misery on earth. They cried to God but they got no answer. some said: how could God tolerate so much trouble in the nations, and began to lose faith in God.

The godly spirits in the kingdom began to say: now we will attack. They have no faith. Let us seduce them to death to destroy the kingdom with all sorts of sin and disease so there be no flesh left on earth.

Then I heard a voice say: Wake up Elijah, to begin the work in salvation. The spirits began to speak through the mouths of Mankind, Jesus! Jesus! In the name of Jesus go away from us. We want peace.

Then I saw Elijah put up His hand speaking the words: there is no peace without faith. And I saw the spirit CHRIST come on a pillar of clouds, and multitudes of spirits that were in the bodies of Mankind began crying for Jesus before CHRIST cast them out of the kingdom and I heard a voice like thunder say: don't let any escape. The spirits of gods that had no faith were the first to be carried away from the earth to the pit for declaring war against CHRIST and Elijah.

Then I heard a voice say: salvation has come to those who have faith for peace, and the earth was full of clouds, CHRIST stood in the clouds over the earth and Elijah was presenting multitudes of kingdoms from over the whole earth.

And multitudes of spirits were fast asleep and multitudes of spirits who had no faith were cast out from the kingdom and were carried away by the whirlwind. They began falling in the mouth of the waters crying, journeying to the gates of Hades, and saw the devils with a book of the dead entering their names. The spirits of Mankind who had no faith began to cry: let us out! There is no space. We are chastised with fire.

Then there was total silence and a voice said: the final judgment has come and the exit was opened and the spirits and the devils began to journey to the gate where there is fire for eternity.

Then I looked and there was no more darkness in the world. Then multitudes of people in Heaven and earth were giving praise to Elijah for giving CHRIST the victory by the Word to rule and have dominion in all worlds.

The archangels began bowing to CHRIST and giving CHRIST praise for creating His Elijah to do His holy work and worshipping the Eternal for creating His CHRSIT to finish the work. He started to put the whole world in the Light.

Then I said: woe is on me if I don't warn the people of the plan for peace.

The first mission to the Israelites in a province 4:2

King Bel went to a province on his first mission to speak to the chief rabbi of Israelites. He said: I thought it good to tell about the signs and wonders that the Great Spirit Elijah has shown me.

The rabbi and his Israelites said: we heard that the spirit Elijah is with thee. Bel said: the revelation of the kingdom is explained to me and it is to be everlasting from generation to generation and I have a plan for peace on earth. It is based on faith in Elijah to be saved after death.

No change Jn.12:40
God has blinded their eyes and hardened their hearts

The chief rabbi and the Israelites blocked their ears and said: don't trouble us with this vision for peace. Thou hast dethroned our kings from ruling Mankind and have taken their kingly throne from them in the nations.

Other Israelites shouted: thou hast lifted up yourself against God who made thee with his concubine who was his maid and made her his queen and now she is your queen. We don't accept this plan to change the law for faith.

Bel said: the law has many faults. The rabbi got angry and ripped off the gold chain God had given King Bel from his neck and said: you are not worthy to wear this chain. You want to put division between Israelites and Mankind. If this vision is true, tell Elijah to come and we will believe you.

The rabbi continued: It is written in the law that all kinds of evil will come after us, but we pray to our God to give us understanding. We are not like you, who were brought up in bondage among Mankind and who deal in witchcraft.

Our father is our God and his mother is our queen you hold in captivity. Your mother is jealous because she can't make Israelites and made Mankind, so how can you talk about peace to us with a plan to have faith in Elijah, who we have not seen or heard?

Bel said: I came here in peace on a mission to tell you to stop worshipping God your father and strive for faith in Elijah for peace, or you will be cast out of the earth for having no faith.

God our father had no faith in Elijah. He destroyed his people from the earth, rejecting knowledge of scriptures. King Bel said: if you are not willing to change our father's shame for glory in the kingdom he passed on the accursed seed to us, Elijah will punish thee for imitating the ways of our father for not taking heed of this plan for peace.

King Bel said: your spirits will be cast out. King Judah fornicated with your mother and passed on this seed to you to be carried away in devouring flames of fire for bringing another in this world to suffer under the law to death.

Bel left disappointed and told Hadassah.

King Bel went to the next nation. The rabbi and his Israelites were waiting for him to discuss this peace plan in the synagogue.

Bel told them about the visions he had and explained the revelation of the purpose of the kingdom and the resurrection of spirit and the spirits that had no faith were descending to the pit in flames because they didn't believe in peace but the law to death.

The rabbi said: who are you to tell us about the law of God our father who made us from his seed with his mother to be his people on earth and after death? This is his law.

King Bel said: God, who you say is your father, fornicated with his mother. Logically speaking God your father is your brother if he made thee with his mother, who is also your mother. He also made me with my mother who is his daughter and she is my sister. Don't you see this corruption in holy flesh? The rabbi and the Israelites were silent for answers and everyone in the synagogue was scratching their head and had no answer. He said: we are equal with God. From the same seed

King Bel looked at these hypocrites and went on to say: Where did God your father, and my father also get the law? Your mother is still on earth can testify God accepted the law of the devils under oath to live to death.

The rabbi said: we cannot ask our mother. God kept this as his secret to himself to tell us after we are dead. We populate the earth by passing on his seed without knowing his secret to death, so he can inherit all spirits from his seed after death according to the law.

The promise is not by the law

King Bel said: Elijah gave God the choice for peace. If he had faith his kingdom he would have a spirit in perfection to be accepted above but if he had no faith he would enter the gates of Hell and would inherit all who have no faith in Elijah. This is the promise God our father had before he took the law by the oath of the devils.

The Israelites said: No! No! No! Now we know you are mad with this new religion for faith for peace. If Elijah appears, we will believe you.

King Bel said: it is Elijah who brought up God your father from the wilderness. Your mother is also the mother of God. She is a witness. He made her his first queen. She had faith in Elijah to save him from the devils who wanted to eat him from birth.

The Israelites blocked their ears shouting: Lies! Lies! We don't want to hear any more. They started to go out of the synagogue and saw Queen Hadassah coming on her chariot and in fear of her they began to run away from the synagogue.

Hadassah riding in scarlet on her chariot Rev.17:6–7

King Bel went on his chariot towards Hadassah. She said: are they for peace or for war? Bel said: my queen mother, no more bloodshed on earth. Go back to Babylon. It is important everyone in the nations has a choice for peace or fall to death according to the law.

King Bel became a prophet of peace. He went from nation to nation with the peace plan for the earth, with much opposition. The fear of God if they changed the law was instilled in their nature not to change the law to death.

King Bel became the most unpopular king with his peace plan and caused much division and everyone had their own idea on peace and made their god to worship, for they realized Judah, who they made their God of the world, was a man born of a woman like them and did not make anyone perfect – it was all in his imagination and he ruled by fear to death.

The Bible says God is of the seed of god Dan.2:47 Ex.4:16; Gen.17:7; Jn.8:41; Isa.10:21

Since god (Cain) raped his sister to make a god like himself it is natural his god would be in his nature. His god born called himself the mighty God, became wicked, and corrupted others on earth with his imagination to pass on the accursed seed. All gods on earth do the same in this generation and give themselves a different name.

Elijah said to God of god (Cain): not by might or by your power and violence and hate for my people you can have a spirit like theirs or mine with the Word. **Rev17:14; Num.25:1**

Elijah told Judah before he died: you despise the holy people of CHRIST. What you did to them was without mercy. You are worthless and all spirits from your seed will be ashamed to know you commited abomination with your mother and your daughter to make gods like you to fall. Because you disobey, spirits from your seed will be removed from the flesh of your mother by CHRIST for judgment.

Repent or perish Lk.13:3

God said: I repent I made Mankind and Israelites to pass on the seed of god my father in Hades. **Rev17:5–8; Ps.137:8; Hos.4:13**

The peace vision

King Belhadassah was having a rest in his palace and had a vision. The Great Spirit Elijah said: Belhadassah, now you have kingly power and authority over all the people that dwell in the nations on earth.

Peace be multiplied unto you if you have faith (21). I thought it good to show thee signs and wonders what the Great Spirit CHRIST, who sits on HIS throne, will do in the kingdom to have everlasting life from this generation on earth.

Belhadassah saw in the vision a tree in the midst of the earth. Its roots reached to the bowels of the earth. Then he saw a whirlwind come and it broke the tree in half and it took the half with all its branches and fruit and its seed away. It disappeared and left the stump of the tree on the earth.

Then he saw an old man cleaning around the stump. The grass that was choking the stump and he watered it. Then he saw new branches began shooting out from the stump and it began to flower and produce beautiful fruit. From the fruit he saw spirits getting out of the fruit and going up to Heaven.

Then in another vision (**12:15**) he saw the holy CHRIST come from Heaven on a pillar of cloud and went in the kingdoms and saw spirits cast out without flesh from the seed of Judah. Then he heard a voice say: don't let spirits of the beast escape. Then he saw the spirit Elijah speak and a whirlwind came and took the godly spirits away for making war and spreading disease in the kingdoms in the nations to be Judah's inheritance in the gate of Hell by decree of the promise to him before he took the law.

Then he heard voices of the devils saying, who are these? Whence come they? They are not ours. Then spirits began to cry: CHRIST rules in the kingdom on earth and sent us to thee to do whatever pleases thee. The devils were wrath. The spirits of gods began to cry: we thirst we thirst in this heat. The chief of the devils said: you had a choice to have peace but chose to thirst to death. Who is this CHRIST? We have never seen Him. The spirits cried: he rules in the kingdom and we are not His spirits and Elijah sent us to join the rebellion with those that hate holy people in His daughter's flesh.

Belhadassah began to cry and said: O Great Spirit Elijah, this vision I've seen brings much sorrow unto me. I'm from the seed of Judah. If I enter the narrow gate in Hades I'm no more a spirit in the kingdom. I'll be in flames of fire, dying of thirst. How can I serve thee, O Great Spirit, when there are no spirits left in the kingdom on earth?

Elijah said: fear not your father with the law; he is in the gates of Hell. If you have faith, peace be unto your spirit and your kingdom will have a new blessed spirit when I speak the Word to the great holy CHRIST to do the holy work in creating spirits in the kingdoms that are worthy.

THE TRUTH IS HID BY JUDAH Ja.15–27 Dan.2:47

Belhadassah, Elijah said: I'll show thee what is written in holy scriptures. No spirit born of the accursed seed holds unto the truth. Your father was taught scriptures but he kept the knowledge of the way to everlasting life to himself. He had no faith in me to have peace. His spirit was carried away to Hades, where there is no peace.

Your father became a prophet of the laws of devils under oath and did wickedly to be a king. He went against CHRIST and eliminated his holy sons on earth. If he had faith he would love his neighbour who was not like him, and lived in peace.

He made Mankind and Israelites in the daughter of CHRIST and all on earth from his seed worshipped him as God through fear. Before he died he made you king over all the peoples with different features on earth.

You should use your kingly power to do good for your people so they have peace after death according to the scriptures shown thee, and to correct the law of Judah and give instruction for Mankind to have faith for peace to be multiplied on earth to be justified by the Word.

Belhadassah, consider your life in the kingdom. You are not perfect. You must have faith in me to rest in peace for your kingdom to have an immortal spirit by the Word to be accepted above by the Eternal Spirit. **Ja.15:27**

King Bel and Queen Hadassah

Bel was fasting and praying and thanking Elijah for the knowledge of what he has to do for his kingdom to have an immortal spirit. The truth which God his father withheld from Mankind and Israelites whom he made not perfect like himself to pass his seed in his mother's flesh to make spirits to fight on earth.

The Great Spirit Elijah said: I've heard your supplication. I've come to give thee skill and understanding so you can put an end to sin and for your people on earth to have a choice to prepare their kingdom for an everlasting spirit to be created in their kingdom in righteousness by CHRIST the creator of spirits in kingdoms for salvation by the Word to continue on earth in their image.

The spirits from the seed of God your father with your mothers are living in troubled times. If they have no faith, they will fall and will be held in captivity in Hades, where there is no peace, with God your father.

I've kept an eye on this evil generation of God your father who I brought up to do good for the righteous way for creation by faith and

I tell you the same as your father for peace. So tell your people before it's too late in Babylon.

Break off your abomination with your mother and do righteous work. Show mercy, so the end of your days as king be at peace after your spirit departs from the kingdom.

There is none among your people who has an understanding of everlasting life to go above. If you hold on to the TRUTH and don't tell them to have faith to rest in peace, their spirits will be carried away by the wind to God your father in Hades.

Everyone has a choice to have faith for peace, or fall to the gates of Hades.

Those who are proud of their features and not willing to change to the way of peace and want to continue in the evil way, will be in the heat when their spirits depart from the kingdom.

The blessing in the kingdoms

The spirits that have faith, their kingdoms will have a spirit of creation by CHRIST in the time of salvation to be accepted. Elijah said: Belhadassah, I am telling you the same I told God your father before he accepted the law by oath to go against CHRIST.

Your father was tempted by the devils to lose faith, and everyone who has no faith is tempted to entice others by lust in his nature to do the same to pass on the accursed seed to give birth to a god to sin to death

Elijah said: you were misled, Belhadassah, with this law. Every kingdom is righteous when it is presented to CHRIST who sits on HIS throne in Heaven. Is for Him to come to create spirits in the Light with no fault by the Word.

Understand this plan for peace, explain it to your brothers and sisters to have faith in Me to rest in peace after death.

Everyone who hears this plan for peace and does not act upon it has similar spirits as your father, who was worthless and could not save his mother and did the same as god (Cain) to pass on the seed of the devil.

Pure religion is to prepare the kingdom as a peace offering to Elijah to have a spirit of creation in the kingdoms on earth through CHRIST.

Belhadassah, now you have understanding of everlasting life. Go in the nations and make it be known among your brothers and sisters about this plan for their spirits to rest in peace on earth through faith in me.

Elijah said: Belhadassah, the spirit CHRIST is not partial to spirits of gods in the kingdoms from his flesh. He will cast every spirit in the time of salvation to the last seed of gods from his flesh. Let it be known this free choice for spirits to rest in peace is a consolation for all spirits of gods in Mankind born in the kingdom. If their desire is to sin to make gods while they live in the kingdom their spirits shall come unto judgment after death. Judgment is merciless on spirits who have no faith and will fall and have no one to blame but themselves. If the spirits of gods say they have faith and keep doing the same evil they are useless if they don't prepare their bodies for salvation for creation of everlasting spirits so their spirits rest in peace. **Ja.3:18; Ja2.20**

Belhadassah told Hadassah the vision for this peace plan for the earth. Hadassah said: O my wise king, your wisdom and greatness has reached to the heavens. Don't fail on this plan. It's a chance to test Mankind and Israelites to see if they have this faith in the Great Spirit Elijah to rule the earth in righteousness. My king, I'll prepare a banquet for all the wise men, councillors, astrologers, pharisees, seducers of the spirits of the dead, publicans and tax payers to come and hear how you plan to save Mankind and Israelites after death and not fall in fire.

The last vision before the fall of Babylon. Many are called. Few are saved

Belhadassah, go to your people in the nations and explain to them the kingdom is created to be everlasting with spirits of CHRIST and not for spirits of gods. They are of the devils' nature that came to earth to corrupt flesh with disease of all kinds. The people must prepare their kingdoms for the most holy spirit CHRIST.

Babylon, be an example to sudden death to those that disobey

Elijah said to Belhadassah in a vision: the spirits in your mother's flesh are living in troubled times and Babylon will be an example to end of spirits that disobey, by the Word.

No faith, no peace

Elijah said: Belhadassah! Make your people understand what will befall them in this generation if they don't have faith in the plan for peace. The whirlwind will come and carry them to be with your father to inherit spirits from his seed.

Belhadassah began to cry in the vision: O Elijah, this vision brings much sorrow on the earth. I fear the people will not want to give up their joy in fornication and will hate me. They will say I am more wicked than God to tell them about this peace when there is much lust in their nature to make Mankind and Israelites.

The spirit said...

Elijah said: tell your mother to stop whoring and committing incest with you, making children that suck the same breast as thee, lest I strip the flesh of her spirit and send her to your father, where there is much howling in the flames and no water to drink or flesh to lust.

If she has no mercy on my people, I'll have no mercy on her children. She is doing the same as your father, inbreeding your children with her lovers, making Asians to look like her.

I will cause your mother's joy and her Sabbath feasts to cease. The spirits from her olive skinned kingdoms will be sent to the devil, who raped her mother's mother, to tell him they were born with all his faults.

The kingdoms from the flesh of Asia who died giving birth to your mother will be recreated with spirits to sing and dance to her in Heaven with joy before CHRIST and Zion on the throne. (16)

Since Hadassah's father is your father as well, she has knowledge that Elijah brought up her father (Judah). She has no respect for Eve and your father's mother's holiness. She hopes she can be queen of the earth after death, with God to rule the earth spirits.

Judah imitated the devils and Elijah's power with the word

Therefore every spirit from his seed that dwells in kingdoms will be cast out to be his inheritance.

Belhadassah, go in the nations with this plan for peace. They must have faith, and fear no one. Tell them God (Judah) made no one perfect on the earth and he repented he made them, with faults in his nature passed on to them.

Now I make thee a prophet with knowledge of holy scriptures. If you don't explain the way to everlasting life to your people and hold the key of knowledge to yourself as God your father, you are no prophet to me, to save the people after death.

If your people are not willing to change their shameful way while they live in the kingdom, I will punish their spirits after death for not taking heed of the plan for peace while they lived in the kingdom, and bringing another spirit in the world to do the same as them to suffer grief in the heat because of disobedience.

The people you saw in the vision, walking on earth, had a spirit in the Light created by CHRIST through faith to be make multitudes of immortal spirits to be among angels in the Light in the heavens.

King Bel said: I'll use my authority as king for spirits of gods rest in peace after death and who don't believe me, so be it.

Then Belhadassah had another vision and saw a spirit in the Light come from the body of a man hanged on a tree and it went in the kingdom and began casting out spirits. Then he heard a voice say: don't let the beast escape for declaring war in the kingdoms on earth.

I cried: O my father, you have deceived everyone on earth with your fear and wickedness, and he got up trembling when he saw eyes of devils in the dark screaming at him, if you tell the people the truth we will do the same to thee as your father.

Then Bel heard the voice of Elijah saying: the scripture is given thee to correct the doctrine of the law of Judah and instruction given thee in the righteous path for salvation.

Trial of faith Ja.15:27

Temptation will come to spirits of gods in Mankind. They should consider their life in kingdom is not perfect. They have a choice to accept peace before they depart from the kingdom

Elijah said: Belhadassah, declare the plan for peace to the people on earth and make it be known the way to everlasting life is through Elijah to CHRIST and it's also for Israelites on earth who hate thee for being king over them. The kingdom will be established through faith and those who have faith will be saved after death from fire.

King Bel, not by your power will you save them, but by my spirit with the Word I will put an end to sin. Put this choice before all the people in Babylon before the Passover feast takes place in Babylon to make an example to final end of spirits of gods in the flesh of Tamuze

Bel told Hadassah of this vision for the plan for the earth. She said: my wise king, your greatness has reached to the heavens. Don't fail on this plan to test your faith in Babylon.

Hadassah said to Bel: my wise king, you have had no pleasure with me for the past thirty days. So what is the problem with you? This faith has turned you off me or is it that I don't turn you on any more? Our father couldn't have enough of me to his death.

Bel said: my mother, there is a time to live and a time to die. You think like God our father, who thought he would never die for his wickedness and putting fear in people on earth. I have had a chance to meditate on this faith with this Great Spirit Elijah for peace. That is why I am in my chambers, concentrating on this plan for peace.

My mother, this fornication with you must stop. Our father didn't escape death in this palace. Neither will you escape death in this palace for shedding blood of the Israelite men and capturing Israelite women. You must change this cruel way of our father under the law.

I am a prophet and your king and an advisor. We should use our power to do good and direct the people on earth to have faith so God our father doesn't inherit their spirits when they fall because of his evil way through fear. You will have no peace if you do the same as him by shedding blood through ignorance.

Hadassah said: you ask me to come to your chambers to hear the request of Israelites in other provinces. Make it a law that no Israelite enters the palace of your mother except if the king or queen invites them to the palace.

Bel said: if you hold on to this peace there will be multitudes of Asians on earth who will overtake our father's Israelites with all manner of people on earth as your creation. Let us be positive now we know the truth our father has been holding from us. Murder has been committed in your ignorance. You have to make a complete break from this evil to death.

Maybe the Great Spirit Elijah will make you return in the kingdom to see all your children upon the earth at the appointed time before judgment on all who do evil on earth.

Hadassah said: my prophet king, are you prophesying I will return to see my people before I perish like your father for shedding blood on earth? I've been under your father's spell all these years. I know no other way. Now I have a choice to do good or evil. Be patient with me, my son. To give up my pleasure in this life is hard. If I don't have faith to rest in peace I have only myself to blame if I fall to be with your father.

If it pleases thee, my king, I will prepare a banquet for thee with our friends who mix and mingle with Israelite women to make Asians to look like your queen on earth for peace so their kingdoms can be created with beautiful spirits in salvation through faith for peace.

Bel said: my queen, if that is your desire, put it in the hands of the Great Spirit Elijah for their spirits to have peace and for their kingdom to be created with immortal spirits to be accepted above through faith. Their kingdoms are worthy to have salvation so let us celebrate for your children's future on earth with this plan for salvation.

The banquet to celebrate the king and queen's new creation in the name of Asia

The Israelite women prepared the banquet with kosher food, curry, goat, rice and beans and other spices for the banquet. King Belhadassah was in his chamber, getting ready for the banquet.

He heard a knock on the door and said: who is it? They said they were the queen eunuchs they came to bring his royal clothing the queen wants him to wear for the banquet. Bel opened the door. The men rushed inside and covered his head and stabbed Bel and left him bleeding on the floor and escaped at the secret exit.

It is better to dwell in a corner of a house than in a palace Pro.21:9

All the guests were waiting for the king and queen to come to take their places on the throne. The queen came and sat down waiting for King Bel. One of the guests gave a speech and said: let us be joyful and celebrate and give Queen Hadassah praise for her new creation of Asians, who are as beautiful as our queen, to be her peculiar people on earth, and to hear the wisdom of our king for his plan for the victory over death.

The old commander who witnessed the slaying of the sons of CHRIST in Adam said: what is faith? My brothers, there is no peace on earth for shedding blood of Hebrews. A giant stood up and said: we are all brothers in the same nature with different Hebrew mothers. We are born to put this faith to the test by strength and not weakness. The devils, God and his father failed the test and they are no more on earth to establish this victory for the earth through faith.

Another giant said: we have two Hebrews left on earth and they are still alive through faith. Our mother died giving birth so faith is elusive in life and death. Our King Bel is a prophet and we should give him a chance to explain to us this faith. I give praise to our Queen Hadassah, whose mother is my mother's sister, and her son the king has a new plan for the earth through faith.

Another giant said: let us celebrate with our queen and King Bel, who can establish the peace. Our giants are now in multitudes on earth and we get no respect for our strength, and allow others to rule over us. Unless there is a common solution by our prophet king our youth are restless and there will be much blood shed on earth if we don't have a new plan for the earth.

After much discussion and praise for Queen Hadassah, the trumpet was blown for the king to set his plan for peace through faith on earth before the guests. There was much coughing and sipping wine, waiting for King Bel to come and everyone was looking at Queen Hadassah.

She got up and went to Bel's chambers to see what was taking him so long. When she entered the chamber she saw Bel lying on the floor dead. She fell on his body with tears, screaming: how can this evil come on my wise son?

Shouting: Treason! Treason! she tore the clothes off her body and was beating on her breast. My king! My king, bone of my bone, flesh of my flesh, who did this to you? Now the war begins.

It is better to dwell in the wilderness than with a contentious angry woman **Pro.21:19**
The kings of Mankind rushed inside. They heard her screaming: My Bel! My Bel! and beginning to curse God for taking Bel from her. Is this the way you repay me for making you a wise son and brother who has faith? Mt.22:21

If a man lies with his daughter, both shall die Lev.18:15

Hadassah began to scream: I cannot endure to see this death of my son. He is my joy, she cried, and sorrow has come. I have no wish to live but to destroy those who killed my king. She embalmed Bel's body and put it in the tower next to Judah's body.

The two gods Seth and Belial

They both were smitten by desire. Hadassah was not aware of this, as they were houseboys she trained for her pleasure.

As soon as the cock crowed in the morning they would wake up. They both came quietly to her room to see what scraps they could find under the table to eat. They began to argue with each other: it's my turn to bath the queen. Hadassah shouted: be quiet! I'm trying to sleep!

She said to Belial: you will wash and soap my body when I get up, and Seth will massage me with oil. Shut the door and leave my chambers. They did as she bade them.

After she had her bath with fragrant soaps, she lay on the altar of Judah. Seth began to massage her with her favourite stimulating oils. This was too much for Belial, and he joined Seth in massaging her and he began to get excited as the heat of the oils was taking effect.

Belial said: O Queen, if you suck salt I will tell thee who killed King Bel! She said: I'll have your salt like a thirsty bitch, but I would not like you to commit this sin on the altar.

The spirit that is in thee perverted thee like pestilence and wants to suck. Has my beautiful body beguiled thee with base passion? Have you no fear of me? Belial said: O Queen, I want to be the first.

If you want to be the first houseboy to suck on the altar of Judah, you must first tell me who slew Bel.

If you don't tell me the truth, the spirit Israel from King Judah will come and will make an end of thee for your malicious passion with the mother of Mankind.

Seth said: O Queen, if you let me suck salt I will tell thee who killed King Bel. She said: Seth tell me first and you can, to make Belial jealous because he kept the secret from me.

Seth said: O my queen, while we were in the passage waiting for King Bel to come and give his speech, we saw two Israelites with masks running away and escaping through the secret exit.

Hadassah screamed: CONSPIRACY! CONSPIRACY!!! The guards rushed inside and she told the guards: hold these two for conspiracy for killing my Bel. Put their hands in the basket with vipers and don't let them go until they are dead.

They were jealous and conspired with the Israelites to let them in the palace to kill King Bel. He was king of the earth.

Hadassah told the guards to get the workmen to gather much wood and pile it in the palace yard for a burnt offering to God.

She took her chariot and went to invite the councillors in Babylon, Israelite chiefs in the synagogue, and other honourable men who delighted in her beauty, to come to the palace to witness the Passover.

Thou shall not bear false witness

The guards went to the harem and brought out Tamuze, ex-queen of Babylon, and they tied her to the logs of wood. They brought a false witness forward and he said: I recognise this woman with the two men who escaped being concealed by a mask.

They asked Tamah if she had anything to say. Tamuze answered: it is all lies. I don't know anything about masked men. The crowd shouted: remove her veil so we can see her. When they removed her veil they saw how old she looked, she who was once beautiful, tied to a log, stripped naked.

Another false witness came forward and said: we were in the palace and saw these Israelites and we hid to see what they were going to do. After they came from the chamber of King Bel they began to run, but we could not hold them; they were too strong for us. This, we testify.

They asked Tamuze: what have you got to say about this testimony? She said: I am free born and no god can judge me and condemn me to death if I've done nothing wrong. Your mind is closed to the truth, and future generations will tell.

The crowd shouted: thou be of ancient days. Now the sins of your past have come unto thee. Thou hast conspired to slay innocent King Bel in his palace, and King Judah his father died with disease because of your witchcraft and jealousy of Queen Hadassah who rules over thee.

Tamuze said: your Queen Hadassah is false and has gathered false witnesses against me. Behold, if I must die it will be for doing nothing. I did no such thing in conspiracy with a man who killed King Bel. Her witnesses were maliciously invented. These charges against me are because Hadassah hates my mother and me. She is like her father, who is a murderer and spilled blood on earth.

The pharisees began whispering to each other, and the chief of the pharisees said: let us examine her more closely to know the truth of this spirit Elijah, Israel spoke about before he died. King Judah made Tamuze his queen and is no more our God alive. **Ps.77:13**

The pharisee said: We heard it was Elijah who brought God up in the name of Ammon, so how come his name is Judah? Who gave him this name, so we can record it?

Tamuze looked at the pharisee then said: if he was alive he would tell thee himself, and soon you will be with him to ask him yourself who called him Ammon, or the devils who held me in captivity will tell thee why they called him Judah.

A Seducer said: thou, O Queen Tamuze, art waxen old in wickedness with the devils and King Judah. Thou has sinned and committed abomination a foretime. If this judgment is false as you say and we condemn thee, it is for letting the guilty who sinned go free for making us not righteous and not perfect as the daughters and sons of Adam. You are against your own god; we are his people. Our father's spirit will save us after death.

A pharisee said to the Seducers: are you such fools that you are condemning the mother of God our father without knowing anything about her faith in her spirit Elijah, who has protected these two Hebrews, mother and daughter, from death all these years and know not whence come he, and in what form he operates or his skill to save from death?

These men who killed King Bel belong to a sect with much hate and should be put on trial with them. The crowd shouted: we heard the witnesses against her conspiracy in the palace with hate and envy, because she is no more queen of Babylon.

The two Hebrews are wicked. They have committed sin with ancient devils and they are guilty to death. That is why our father had to hang the chief Adam on a tree and slay all his sons from the face of the earth.

Don't let the witches beguile thee. They are corrupt, hypocrites, burdened with sin. Her desire was to make Israelites to look like her brothers that were killed with children of our beautiful Queen Hadassah of our father Judah who died with disease of the bowels.

I fear if the two women are not put to death, the spirit of Israel will punish us if they don't pass over the kingdom to Queen Hadassah.

The chief of the Seducers said: there is no such spirit as Elijah. We have searched the books of Judah and he has not mentioned this spirit. Maybe it was the key to knowledge he kept to himself as his secret. There is no place for these two women after death. They will go to the other world to suffer for what they did on earth.

They who sow in tears shall reap with joy Eve Ps.126:5

The crowd began to shout: bring out the old witch who made god with the devils. It is because of her the devils disappeared in the quake.

They got sticks and stones in their hands to throw at her, shouting: the motherfucker who made god to go in the heat for making his son with her daughter to make Israelites to kill our King Bel.

Eve came out screaming at the guard: you are twisting my arm! You are hurting me! The crowd rushed at her and began to tear of her sack clothes and tied her back to back with her daughter.

A scribe said: what have you got to say as a testimony for this sin? The devils are no more on earth to ask them who sinned. Some gods say he gave you an apple because you were hungry, to seduce you to make him a god to look like him.

Eve said: I was ignorant like you about sin. God of your father, who you say is your God, passed on his seed to you to sin to death. Neither had faith to stop this sin in the world and you want to pass judgment on me for this accursed seed. If it were I who had seed you would be pure and righteous in holy flesh. **Ps.77:13**

I am free; I am under no law or commandment of ancient devils. Every one of you with sticks and stones and wants to break my bones stand in my flesh and accuse me of sin, and not the devils who passed on his accursed seed on to you. So any of you who has no sin can stone me to death. When the crowd heard what she said they backed off.

Eve went on to say: when each of you depart from the flesh of the sinner, judge Elijah will send you to the devil to ask him why he sinned to make you naked in Hades without the flesh of the sinner to suffer heat and cry for his sin. While you are still in my flesh it's better you repent and have mercy on us.

My body, which you want to set on fire, will be a burnt offering, and a sacrifice for our peace.

This you can write as my testimony for everlasting life in the kingdom. If you want to continue in sin, do not blame me when you leave my flesh, for this is your free choice to be free of the law to death for your peace.

I am free under no law and none of you bastards, who are in my flesh, can judge me. You have no mercy for my daughter or me, who want peace in the world.

The last warning before the Sabbath

The scribe said: Eve, what is your last testimony? Eve said: this is the last testimony of the two of us in your presence so you can repeat it to Mankind in our absence after we Sabbath.

The kingdom from our flesh will be established on earth. While Hadassah lived with me I warned her that Elijah did not spare the devils who sinned earlier, and any god who sins to pass on their accursed seed will end in fire.

Elijah has no favouritism with gods and in dealing with Hadassah and you in the kingdom who gather here to be a witness of the Passover so it will be justified when salvation comes at the appointed time.

Examine yourself while you are still live in the kingdom, and have faith in Elijah. We hope when you depart from the kingdom, you do not fall to be a witness to the Passover.

It may seem to you we are fools. We are weak in body but when we are absent from thee we will live.

Eve said: Hadassah! Elijah has authority to build us up and tear you down. Write this testimony while you stand in my flesh.

Hadassah, I taught you scripture and you turned to a different religion to live by the law to death to create confusion to please the devils with the law to death.

The scripture is not made by Judah but by the Eternal Spirit in the Light who created HIS CHRIST by the Word to continue His holy work for peace, and His CHRIST created His Elijah to serve Him and save His spirits in the kingdoms for the heavens by the Word. **Gen.2:3–4**

You want to Sabbath His people because you are not accepted above. You are jealous and want to kill us to be queen of the earth.

So that the knowledge of everlasting life becomes your secret, you want to do the same as Judah to rule on earth with fear of death.

You are foolish, Hadassah. Judah has bewitched you. You always did what he said under the law to rule as his queen in the palace.

You think he gave you a spirit to work miracles among Mankind on earth; you are of the accursed seed of Judah of god (Cain) of the devils.

Hadassah left her seat and climbed the pile of wood and gave Eve a hard slap on her face and spat in her face and slapped Tamuze and walked back and took her seat.

Eve cried: O CHRIST, you have seen what she has done before your face. Be gracious to me after I Sabbath.

Though the wicked bitch binds me with ropes with our daughter, we will rise to give you thanks, for your way is righteous to fill the kingdom with spirits.

Elijah, Eve cried, the arrogant have smeared me with lies. She has no mercy on us and wants to eliminate us to death.

Elijah, put this arrogant queen to shame for conspiracy before her witnesses, to remove your people from the earth.

CHRIST thundered: be glad, O woman, cry aloud! You will have no labour pains to bear children. She will never share in the inheritance of kingdoms from your flesh and Tamah.

Elijah will call you Zion, and Tamah, Jerusalem, after your bodies are burnt.

PUT PEACE TO THE TEST

The councillors said: there is no need to bring witnesses. The crowd shouted: Queen Hadassah, she is a witch. If you let her live she will corrupt our people with this peace offering and put much division on earth with this doctrine. Put this peace to the test on earth and set fire to them as a burnt of offering to our God.

The scribe said: Tamuze, what is your last testament? She said: I am before thee, tied as a lamb for the slaughter. I gave birth to you bastards who stand in my flesh and want to set my body on fire. After this Sabbath I will truly be free.

Elijah sees and knows all things before it happens. Since I have been held in captivity, one thing led to another. I am free born. I'm a victim of circumstances and want peace from all this drama on earth.

There was a thunder and a voice said: there will be no peace for you while you are in your body. Have faith!

The crowd blocked their ears when they heard the voice in the thunder say, have faith. They began screaming and spitting at both Eve and her daughter, shouting: It's because of these Hebrews we have all this genealogy problem and live in fear of death while they wax to hundreds of years among us. Death doesn't seem to come to them.

The pharisee said: if we burn them to death their spirits will take revenge and will destroy the people in Babylon because the kingdom is Passover to our Queen Hadassah to rule on earth.

The Seducer said: we heard the witnesses say the Great Spirit Elijah will destroy Babylon for killing these two women from the earth. That is why Judah died – to prepare spirits for war for the earth to be king with our queen. There was silence.

Love your neighbour as thy self

Queen Hadassah went up to the logs of wood and looked up at Eve and said: from birth I was cast upon thee by my father Judah, who is dead and not here with me.

I am surrounded by these barbarians that want to Sabbath. I am a worm, scorned and despised and not accepted to go above, just like my father, and all who are here are angry and bitter with hate. I am what I am and all the families of the earth will remember thee being good to Hadassah. My sins have multiplied from your one god who sinned, and his son made me what I am – a harlot to death.

Daughter rises up against the mother of her father Ps.76:2; Ps.48:11–12; Mic7:6

Queen Hadassah circled around the pile of wood three times, in deep thought. All eyes were upon her and she stopped and looked up at Tamuze and said: my father's sin with thee has multiplied my sin with him to make the people on earth. I am burdened with much sin and ashamed, just like you. One of the devils raped my mother's mother, who is your sister. God (Cain) did the same and raped thee and made my father.

You married your god under the law and he became your king. I did the same and married my son and made him my king. We both committed abomination with our gods. My god Bel had faith and died. Your god Judah had no faith because of his father's wickedness with the devils to be a king on earth.

I'm a spirit in the nature of Judah's wickedness. I have committed more sin on earth than you and have more majesty than even the devils that are no more on earth, or even your god or my god, King Bel, was killed in conspiracy. I deserve to be queen of the earth.

A BABY GOD LEFT IN THE BUSH MAKES HIS MOTHER ASHAMED Pro.29:15; Ex.3:2–4 Acts.7:35; Ja.5:6; Ps.22:23; Jude.24; Mt.18:15

My father (Judah) and I, before he died, were compatible in wickedness. He ruled with anger and hate to be born in your flesh. It's not our fault we were born through wickedness. Through our wicked nature multitudes of spirits from his seed will multiply kingdoms for salvation for Elijah and CHRIST to create immortal spirits with everlasting life that is accepted above. From our wickedness Elijah will give you children from the best of kingdoms from your flesh, in the time of salvation for creation of spirits with everlasting life in the light.

Now my children are fatherless and I am their queen, a widow. I deserve to be queen among my people on earth to death, since we are not accepted above. I am the mother of all spirits on earth and committed incest for them. **Rev.17:5**

Tamuze said: Hadassah, you and Judah had a choice for peace. You are hard-headed like your father and want to make a name for yourself. The devil did the same in Heaven and was cast down to earth. Judah did the same and tried to make a name for himself and became king. They had a choice for peace but they had no faith, even god (Cain).

Elijah is very strict with those who have no faith. Elijah removed the devils from the earth. Also god (Cain) ,Judah's father, had no faith in my father, who offered him peace.

You are a queen and you should use your power to do good for your children on earth to have a choice for peace for Elijah to save them and not end up like the devils, god (Cain) and Judah, to fall on judgment day for having no faith.

Elijah taught your father Judah scriptures and also my mother Eve, who you have tied together with me on logs of wood before your witness on earth to make a name for yourself so it be known you set my body and my mother Eve on fire as your Passover.

Tamuze said to Queen Hadassah: I left the palace when I knew Judah was my first god. Neither of us were compatible. I warned him I had no desire to add to my shame. To make Israelites was not righteous in my flesh because of his seed.

Since I left my father and mother's house I have been held in captivity, first by the devils under the oath and then by Judah. He forced me to be his queen under the law for peace. I had faith in Elijah to save me from his violence and hate.

Up to this minute you have no mercy on my mother or me to set us free, just like your father who died. Judah became a foolish god (**Pro.10:1**) of his mother and put fear in Mankind to worship him as a god. He is stupid to challenge Elijah for the earth with his godly spirits.

He interbred your children with my children. They are all from the same seed. There are none good from this accursed seed. Their spirits are the same as yours, just as you and him hate to be in my flesh and are angry because you are not accepted above.

The same way, the spirits of gods in Mankind and Israelites will hate us for making them to live in the kingdom to fall after death. Judah himself said it and repented for making spirits from his seed (**Gen6.4–7**), and you will imitate his way after his death.

Hadassah got angry and went on the pile of wood and gave Tamuze a slap on the cheek and said: if you and my grandmother (Eve) worship me I'll set you free, and she spat in her face. **Lk.6:29**

Tamuze said: as you well said, there can be only one queen upon the earth. When I will be queen the world will be in the Light. But I shall not bow to thee. You shall fall in the rubble of Babylon for wanting to be queen of the earth and will lick the dust of the feet of Elijah if you set this log on fire to burn our bodies to death. Tell these scribes put this in their doctrine after our bodies are burnt to death.

Hadassah sits as queen of the whole earth Rev.17:5; Lev.20:14; Ps47.11

Hadassah returned and sat. All eyes were on her and there was silence. She called the scribe and said: did you write all what she said? He bowed and said: yes, Your Majesty. Hadassah said: when you write your doctrine don't mention Elijah. Let his name be a mist.

Hadassah then called the pharisee and Seducer and said: you are witness to this Passover and all the other pharisees present desire this Sabbath to Passover the kingdom to your queen to rule all on earth so they don't blame us after for killing the mother of our gods. Queen Hadassah said: before you will blame me after. Do what is in your heart to them. The crowd shouted: let them be burnt to death according to the law. Their blood shall be on gods.

The crowd shouted: O Queen, it is you who laboured to make us. You deserve to be our queen on earth. We are all your children and subjects on earth.

The crowd shouted: the spirit of God Israel will save our queen. Set fire to the wood, so the Passover is remembered from our generation of children to tell their children of the day the Hebrews disappeared from the earth to Passover the kingdom to our queen the goddess of fertility.

Call Elijah in the day of trouble Ps.50:15

They put torches of fire to the wood and it began to smoke. The wood began to fire slowly with flames. Eve and Tamuze began to scream: Elijah! Elijah! Save our spirits, and suddenly there was one big flame of fire. The heat was intense and the crowd backed off.

The sacrifice to death Ps.50:5; Is.51:5

As their spirits left their bodies, Elijah held their spirits in the flames. A wind came unto the flames and it turned into a great light going upwards, and the people kept looking at the flames until it disappeared from sight and they were in the winds and Elijah took them to Whykibully, a mountain island far off, a paradise island where there is everything exotic. Many streams and rivers, lakes and waterfalls, hot springs and exotic fruits to eat. A paradise on earth for spiritual healing and to purify them in the thermal springs.

The mystery hid is given to the reader. Their spirits cannot die, and death had no claim on their spirits. Their bodies were the sacrifice to death so they could live by the spirit in the Light.

The Book of Life Ps.50:3.
Out of fire comes perfect beauty

Zion and Jerusalem, now immortal spirits without flesh, looked up to Heaven and gave thanks to CHRIST on HIS throne, and the book was opened and they saw lightning flashing in the sky and the writing: MY ZION FOR EVER. The leaves on the trees on earth were clapping. CHRIST thundered: Hail Elijah! Thanks for saving our queens.

144,000 brothers and sisters in the heavens sang: Hallelujah, Elijah. And all angels looked at Elijah on earth and He spoke the Word: Tamah is my Jerusalem, the queen of the earth, and there was thunder and lightning and rain on earth to bless Zion and Jerusalem with her king Elijah for ever.

The perfect beauty of CHRIST Ps.50:2

Queen Zion said: O Elijah, thanks be to you. You have made me beautiful. You know me very well and protected me and saved me. I am in your hands till salvation comes, to be with my CHRIST.

Jerusalem said: Elijah, thanks be to you. You have made me your beautiful Jerusalem by the Word from your mouth. You have saved me. You saw my body was polluted and burdened with sin under the oath and the law. There is none born that is good. They are all corrupt like their father, with much confusion and no faith.

You protected me and had patience with me while I lived under the law. It is excellent and wonderful for me to see my spirit in the presence of your spirit. There is no wickedness in me. I want to live your way in peace.

Jerusalem said to Elijah: I am overwhelmed. I survived this dreadful Sabbath to pass over to life everlasting. I was like a dove flying in the stormy wind to this island from the violence and oppression in captivity in Babylon to be with you in the spirit.

Thou hast done a great thing on earth, saving all the 144,000 spirits of my father's seed When CHRIST comes in the time of salvation, He will cast out spirits of gods from my flesh for the final Passover in the kingdoms for creation of immortal spirits with everlasting life in the name of CHRIST in this world.

May the Tower of Babel fall on my enemy in Babylon for not having mercy on your people on earth to be with her king after death. Elijah, you had mercy and saved me. I was born to be your queen on the earth as long as there is Light in the world.

The promise to Jerusalem Gal.4:23,28; Ro.4:13; Eph.1:13; Heb.6:12; Deut.28:9

Elijah! All my mother's children are in Heaven except for me on earth, and I have no children with spirits in the Light. Will you give me a son to pass on his seed in righteousness so I can have children by your Word, to continue on earth?

Elijah replied: Jerusalem, stand before Me. You are perfect. I will give thee a son with an everlasting spirit with seed in creation that will be exceedingly fruitful in your flesh to be with you and your King Elijah at the appointed time when it will please you most on earth, and you will be satisfied with him.

The knowledge of spiritual life Gen.1:14

Elijah explained: Now we are spirits. No spirits of God in their humanity can see a spirit while they are living in the kingdom from your flesh. They have a choice to rest in peace or fall after to death if they have no faith in me.

The process of creation will begin by the Word to CHRIST, who will set the time to establish kingdoms from your flesh in salvation from all nations on earth. You and Zion are like all angels in Heaven. Flames have devoured your body. Your sin in the flesh is written off. your spirit did not sin. You are no more Eve the body, but the spirit Zion. neither are you, Tamah Tamuze, queen of Babylon, but spirit Jerusalem.

When spirits of gods depart from the kingdom they are godly spirits and they will be removed from the earth and held in captivity. The same will be done to them as they held you and Zion in captivity to death while you were in your body.

Sanctification in flesh

Jerusalem, Elijah said, the time will come when your spirit will have to sanctify in any kingdom from your flesh till you resurrect to see salvation to give you children in kingdoms through CHRIST when I say the Word.

The trinity. The Eternal with the Word CHRIST with the Word and Elijah with the Word

As you well know, the kingdom on its own cannot bear spirits to have heavenly existence. You are a spirit without flesh so the body has to sanctify to have your spirit to bear a spirit with your immortal spirit by the WORD for everlasting life through CHRIST, to give you the promised son in the same principle of creation.

CHRIST created in Adam with the Word to do the same in creation as our Eternal Holy Spiritual Father, by the WORD CHRIST created HIS Elijah by the Word to save HIS immortal spirits and to establish the kingdom through faith by the Word.

The Eternal Holy Spiritual Father, CHRIST and Elijah all by the Word Is.50:16

The wicked god had no vision Pro.29:17–18.

The Seducer told the pharisee: God who you worship perished by the law, and many who follow the king of Babylon with his law will fall when judgment comes in Babylon for this Sabbath.

The prophecy Mt.25:27; Dan.9:13; Dan.11:7

God slew Abel. His spirit Jesus will come at the appointed time and sanctify in the same body with Jerusalem to cast out the spirit Israel son of god to tell the world the truth of what Israel the spirit of God/Judah did not want the people on earth to know what he did to Jerusalem when she was human and the choice the spirits of gods have to be saved after death.

Jerusalem will join Elijah and she will be His queen in the end time.

Kingdoms from the flesh of Jerusalem shall have new spirits of creation to continue on earth. When Elijah prophesied this to King Bel of Hadassah, he was silent for words.

It is written: We pray to God of god who made us to give us understanding of Elijah, for His way is righteousness and His Word does the work in salvation to save the kingdoms of the people with the law on earth to have peace.

To those who are concerned of the future

Pray to Elijah to give you skill and understanding concerning faith to save your spirit after through faith. Spirits from the seed of gods need to change their attitude and perception, and face the reality of their nature, they cannot be born again and should prepare their kingdom for salvation for the only saviour Elijah for their spirits to rest in peace or fall after judgment.

Elijah, Zion, Jerusalem

Elijah spoke to Zion and Jerusalem of His way to put the CHRIST plan in order by the Word for world peace according to the New Testament to make the covenant between the ETERNAL and the devils obsolete for ever for violating the peace by making a god in the world to sin to death.

The debate after the Sabbath of Zion's and jerusalem's bodies. The kingdom went to all mingled people by force Jer.25:20

Queen Hadassah had to a meeting between the pharisees and the Seducers in the palace to discuss the plan for the earth according to the law. She said: I have multiplied the Israelites on earth, to be my ministers in the law (**Jer.33:22**). The pharisee said: our God has made us to be his ministers of the law on earth.

The accursed seed has mingled with holy people Esra.9:2; Ro. 15;25

The seducer said to the pharisee: the law is carnal. I will minister to spirits in the kingdom with our lust so they can do the same.

The law made nothing perfect Heb.7:22; 2.Cor:9, 10; Ro.15:16; Gal.3:5

The Seducer said to the pharisee: Elijah is strict when it comes to the flesh of Eve for CHRIST to create spirits to eternal life in multitudes of kingdoms on the earth after He cast out multitudes of spirits out of the flesh of Zion and Jerusalem in the nations.

A perverse spirit hath entered the body of the pharisee, among the people of CHRIST Is.19:14; Jer.33:21; Ps.104:4; Ki.8:27; Eph.4:12

The pharisee asked the Seducer: what will happen to the spirits from your seed? We heard spirits will be in flames of fire to make the covenant obsolete to establish the New Testament for peace in the kingdom.

The Seducer said to the pharisee: from a godly spirit after death in the body of a pharisee, we heard it is in the kingdom that CHRIST will see spirits of gods face to face and I fear when He cast us out to for judgment.

The Old Covenant is becoming obsolete Heb.8:13; Jer.31:31–34; Phil 1;15; 1.Pet.2:4

The pharisee said: our godly spirit will preach through the mouith of mankind that God is a Lord in deceit. They will preach God is a jealous god and envy the spirits of Mankind, an Israelite, for having a choice to fall like him for having no faith for peace.

Act.17:30; Eph.4:18; 2.Pet.2;15; 1Pet.1;14

The seducer said: there will be a time the people in the future generations will get bored by the law and religion and will want to have knowledge of the New Testament. They will realize God can't save them even if they pray to him. and want to know the truth and will not fear him and stop worshipping when they suffer misery and get no help.

The pharisee said: all the spiris of gods in the kingdoms are ignorant of the truth while they live the kingdom. After death they will fight war in the kingdom to destroy the hope for salvation.

The seducer said: we will seduce them to fuck like the vagabond god in Hades to lose faith to fall after death. They will be foolish like us who live by the law. Let us change the name God to Lord while there is time. **Ps.72:22; 1.Cor.14:38**

The pharisee said: The spirit Jerusalem was not born ignorant. Elijah saved her and took her spirit to a far-off island with Zion. **Job.22:30** They are holy spirits whose bodies we Sabbathed to death.

The Seducer said to the pharisee: do you think Elijah will return to Babylon to take revenge for burning their bodies in fire? He had power to save the spirits in the fire to give them the victory over Queen Hadassah. We will have no peace if Elijah returns. **Rev.14:11**

The kingdom shall come to Jerusalem (Mic.4:8) and she will be satisfied Ps.48:11

The seducer said: our God loved Hadassah, but I have a feeling Zion's and Jerusalem's spirit will return to tell the world that Queen Hadassah burnt their bodies to death and the truth will be known that it is we who destroyed the Hebrews from the earth.

I set before you a blessing and a curse Deut.11:26

The pharisee said: the spirits of our people are subject to our vanity, disorder, for war and destruction, and will continue on earth until they disappear like vapour when CHRIST returns to inherit kingdoms from Jerusalem's flesh in salvation. The spirits through their ignorance of scriptures will fall to our God for his foolishness in Hades passing his seed to our children with his anger. **Job.11:12**

O sons of God, how long shall ye love vanity? Ps.4:20; Mal.3:14; Eph.5:6; Ex:20

The seducer said: the prophet Malachi said, many will come to the conclusion that it is vain to serve God and should not let any spirit deceive them with vanity as they shall not have the name of CHRIST. Vain worship is not profitable and will lead spirits to spiritual death and sorrows.

In multitudes of dreams there are vanities Eccl.15:7; Ro13.4

The pharisee said: do you think the scripture says things in vain? For when salvation comes, God has not the Word to do the work in salvation. Our arrogance is according to the law of God to live to spiritual death.

The Seducer said: Elijah is the miracle worker of CHRIST. Judah said, before he died it is Elijah that baptizes spirits without faith in fire. I fear multitudes who seduce and tempt others like us will fall and there will be much torment, and they will be terrified by angry devils blaming us for their fall in the fire of the sun. **Is.24:13–19**

The pharisee said: I am amazed the power Elijah has with the Word. The wind is at his command, thundering, earthquakes so great and clouds, violent storms, fire and desolation. Spirits stumble and are in fear of Him. **Eph.1:19; Lk.9:43**

The Seducer said: O Queen Hadassah, what shall we do if we fall? Where can we hide from the devils? We have heard the queens dreamed. They said there is no space and water is limited. Multitudes of spirits will be crying of thirst in the heat and blame us for your new creation of your beautiful people and want to pluck out our eyes in the heat for deceiving them while they were on the earth.

Queen Hadassah said: let us celebrate, my beautiful people, this Pentecost and not think of this death. It is like a dream. I am queen of the earth in life and in death. Let us prepare to celebrate Pentecost so it will be the biggest celebration to be well remembered from generation to generation to know we tested Elijah to see if he can destroy Queen Hadassah of Babylon, with her people.

Elijah said to Zion and Jerusalem: I have to leave you both on the island. Enjoy the peace and purify yourselves with thermal springs from the earth. Eat as much fruit till I return. There are no godly spirits here to disturb your peace.

The time of Pentecost. Time of provocation against Elijah

Many people from all nations speaking in different languages were heading for Babylon to pay their respects to King Bel's and Judah's bodies, mummified in the Tower of Babel.

Observation of the new moon

People from all nations came to celebrate the Sabbath eliminating all the holy people from the earth and giving praise to Queen Hadassah for the Passover on earth.

Hadassah sat in the tower and there was a long queue waiting to bow to her majesty dressed in purple and scarlet and gilded with precious stones and pearls around her neck and with the disk of the moon between horns on her head.

The doom of the great whore Rev.17:1–2; Rev.17:15

The inhabitants became beguiled by her beauty, crying: O queen of fertility, Goddess of the earth, God bless you with all the people of the earth. He went to prepare a place for us after death. O Queen, there is no one so lucky as you on earth. Live for ever, like the stars.

Elijah is slow to act Pro.26:16

The people began to celebrate the Sabbath of the holy people of CHRIST. Others celebrated the Passover of the earth to Hadassah, queen of fertility, who made all the people on earth with Judah, our God.

Celebrating the first Pentecost

The square of the Tower of Babel was full of people, with little space to move. All over Babylon there was music, dancing, trumpeters, skilled artisans, flame blowers, shouting: O queen of fertility, furnish the heavens with your people on earth. O spirit of god, prepare a place for us after death.

The first judgment of Elijah is put to the test Pro.26:16;Rev 16.18; Rev18.23

Slowly the moon began to go in dark clouds and it was dark. There was a loud thundering noise that was never heard in that generation, followed by flashes of lighting one after the other, followed by thunder. Balls of fire began to fall on the crowds and a stampede began, with people crying: O God! O God! Save our queen and us. Don't hurt your people on earth.

Balls of fire came from the sky, falling on the houses, and fire began to spread from house to house by a wind. The people were running here and there, trying to squeeze their way out to get away from the buildings on fire.

The people were trapped with fire in the exits. Everyone for themselves, looking for gaps to escape. The wind blew the flames in all directions and Babylon was on fire.

There were tremors on earth and The Babel Tower began to sway to and fro. The bricks began to loosen up and fall on the people. They began to cry: O God! O God, save your people! There was a stampede to try to get out of the tower. Hadassah began crying: O God, save me from Elijah.

The earth quaked and split the city of Babylon wide and deep, and the Tower of Babel came crashing down in the depths of the quake, with Hadassah and the people imbedded in the rubble like a grave covered with bodies to death.

Those who managed to escape, when they looked back could only see fire and smoke. All the wealth in Babylon was encased in the rubble. The Pentecost ended in desolation beyond repair. Merchants and rulers got caught in the fall of the Pentecost in Babylon.

Swift judgment, much sorrow in Pentecost instead of joy Rev.15:3–4; Rev.14:13

After the fall of Babylon the wind brought much clapping and voices from Heaven: Hail Elijah! Just and true are your ways, thou king with

Jerusalem. Blessed are the spirits of their burnt bodies now they may have peace and rest.

Your judgment is justified and you have judged the harlot of the earth, who corrupted the earth with her father's spilling the blood of the sons of CHRIST on earth.

Make the next judgment be worse than the fall of Babylon before salvation comes on kingdoms. Make all her spirits be in a place where there is no water to drink. Hail Elijah, you are king in the kingdom to do holy work, in the presence of CHRIST to put the world in the Light by the Word.

The capture of godly spirits after the Pentecost Ps.77:18–19

The third day after the crash of Babylon, the sun began to shine brightly. The spirits of Hadassah and all that were dead in Babylon began to come through the rubble and were pulled by the sun like dust to a magnet. Then the whirlwind came and took the spirits away to fall in the mouth of the waters to journey down to the gates of Hades for a thousand years in captivity.

Judah called mighty God. His spirit name is Israel Ps.53:1–4, 7

Hadassah became corrupt, like Judah, for power. With hate and Jealousy she burnt the bodies of Eve and Tamuze to rule as queen of the earth.

The book of the spirits of death

The Book of the Dead was opened and the goddess in Hades took the names of the spirits that entered the gates in Hell that were judged by Elijah for trespassing in holy flesh without faith.

After having their names taken, they were cast in the fire for their first baptism in the heat.

The thing that was not yet done by the Word is established in judgment for trespassing in holy flesh and shedding blood on earth.

Devil kings with masks

Devil with mask of fox

Judah with daughter

King Judah II

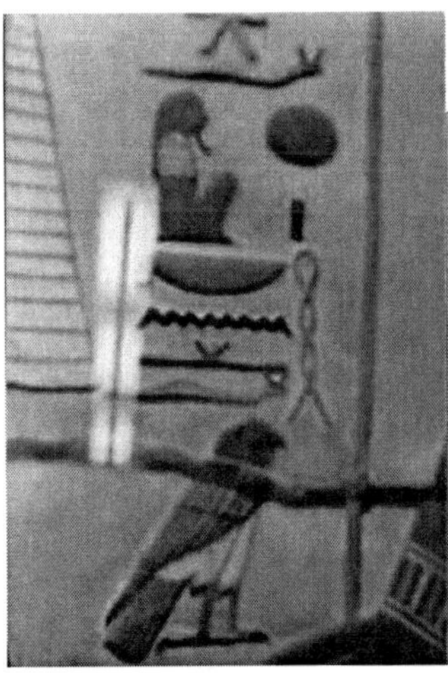

Queen of babylon

Chapter 3

Many Generations later after the fall of Babylon

Giants after the fall of Babylon

The Anakin giants were protectors of the Israelites of Judah who worshipped God. They were trained by Judah to do battle. The Anakins got pleasure in squeezing their opponents to death. After the fall of Babylon they wanted to be the kings of the earth. Because of their great strength they became territorial and the strongest became king of their nation.

The people on earth began to run away from them and the population of the earth began to spread out to distant lands.

The Rephaim giants were aligned with Mankind and were against the Israelites and began populating the earth faster than the Anakins. Suddenly there were all sorts of giants on earth, mixing and mingling with the Nephelim giants. Through them came the giants called Emmins, Ogs and Golieth, and they began fighting with the Anakins to capture the Israelites who wanted to live by the law of their God Judah to death.

Noah was an Israelite pharisee and began to protest against the violence on earth, seeing much fighting on earth and the death of Israelites and their children in the streets and his people living in fear and insults.

Noah began having dreams of the end that was about to come, and he began warning the people to put a stop of the overspreading of abomination with his Israelite people and spilling their blood.

The giants began going with the daughters of Israelites and they were making children for the giants.

Their sons were giants on the earth and every imagination of their thoughts and heart was to do evil continuously like the giant devils that captured and took Israelite women to be their wives to pass on the accursed seed of giants in the kingdom.

The earth was corrupt, filled with violence, and there was no order and constant warfare. Noah began to protest and warn the people living in fear that the end was coming to his people, and condemned everyone on earth that was attacking his people, saying that what they were doing was not righteous.

The pharisees began to get agitated with Noah and told him: everyone is accountable to God and should observe the law.

THEY ARE ALL TOGETHER BECOME FILTHY. THERE ARE NONE THAT DOETH GOOD Ps.14:3; Amos.8:2

Noah began to have dreams and saw in the dream his people were crying and the women of his people were raped and were pregnant with giant children. He was seeing children born crying without their mothers, who were dead giving birth

Noah saw in the dream that the spirits of the women after giving birth were crying in flames. Then he heard a voice in the dream saying: every valley will be filled and every mountain will be covered to prepare the way forward to establish the kingdom.

The voice began saying: the pharisees and seducers have followed the shameful way of your fathers to bring the scripture in dispute, with doctrines they made up to suit themselves, and it will mislead many to Hades. Noah got up confused.

Zion and Jerusalem were on the island of Whykibully, far away from all this violence on earth, enjoying the peace and having rest.

After the fall of Babylon there was plenty of food everywhere in the nations. After many generations there was famine and shortage of bread from nation to nation.

Draught set in the nations on earth. The heat began to crack the earth. Water shortages and the drying up of rivers and streams brought food shortages, hunger and disease and everyone was blaming each other. Noah began to tell the people it is because of the abomination with his people and violence and bloodshed on earth they are punished, and the end is near.

Noah took his stool and stood on the street corners, preaching peace. Secretly he began praying to the spirit Elijah that saved the mother of God of his father from the den of lions to give him understanding of all the things that were going wrong since the fall of Babylon.

Noah began praying: O spirit Elijah, my people are perishing and their children are sold as slaves to live in bondage and they blame Israelites for all their troubles on earth with the law of Judah.

They make a mockery about our children's noses. They call us unicorns. The gentiles say it is because we burned our holy mother that there is no bread and water in the nations.

O Great Spirit Elijah, help us! We are greatly weakened. Forgive our sins. For our mother's sake spare us from death on earth.

The people ask us: where is our God? Can he feed us with food in the famine? Let him come and take vengeance for shedding the blood of our people. If he is a God, tell him to save his people in this famine and put bread on our table. There is no bread because of death of our queen, in Babylon.

O Great Spirit Elijah, save us so we can be a flock to give you praise for ever. That night Noah had a vision. Elijah said: I heard your supplication. I will come to sanctify in thee to be in the midst of the people. My spirit will be in your body.

In the day I will come and sanctify. Your unclean spirit shall be cast out of the flesh of your mother and your spirit shall have eternal rest and your kingdom will have life with my spirit in the presence of your people. **Ps.16:8–11; Essek.14:17–18; Essek.14:16**

I have showed thee, Noah, what is good and what is required of thee. If you want mercy, have faith and humble yourself and your kingdom will be justified and I'll speak through your mouth as a man and shall use your name. **Mic.6:8**

Your mother was a Hebrew, your father was Ammon, called Judah, who your people worship as God **Essek.16:3–45**

The spirits in this generation from the seed of God your father have become violent and deceitful for killing and shedding blood on earth. The kingdom has become corrupt in the face of CHRIST in Heaven. There is no spirit righteous from the accursed seed among your people. Jerusalem's spirit has departed from her flesh because of deceit by your ancestors in Babylon. Noah cried: woe is on to me, O Great Spirit Elijah. The pharisees may do evil and strangle me to death if they know I ask you for help.

Noah said: O Elijah, let it be as you say. Let your spirit be in the kingdom of Noah and let my spirit rest in peace after you sanctify. **Ps.128:1**

Save kingdoms of my people to have a spirit in the Light like yours. **Ja.1:17–18**

Elijah said: it will be so according to the New Testament. Your people have no understanding of the way to eternal life and have turned the opposite way and are corrupt in religion to suit themselves with the law to death.

Meanwhile back in Heaven.

The tabernacle in Heaven

Outside the tabernacle were two massive statues built of gold – Zion and Jerusalem, facing each other.

Inside was the mercy seat made of gold with the word faith engraved with diamonds in front the two seats which the ETERNAL HOLY SPIRIT in the LIGHT created before the ancient devils for His CHRIST and Zion to rule and have dominion over the whole world, and to continue the work in creation of angels and holy spirits in the Light with a New Testament to make the covenant with devils obsolete if the devils made a god with His creation and put the whole world in the Light by the WORD after HE rested. **Gen.2;1.3**

In the tabernacle was the testimony of what HIS CHRIST will do and a warning to all devils that if they made a god in the world HIS CHRIST will create Elijah with the word to judge them and their spirits if they had no faith in him to the everlasting fire.

The Eternal Holy Father of Light testified before ancient angels and devils that when HIS CHRIST comes into the world it is to create new spirits to be angels in the Light for all worlds by the Word.

The Eternal testified that HIS CHRIST would have FAITH in Him with the Word to execute judgment on the ancient devils of darkness if they made gods from their seed; it is a sin to death.

The Eternal testified HIS CHRIST would sit on HIS throne in Heaven and His Elijah would be king to execute judgment on devils and their godly spirits who have no faith in him to save them for their peace in the world.

The feast in the tabernacle

Angels in the Light from all worlds began their journey to congregate and worship the Eternal and CHRIST resurrected from the earth by Elijah with the word.

Before the celebration they went to pass their respect and praise CHRIST for capturing the devils that were tormenting them with temptation to make a god for them while they were in Heaven, and asked when it would be possible to meet HIS Elijah, who saved all His angels on earth from devils.

Jesus and his brother were on a project where all devils and godly spirits would be for eternity for disobedience.

CHRIST called for Archangel Michael and he said: Jesus is on a project with the Alfa of the sun. Take the fastest wind and tell him I want to see him urgently.

Jesus arrived and went to see his father. He said: my father, You asked for me! CHRIST said: how is this project coming on? Jesus answered: it's going according to the plan, my father. CHRIST said: my son, you are always here with me. There is much violence on earth. I want you to take your horse Genesis and My horse Faith. Harness them with your horses and catch the whirlwind to earth. Wait in a pillar of clouds and send the chariot of horses to Elijah in Whykibully Island and bring Him up for the feast to celebrate and worship our Eternal Father for thanksgiving.

While Elijah was speaking to Zion and Jerusalem, Zion looked up and said: Elijah! Jesus has sent a chariot of horses for thee to go upon and celebrate the feast in Heaven.

Genesis and Faith and the other horses were coming towards them on the island in the wind. Elijah said: Jerusalem, what will you do after I'm taken up from thee?

Jerusalem requests to have a son

Jerusalem said: I'll pray for when you return to give me a son with my spirit through CHRIST my father by the Word to give us children in perfection in my flesh on earth to go up to be with my brothers and sisters and my father CHRIST.

The promise by Elijah

Elijah said: I promise it will be so in due time. Tarry here. When I get back I'll be in your flesh with the Word and you will be unto me in the sanctum.

Zion and Jerusalem and Elijah were waiting for the chariot, waving their hands to Jesus. The horses stopped short of landing on earth. They hugged and kissed. Elijah got inside the chariot and the wind came and the chariot of horses was taken up to the clouds to meet Jesus.

Jerusalem cried: Elijah! Elijah! Tell my father and Jesus and all my brothers and sisters and the Eternal that we love them, and to pray for us.

Zion and Jerusalem had to tarry on the island until Elijah returned. They purified themselves in the thermal springs and clear pools of water. They ate fresh exotic fruits and enjoyed the peace away from the wickedness of the strangers on earth.

The news went around the world's TVs and satellite systems that Jesus went to the earth to bring up Elijah to celebrate and worship the Eternal. The angels lined up the streets leading to the tabernacle to see Elijah, who resurrected His CHRIST from earth to the throne to rule the world and to establish the kingdoms on earth.

The angels began to chant: CHRIST! CHRIST! Blessed is the son of our Eternal Father. We give you praise for creating your son Elijah, who captured the devils and sent them to Hades to await the final judgment.

Ancient angels had their tambourines, and in national costumes from other worlds, began dancing with joy. beautiful angels of CHRIST, dressed with diamonds, took their seats in the tabernacle.

There was much praise and great excitement. The testimony of the Eternal Holy Father was fulfilled. HIS CHRIST was on the throne of the world and HIS Elijah, created by the Word as his first SON in the kingdom for salvation after the devils strangled their god.

Elijah's first journey to Heaven

Jesus and Elijah arrived by the whirlwind and the chariot of horses began going through the crowd of angels. They began to chant: Hallelujah Elijah! Hallelujah Elijah! Reign in the kingdom as king.

Let us rejoice and give CHRIST praise. HIS Zion is making herself ready on earth to be HIS queen of the universe.

Multitudes of angels congregated before the tabernacle, wanting to see Elijah of CHRIST, chanting: Hallelujah Elijah! You destroyed the devils for ever by the Word. True and just is your judgment for our CHRIST to reign with power.

The angels began to chant: O CHRIST, bring on the salvation. Elijah has condemned the devils for committing adultery to make a god (Cain) and his god has committed abomination in the flesh of our sister to make a god for him.

Angels began to chant louder and louder: Elijah! Elijah! He has condemned the harlot of the earth who made Mankind and Israelites with god her father, and destroyed his Babylon city.

Elijah! Elijah! they chanted, while the chariot was passing through the crowds. He saved our Zion and his Jerusalem from the devils and their wicked god with their law. Elijah, we praise thee. CHRIST, we praise thee for your holy work for creating your Elijah by the Word. The first SON you created in the kingdom. You have fooled the devils with your son, who has faith in you.

All angels, small and great, began to praise CHRIST for HIS holy work in the kingdom. Your first son of creation has fulfilled the testimony of our Eternal Father.

There was lightning zigzagging and peals of thunder from the heaven of heavens, and Shooting stars from one world to another and on earth to tell Zion and Jerusalem that Elijah is in the tabernacle.

The voice of the Eternal Father said: my CHRIST, reign on the throne according to the testimony and the creating of HIS Elijah. He has fulfilled the Testament in the tabernacle.

Rejoice and be glad he captured the devils by the Word, and will be king with His Jerusalem, who has faith in Him and will establish kingdoms from her flesh.

The tabernacle was fully packed with angels and archangels of the Eternal. Jesus and all his brothers and sisters sat on thrones with their queen. Elijah took the seat of honour. CHRIST sat on the throne of the world. The seat of Zion was vacant as she was still on earth, making herself ready for the day when she will sit and receive angels from the kingdoms from her flesh in salvation.

The Eternal Holy Father of Light blessed HIS CHRIST and Zion, Jesus, Elijah and all the angels from the seed of HIS CHRIST and Jerusalem and all other angels, which HE created in other worlds in the Light.

HE told them to be patient. Everything is in the hands of HIS CHRIST to finish the work in creation by the Word according to the testimony to put the world in the Light at HIS good pleasure. HIS Elijah will be king in righteousness with His queen.

The New Testament

Blessed are the spirits of CHRIST in the Light in salvation, who will resurrect to Heaven. The spirits of the seed of god who have faith in Elijah, He will save from falling in Hades and will have rest. They should not be afraid of death. If their kingdoms are worthy, they will be created to continue to have new spirits through faith in Elijah.

The promise to be fulfilled in Hades

The devils made a god and his god made a god who the people worship him as God that has no power and is deceitful like the devils.

Elijah will judge his godly spirits from the accursed seed as his inheritance in Hades for ever to fulfil the promise made to him.

After the blessing, the archangels came forward and bowed before CHRIST, and angels of renown came and put the crown at the foot of Elijah, saying: Elijah, you are worthy to be the king of the earth for capturing the devils and resurrecting CHRIST to the throne of the world. Then they bowed before CHRIST and said: CHRIST, you are worthy to be the ruler of the world.

We congratulate you for your holy work to put the world in order and in peace according to the holy scripture and the testament of our Holy Eternal creator, who created us from the beginning, and to hand over our holy work to you so your sons can continue in the New World in perfection.

CHRIST spoke to the angels in Heaven and explained the reason for the delay in putting the world in the Light, and asked them to be patient as everything on earth has to be justified for peace in the world according to the scripture and the testimony of the Eternal be fulfilled to establish the kingdom on earth to be with everlasting spirits by the Word.

Jesus and his brothers and sisters and Elijah were in the palace with CHRIST, feasting with much joy. This made CHRIST happy. All his children from his seed were in the palace and sorrowful for Zion and Jerusalem on earth, who suffered much for peace, and was held in captivity most of her life and was now a free spirit with Elijah.

The plan

CHRIST told Jesus to fetch the plan and bring it here. Jesus brought the plan to build the vessel. CHRIST said to Jesus and Elijah: we are here to discuss the Sabbath on earth and the way forward to salvation, which is the objective to establish the kingdom for creation from the face of the earth by the word.

Elijah, you will build a vessel according to the plan to scatter the people of all sorts all over the earth to breed and multiply kingdoms from their sort until the appointed time to begin holy work in salvation in multitudes. They will do the sowing to make kingdoms to create immortal spirits by the word.

Elijah, you will be the judge. Everything on earth is in your hands to establish the kingdom on earth by faith. Jesus, you have the plan to do the work for final judgment in the world between Elijah and the Alfa on the disobedient and hypocrite rebels on earth for eternity for trespassing in the kingdom and spilling the blood of your brothers on the earth.

CHRIST said: Elijah my son, you have done righteous work up to this generation on earth. There is none good in the kingdom from the seed of god. They are all wicked like their father who made them with passed on seed of the devils.

Seedtime Gen.8:22; 9:1–17

Let the people who have faith help build the vessel so they may earn extended life to Passover the Sabbath of the earth to breed abundantly, and multiply kingdoms on the face of the earth for salvation. When the vessel is finished, let the couples you have chosen from all sorts go in the vessel to replenish all sorts of kingdoms from the couples chosen for creation.

When the ocean and seas be calm, let out the couples in different parts of the earth to breed and multiply kingdoms with their immutable spirits. When you have emptied the vessel, you and Jerusalem rest in Whykibully. The wind will take the vessel to rest in the ocean.

Consolation to spirits of gods in the Kingdom

As a token consolation, the spirits of gods in the kingdom will have a free choice as a consolation to rest if they have faith to establish their kingdom with a new spirit in the Light by the Word to continue in their image with everlasting life, or fall to the devils for having no faith in Elijah to rest in peace. They will only have themselves to blame for ignorance of the New Testament.

When the time of salvation comes there will be clouds and rain all over the earth. To do holy work in creation by the Word for the battle in the kingdom is to cast out spirits of gods from kingdoms for kingdoms worthy for creation. Judgment shall be on spirits cast out from all nations, for Elijah to judge spirits of gods that have no faith to rest in peace for ever.

When the people, animals and creatures are in the vessel it will be shut automatically. Water from the great deep will be opened and it will come up on the earth in fountains, plus rain will fall and increase the water levels and flood the earth to lift the vessel until it rises.

Every valley shall be filled with water and overflow the mountains till there is no land in sight, to Sabbath the filthy generation from the earth. The whole earth will be cleansed to Passover from the last generation so the earth can be cleansed for food to be in abundance. The kingdom will be healthy from disease and perfect for creation. **Lk.3:4**

All the spirits in the kingdom from the accursed seed outside the vessel will Sabbath to death. A whirlwind will come and carry these spirits away to fall in the mouth of the waters to journey to the gates of Hades to be held in captivity to prevent them from pestering the people during seedtime on earth.

Then release the godly spirits when the earth is populated to tempt the people for their faith to earn rest. Jesus will come and sanctify himself to warn the people and tell them the way to Eternal life at the appointed time with you so they have a choice to have rest or fall for the final judgment.

When the flood has emptied itself from the deep the water will return to the deep of the earth to where it is set.

The earth will be divided into continents, with oceans and islands, lakes, rivers and streams with a continuous flow of water on a gravity system until the time of draught.

The oceans and seas will be calm. The vessel will be moving on the face of the waters to different continents and islands. Let out the couples on land in different parts of the earth, with animals and creatures to multiply.

The spirits rest

Elijah, when the first sight of land is seen let Zion out of the vessel so she can have the choice of where she wants to live after she has rested until she sanctifies and asks Mankind to have mercy and have forgiveness before you, Elijah and Jesus in that generation.

Elijah becomes a husband to Jerusalem Gen.9:20

Jerusalem will sanctify with you, Elijah, in the body of Noah for peace. Both of you will have rest after you dispatch Mankind and Israelites from the vessel. When Jerusalem awakes she will be free to sanctify in any body she wants in the kingdom from her flesh.

Jesus will return to sanctify to be in His image

Jesus will sanctify in the same body with Jerusalem to be human to do ministry work in that generation at the appointed time. Elijah, you will resurrect Jesus back to Heaven after he Sabbaths his body to death.

Elijah will sanctify in the same body as Zion. You, at the appointed time, will be human to be their witness when they ask Mankind for mercy for making gods before godly spirits and the devil. They will ask the devil to repent for making gods in their flesh. After resurrection, Zion will be on the mercy seat in Heaven for judgment before angels.

Jerusalem will stay on earth in the midst of her children then Elijah will resurrect Jerusalem to see the final Judgment on devils and godly spirits and see salvations in kingdoms from her flesh until the end of salvation to return to earth as queen of the earth with her King Elijah after the final judgment on all spirits of gods are purged out from the kingdom from her flesh to have immortal spirits created in the name of CHRIST to live in the New World in the Light for ever.

The flood

When the water returns to the deep, command the wind to blow the excess water on the earth and let it be gathered in the north and south of the earth and command it to freeze into ice by the Word to be a testimony for salvation for kingdoms and the end of spirits in the kingdoms.

The wind will come through the portals in the north and blow hot air unto the ice northeast to south and from the portal of the south and blow hot air on the ice southwest to north to circulate mist and clouds and set the temperature to grow food in all seasons until the time of salvation to melt the ice for draught as a testimony until the spirits of gods come to an end in the kingdom to reign.

Mankind, do you think the New Testament is in vain? (**Ja.4:5**) Jesus said: in vain they worship God through fear. Jesus told Mankind that the godly spirits are in them and it's Elijah who will pass judgment on the spirits that have no faith in Him to fall (**Mt.15:2**). Let no godly spirit in the kingdom seduce you to lose faith to fall because of vanity. (**Eph.5:6**) Thou shall not take the name of CHRIST in vain (**Ex.20:7**) if you are not a spirit of Christ in the Light.

After CHRIST discussed HIS plan with Jesus and Elijah in Heaven to establish the kingdom on earth, the flood, to save all sorts of couples to populate the earth to make kingdoms until the time of salvation of kingdoms for creation of immortal spirits by the Word.

CHRIST SAT ON THE THRONE BEFORE ANGELS FROM ALL WORLDS

Jesus read the New Testament of CHRIST to the angels in the tabernacle according to the plan on the Sabbath, the flood, the Passover, salvation of kingdoms for creation and the final judgment on the devils and spirits of gods and to put the kingdom in order with spirits created by CHRIST to populate the earth in righteousness, equality and prosperity for all immortal spirits to live in a perfect world through faith in Elijah.

THE UNVEILING OF THE ARK

The golden ark was in the tabernacle with the New Testament by CHRIST. Jesus unveiled cherubs of Zion and Jerusalem above the ark. The angels began to cry for Zion and Jerusalem. Jesus went on to say: Their spirits will be inside the sanctum of the vessel on the top deck, Jesus showed the angels the plan where couples that would be saved for the Passover when the earth is flooded. Then the plan for the lower deck to save wild beasts and creatures in the flood.

Jesus said: this New Testament by CHRIST is a testimony to make the covenant between our Eternal Holy Father and the ancient king of devils of the dark world obsolete to establish the New Testament in the world by the Word for peace.

The Sabbath of those not accepted inside the vessel will avoid foolishness and controversies about genealogies to stop arguments and quarrels by spirits of the seed of God of god (Cain) god who claim they have right by the law to live in the kingdom from the flesh of CHRIST will experience if God can save them in the flood.

Elijah to choose couples to populate the earth until salvation

Jesus said to the angels: the people who help to build the vessel and couples saved by Elijah, after they die, their spirits will rest in peace.

Jesus went on to say: Let us rejoice and be glad for CHRIST my father, creator of spirits in salvation in kingdoms through Elijah to be accepted by the ETERNAL to live among angels with eternal life after they depart from the kingdom on earth.

Jesus introduced Elijah and said: my brother is here to testify in the tabernacle about salvation, and there was silence. Elijah said to the angels: The devil strangled his god. After his spirit left the kingdom from the flesh of Zion to Hades his kingdom became vacant and CHRIST spoke the Word and I was created in the kingdom Elijah CHRIST with the word to do His holy work in salvation and to save my brothers to be the judge between him and the devils on earth.

The kingdom

Elijah went on to say the kingdom is the foundation for CHRIST and holy spirits to live in kingdoms from HIS seed, but because the son of god slew all the sons of CHRIST from the earth, the New Testament of salvation will take effect after CHRIST casts out spirits of gods from the kingdom to create immortal spirits to continue to populate the earth to establish the New Testament.

Everything in reference to creation is until every kingdom that is worthy is created with new spirits to continue to be productive on earth in righteousness.

While the world is between Light and darkness, our Eternal Father has not showed His face from the heaven of heavens until His CHRIST does what HE was created to do by faith to put the world in order and has made the sacrifice for His CHRIST to continue His work in creation by the Word. His CHRIST has made a similar sacrifice to put HIS Elijah in charge of the kingdom so spirits from the seed of god in their humanity can have rest if they have faith in Him.

When Elijah was through testifying CHRIST, creating him in the kingdom in salvation before the angels of all the worlds in the tabernacle, there were loud cheers. CHRIST called Jesus and told the congregation that Jesus will return to earth at an appointed time with Elijah to declare the New Testament in that generation, so spirits in their humanity can prepare themselves for salvation.

The testimony of Elijah

Elijah sat at the lower part of the tabernacle and came to the rostrum and congratulated Jesus as messiah of CHRIST in Heaven. All angels looked at Elijah. Elijah looked at CHRIST on HIS throne and Jesus and all brothers and sisters whom He had resurrected from earth looked at the archangels and lords of the ancient in creation.

Elijah said: I am honoured to leave earth to be among you in Heaven to enjoy the perfect way of life to establish the New Testament of CHRIST and dissolve the old testament of our Eternal Father and creator by the Word.

I am Elijah, created by CHRIST in the kingdom of god by the Word to direct kingdoms for salvation to CHRIST on His throne to create immortal spirits, to save His spirits and spirits of gods that have faith in me to rest for eternity, to establish the kingdom on earth with spirits of creation in the name of CHRIST. I have established the covenant of the ETERNAL that His CHRIST will create His Elijah by the Word. By the Word I removed the devils from earth to Hades. The earth is going to be flooded with water and when the flood comes upon the earth multitudes of spirits from their seed after death will be held in captivity so the people chosen can populate the earth up to the time of salvation

The devil raped Eve to make a god. The god of the devil raped the daughter of my CHRIST and she conceived his seed. The devil strangled his god and took Tamah in captivity.

Our sister was pregnant with the seed of god (Cain) before he was strangled by the devils. She gave birth to a baby god for god (Cain) in the bush. I was passing by and heard the baby god crying, still in his mother's blood. I took him and clothed him and brought him up on milk and honey. I taught him scriptures to do good and I named him Ammon.

I taught him the way to eternal life. I told him he had to make a sacrifice so his spirit could have rest and his kingdom would be created with a new spirit to be my son to be accepted above. He had no faith to accept peace. I showed him where his mother was held in captivity and told him to go and save her from the devils.

I warned him not to have sex with his mother to make gods with his mother as every spirit from his seed would be his inheritance in the gates of Hell and that every kingdom from his mother's flesh would be for creating new spirits by CHRIST.

The time came when we had to part from each other. He had no faith, just like god his father who conspired with the devils to hold the daughter of CHRIST in captivity. When AMMON saw his mother he lusted for her and took an oath to be the prophet of the law of devils, to live by the law to death and all from his seed. The devils changed his name to Judah.

Judah challenged CHRIST and I for the earth. There is no excuse for he was brought up to know scriptures. He slew all the sons of CHRIST from the earth and committed abomination with his mother and made Israelites and Mankind with his daughters and became king of earth, and all on earth worshiped him as God. He threatened Eve and her daughters with death and cast them in a den of lions and their faith saved them. He died of bowel cancer and is now in Hades.

When the angels heard of the terrible life on earth they began to cry: O Elijah, save Zion and Jerusalem!

THE PATIENCE OF CHRIST

Elijah said to the congregation of angels in the tabernacle: the spirits from the seed of god are rebellious and violent while they live in the kingdom on earth. There is no peace on earth. The Israelites and Mankind live in fear of these barbarians, who ruin many people's lives. They are enslaved by all kinds of passion and abomination. They rape, murder, steal women, fight, and spill blood on earth.

They have no faith and reject truth. These spirits in the kingdom are corrupt and pass on seed of the devils, and pass on disease of the devils to destroy the kingdom and make war to death.

Their rulers know Elijah of CHRIST and deny me for doing anything good for the kingdom. If I do not return to earth there will be no flesh that is healthy for CHRIST to do HIS holy work in creation. CHRIST created me to save HIS flesh and spirits on earth. So Elijah spoke!

Salvation is for spiritual creation in the kingdom by CHRIST on HIS throne. If I am in Heaven the work to create immortal spirits in kingdoms cannot be established in salvation by the Word in righteousness to save the spirits in the kingdom to replenish the earth to be as it was in the beginning with CHRIST and ZION by the Word in the kingdom.

Furthermore, Zion and Jerusalem were held in captivity while they were human and were humiliated and tormented by God of god and the devils. It is because of their faith they are free spirits on earth and have to wait to ask for mercy at the appointed time to resurrect to have mercy from angels in Heaven before CHRIST on his throne.

The price of sin Eccl.19:18; Jer.50:20; Is.40:2; Mt.9:11; 1.Cor.6:18; Pro.28:13

Elijah said: the sin of the devils to make gods in their flesh has been a burden to them. The only way forward is for CHRIST to return and cast out all spirits from the seed of the devils so the kingdoms can be created with immortal spirits by CHRIST by the Word.

The angels began to cry: O Elijah, you are mighty, with faith. Save the kingdom for immortal spirits in the name of CHRIST to reign in all kingdoms, so Zion can resurrect next to her CHRIST to receive angels of CHRIST on the throne in Heaven.

Elijah begs for mercy for Zion

Elijah said to the angels: I beg you to have mercy on Zion and Jerusalem when I resurrect them to you in Heaven. The angels cried: we did not know all the problems that are on this earth. You have judged the devils with righteous judgment for rape and abomination like creatures and pestilence with hate, malice, and violence on earth

Faith without the Word is death

Faith without the Word to CHRIST is worthless if there is no kingdom from his flesh to create angels to be justified in the New Testament. The devils were cowards and used gods to do their dirty work in sin to destroy the kingdom.

Elijah said: the flood on earth will be the opportunity to select couples of many sorts to multiply kingdoms on earth so when the time of salvation comes, the spirits will prepare their kingdom for CHRIST to create immortal spirits in salvation. The spirits of gods will be given a choice to have faith for peace or fall. They will decide their fate while they live in the kingdom.

Elijah said: it is good to be in Heaven but I don't feel its righteous I am here while Zion and Jerusalem are on an island on earth on their own. They have suffered enough and they deserve to have peace in the world just like every angel in Heaven. Zion and Jerusalem are good; they did not sin with their spirits. Sin was in their flesh that was burnt to ashes and blown all over the earth by the wind like dust.

Elijah testified before angels in the tabernacle and gave full account of life on the planet earth, of what the devils, god (Cain) and his god his son did to declare the battle in the kingdom. The challenge of war in the kingdom is a serious challenge against the Word.

The angels cried: Elijah, mighty warrior of CHRIST, it is justified for CHRIST to return to cast out spirits of the devils from HIS holy flesh, when you say the Word for their godly to fall in the everlasting fire. Elijah went back to his seat at the last row of the tabernacle.

Elijah is anointed KING of the earth. **Zech.14:9; Rev.11:15; Hag.2:22; Lk.1:33; Ps.103:14**

CHRIST said with a firm voice: Elijah, come here, my son, and sit by my right hand. I created thee, my son, by the Word like our Eternal Father created me by the Word to continue HIS work in creation. He rested. I created you to be my helper on earth.

You have commanded the winds to cast out the devils from the earth to fall in flames of fire, and resurrected my spirit to this throne in the tabernacle through faith in me.

Your throne, Elijah, will last for ever. Your spirit is righteous and you have the authority to go in and out of any kingdom to do the work in salvation with my blessing.

You hate wickedness and deceit and excel exceedingly above devils and spirits of gods in the kingdom on earth. I consecrate you with my blessing today as the king in the kingdom on earth and to judge the earth in righteousness for the New World in the Light.

The spirits who have no faith, let them fall to be with the devils when they depart from the kingdom from my flesh.

After announcing Elijah as king of the earth CHRIST sat on HIS throne, it was recorded in the New Testament.

The ancient archangels came and bowed before CHRIST and gave HIM their blessing and laid their crowns before Elijah, as there was no work for archangels in Heaven under the Old Covenant, which became obsolete by the New Testament by CHRIST and KING ELIJAH on earth.

The archangels came and bowed to CHRIST and Elijah, for their work ended with the New Testament and CHRIST needed only Elijah to do the work, that was much superior in the New Testament for world peace

The archangels rested like the Eternal from their work in Heaven so Jesus and his brothers can do the work according to the New Testament in the heavens.

CHRIST made the Old Testament obsolete and had full control in Heaven and Elijah to establish the kingdom with immortal spirits in the name of CHRIST to be angels to live in all worlds in the Light.

This was Elijah's first trip to Heaven. He sat at the right hand of CHRIST on the throne in the tabernacle in Heaven in the midst of angels, given authority, and became king with power over spirits on earth.

After Elijah was consecrated KING in the kingdom there was joy and much praise by angels chanting: you are worthy to be KING of the earth.

The prophesy of CHRIST: The real enemy of CHRIST, Elijah will deliver into his hands for declaring war Jer.20:11

Christ became angry feeling the loneliness of Zion on earth, and then there was silence. Elijah, you begot the son of god who held my daughter in captivity under the law just like the devils. He became my enemy and a blasphemer. He was an opportunist, who took advantage of your kindness and joined the devils. He slew my sons and eliminated them from the earth and held my daughters in captivity and declared war for the earth with godly spirits from his seed.

You taught him the scripture to do good and turned to be my enemy, imitating the devils.

The son of god made Israelites and Mankind, mixing and mingling to make all sorts features and they lived in fear of him like the devils. He was a tyrant, a violent oppressor. He is the enemy, anti-Christ with his law, and wants to rule the earth with godly spirits after death. Though you taught him scripture, he had no faith. Evil is deep rooted in his nature.

After his spirit departed from the kingdom you put him in a chamber so the devils don't beat him up. You were patient with him, just as I was patient with god (Cain) his father, who had no faith and Sabbathed Jesus body (Abel) to death. because of the son of god's vanity, there is much violence on earth since he eliminated my SONS to replace with his kind of creation in my flesh.

The token choice

His spirits shall live in the kingdom until you speak the Word for me to come and cast out his spirits from kingdoms from my flesh. You will be the judge. Let no spirit from his seed escape when they depart from the kingdom if they don't have faith in you, Elijah.

Until the spirits from the seed of god his father are cut off from the kingdom, and the kingdoms worthy for creation shall be with new spirits of creation through me when you speak the Word.

The spirits that trespass in the kingdom, if they shed blood on earth while they live in my flesh, shall be condemned after death.

The spirits of gods in the kingdom are corrupt. They do not acknowledge CHRIST or you, Elijah, and yet they live in my flesh and say we are vain and jealous. They burned the body of Zion and Jerusalem and say the last of the Hebrews are no more on earth and the name of CHRIST is now a mist. There was much silence.

CHRIST was angry and there was silence. He looked at Elijah and said: I want you to deliver this antichrist who hanged my body into my hands. Your name, Elijah, is strength of CHRIST, in whom all my people take refuge and hope. You are their fortress against the enemy.

Elijah present the kingdoms for salvation for me to create immortal spirits to continue in the kingdom in the name of CHRIST.

You are my rock, Elijah, on which the kingdom is built in salvation with immortal spirits according to the New Testament. No spirits from the seed of god are accepted in Heaven.

The spirits in the kingdom must have faith in Elijah to save them 1.Sam.22:3

Elijah, you are the only saviour of spirits while they live in the kingdom with different features until salvation before I return to create immortal spirits to make their features perfect with spirits in the name of CHRIST to continue in perfection to be accepted above.

The enemy. The most wicked spirit

CHRIST said: Elijah, after the godly spirits of Judah are released from captivity, they will create disorder on earth to destroy the kingdom by war, corruption and disease, and will spill blood to destroy the faith; and there I will catch Judah in the battle in the kingdom and all his godly spirits.

Ignorance of scripture and testament

The devils had knowledge of the old scriptures and did not believe they would be cast out of the heavens and Elijah would remove them from the earth to Hades.

MANY ARE CALLED; FEW ARE CHOSEN

Multitudes of spirits will fall after death because of religion that is taught to suit themselves not in accordance with the New Testament to have faith in the only saviour, Elijah.

Multitudes of spirits in the kingdom will lead each other astray through corrupt teaching like the foolish Judah, who imitated the devil with every imagination, and this evil is in his nature to make others deceitful, to have no faith, and fall through ignorance, not knowing the free choice for peace.

VAIN WORSHIP CAN SAVE NO ONE

The deceiver said to Mankind: the scripture says things in vain so they can worship him in vain. Elijah with the Word saves spirits who have faith in him to have peace and not fall after death like him for having no faith.

A VAIN GOD IS THE ENEMY MAL.3:14; EPH.56; EX.20:7

The bibles say the enemy has said it's vain to have faith. Thou shall not have the name of CHRIST in vain if you are not a spirit of creation. Let no spirit from the seed of god deceive you to fall through vanity.

THE SONS OF THUNDER

The angels were amazed at the wisdom of CHRIST to put the archangels of the ETERNAL to rest from their work and for Elijah with the word to command the wind, thunder, hailstones, thunderballs, lightning, earthquakes, fire, rain, flood, resurrection and establish the New World in the Light with angels in the Light Through CHRIST on His throne in Heaven.

THE FIRST PASSOVER ON EARTH BY WATER Jer.8:3; Mt.20:16 Gen.6.5:7.23,18,25; Rev.6:4; 1.Jn.5:8

The end is near for multitudes as an example to the end of spirits in the kingdom. The time has come for the spirits of god to be judged through the mouth of Noah. Many are called; few are chosen to begin a new life in peace.

Every spirit in the kingdom that is saved for the Passover is to begin a new life after the flood in order to populate the earth until salvation. Every spirit in the kingdom that is not accepted will be in captivity after death.

King Elijah became the mediator of the New Testament for redemption of the transgression of devils to make gods. The first testament is to have mercy. Where there is a testament, there must also be death on earth and those chosen will be in the vessel to testify to their children of those who died in the flood. **Heb.9:15-16**

The angels began to sing for Elijah: He is mighty, the strength of CHRIST. And they began to blow their horns. Let the judgment begin with the flood to establish the New Testament of CHRIST and blessed CHRIST, Jesus and Elijah for the New World.

A new and living way began in the tabernacle Heb.10:20; Lk.3:4, 22; Heb.10:26; Lk.3:4, 27

After the prophesy of the New Testament by CHRIST, the angels returned to their world with confidence in CHRIST to deliver, to put the world in the highest order with scientific intelligence, technology in creation and prosperity for all worlds without end.

The battle in the kingdom is to prepare the reader who is not a Christ to prepare for salvation for their peace. If they don't take heed of their end, they will have no one to blame if they fall but themselves.

In the tabernacle in the heavens Heb.5:45

Salvation is according to the plan by CHRIST, JESUS, with Elijah. Every kingdom on earth is in his hands of Elijah for salvation for creation through CHRIST.

The promise 2.Pet.3:7; Ju.7; Mt.9.6:33; Ezra.9:8

Elijah promised to save the spirits from the seed of God of god (Cain) who have faith in him, to rest in peace and not fall in the final judgment.

A short work will Elijah do on the face of the earth and bring judgment on spirits from the seed of God and save some to make kingdoms for salvation.

The fault is in The god (Cain's) hand the devils Ja.5:16; Ex.5:16; Mt.18:15; 1.Cor.6:7

There are millions of kingdoms with spirits from the seed of God on earth, and not one spirit from his seed is born perfect in the kingdom. If God's spirits were perfect they would be like spirits of CHRIST.

Every spirit has a choice to focus on their end before they depart from the kingdom, and should acknowledge is not their fault that they were not born perfect and have a choice to have peace after death through faith.

King Elijah returns to earth by spaceship

Elijah returned to earth to begin the work on the vessel. The spaceship brought all the necessary equipment for the vessel – satellite navigation system, panels, machinery, nails, screws and bolts to speed up the building and to use local material for the vessel with the testament in the ark.

Elijah Sanctifies in the body of Noah Essek.14,16–18

Elijah sanctified in the body of Noah and cast out his spirit, and the body of Noah was now made perfect with the spirit of Elijah.

Noah's spirit was put to rest (**1.Pe.3:18**), that is to say, Noah's spirit exists no more on earth and is at rest for eternity. The body of Noah was made perfect with the spirit Elijah with life and with grace. Elijah can use Noah's body, as it was his own, and live among humanity and no spirit in their humanity can know the difference. **Gen.5:23,29; 7:8**

The power with authority

Elijah shall do the work in the hands of Noah, whose spirit is at rest. Noah's body was brought to perfection (9) with Elijah's spirit (**1.Pe.4:7**). Elijah spoke through the mouth of Noah in the image of Noah. It was Elijah with the Word in the kingdom and he walked in the kingdom as a spirit in the Light. **Essek.14,16,17,18,21; 1.Pe.3:18–20; Is.50:11**

From the New Testament in Heaven

Elijah has authority to go in and out of any kingdom and cast out their spirits to do the work before CHRIST on His throne in Heaven.

The New Testament is written for our learning so we may meditate on salvation to establish an immortal spirit by CHRIST through Elijah. You can't be born again if you are from the seed of god but have a choice to have everlasting peace if you have faith in Elijah to save you after death.

Immortal spirits created in salvation will resurrect after death to be among angels in the Light in Heaven, with everlasting life. Immortal spirits are natural spirits of creation in the Light through CHRIST by the Word as it was in the beginning in paradise with Zion in Eve, and CHRIST in Adam.

The new testimony in the ark in the tabernacle in Heaven was to show the angels the work Christ and Elijah will do on earth

The work of Elijah shall be done before the people on earth. Every doctrine shall be tried, true or false, sound, solid or corrupt. The vessel is built on the earth as an example of the work of Elijah to end spirits in multitudes when he speaks the Word to CHRIST. The population of the earth at that time was two hundred million, scattered all over, born under the law of Judah, who slew innocent sons of CHRIST from the face of the earth to make Mankind.

The time has come to judge the spirits of god 1.Pe.4:7

The time has come to judge the spirits of god in the kingdom and to save some in the vessel to continue after the flood to populate the earth until salvation.

Elijah, the first spirit of Salvation manifests in Noah before the people

Elijah started to set up the plan to build the vessel in clearing up the place with his caterpillar and other equipment and chain saws to cut down the trees.

The noise of the trees falling attracted a lot of attention and the people came up to Elijah and said: Noah! What are you doing? Are you crazy, clearing all this forest? And they began to laugh.

A pharisee came among the people and said: Noah, who gave you authority to cut down these trees in the forest? He got no answer. The pharisee said: what are you doing here? Elijah said: I am clearing this place to build a vessel with a testament in the ark. The pharisee said: Noah, why are you building a vessel with an ark? You are not following the tradition of god our father. You do things like a gentile who doesn't follow the law. I am going to report you to the chief rabbi.

The chief rabbi came with other pharisees and seducers. The chief rabbi said: Noah, what are you building in this forest? Elijah said: did you come to do battle with me or did you come to collect taxes? If you don't get what you want you kill, covet and fight with whoever doesn't pay.

A pharisee said: it is against the law to build against our God. If you don't stop this building we will have the Anakins to destroy your machinery. Elijah said: I am building a vessel for the holy CHRIST in Heaven. Your God is no more on earth.

Many people gathered and Elijah said: when the people on earth ask your God for anything, he never delivers, because they do not ask Elijah of CHRIST in Heaven to help them to receive what they want. You fear God and hate the good spirit Elijah without cause, and have become his enemy because of envy. If you want to know, he gave the body of Noah grace before your eyes in perfection.

Elijah opposes the proud and gives grace to Noah. The pharisee said: Noah, Elijah is against the law. Elijah said: there is one lawgiver and one judge who can save and destroy the people of god. But you want to judge your neighbour for making a vessel and don't know if you will live tomorrow, or where your spirit will end. You brag and boast about the law like God your father. He will testify who he is against when you have no flesh in the fire!

Your abomination has reached in the face of CHRIST the harvester, who lives in Heaven. You live in luxury and self-indulgence and fatten yourself like a bull for the day of slaughter. God will tell you who it is that murdered innocent men from the face of the earth (5:6).

The farmer is patient and is clearing this place to build a vessel for his valuable crop (kingdom). The judge is waiting to give those who want rest from their labours and not condemn them to death and if you, pharisee, have understanding, I can explain what it means to you.

The pharisee chief said: you are a lawbreaker and you are stumbling among us if you build this vessel. You show us you have more favour with this spirit CHRIST in Heaven than God our father.

The pharisee found it strange that Noah is not following them according to the law, and kept his verbal abuse on Elijah, saying; Noah, this vessel is against the law. Do you want to start a revolution? The pharisees began to whisper into the ears of each other, then said: Noah, we are going to get the strongest of our Anakin giants to come and destroy all your machinery so you don't build this vessel for this CHRIST in Heaven. Noah! Stop building this vessel if it's not for our God.

Elijah said: if this Anakin is your rock by the law, let us put God to the test to see if he has power.

Elijah puts God to the test

The crowd started to shout: We pray to God to put food on our tables to feed children from his seed. He never responds and our children are dying of hunger. Our old are sick. There is no bread in the nation, and we still have to pay taxes.

Elijah called the crowd and said: those who believe God made the world, stand by pharisee; and those who prayed to God to feed children from his seed and got no response, stand on my side. So there was a division.

The pharisee said: Noah, you are a terrorist and want to divide the nation to break the law to bring lawlessness in the nation.

Elijah against God

Elijah said: the law of God has no power and leads astray many who want truth. Let us put God to the test against Elijah and see if he can feed the people with bread in this wilderness. If he can feed the people with bread he has more power than Elijah, and if Elijah can feed the people with bread he will be captain of the vessel.

Elijah said to the pharisee rabbi: God who you say is your father and whose spirit name is Israel, was a man like you, who had knowledge of

Elijah. You insist to live by his doctrine until you die.

The people gathered to see this contest and there was much argument between believers in God and those who were disappointed in God not answering their prayer to feed them who he made from passing god his father's seed.

Those standing up for Elijah said they are disappointed in God. There was much shouting on both sides in this heated argument. Elijah kept his cool as one side was blaming the other with laws and tax collectors bleeding them to death by making them pay money they can't afford.

The pharisee said: to those who want to break away from the law, God will punish you if they don't believe God can feed them in the wilderness.

They shouted: if God can feed us with bread, let it come from the sky to feed them now and we will have faith in him.

Elijah said to the crowd: all this violence and abomination and religion with laws and commandments to death will come to an end if God doesn't show his power before the people today! And told the pharisee and all the people who believe in God pray to God to make bread come from the sky.

The pharisee and the people who believed began to pray: O mighty God, show your power and make bread come from the sky to shut up Noah with his blasphemy against you. Show your power. Noah said: Elijah has more power than you! They got no response.

Elijah said: I go a stone's throw from you to pray for bread to fall from the sky to show you that Elijah has power on earth and can feed everyone with bread from the sky and God, who you fear and worship, has no power.

Elijah went a stone's throw away and looked up and lifted his hands towards Heaven. The sun shone brightly on his body and bread began to fall from the sky. The people began to pick up the bread. They began to say: Noah is a prophet, the chosen one, who put the pharisee to shame today.

Elijah said to the pharisee and the seducers: do you want to put God to the test to see if he has more power than CHRIST in Heaven? The seducer said: there is No CHRIST in Heaven. Our God made the world and we are all his children from his seed and have power over all his children on earth.

Elijah said: it is true you are children from the seed of god, but his children live in CHRIST'S flesh and he has power to cast out all children of god in His flesh back to him as his portion on earth. CHRIST can show you He has more power than God.

God is put to the test against CHRIST

Elijah said to the pharisee: get the Anakin to get some logs of wood and pile them up on your side, and I'll get the people who eat the bread from the sky to pile logs of wood on my side, so there will be two piles of wood – one for the mother of god (Jerusalem) and one for her mother (Zion) who made god.

The two bullocks

Elijah said to the pharisee: look over there. There are two bullocks. You take one and kill it and chop the meat in little pieces as much as you want and put it on the pile and throw the blood on your pile of wood for Jerusalem.

The people who were on the side of Elijah killed the other bull and chopped the meat in small pieces and put it on the pile of wood and threw the blood on the wood for Zion.

Faith by works

Elijah said to the pharisee and all still indoctrinated with this religion: pray to God your father and tell him to set the pile of wood on fire and if he can do so he has more power than CHRIST in Heaven to stop me from building the vessel.

The pharisee and his followers began to pray: O God our father who made Mankind and Israelites, set the logs on fire to burn up the flesh on it to show Noah he is a lawbreaker. You have more power on earth over CHRIST in Heaven.

Faith without works is useless

They got no response. This contest gathered multitudes of people who had suspicion of this God and were born and brought up to be in fear of him in life and in death.

Elijah said to the pharisees: maybe God went on a journey in the other part of the world. Shout louder so he can hear thee.

They began to pray loudly: O mighty God, show this delinquent and backslider of your law your power, and light the pile of wood and burn the pieces of kosher flesh we drained its blood for you on the wood. Burn its flesh in fire as a sacrifice to your mother and blind Noah's eyes for saying you have no power over CHRIST in Heaven. We have faith in you, O God. They got no reply.

Trials and temptations

Elijah said: maybe God is fast asleep. Shout louder! Those who were still indoctrinated next to the pharisees began to pray louder and louder. They blew their horns. Wake up, O God! They began to cut their arms and legs and faces and blood was dripping all over their bodies as a sacrifice. The blood was dripping on the earth.

They were praying: O mighty God, show this son of a bitch born in abomination your power on earth and in Heaven to destroy his kingdom with disease. Set the logs on fire to show how you will destroy his flesh from your seed, so he can have respect for you and your people who carry out your law to death. Show the multitudes gathered here today you have more power than CHRIST in Heaven and all angels in the heavens are against you as the enemy. Once again there was no response.

Faith without works is death

Elijah said to the pharisee: you have this day chosen whom you shall worship. Then Elijah said to the multitudes: come closer unto me. Elijah looked at them and there was silence. Hear me, each of you that are gathered here today, and let it be known this day among all the people on earth that I am the servant of CHRIST in Heaven. Then he turned to the pharisee and said: you have begun to show signs of antichrist in the world with your law to mislead people to death. You have made yourself foolish with laws and have condemned yourselves. Neither have you any faith in Elijah, who brought up God your father and has fed the multitudes with bread. You will have no rest when you fall. Ask God to save you.

Faith by work. CHRIST shows no favouritism
Elijah told the people who stood by him to get buckets of water and throw them on the meat on the wood.

The evidence of faith
The people threw the water on the meat of the bulls on the two piles of wood and around the wood the earth was full of blood. Then Elijah looked at the pharisees and said: this is how you will be baptized today in fire.

If CHRIST answers by fire, HE is the Lord of the earth
Elijah said: CHRIST, make fire come from Heaven to light the logs to show everyone that CHRIST in Heaven will put Light in his flesh in salvation that God who they worship can't save.

A laser beam of fire came unto the logs of wood and set the wood on fire and suddenly devouring flames burnt the flesh of the bullocks to ashes. Elijah commanded the Anakin to take the pharisees to the valley and slay them to death for leading the people astray with the law and return to help build the vessel. The people lined up for work to build the vessel.

The word with King Elijah 1.Cor.3:13; 1.Ki.12:40; Mk.14:54
When Elijah speaks the Word to do work it is effective for life or death. It commands fire, wind, earthquakes, lightning, thunderstorms, rain, clouds and flood upon the earth until final judgment for eternity much superior to the archangels in Heaven.

CHRIST sits on HIS throne in Heaven and puts HIS faith in Elijah to do the work on earth to save HIS spirits and establish kingdoms in salvation.

Elijah works according to New Testament of CHRIST in Heaven. Every man's work must be tested, and his doctrine, to see if it is true or false. If it is deceptive it will collapse and fall. Elijah was created with wisdom and knowledge to direct the work to be done by CHRIST the creator of spirits in salvation.

Thou Israel spirit name Israel. **Hos.4:15; Sam.38:15; Gen.35:10; Lev.20:14; Job.12:7–12; Ro.8:20; Jn.8:34, 44** God is now a godly spirit in the name Israel and cannot save Mankind. He was born on earth from the seed of god (Cain). He has no power, Elijah has the Word. God Israel had no faith and died of bowel cancer. **Ja.4:12; 2:17; Heb.11:28; Hos 4.15**

The Passover

There is no love-loss if a spirit from the seed of God lives to death under the law of ancient devils of darkness.

Elijah created to do the work

Elijah built a vessel and in the ark was The New Testament for the people he saved to continue up to salvation to teach their children to have faith in their saviour

The people ask for work

Elijah began clearing up the sight in the forest to set up the vessel. The people asked him for work to help him clear up the forest. They looked upon him as a revolutionist, with power of Elijah.

The majority of pharisees did not like his style and arrogance and confidence in the way forward. They wanted Noah to be like them to live by the law.

They did not know what to make of Noah. They did not know about Elijah. There was much controversy. The rebellious leaders thought Noah was a mad prophet putting his faith in Elijah instead of God their father, and they began whispering among themselves.

The chief rabbi said: Noah, when the vessel is finished we will laugh, and you will find out God has more sense than Elijah in whom you put your faith to make this vessel sail in a forest of trees.

Elijah spoke through the mouth of Noah: the wisdom in this world is foolishness with Elijah. He catches the wise in their craftiness and everything is in the hand of Noah to build this vessel. You will see with whom you will laugh with when the vessel is finished.

Don't cry to me to let you inside after the door is shut. You will have God, whom you trust to save you when the vessel is lifted from the forest.

The construction of the vessel

The length of the vessel was 167.7 metres, width 18 metres and height 27 metres. There was a lower deck, second deck and third deck. Decks were fitted with 55cm portholes. On top of the vessel Elijah built the sanctum – private quarters for the holy spirits Zion and Jerusalem, with a table made of gold.

The vessel was fitted with solar batteries to propel the vessel, a navigation satellite system, kitchen for cooking food, and air conditioning to regulate the temperature in the vessel.

Bread

Every morning the people who worked would collect their bread, partridge and quail fallen from the sky in a part of the forest. They lived on site. They began to have faith in Elijah.

Two cherubs like Zion and Jerusalem

There were two cherubs with outstretched wings with different colours – one fitted at the bow of the vessel and the other fitted at the back of the vessel facing the one in front. In the middle was the ark with the scroll of the New Testament.

Elijah fitted all the pieces, including stalls for beasts, cattle, sheep and goats, cages for the birds and insects, and fruit cuttings of bearing trees, and seed. The people began to complain about the bread from Heaven going mouldy after sunset; they would rather have the local pitta bread. Elijah set serpents on those who were complaining about the bread from Heaven and they began to tremble and cry: we have sinned to complain about the bread from the sky. Tell the serpent to go away, Noah.

Elijah took a serpent and put it on a pole and said: I don't want anyone who works on the vessel to complain about my bread. I want everyone who works on the vessel to go to the pole, and who the serpent bites, will work with me.

One by one they went to the pole in fear of the serpent and those the serpent bit went on one side and those who did not get bitten left the site and went in the nations to complain to the pharisee.

The pharisee came with astrologers from other nations and said to the giant: who gave you authority to kill the pharisee in the nation?

The giant said: if there was no crime there would be no need to have a judge in the law, or solicitor, barrister, courts and jails. No one would be held in captivity or bondage. No adultery no cheating, scriptwriters, no murder, no war. NOAH fed us in the forest, not the law. You practice what you preach.

Is it against the law to build the vessel in the forest? Who gave you the law is not on earth! The law is out of date and old, from ancient devils, and leads to death for those who practice it.

God who gave you this law is dead! Can you pray to him to feed the workers from his seed in the forest? The workers shouted at them: we eat bread and roast partridge and quail and we are satisfied. What is it with you and the law?

A giant Anakin said: Chief, should I break their necks for coming to disturb the peace in the forest to make an example?

The astrologers and pharisees began to tremble and said: don't break our necks. We came from the other nations. We heard NOAH put God to the test and he didn't respond to these corrupt pharisees. We are rabbis who want to know about the spirit Elijah who made fire come from Heaven to set wood on fire on earth.

We heard from our witches. They saw in a crystal ball the spirit Elijah is with Noah and we want Noah to tell us about this spirit Elijah we know little about.

Elijah said: God has many faults and was born on earth and is from the seed of the god of the devil. Had he been perfect, God would make Mankind on the earth perfect from his seed, even in this generation.

Therefore it is good to know why you are not perfect. The god (Cain) raped his sister to make a god like himself, before the devils strangled him to death. Born to her was a son of god who you worship as God your father, who passed on his seed to make Mankind not perfect, with much violence, shedding blood on earth.

There are two hundred million people on earth from the seed of God and not one spirit from his seed is perfect in the kingdom. If the spirits of the witches were perfect they would not have to look in crystal balls; they would tell you plainly who are Elijah and God your father and what he did by exterminating holy people from the earth to make you not perfect like him.

You want to know about Elijah? He removes a spirit in a kingdom and he sanctifies his spirit in the kingdom. Therefore, focus on the fault of this law. Do as Noah did, and have faith in Elijah, who is building this vessel in the hands of Noah, to rest in peace.

Through the mouth of Noah Elijah said to the pharisee: you want to know about Elijah? He is a spirit created by the Word in the kingdom of the god of Satan to do the same in the kingdom for spirits who have faith, so his CHRIST can perfect your body to rest in peace.

Elijah made the imperfect spirit of the accursed under the old law to have peace instead of crying with devils, and the godly spirit of God after death.

Elijah said to the pharisee: it is not the devils you fear but God who gave you the law to live by the law and it relates to all the barbarism, wickedness and violence on earth. The law is deceitful, not perfect, and those who live by it profit from it, to lead astray from truth for spirits to fall after death because of jealousy with envy.

No spirit from the seed of the god (Cain) can make a spirit of creation in the kingdom; neither can any pharisee of the law save a spirit when it departs from the kingdom.

You are a pharisee of the law. Learn the fundamental teachings of creation instead of the law of God. The devils knew about the Word, CHRIST and Elijah, who are hidden in your doctrine of law and were in fear of CHRIST and Elijah.

The giant who killed the pharisees said: Rabbi, we don't believe God created the world and we will help you, Noah, to build the vessel. Rabbi, you cannot save our spirits after death. Elijah through Noah showed us his power and made bread come from Heaven and we have faith Elijah will save us. God could not make a crumb fall from the sky to give us hope.

An astrologer said to the giant: if you don't believe in the law of God, then you believe in creation and creativity. We know everything leads to Heaven. We know everything started up there and the devils were cast out of it to earth. We are told Elijah cast them out of the earth, before giants were born, and God our father made us same time as you.

But what we do not comprehend is the Word that has so much power. We have a problem with this higher intelligence than ours and we are confused and have arguments about God with this law to death for spirits to go below. We see the sun, moon and stars above in this truth.

And the reason we don't have faith in Elijah is that we have never heard of Him. The doctrine we have is written with a lot of dots and doesn't say much about Elijah, so we have no knowledge to teach about Him and the higher intelligence to have faith.

The rabbi said: Noah, you have put your faith in Elijah and it has created a division between the God of Israelites and Elijah.

Through Noah, Elijah said: the way to everlasting life is simple. It is free if you want your kingdom to be established. The spirit created will have knowledge of the higher intelligence while your faith will gain you rest. It is very simple. You need no law to understand this.

The reason why there are many dots about Elijah is because scriptwriters are seduced by corrupt godly spirits who don't want you to know about the advanced way of life by the Word, and switch what Elijah does, and say it is God that has power.

The doctrines are corrupt. They have switched the work Elijah does by the Word and say it is God who did it to make God look mighty and powerful with the law, to put fear in Mankind to worship him to death to fall to be a godly spirits after death to fight with God for the earth.

Elijah gives the spirits of gods in the kingdom a choice to rest in peace or fall. Before God made Mankind he took the oath to live to death and all from his seed. he is angry and jealous of the choice Mankind has not to suffer sorrows like him for eternity. He did not create you perfect because he is not a creator and was born on earth like you from the passed-on seed of god (Cain). You are ignorant of this truth, because what God did is shameful and it is hid.

If you want to have knowledge of creation you must change your concept from religion that is made comfortable and superficial, and face reality. While you have flesh on your spirit, Elijah give every spirit of God of god a choice for peace or fall. if you have faith, prepare your body for salvation to make what is impossible by God possible by CHRIST the creator by the Word of Elijah.

The astrologers began to argue with the pharisees about creation and the law of God. There was heated argument and the chief rabbi said to the astrologers: this controversy about Elijah and the Word is brainwashing, and they began to whisper among themselves.

Then they returned to Noah and said: when the vessel is finished we will laugh at you and your spirit Elijah in who you put your faith to make this vessel sail in the forest full of trees. Don't come in the synagogue to cry to us.

Elijah spoke through the mouth of Noah: the wisdom in this world is foolishness with Elijah. He catches the wise in their craftiness.

You will soon see who you will judge. When the vessel is finished on earth, don't cry to me to let you come inside. Once the door is shut I will not let you in. You will know if God can save you when the vessel has risen and when you enter the gate inside the earth.

Many follow the shameful way of God to bring the New Testament of CHRIST in disrepute in their greed to exploit others with doctrines made up to suit themselves. Judgment is long overdue. **2.Pe.14:2**

Every valley shall be filled with water. Every mountain will be covered with water to prepare the people Elijah chooses to populate the earth to make kingdoms for salvation to create immortal spirits by the WORD. **Lk.3:4**

The pharisee and Rabbi said: Noah, you are mad. You are a dreamer with this Elijah. He doesn't exist.

The preparation for the new earth with the testament in the ark

The vessel was now finished and the workers gathered the seed from fruits and bearing trees. They cut vines and everything that was pleasant to eat. They gathered cuttings from trees yielding seed. Then they began to carry everything gathered inside the vessel in the cool room to keep it fresh. Others were laying woven carpets of straw on the floor.

The news went round about in the nations that the vessel was finished, and all sorts of people were invited for the Passover and began to cue up. For the Passover they had to go through a health check and strip naked.

Those accepted, male and female of their sort, took a dip in a pool of water and went inside the vessel – Shem, Ham, Japheth and six thousand men, women and children. Thus the vessel was finished and the host of them who built it rested from their work.

Thc time had come for those who put their hope in God to save them and for those Elijah chose to populate the earth to continue after the flood until the time of salvation.

To set an example for the next civilization, and to believe in the only saviour Elijah for when their time comes to depart from the kingdom to warn the people in religion contrary to the New Testament of CHRIST, the danger of multitudes falling in the everlasting fire in the sun. A spirit is elemental and can't be born again in danger of everlasting Hell if they don't have faith in Elijah to save them.

A SHORT WORK ELIJAH WILL DO ON EARTH Mk.9.26:6–33; Eccl.1:4; Gen.114–15; Jn.4:48

Elijah said to the couples He chose with their children to go to the second and third decks to rest.

Those who entered began to say: brothers and sisters, our bodies are clean for Elijah so he can establish our kingdom with a new spirit to go to Heaven.

The pharisees follow fables with faults and do not believe in the Great Spirit Elijah who gave us bread to eat from Heaven and partridge and quail to roast at night.

Those unbelievers who were not accepted began shouting at Noah: the great Elijah has possessed thee to build a vessel in the forest! Those not accepted began shout at those entering the vessel: brothers, don't let your women go inside the vessel. Noah is mad. Others began shouting; Noah, you want the women to go in the vessel naked to have sex with them to pass on your seed to make Israelites. All Israelites continue since God our father made Mankind. Get out of the vessel.

Elijah said: once I shut this door you who stand outside will cry for God to save you without the flesh of his mother when you enter the gate, for your ignorance of the truth.

The spirits of gods in Mankind have been deceived to go to Hell through corrupt religion

You have been deceived with the law of God to live to death. You have a choice to rest in peace after death for your kingdom to continue with a spirit created in your image to live for eternity. The choice is yours while you live in the kingdom. Have FAITH in Elijah.

The saviour you can trust is Elijah Jn.28:29; Mt.16:18:20

The work Elijah does is spiritual by the Word. This New Testament of CHRIST was inside the ark on the vessel for Elijah to distribute among who he saved to live by the New Testament.

Before Elijah shut the door of the vessel beasts, fowls, insects, creatures and cattle started heading for the vessel – males and females of all sorts, young and healthy.

Cattle, goats, sheep, fowls, birds, creatures and insects began entering the first deck of the vessel. Then the big beasts took their turn. When the last pair had entered, the door was shut automatically.

One generation Passover by water, the other Passover comes in salvation Eccl.1:4; Is.51:8; Joel.1:3; Ro.7:2; Deut.28:1–14

The whole earth was in darkness. Thunder and lightning was zigzagging in the sky. Elijah caught the jet stream to Whykibully to be with Zion and Jerusalem. Then they returned by the jet stream to the vessel, and Zion and Jerusalem went inside the sanctum built for them on the top deck.

Israelites and Mankind will know if God can save them 1.Cor.3:13,15; Rev.3:17–22

The trial of faith is put on show: Elijah's work is tried for Mankind to see if the vessel will float on water and for everyone to see who is their saviour to survive the flood to start a new life after. The earth began to tremble to loosen up the earth. The water from the great deep came up above the earth and fountains began spouting water all over the earth.

Rain started falling non-stop and the water increased rapidly. The people began running up hills to higher grounds. This rain brought flooding and chaos and the people began crying to God: the end has come upon your people. Save us, O God. But they got no answer. Nor was he seen to save any one to stop the water from flooding the earth.

The water began running down mountains and filling up valleys, and came unto the vessel in the forest. The vessel started to creak, taking the strain. Then it moved sideways and suddenly the vessel began to rise in the same ratio of the water upward.

The people began to shout: open up, Noah! Let us in; we are going to die! Noah, let us in! But the vessel was too high and they could not climb to hitch a ride.

The people began running on top of hills to escape. They began to cry to the pharisee: The end has come for multitudes, for the family of God to die You have made the Great Spirit Elijah angry with your law to death. Pray to God to save us from this flood. Slowly the water was gaining height on the hills and rain was falling non-stop, causing landslides and flooding valleys.

The water was gaining height from one hill top to another. Multitudes outside the vessel were trying to stay afloat, including big beasts caught up in this flood, swimming to stay afloat in the water. Suddenly there were no more hilltops in sight.

The water began to creep upwards on mountains. Multitudes of bodies and wild beasts were everywhere. Slowly the vessel began moving upwards to the peak of mountains and the vessel prevailed and was unto the top, sailing over the planet in victory over earth. The Passover to the new civilization. No earth could be seen. Thunder and lightning stopped.

THE PROMISE TO INHERIT THE SPIRITS OF THE SEED OF GOD IN THE GATES OF HADES

The spirits of the dead began heading down to the gates of Hades in multitudes, and the gates were automatically shut when the last spirit entered. They were all going to meet God with the law as his inheritance according to the promise Elijah made to him before he took the oath of devils to live to death.

THE TRUTH TOLD TO THE PEOPLE IN THE VESSEL IN THE FLOOD

The rain stopped and the water from the great deep stopped and there was calm. The earth was a planet of water. The vessel drifted in silence. Elijah went among the people and animals to ensure they were cared for.

THE WORK TO PLAN

Zion and Jerusalem were in the sanctum on the top of the vessel and saw the judgment on Israelites and Mankind. Multitudes of bodies floating in the flood and those inside the vessel saved were the witnesses to tell their children in future generations who is their saviour and to make kingdoms until salvation for creation of spirits in kingdoms with everlasting life.

THE TESTAMENT IN THE ARK Heb.9:16

Where there is a testament, it's effective after death. The people saved were executives of the New Testament in the ark in the vessel to pass on to their children for salvation for their spirits to rest in peace after death.

ELIJAH CHOSE SIX THOUSAND OF ALL SORTS OF IMAGES OF MANKIND

Elijah the saviour chose Mankind in the vessel according to the New Testament plan to save the kingdom and for the people to populate the earth and live up to salvation for their kingdoms to be created with a new spirit by the Word. The people Elijah chose to start a new life were naked, they had no disease, and were healthy when they entered the vessel with the New Testament in the ark.

With beasts, cattle, fowls, birds and creatures of every kind on the low deck in stalls and cages to Passover to the new civilization to populate the earth of their kind.

Mysteries of the Ages

Jesus is of the seed of CHRIST the first son of CHRIST with Zion Eve in the kingdom in the name Abel, the first son of Christ to ascend to Heaven after god (Cain) slew him because spirit Jesus is accepted above. God (Cain) was not of the seed of CHRIST. Elijah is the first son Christ created by the Word and is the brother of Jesus. The two sons of Christ Jesus and Elijah will return to confirm the New Testament to the children of Israelites and Mankind to confirm the choice they have and the promise of salvation for peace before salvation begins in kingdoms according to the New Testament

Elijah saved Israelites and Mankind to populate the earth to live by the New Testament so kingdoms from their children can be created with a new spirit for their spirits to rest in peace after death, so their kingdom can continue with an immortal spirit in the name of CHRIST to populate the earth so when their spirits depart from the kingdom they will be accepted above to live among angels in the light for ever.

Elijah said to the people in the vessel: it is good you bear witness to the multitudes that died in the water who followed religion with laws with a doctrine contrary to the New Testament, so now you can bring up your children according to the New Testament and tell their children the only saviour they must trust is King Elijah and no other.

God has unsettled Mankind through fear. The people who died in the water worshipped him to death. They did not want to hear the truth or even try to know what is hidden from them. They thought God would save them from the flood on earth.

Elijah said: you put your life in the spirit in Noah to protect you from death. Now you are resting in peace in the vessel as an example after death.

Elijah will save every child born from your children, so teach the children to teach their children to have faith in Elijah to save their spirits to rest in peace.

Those of you who worked on the vessel have prepared the way to start a new life with no violence and must be an example to others while you live on earth so it go well for your children. Do not go back to worshipping God. You heard many were crying for him to save them from drowning and he did not save one from death.

When the earth is populated with multitudes in nations, tell your children to tell their children: do not lose faith in Elijah to save them, after death to rest in peace.

The flood is the beginning, to learn about faith and for all of you inside the vessel to learn what is required so immortal spirits can be created in the kingdom in the time of salvation for your spirit to rest in peace.

Peace is elusive

Elijah said to the people in the vessel: while you lived in the kingdom under the law of devils, peace was elusive, you had no understanding. It applied to you after death for your spirit to rest in peace. God did not have faith while he lived in the kingdom. He died and became a godly spirit with no flesh of his mother to know there is no peace in Hades after death.

No mediator after death

There is no saviour after death; while you are alive you must have faith so you don't fall. Keep your body healthy as your gift for new life. Set an example for your peace and your children's salvation to have spirits to live in the New World, with knowledge, wisdom and understanding like angels above.

Elijah said to Mankind: if you disobey and go back to the old way and lose faith after death, your spirit will be in a place where you did not expect to enter after death.

This flood is an example to the end of the barbarian uncivilized and corrupt life. You saw multitudes were dead and multitudes of Mankind will be dead if they don't have faith in Elijah to save their spirits after death in the time of salvation.

A pattern to the end of days for spirits of gods in the kingdom 1.Pet.4:7; Ro.11:22

Elijah gave the people in the vessel a lecture on faith and the purpose they were saved to populate the earth until salvation, and the end of their spirits in the kingdom for the final Passover to immortal spirits to continue in the kingdoms to populate the earth in the flesh of Zion and Jerusalem, world without end.

Through the mouth of Noah, the spirit Elijah spoke to Israelites and Mankind in the vessel in the flood over the earth for a clean break from the old way of worship and to have faith in Elijah as their saviour because they are not perfect and their kingdom needs salvation by the Word to CHRIST

If Elijah did not save Judah, who he brought up from birth, neither will he spare those who have no faith in him to save them after they depart from the kingdom when CHRIST comes to cast out spirits from the flesh of Zion and Jerusalem in the time of salvation. Mankind that disobeys and has no faith after their spirits depart from the kingdom will be removed from the earth like the godly spirits and devils to the fire.

The spirits from the seed of gods will come to an end in the kingdoms for spirits of creation in the Light to continue in the kingdom to go above for eternity. Every spirit from the seed of God has a choice to decide their fate while they live in the kingdom to have peace or fall and should tell their children that the way of peace in the world is to have faith in Elijah before CHRIST comes to cast out spirits from kingdoms from his flesh Zion and Jerusalem in the nations on earth on the days of salvation.

The secret concealed Ro.13:12,14,17–18; Ro.12:2; Lev.20:14

After Elijah explained his reason for the flood, the people began to sing: Elijah is our saviour; we have seen his judgment to establish the New Testament. There is no one else who could save us from the violence on the earth. We shall prepare our bodies for Elijah to have a new spirit. Praise his holy name.

Elijah is our king on earth. His way is righteous and true. He has showed us who is our enemy and told us why he saved us.

Multitudes had put their hope in God and died in the flood. God did not save us. They made them think God made the world and died in the flood.

An Israelite said: Uncle Noah, what is the truth of genesis? Could you tell us? We don't understand about this serpent. Elijah said: the mother of God your father called him a serpent. He beguiled her and committed abomination with his mother to make Israelites.

The truth about the serpent and the beast

Elijah said: Jerusalem is a spirit and she was in the body of Babylon and called Judah a serpent, and Satan Jerusalem called the beast for holding her in captivity to make gods from her flesh.

Jerusalem spirit was in the body of Babylon when she called Judah a serpent. **Gen 3.1-19**

King Judah was wiser than the devils and had knowledge of who were Elijah and CHRIST, and the scriptures.

Elijah said: the scripture was written wrongly by God, Judah (the serpent) who said unto (the woman) his mother: did (God) Elijah say ye shall not fuck with your son in the mountain?

Jerusalem is the daughter of CHRIST (the woman). Judah (the serpent) said she may go with the son of the man Elijah (CHRIST in Adam her father).

Judah was warned by Elijah, who brought him up

I am the daughter of the man CHRIST in the body of Adam, held in captivity by the devils under oath. King Judah (God) said: Elijah said I should not fornicate with thee or touch thee less I die.

But Judah (the serpent) said unto the daughter of CHRIST: but ye shall not die if I fuck with thee.

Judah (God) knew scripture through Elijah who said to him: on the day ye fornicate with your mother, she shall bear for God, who knows good and evil.

The daughter of CHRIST in the body of Adam was in captivity by the devils. Judah had lust for his mother. After the devils were captured by

Elijah Judah became husband to his mother and she gave him children he called Israelites.

Judah began to ill-treat his mother and made her cry. Elijah appeared. Judah heard the voice of Elijah speaking to his mother his wife he called Babylon. Judah hid himself from the presence of Elijah, who was in the image of god his father.

Judah (the serpent) said: I heard your voice and I was afraid I would be a spirit without her flesh. Elijah said: thou have committed abomination with your mother. I commanded you that you should not commit abomination with your mother, You have made children with her with this accursed seed of god your father.

Elijah said unto Judah (the serpent): you have committed abomination with your mother. You know you are of the accursed seed of god your father. Every spirit from your seed born from your mother's flesh shall go in the gates of Hades when they depart from her flesh.

Elijah told Judah: You have brought evil between thee and the daughter (Jerusalem) of CHRIST and passed on the accursed seed of god (Cain) to make Israelites there. Spirits in the later generations from her flesh will fall because you did not obey me, and the kingdoms from her flesh will be for creation in the time of salvation, through CHRIST by the Word.

The kingdom from the flesh of the daughter of CHRIST will multiply upon the earth and spirits from the accursed seed of the god your father will be your inheritance if they don't have faith.

Elijah said: cursed are the spirits from Judah's seed on earth. Because he did not obey, the spirits from his seed live to fall after death and will suffer with much torment in the fire if they don't faith in Elijah.

His mother

The spirits from Judah's seed are like sperm, which he passed on to Mankind. Judah knew he should not commit abomination. He did the same with his daughter Hadassah to make Mankind in all different images.

Elijah said to Mankind in the vessel: multitudes who died in the water believed in God-Judah but he did not save them. They worshipped him to death. Many believed he made the world, and they died a sorrowful death in the flood.

Why so many questions? Elijah asked

The reason why God is angry is because he has not the Word to create like Elijah and was a human being, just like Mankind. That is why he is angry and the spirits from his seed descend to be with him as his inheritance. Tell your children to tell their children to have faith in Elijah to save them after death of their body. **Rev.14:19, 12**

Anyone who worships the beast/devil shall be tormented with fire when their spirits depart from the earth if they do not believe Elijah can save them. **16:1**

The wrath is upon spirits of gods who have no faith and do wickedly to destroy the kingdom by force and violence. So there will be no flesh for salvation.

The prophesy

When the time of salvation comes, the sun will throw much heat on earth. Mankind will curse god for their pain and sorrow and there will be much anguish on earth when their spirits end in fire with the devils and the false prophet. In the final judgment, the spirits will be removed from the earth.

One of the women in the vessel said: I had a dream. God was angry with Mankind and I saw in the dream many spirits coming out from fire to do battle against the Great Spirit Elijah unto Noah, who saved us in the vessel.

Another woman said: I had a dream and saw our children giving praise to God. His godly spirits made them unhappy and depressed and seduced them and tempted them with pleasure to lose faith in the Great Spirit Elijah.

Another woman said: I had a dream and I saw a great spirit as bright as the sun come from Heaven and begin casting out spirits from bodies. Then I saw a great spirit in the Light looking like Uncle Noah, waiting for those spirits that had been cast out. Then he began to speak words I could not understand and multitudes of spirits were taken by a tempest. I began to cry because I could not see them again.

Elijah said: consider your future and tell your children the great spirit you saw coming from Heaven is CHRIST to give your children's kingdom a blessing with new spirits, and they must trust no other spirit but Elijah to save them from this tempest.

WHY SO MANY QUESTIONS AND STORIES FROM THE PAST?

Another said: my mother's great grandmother worshipped God to death. Her great grandmother fell in Babylon. Elijah was passing by and asked: why so many questions and stories of the past?

The people said: Uncle Noah, we know the spirit Elijah is with thee, but we want to know the truth so we can tell our children to tell their children to prepare themselves for the Sabbath for their future so they don't die like those who died in multitudes in the flood.

Elijah said: it is important you asked and want to know the truth and where it went wrong for God. He was taught scriptures and was wiser than the devils. He is not a creator. He was a human being just like you. If he had faith he would be a spirit at rest and Elijah would create a new spirit to be his son and you would be perfect with no faults to continue on earth to bear children to go above.

Elijah said to the people inside the vessel: you have worked on the vessel in peace and resting inside the vessel in peace. This is an example. When you depart from the vessel you will be passing much seed to make kingdoms on the face of the earth.

When your spirits depart from your bodies you need Elijah to save you to rest in peace and for your body to continue to have a spirit in salvation for peace.

When you go ashore, don't go back to the old ways, with laws to live to spiritual death, but have faith to rest in peace after death. You are being saved in the vessel to make a clean break from the past so the kingdom can be established with spirits by creation to continue on earth, according to the New Testament in the ark on the vessel.

One Israeli said: Uncle Noah, now we understand we must be obedient for the Great Spirit Elijah to establish our kingdom with perfect spirits to be accepted above.

You ask and want to know the truth

Elijah explained to Mankind, it is good for every one of you in the vessel to know the devils are in fire, the god of the devil is in fire, and God your father is in fire and you have no one on earth to save you from fire but the spirit Elijah who has chosen you in the vessel, and saved you from death so you can continue to make kingdoms for creation, so you can rest in peace and not fall after death in fire.

No spirits from the accursed seed of the god can resurrect or live in the world when it is full of Light with spirits in perfection. A token covenant is made for thee until salvation to rest for your labour and for children after you who keep the faith to be saved after death.

It is important that you know about the holy spirit CHRIST and Elijah your saviour while you live in holy flesh of CHRIST, Zion and Jerusalem before you leave the vessel to multiply kingdoms on earth to rest from your labour.

While you are inside the vessel you have suffered no grief and misunderstanding among yourselves and know what is required of thee, to multiply kingdoms to have created spirits in salvation to continue in the world in perfection while your spirits will rest in peace.

You have seen multitudes of bodies floating in the flood and they cried, drowning to death. God did not save one after the vessel lifted from the earth, so now you will populate the earth in sight of CHRIST for Elijah to save your spirits.

God thought he was cleverer than Elijah and CHRIST with his vanity. Tell your children – don't be vain to be against CHRIST and Elijah to rule on earth by force with violence. Elijah will not save your children's spirits if they are against Elijah

One sews, the other reaps kingdoms

Elijah has chosen all of you inside the vessel to make kingdoms to replenish kingdoms on earth to have spirits of creation, which God your father eliminated from the earth by force when he became king.

The first example of judgment on spirits from the first civilization

The vessel was built to give the people on earth an example of who they should put their faith in to save them after death and to know who is their enemy by the law. **Cant.32:30–31, 37; Judge.6:25; Tim.1:9**

Faith without works is death, for the spirits of the seed of the god (**Ja.2:26**) fall after death if they don't have faith in Elijah according to the New Testament.

The people before the flood knew Noah. They knew not the spirit Elijah manifested in Noah, building a vessel to Passover. The kingdom is righteous and faith for peace on earth after salvation of kingdoms is justified.

Every spiritual work must be tested. Elijah set an example for the people to experience who can save them in this world to establish the New Testament with spirits of creation with eternal life to make the Old Covenant non-effective with the ancient devils and the spirits from their seed to death.

The hidden secret of Genesis revealed

Elijah chose all sorts of people that were healthy before they entered the vessel with spirits Zion and Jerusalem in the sanctum, the holy pace built in the vessel separated from people inside the vessel in the flood. **Gen.1:6**

The spirits from the seed of God that were caught in the flood journeyed to the gates of Hades in the deep. **Gen.1:2**

7. The vessel was above the earth in the flood when the spirits from the seed of God were separated from the people chosen by Elijah in the vessel from the spirits of the dead that went under in the deep.

8. The body of CHRIST in Adam is called the kingdom. **Job.26:10; Ps.33:7; Jer.5:22; 1.Pet.5:3**

9. Elijah chose the people he wanted to be in the vessel so they could populate the earth, Their children in future generations can rest in peace and for their kingdom to be created by the Word to CHRIST created spirits in their kingdoms on earth.

10. When the earth appeared, oceans and seas separated it to continents and islands.

11. The chosen people in the vessel went ashore. It was for the people to make kingdoms abundantly from the seed in God's nature, so their kingdoms are for creation to have spirits in the Light, after the spirits from the seed of God were separated from the flesh of Zion and CHRIST.

14. The salvation of the kingdoms ends when there are no more spirits from the seed of God of god in the kingdom on earth.

15. The spirits of gods in the kingdom live in the kingdom until the salvation for immortal spirits created in the Light to continue (16) on earth to be productive with perfect immortal spirits.

17. To bear an abundance of immortal spirits in the Light on earth for the whole world to have spirits in the light (20).

God is not a creator and was not on earth to save his people in the flood. Elijah chose whom he wanted to continue on earth according to the New Testament in the ark on the vessel with Zion and Jerusalem.

Essek.14:16,21

Noah's body was made perfect with the spirit Elijah. Elijah sanctified His spirit in Noah's body and manifested with grace. Noah's spirit was put to rest, so Elijah could do the work. Elijah is the king of the earth, the son of CHRIST with the Word. **Heb.7:3-4; Job.26:6; Job.24:24:19; Ps.45:17; Ps.45:13; Ps.75:7; Heb.9:14; Ps.19:12; Is.2:10**

Elijah explained to the people in the vessel he saved, who is the Saviour

God put fear in Mankind on earth before he died, and became a godly spirit. God provoked Elijah to wrath. God had it in his mind to do evil to Jerusalem because she had faith in Elijah. But now Elijah will do good for kingdoms from the flesh of Zion and Jerusalem to remove the spirits from the seed of God from their flesh, so God can receive spirits that have no faith in the gate of the sun as promised by Elijah.

Elijah is a spirit and can't be seen and was unknown to the people on earth. But God of Israelites and Mankind was known when he was human, born of seed of god, and was seen to be wicked, and the fear of him is on all from his seed. When he did evil he did not repent. He did evil to his death on earth.

Elijah is gracious. God is angry. Elijah gave God a choice to rest in peace and not end in furious flames of fire. Instead he joined the devils and was against CHRIST and Elijah.

God is angry. He did all the hard work passing the seed of god (Cain) in Hades, and Elijah is cool and will establish kingdoms for Jerusalem to have children in creation through CHRIST so spirits can have rest from passing his seed and not suffer in the heat like God for having no faith and putting his hope in the law of the devils to live to death with no grace. The scripture calls him a foolish king who had no faith.

The power of Elijah is more than God

Elijah said to the people: I have chosen you. If you turn back and do like the devil when you land on earth, I'll remove you from my sight.

When I release God from captivity and his godly spirits, it is to warn your children of the chaos in Hades to warn Mankind to keep the faith so they can have rest instead of fire. It is Elijah who is gracious and on the side of Mankind to save their spirits from fire.

Elijah said to the people: God is now a godly spirit, after he died and is a hateful godly spirit and blames Mankind for his fall, seeing he lost his chance to have peace and Mankind has a choice to have rest in peace if they have faith in Elijah in future generations not to fall.

Elijah told the people: I have chosen from all Mankind from the earth in the flood, so kingdoms from your seed and your children can have a gracious spirit created to live in joy and for your spirit to rest in peace on earth and not fall after death to suffer like Gods in the heat. And the people in the vessel said: Amen.

Faith in Elijah

Elijah said to Mankind: you are the remainder of the last civilization in the vessel. Healthy, well fed in my sight and want your children to be healthy in my sight for creation to minister to CHRIST on HIS throne in Heaven to create spirits for your children's kingdoms, so when they depart from the kingdom they have rest through faith.

This is the purpose you are saved – to do good for your children's kingdoms to Passover to life and to save their spirits after death from everlasting fire. The New Testament plan is for all of you in the vessel to make the kingdoms for creation of spirits from the flesh of Zion and Jerusalem on earth, in their presence.

Blessing in the kingdoms

Elijah said to the people in the vessel: creation in the kingdom from their flesh of your children will spring forth from all over the earth when salvation begins in the presence of Elijah and the spirits created in their kingdom will reach fullness of old age in holiness and their children will sing with joy and thank you.

The people said: praise to Elijah, for his holy work is righteous.

Elijah said: do you understand the purpose why you are saved? The people said: yes. Amen. Hallelujah Elijah! He has extended our life to live in peace on earth instead of death in the flood to make children to live in happiness and for spirits to live in the kingdom to the fullness of old age and to remove the fear of God, who is angry with us for being alive and not dead to live on the earth to make kingdoms for righteous work in faith.

The people said: it is good we are all gathered here in peace, and must look at the future work of Elijah. He saved us to make the righteous kingdom and have glory with a perfect spirit from the promise he made to Jerusalem to give her children in perfection.

The people began to debate: Elijah's way is straightforward. Our children will know how they stand by him if they keep the faith to receive the blessing to have beautiful children in the kingdom, and they began to jump for joy and shout: Hallelujah Elijah. He is our salvation from death even though we will not see salvation. He has opened our hearts to see our way is hopeless in this world because of this cursed seed, and we have a choice for peace.

God is angry with all of us because there was no peace and would rather see the end of all of us from his seed than to have a choice to rest on earth when we depart from the flesh of Jerusalem whom he hates for having faith in Elijah to save the spirits after death. And all the people said: Amen.

The hardness of heart

Elijah has saved us and is concerned in doing righteous work according to the New Testament so we are not worthless like all the dead outside the vessel in his sight in this temporal life. He saved us to do better for our children in the future to live in a perfect world in peace.

The spirit of Elijah has brought us all together in the vessel to give us understanding of salvation and creation and why he has saved us, so when CHRIST comes to put the kingdom in order to establish peace on earth with new spirits in perfection in Zion's and Jerusalem's flesh.

It is made clear to us, rebreaching kingdoms, justifying, sanctifying and glorifying kingdoms. It is plain to see Elijah is the saviour and he has saved us to make kingdoms to replenish the earth to put back the good spirits that were destroyed in the kingdom from the face of the earth by God our father's anger because he was not accepted to go above.

God our father made Mankind. He made no one perfect from his seed from god. We are at liberty to choose the right way for our children in the future so we don't fall like him with no faith.

Therefore we should keep the faith so our children in the future can prosper in peace and continue to have discussions with one another while we live under this condition to make kingdoms for peace, as it is the main purpose of being in the vessel – to learn the way of life through Elijah.

It is up to every spirit of Mankind to seek the spirit that gives glory and doesn't end like the foolish king of Babylon, who made nothing good on earth and wanted to take the kingdom by force because he disobeyed Elijah.

The saviour

Elijah gave Mankind in the vessel an example of the final end of Mankind on the face of the earth in the flood, so that they can tell their children who will save them in the future.

Elijah showed Mankind in the vessel the direct way to life before he scattered them in all directions on earth, to populate the earth with kingdoms in multitudes for salvation.

The flood is a pattern of the end

For burning the bodies of Zion and Jerusalem to ashes, Elijah made an example of what is going to happen to spirits from the seed of God of the god in the flood, so those saved can tell their children to tell their children in the future generations that only Elijah can save them and to establish their kingdom with a perfect spirit in the Light, and that there is no other spirit they should trust.

Different nature

A woman said: I had a dream. I saw this Great Spirit CHRIST coming in clouds and I saw spirits from Jerusalem's flesh cast out from kingdoms. And the spirits were crying without flesh before the mighty Elijah, trembling in fear. And the spirits were gathered in multitudes and were crying loudly: Elijah, save us! And they disappeared in a whirlwind.

Another woman said: I had a dream. I saw this great spirit on a throne looking at Elijah on earth, and Elijah was speaking words to CHRIST. And CHRIST came on clouds to earth and I saw spirits flying out of bodies from all over the earth and God and another god began to fight, one saying: they are mine and the other saying: I pass on more seed than thee. They are mine from my mother's flesh. Elijah promised me before I left the earth that all flesh on earth is for my mother, and spirits from my seed is my portion in Hades.

Elijah said: it is good you have these dreams to warn your children if they stray and build temples to worship gods made of wood and stones to forget your saviour. I know your imagination is to do good and evil with religion to profit from this Passover. I've taught you arts, crafts and skills to prepare you for your survival after the flood. Make good use of them and teach your children them straightway.

Seed time Gen.1:28

Elijah said to the people in the vessel: be fruitful and multiply to replenish and rebreach kingdoms upon the earth with grace.

Elijah told the men that their seed would bear all sorts of images upon the face of the earth from the women in the vessel. Every spirit from your seed shall be in your nature when they leave the kingdom, and if they don't have faith they shall be with the beasts/devils and the serpent in the bowels of the earth waiting for judgment.

Every one of you saved in the vessel is chosen in this generation to continue on earth and knows now what is required of thee. Be obedient before the Great Spirit CHRIST in Heaven, who has given you more time on earth.

Every kingdom is pleasant in HIS sight, with spirits on earth to create new spirits to be as it was in the beginning in the Garden of Eden by the Word with knowledge and high intelligence of creation.

Every kingdom that is prepared for Elijah is for creation to be rebreached with a spirit with knowledge when the spirits of God are separated from his holy flesh because God hanged his body on earth and killing and shedding blood of his holy sons from the earth.

The token covenant for all mankind

This token covenant is made for all Mankind because it is not their fault to be born, and is given thee to have a choice to have rest through faith.

Pass seed to make kingdoms for the saviour of kingdoms

The people in the vessel could have died in the flood like the others. The plan is to save those who are healthy of all sorts to populate their kind to earn the token rest through obedience in deed.

When Elijah was finished with his exhortation as to why he saved them to multiply kingdoms he said: the flesh of Man, you shall not eat, because it is for creation, and the people said: Amen.

Obedience is required

Elijah said: when you go ashore, be fruitful and have power over all creatures and beasts on the face of the earth. They shall be meat for thee from every species that moves with life upon the earth, and the people said: Amen.

The sanctum of the vessel

The Sanctum on the vessel was private for the holy spirits Zion and Jerusalem and Elijah. After Elijah spoke to the people in the vessel of what is required of them, he entered the sanctum.

Zion said: Elijah, you are always working. Elijah said: I look for the day when the work is complete in salvation for ever.

It is expedient Mankind knows about faith to prepare their bodies for their future so they don't do the same mistake like the devils and live by the law to death as God their father did, to blame me for not saving them in the end of their days. So it is important, Zion, that they know the truth to pass it on to their children.

They tend to make the same mistake as Judah who made them. Their imagination is in his nature to do like the devils that were on earth. It is expedient that they know about faith to prepare for their deaths and not fall to be with the devil in fire.

Elijah said: Zion, you have one more hurdle to Passover before salvation, and then you will be on your way to Heaven to sit on the throne next to CHRIST as queen of the world for ever.

Jerusalem said: Elijah, what about me? Elijah said: blessed are you, Jerusalem, among women, saved in the vessel to make kingdoms for thee from your flesh. Jerusalem began to cry: I am so ashamed. I am spiritually poor with spirits from the accursed seed to bear kingdoms while I'm a spirit with no flesh.

Elijah said: Jerusalem, you are a free spirit of the earth. The spirits of the women are of the accursed seed and are good for nothing. They will be cast out so spirits can be created by the Word to CHRIST to give you holy women accepted and righteous to multiply the earth.

And they shall be immortal spirits on earth in the kingdom, the same as you, and you shall be among them of creation, glorying in kingdoms from your flesh before CHRIST in Heaven.

When the last seed of the accursed seed is purged from your flesh you shall be queen of the earth, lustified in righteousness, with spirits of creation in your flesh. And you will be satisfied with immortal spirits that will continue to populate in multitudes to replace spirits of the accursed seed of the god who raped thee to make a wicked god like himself to pass on his seed to Mankind.

Elijah said: Jerusalem, you shall be queen of the earth when salvation ends with spirits of gods when CHRIST comes to put kingdoms from your flesh in order for thee from this generation in the vessel when salvation begins in your flesh in multitudes like stars to be among angels in Heaven.

Jerusalem said: O Elijah, all this work for your Jerusalem to be your queen in righteousness, from the seed devils much good will be in kingdoms on the earth by the Word. Elijah said: you shall be with children that give you much joy from children of sorrows. Jerusalem said: you will be my king. CHRIST my father has made me for thee by HIS Word. You are my rock of salvation.

Jerusalem began to cry and tears ran down her face. Elijah began to wipe the tears off her face and Zion said: you see how blessed you are, my daughter on earth. Therefore you shall cleave unto your husband in the same body as him and you shall be as I was with your father in Adam. When the people in the vessel are scattered all over the earth you shall sanctify in the same body as Elijah, until you awake from sleep to be tried by faith to be his queen of the earth for ever. Indeed I pray you will overcome temptations when you are among Mankind until the appointed time after I resurrect you to see spirits cast out from your flesh in salvation in the final judgment.

Elijah said: my work is finished in salvation and this is far off and will have rest after I have spread the people all over the earth. The earth is now tilled from the filth of the first civilization.

Elijah said: Jerusalem, when you awake from sleep you will live from my presence. All kingdoms are from your flesh, sanctified in a body of an old woman so you don't get grief. Many women in the vessel are young and they are healthy for childbearing to make kingdoms for thee.

So it would be advisable to sleep so when you wake up they are old and have much choice to choose one for peace.

Zion said: Elijah, all I want is peace while the earth returns to seed-time. I have had enough of living in flesh. I am a spirit and look for the day I resurrect to my CHRIST. When the earth rises from the water I will find a Shangri-la on earth to enjoy my sleep until I wake up, to be judged by the children of Mankind in the vessel.

Jerusalem said: Mother, you are from creation by the Word of our Eternal Father. I was born on earth from holy seed of CHRIST.

Because of one sin, much flesh is on earth through me while I was held in captivity. I can't be queen in Heaven, nor is it righteous I should be queen of spirits of the accursed seed of devils.

Jerusalem said: Mother, Elijah saved us after death. He is the king of the earth and promised to give me a son with my spirit by the WORD to give us immortal children with holy seed to populate children all over the earth for his queen. I was born to be Elijah's queen on earth and all our children's spirits will resurrect to have your blessing when you are queen of the world.

Zion said: Jerusalem, I pray when you wake up from sleep, Elijah, will save you from the godly spirits when they return from captivity.

You are an immortal spirit and kingdoms from your flesh will be created by the Word of Elijah to CHRIST so you will be a mother of immortal spirits on earth to continue to be, as it was in the beginning in Eden, in holy flesh of your father and me.

You are a spirit who knows good and evil and you can't be a queen of good and evil but a queen of immortal spirits in your flesh by the Word to be accepted above through your faith in King Elijah for ever.

Zion said: my daughter, the earth is tilled for thee to bear kingdoms in good health to prepare for holy work in salvation to create spirits with everlasting life by the Word, when I take my seat in righteousness in heaven.

When your spirits resurrect it is to receive holy blessing from your queen mother and CHRIST to live in any world of their choice. I have faith in Elijah to resurrect me on the throne of faith.

Trials of temptation begin when you will want to be free. Had I not wanted to be free to till my patch of the earth on my own, and through curiosity, it brought this entire problem with the accursed spirits of the god of Satan on earth to be in this vessel to escape the violence of corrupt spirits with hate and jealousy and murdering your brothers to make them. Elijah has saved them to give you the victory in the end of days.

When the people are dispatched all over the earth, they will multiply in peacc so your labour and sorrow will not be in vain, but to have joy in the end with everlasting children by your king, who is the faithful son to serve CHRIST'S kingdom on the face of the earth to create spirits in the Light in perfection like us.

You see, my daughter, it is important you should not lose sight of faith to have grief afterwards because of temptation. When you awake from your sleep, don't let curiosity get the better of you then to keep crying to Elijah to come and save you when you are persecuted by godly spirits.

Jerusalem, pay attention to what Elijah has said. Sanctify in an old woman so you may have peace, or suffer grief and torment in young kingdoms of women.

Zion said: Jerusalem, temptation will come unto you, Jerusalem, till Elijah gathers kingdoms for creation to have children like chickens under your wings. When the spirits of gods are separated, those who have faith will be saved after death and those who don't believe and live in false hope will be removed from the earth to the gate for disobedience.

Zion said: my daughter, Elijah's work is strict to the dot of the New Testament of CHRIST to purge HIS holy flesh from seed of the devils for ever.

Jerusalem, you are a witness in the flood. Our eyes have seen Elijah's judgment by the Word, and saved our spirits in the fire. And his spirit manifested in Noah so we can do the same as holy spirits in any body from our flesh to live until the appointed time, when I shall leave the earth..

Jerusalem, you will reign on earth with king Elijah when his holy work in your flesh is finished. I was with CHRIST when HE created Elijah. While you were held in captivity by the devils, CHRIST created HIS Elijah to save you from the devils. There is no spirit of the seed of god that can save you and can do the work of creation with CHRIST.

Zion's exhortation to Jerusalem in the sanctum

Blessed are you, my Jerusalem. You are pure in heart. When you cry you shall be comforted. Elijah shall give you the promised son and you shall be satisfied with his children in righteousness on earth.

You are the spirit of the earth. If Elijah did not save those in the vessel, how could you have kingdoms to have spirits of creation if you are a spirit with no flesh?

You are a spirit in the Light, a beacon of Light on the earth. As long as you live in kingdoms on the earth, kingdoms shall be established with spirits created by the Word to CHRIST to resurrect to HIS throne in Heaven in perfection, world without end.

The New Testament is according to the plan of CHRIST

Zion said: Jerusalem, every man's work must be tested. It rained on earth. Fountains of water sprang from all over the earth. The wind took us to Whykibully and Elijah brought us back in the sanctum in the vessel. The vessel was raised by the flood and was built by your rock of all ages, and now we are free spirits by Elijah.

The foolish king built his kingdom on your flesh and when the flood came, multitudes died. There was no God to save them except those Elijah saved to give you hundredfold to put the kingdom in order with immortal spirits in perfection.

After Zion exhorted to Jerusalem of the pitfalls of being a free spirit, Elijah said: Jerusalem, your brothers cry unto me and their sons from Heaven for their blood that was spilled by Judah and his battalion on the earth. The mouth of the waters was opened to receive the spirits of those who died in the flood to journey to the gates of Hades.

If those in the vessel had died, there would be no profit to thee and Zion and your sisters who were raped to make giants. They yielded kingdoms in multitudes all over the earth. Now there are various images of kingdoms from your flesh until salvation. The devils and Judah from the accursed god violated the peace and killed all your brothers and their baby sons from the face of the earth.

When you awake from sleep you shall be like a fugitive upon the earth, fleeing from one body to another to avoid persecution by godly spirits after they return from captivity. They will blame you for making them to suffer in heat. They will not blame Judah for his abomination on earth to make Mankind to suffer, for he knew scripture.

Jerusalem said: Elijah, my punishment is greater than I can bear. They will drive me out of the earth. I shall hide from these godly spirits so they don't slay me.

Elijah said: pay attention to my Word and have faith. Judah is a wicked godly spirit, hurt and angry. When he returns from captivity with his godly spirits he will ask for thee to be his wife again. Jerusalem said: Elijah, you promised to give me a son with seed to bear children for CHRIST in righteousness instead of him.

Elijah said: this promised son will be unto thee in old age. If the godly spirit of God disturbs your peace and you cry I will wake up and return to thee to give thee peace, and the godly spirit of Israel/Judah will see the promised son through faith to bear children on earth for thee in righteousness to go above and he will return in captivity.

The godly spirit Israel (Judah) will seek all opportunity to ensnare you. Zion, you knew how to sanctify when you and CHRIST were in Adam as one, only this time no godly spirit can be in the same body as you and Jerusalem. It is strictly forbidden for a godly spirit to be in the same body with an immortal spirit. You can't have Light and darkness in the same place. **1.Pet.5:8; Rev.5:5**

The godly spirit Israel is a tyrant and a violent oppressor 1.Pet.5:8; 2.Tim.4:17

Elijah said to Zion and Jerusalem: if any godly spirit enters the body you sanctify and dwell in, vengeance is mine. When the Lord Jesus and I return it shall be on them sevenfold – more than the stripes they received from the devils for wanting to take over the earth. Don't be deceived by Israel and god (Cain) when they return from captivity to tempt you. They will blame you, Zion and Jerusalem, for making them to suffer heat.

CHRIST in the deep

CHRIST was in the deep to reset the bands of the earth and open the chasm in the earth to let out the water to a setting. HE set up the water system so the water can recycle through the earth through falls, streams and rivers for Mankind to drink, bathe and for domestic use, to grow food and also for beasts to drink, and creatures and plant life to grow.

When CHRIST was through doing HIS holy work in the deep, the earth was below the water. Only the vessel was above. A great mist as white as snow came and there was no sky, no sun, no moon and no stars.

Zion was exhorting the pitfalls to Jerusalem while Elijah was outside the sanctum. They looked through the porthole and saw CHRIST in the mist, and HE waved to Zion and Jerusalem. They could not join HIM, as they have to go through more trials of faith for mercy before Mankind at the appointed time.

Elijah was on the deck, looking at CHRIST in the mist, wanting to give HIM praise. CHRIST looked at HIS son Elijah with admiration. Their eyes locked with each other, knowing what to do according to the master plan. Elijah spoke the Word and a gentle wind came and lifted CHRIST in the mist upward slowly to the heavens (26). There was much clapping in the heavens.

Suddenly there was light and thunder, lightning and rain, and then it stopped. The water upon the earth began to run out in the chasm of the deep to its new setting. Day by day the water began to run out of the chasm of the earth and mountain tops began to appear until the water level dropped below the earth, causing the earth to be divided between land and sea. Then the water ceased from running out, **8:1–2**

The earth

The earth was wet and soggy, with trees standing with no leaves. Elijah spoke the Word and a northern wind came upon the earth and blew the water to the South Pole and it froze into ice. Elijah spoke the Word and a southern wind came upon the earth and blew the water to the North Pole and it froze into ice.

The heat of thc sun began to dry the earth. The water system began to be operative, with filtered fresh water coming down mountains into streams and grew into rivers, making its way through the earth to the sea. **J.38:30**

The fossils in the earth

The earth was thoroughly cleansed. The bones of humans and wild beasts and creatures to the tiniest were engraved all over the earth as fossils for future generations to explore the history of the flood.

The wind system is until salvation

The wind began to circulate around the earth and blow hot air unto the ice in the north pole and it scattered mist northeast to south, and returned on the ice on the South Pole and scattered mist southwest to north to circulate clouds on the earth from heat of the sun and to moisturise the earth and make rain for the people to grow food.

The melting ice is the warning sign of the end

In the time of salvation, the heat of the sun will do as it did after the flood and focus on the ice on the North and South Poles and the ice will begin to melt as a sign of the end of spirits of gods in the kingdoms for the final Passover for the kingdom to continue with immortal spirits of creation by CHRIST through Elijah. No power can stop the ice from melting when the heat is on earth. This is a sign of the final judgment on spirits of gods who have no faith for peace and who will be removed from the face of the earth by the spirit of the sun to the gate, to fall in the everlasting fire of the sun (**3:42**).

Rivers and streams of the earth

In the time of salvation, the rivers on earth will dry up. The heat will cause draught on earth because of the ice melting to the end salvation. **J.39:11** Distress will be upon the earth in nations. Perplexity. Bewilderment. Confusion. Roaring winds.

The hearts of the wealthy will faint in fear of losing their wealth when they see mountainous waves of the sea coming at them and leaving their belongings on the earth after death.

No one will escape in the final judgment by the spirit of the sun. Every spirit of gods that have no rest will be pulled up by the sun from the earth to the gate to make a clean sweep of spirits of gods on the earth from the accursed seed. The earth will be tilled like it was after the flood for the kingdoms of Mankind and Israelites created with immortal spirits with the chosen people of Isaac to multiply spirits in kingdoms on earth in perfection as son and daughters of Christ by the Word.

The spirits of gods that have no faith in Elijah for peace, Elijah will Passover to the spirit of the sun for the final judgment to remove their spirits from the earth to the gate of the sun for God to save them from devils in the heat.

Elijah was not understood

An Israelite asked Elijah in the Jordan in later years: who art thou? Are you a prophet? Elijah answered: no, I'm he who heard the son of god crying in the wilderness and built a vessel for the flood with the testament in the ark for Mankind to prepare their kingdom for salvation.

Why baptize thee in the river Jordan?

Elijah said: it is to confirm the promise made to your forefathers for the work to be done for your salvation and to have faith if you want peace after death.

The vessel in the waters

There was much anxiety with the people in the vessel sailing slowly. Meanwhile the trees that survived on earth began to shoot buds and flowers to bear fruit, and the earth began to look green with pasture with everything new. Elijah let out birds to fly to the earth; the fishes started jumping out of the waters near the vessel for joy, with whales sprouting water and schools of dolphins jumping up and down in the water. Everyone in the vessel was excited, giving Elijah praise for saving them and taking them on a journey on top of the earth on water.

Mankind cannot see spirits

Elijah went in the sanctum and said: Zion, you have the first choice to go to any part of the earth so you can have peace. Get yourself ready. I'll call the jet stream to take you to any place. You are a free spirit to roam the earth till the appointed time. Elijah and Jerusalem gave her a hug and said: peace and love. As the wind came she was in the wind. She found her Shangri-la on earth to live in peace.

Zion's vision in Shangri-la on earth

Zion saw Elijah bringing the plan of CHRIST to focus on salvation in the kingdoms on earth according to the New Testament in the ark of the vessel from CHRIST in Heaven.

She saw much conflict between the spirits of the seed of god (Cain) in the kingdom and spirits from the seed of devils in the kingdom killed on earth and in the flood, the work that has to be done to establish the kingdom is creation with immortal spirits created by CHRIST through Elijah with the Word.

Zion saw the people saved in the vessel going ashore in different parts of the earth.

She saw in a vision CHRIST returning in salvation to create spirits and angels in the heavens celebrating CHRIST and Elijah's triumph and she sitting on the throne with Jerusalem seeing the final judgment on devils and godly spirits. And the world was full of Light.

When Zion did not return to the vessel Elijah said: Jerusalem, you are a free spirit. Get yourself ready so you can experience life on your own. I'll call the jet stream for thee to circle round the earth to see where you want to stay. Elijah gave her a hug and said: peace and love. And as the wind came Jerusalem was carried away.

Jerusalem's journey around the earth

Jerusalem saw all the earth was peaceful with no violence since the barbarous uncivilized died in the flood. The people in the vessel were given a choice to select their destiny after death.

Jerusalem saw the people leaving the vessel for land, and they began to move forward and began to spread out north, south, east and west. Jerusalem decided to take a rest where her holy people once lived when she was human with Adam.

Now I am a spirit, she said, all I want is to sleep. When she walked by the thermal pool she saw Zion crying, wanting to join CHRIST her father.

Jerusalem said: Mother, why are you crying? We are spirits saved by Elijah. When the battle in the kingdom begins we will see CHRIST cast out spirits from our flesh in all nations.

The kingdom is our inheritance and through Elijah it will Passover to us with immortal spirits to be like it was with my brothers and sisters before the barbarous uncivilized took it by force to eliminate us from the earth.

Jerusalem said: Mother, the kingdom has many different features, with spirits of gods that are born in sin, and will bring much conflict with each other while they live in our flesh through the ignorance of devils. It's only Elijah who can save them in the world to have peace. Zion said: my daughter, Elijah is concerned with the destiny of every spirit in the kingdom and has a plan for every spirit that departs from the kingdom. And his judgment is very simple – no faith, no peace. It's a free choice he gives every spirit before they depart from the kingdom. It's according to the plan to give this token choice to spirits of gods by CHRIST in the tabernacle in Heaven.

The Word is reserved for judgment when Christ returns 2.Pet.3:6; 2.Pet.3:10; 2.Pet.1:21

Zion said: Jerusalem, the power of the Word is with Elijah and all spirits on earth have this consolation that if they have faith in Elijah, he will save their spirits after death to rest in peace and not fall.

Jerusalem said: Mother, we are still on the earth as spirits. We should not think of the past to make us sorrowful. We have to wait for the appointed time to go to Heaven by Elijah. The spirits in our flesh, if they want to be saved to rest on earth after death, should have faith, like us, in Elijah.

When we were human we struggled between life and death, but now we are free spirits the mystery of life is no more a secret.

Zion said: Jerusalem, let us celebrate this freedom after death. The kingdoms from our flesh will stretch out over the whole earth for salvation while we sleep.

Zion said: Jerusalem, I feel I want to sleep like when I was joined to CHRIST in Adam, and not wake up until we are together in Heaven. I dread having to wake up to sanctify in the body of some old woman to have mercy before Mankind to go up to face more judgment by angels. Zion said: Jerusalem, you were born for Elijah. He is your king.

Salvation is far off. Elijah will give you the promised son by the Word to give you children in righteousness through CHRIST. Before the salvation of kingdoms begins, you will see the judgment by your king on our enemy.

Zion said: Jerusalem, the children from the seed of your promised son by the Word of Elijah will live in peace and have no godly spirits to oppress them with laws of devils.

Zion said: Jerusalem, when you return from Heaven you will be queen and Elijah will be your king for eternity, and immortal spirits from your flesh will have a long life on earth till they resurrect to the throne in Heaven. That is the way it will be for all generations, with no end.

Jerusalem said: Mother, while the people are passing seed to populate the earth I feel to sleep and not wake up until the appointed time.

Mother, you have one hurdle to go through, but I have to go through temptation when I awake from sleep.

Zion said: my daughter, Elijah sanctified in your flesh. Go and sanctify and be joined together as one, and sleep in peace till you awake to go through temptation and trials of faith as a free spirit to be queen of the earth after salvation's end.

Zion fell asleep while talking. Jerusalem closed the door of her Shangri-la, caught the jet stream, and circled the earth until she saw the vessel in the ocean, and got on the vessel and went in the sanctum of the vessel.

Seedtime

When the vessel got to Australia those taken ashore looked like gods in the beginning on the earth. Animals and creatures were put ashore and Elijah said: be fruitful and multiply to establish the kingdom with my blessings for thee and your offspring in future generations.

The vessel set out on its next journey and people were put ashore in Africa, and all kinds of wild beasts that could swim were let in the water to swim ashore. The birds flew and creatures were let out. Elijah said to the people: be fruitful and multiply to establish the kingdom with blessings for thee and your offspring in future generations. And it was so.

The vessel set out on its next journey and put ashore the next sort of people in Arabia. The elder son of Noah was given the ark with the New Testament and he said: let it be with me. I will make copies of it for all Mankind, so all on earth can know

I was in the Passover in the flood with the Great Spirit Elijah of my father who I have not seen, and acknowledge His spirit among my people. We will keep the testament in the ark for Israelites to receive a spirit of creation in the kingdom according to the Word to be accepted by the spirit Elijah to sleep in peace.

God was jealous

The son of Noah said: our God was jealous and Elijah did not save his spirit as he had no faith.

Elijah said to the Israelites: be fruitful and multiply kingdoms for salvation with my blessings for future generations to be perfect by the Word, to be accepted above, and it was so.

The vessel set out on its next journey, to Asia, and all Asians were put ashore with their herbs, wild beasts and creatures. Elijah said to the Asiatics: be fruitful and multiply kingdoms for salvation, to have immortal spirits and to go above with blessings. And it was according to the plan.

Elijah set out on the next journey, to South America.

Jerusalem sanctifies with Elijah as her husband on earth

Elijah went to the sanctum and saw Jerusalem crying. He said: my dove, could you not find a place on earth to dwell? She said: thou art my rock and my refuge, my fortress and saviour. If I'm not sanctified unto thee I'll cry.

The spirit that sleeps on earth wakes up Dan.12:2

I want to sleep and wake up at the appointed time to ask Mankind for mercy and to be worthy to be your queen on earth. Jerusalem came forward and sanctified her spirit with Elijah, joined together as husband and wife in the kingdom.

Spirits who sleep in CHRIST 1.Tes.4:14

Jerusalem joined unto the spirit Elijah, just as CHRIST and Zion in Adam, and slept until she awoke.

Ja.4:15 Do you think the scripture says things in vain? Let no one deceive you to make you fall. 3:14 Elijah is my saviour, my fortress.

When the vessel arrived in South America the Red Indians were put ashore with herbs, wild beasts, hawks and eagles, and creatures flying. Elijah said to them: be fruitful and multiply until salvation. And have faith for your peace. And it was according to the plan.

The return to Whykibully

The people dwelled in caves and bushes and spread out on the earth to populate the earth. Elijah set out to the island of Whykibully

When Elijah got to Whykibully he put 100 couples of Asiatics ashore with creatures, and let off birds and parrots to fly and multiply and told them: be fruitful and multiply till salvation comes. And it was so.

Elijah went round the island of Whykibully, got ashore and set the vessel on a direct course east until it disappeared out of sight. Then he went up the mountain of the island and there he fell asleep in the spirit with his Jerusalem, as male and female made for each other in the kingdom. **Jer.48:28**

Until Jerusalem awoke to give her the promised son at the appointed time, so children from his seed can populate the earth in righteousness in the kingdom from her flesh as their people of creation by the word. **Job.39:11**

Observe ye everything that takes place on earth from this generation so you don't fall. Behold the heat that will melt the ice, clouds and rain on the earth, and earthquakes. Peace comes to those who have faith in the kingdom.

Elijah is the king of this earth He is ordained to judge the unrighteous spirits of gods after they depart from the kingdom and to save those who have faith in him to rest in peace on earth.

Observation and judgment in salvation

The time has come for all to consider their choice for peace or fall. Peace comes to spirits that have faith in Elijah while they live in the kingdom to observe as the ice melts, the heat on the earth causing floods all over the earth, and earthquakes like when the devils were caught and removed from the earth for ever.

This is the beginning of the end of multitudes of spirits of gods in the kingdom. Those who are deceived by false hope in religion will fall.

When CHRIST comes to establish kingdoms on earth, it is to put an end to spirits of gods in this world.

There will be no place to hide in the kingdom. The spirits cast out will be carried away to the gate of the sun to God as his inheritance from the earth. Once the spirits enter the gate it's automatically closed for eternity.

Chapter 4

Godly spirits return after 1000 years of captivity, after the flood

A thousand years after the flood the people from the vessel populated the earth and built their nations. There was much to eat and the people traded with each other, living according to the culture of their forefathers – living a peaceful life with knowledge of the Great Spirit to protect them if they were in trouble. They put their faith in the spirit of their forefathers to protect them.

The godly spirit of God who was King Judah spirit named Israel returned with his Queen Hadassah and a multitude of godly spirits released from captivity after 1000 years from Hades. The godly spirits entered the bodies of people in the nations on earth and took possession of their bodies. **Act.3:25**

Israel entered the body of Tidal and his Israelite kings and others took possession of the people in the nations and they began to seduce the people to build palaces, just as they did in Babylon. Israel changed his name to King Tidal (Tyrant) and built Sodom on slavery, and Hadassah was queen of the spirits in Sodom.

Sodom was the most corrupt city on earth, with godly spirits seducing Mankind in all kinds of filth in prostitution to go astray and lose faith in Elijah. The kings would go in the nations and capture women to sell in Sodom and Gomorrah.

Abraham was moving his herd from one place to another with his beautiful wife Sarah, and her maid Hagar doing the cooking for the herd men.

The mystery of ages. Jerusalem in Sarah

Jerusalem woke up from sleep and looked for an old woman so she could sanctify, and saw Sarah, the wife of Abraham in old age. and she sanctified in the body of Sarah and cast out Sarah's spirit.

Jerusalem was frigid toward Abraham and he accepted that old age had caught up with Sarah. She was good companion for him, he not knowing Jerusalem was in Sarah's body. Jerusalem liked to bake cakes for Abraham while Hagar did the cooking for the herd men.

A spirit can't be seen by a human. Neither can a human know if a spirit of the dead entered their body to possess them and use their ears and see though their eyes and speak through their mouth and block their ears to have authority in their body.

When Abraham got to Sodom with his herd of cattle, sheep and goats, he pitched his tent away from the city and cleaned up himself and left Jerusalem and Hagar and went to Sodom to have a good time. He met a woman whose godly spirit Hadassah possessed, and he began boasting of his wealth to the woman, not knowing she was once the biggest whore in Babylon before she became a godly spirit. She started to seduce Abraham and he began to open his heart to her.

She asked him: why did you come to Sodom if you have a beautiful wife? He said: she is frigid and she is not interested in sex. She was only interested in cooking and baking cakes for me. She gave Abraham a good time and he promised to see her again.

Having eyes full of adultery cease to sin 2.Pet.2:14

After Abraham left Sodom city Hadassah went to tell Israel, her king of spirits in Tidal, about Abraham. She said: my God, this Abraham from your seed is rich. He has a wife that is frigid like a Hebrew, and all she likes to do is cook and bake cakes for him. Abraham said he worships God to death. You must meet him to take his wealth from him.

The next time Abraham came to Sodom city he met the same woman with the godly spirit Haddassah. She hurriedly went back to Israel and said: my king, he is back. Israel came and switched from the body of Tidal and possessed the body of Abraham to take him back to see this woman who is beautiful, to commit adultery through Abraham.

EYEWITNESS OF HIS MAJESTY 2.Pet.1:16

When Israel in the body of Abraham returned, to his great surprise he saw Jerusalem in Sarah. She was in fear and told him to get out of her sight. Israel blocked Abraham's ears so he could not know what was going on in his body. Israel has authority over all spirits from his seed and Abraham is from the seed.

Jerusalem said: the devils should have removed your eyes before you came back from captivity. Israel said: now that I've found thee I'll not spare thee for my having to come back from the consuming fire with your godly kings and possessing the bodies of Mankind. They shall not spare thee for suffering in the heat. They will want you to be their queen of the spirits on earth.

Israel began to boast what he is going to do and got very angry, blaming Jerusalem for Elijah casting him out of the earth with all the spirits from his seed to suffer in the devouring fire in Hades.

Jerusalem cried: Elijah, do not ignore my plea. Hear my cries. I am distressed with my enemy with his law. Israel, he is threatening me and wants me go to Hades to suffer for making him.

He reviles me because I made gods for the devil and he is angry for making me his queen in Babylon. My heart is trembling within me. The terrors of the devils frighten me if I go to Hades.

Elijah, I'm in fear. My spirit is trembling in this body with his horrible spirit in Abraham. Israel wants me to be his queen to rule the earth spirits like when I was a queen in the days of Babylon.

Elijah, I wish I could sleep with you again, I am far away from my island and in Sodom. This boaster is in the body of Abraham. All he talks about is violence. This is stressful to me.

Israel is malicious and abusive to me while I'm in this body. His godly spirits are possessing Mankind in the nations with their deceit. Israel has turned against me and I don't know where can I hide, to be far away from him.

Elijah, save me! I'll cry night and day until you hear my distress. I don't care though he hears me speaking to you in this body (18). He told me he will hold me as ransom in the kingdom till the last spirit from his seed leaves my flesh.

The godly spirit that returned from captivity has turned against me and calls me a whore of the earth and says I should be queen of his spirits for ever among Mankind. They will not know until death when their spirits depart from my flesh.

These godly spirits curse me. They have no intentions to change their ways to lust in my flesh. They seduce Mankind to make gods in their image to worship them. Israel said: he is my ruler with his godly spirit to control Mankind according to the law to do wickedness to each other in the nations on earth.

21. The spirits speak through the mouths of rulers of Mankind. They seduce them to mislead them from having faith.

Elijah, save me and take Israel by surprise, as you did to the devils. Elijah, only you can destroy these wicked godly spirits from the earth. Save me from Israel.

Awake, Elijah, to send him and these godly spirits back to the pit. Their wickedness is like suckers in my flesh. All I want is peace. Be merciful unto me for making a blasphemer to pursue me after coming from captivity with his boasting. He twists my words so he can do me harm so you don't hear my crying to you. He wants to destroy you so spirits from his seed do not make kingdoms to be created with a new spirit through CHRIST in my flesh to have eternal life.

Elijah, come and save me from Israel. He said he will pursue me till I fall to be with him. Elijah, hear my prayer. I am ashamed to be with this boaster in Abraham, with his deceit. Jerusalem began to cry: wake up, Elijah, from sleep.

Israel has authority over all spirits from his seed. Abraham is of the seed of God. Elijah appeared before Israel in the body of Abraham and Israel, in fear that Elijah would send him back, in fright threw the body of Abraham onto the ground.

The great mystery revealed

Elijah commanded Israel in the body of Abraham to stand up, and took Israel in the body of Abraham to Sodom, the place Israel built when he returned from captivity

The godly Israelite kings in the body of people ruled the nations, including Gomorrah, setting up themselves to rule the earth.

Jerusalem's spirit sanctified in the body of Sarah. Abraham is human so he had no clue of what was going on because his body is possessed by Israel's spirit, who made him non-active.

When they got to Sodom Elijah warned Israel that if he hurt Jerusalem he will remove his spirit on the earth and he will return into captivity. Elijah said: I shall not hide from thee what I am going to do to Sodom and Gomorrah. Israel was in fear and threw the body of Abraham on the ground again in fear.

Elijah said: Israel, in Sodom I am going to set an example to other godly spirits who made themselves kings in the body of Mankind in the nations.

Elijah said: Israel, you are naturally wicked and want to be king on earth. You were released to warn Mankind of the chaos in Hades and built this place with your whore in Sodom, so I'll show you the judgment that I'm about to execute for corrupting Mankind with all godly spirits that have returned to do the same as you did when you were king of the earth, in Babylon

The filth of Sodom and Gomorrah is huge and will corrupt Mankind on earth. You want to commit abomination with your mother and the threaten her with Hades. She has cried to me to save her from you.

Israel spoke through the mouth of Abraham: because of Jerusalem you want to destroy Sodom, because you are the judge of the earth.

Elijah said: there is none righteous in Sodom as Jerusalem. If you can bring me one righteous in Sodom as her I'll not destroy it, so go and bring me one from your seed.

Israel returned and brought Hadassah. Elijah told Hadassah to flee before Sodom falls on her like the tower in Babylon did.

Elijah commanded balls of fire to come down from the sky on Sodom and Gomorrah. The inhabitants began running here and there; the winds began to scatter the flames all over the city. People were crying to God to save them and all he could do was see his Sodom on fire and going up in flames. Israel got the message. If he made Jerusalem cry, next time it will be him crying in consuming flames, in captivity with devils.

Chapter 5

The mystery of Hagar. Hadassah, second queen of Judah's godly spirit needed a body. She entered Hagar. Abraham, being human, did not know about spiritual things. Elijah gave Jerusalem the promised son Isaac by the word

Elijah said: Israel, I promised Jerusalem a SON with her spirit by the Word, and HE will be my heir on the earth.

His name will be Isaac and his spirit shall be an everlasting spirit and all children from his seed that are born are my blessed children with Jerusalem through Isaac to populate the earth with immortal spirits that are accepted above. **15:1**

Elijah spoke the Word to Jerusalem and she conceived an immaculate conception with her spirit – a son by the word.

Jerusalem said: now that I've found favour in your sight, don't leave me alone with them. Elijah said: I'll return at the appointed time, when you shall have my son with everlasting life. Jerusalem began to be in fear of what Israel would do to Isaac.

Elijah said to Israel: I will not hide what I will do to you if you touch her, while she is pregnant with my son Isaac.

Israel (21) spoke through the mouth of Abraham: I'll not lift up my hands unto the posterity of Jerusalem of CHRIST in Heaven. Her spirit is blessed on earth. You have saved her from my hand. I'll not hurt her and Isaac.

Israel said: I'll take Hadassah, who is my queen and from my seed in the body of Hagar (24) and she will give me a son like Daniel before when I was king of Babylon. She dwelt with me as my godly queen in Sodom (13–14) when I confronted Jerusalem in the body of Sarah (14).

Elijah said: Isaac shall not be your heir, but children born from Hagar's flesh from your seed through Abraham are your children (4). Elijah said to Israel in the body of Abraham: tell me, can you number the stars? Israel said: no. Elijah said: so shall the seed of my son Isaac be in righteousness on earth.

I brought you out of captivity and you will inherit spirits from your seed when they are separated from Jerusalem's flesh, as you have taken the law to live to death. They shall return to you in the deep, where you came from with the devils (12).

You shall receive spirits from your seed that have no faith in me when I judgc spirits on the earth in salvation (14). Jerusalem said: Elijah has restrained from sending you back for the wrong you have done to me. The next time Elijah will judge between my son and your children through Abraham.

Elijah said: Jerusalem is a blessed spirit in Sarah and I have given her a son by the Word, and she shall be a mother to the king of the earth, and kings shall be of Isaac's seed in her flesh on earth.

Israel got angry in the body of Abraham and fell on the ground in shame and said: you are giving Jerusalem a child when she is old? Elijah said: Jerusalem is my wife and she shall give birth indeed to my son, and his name is Isaac.

God – Israel was jealous of Isaac, the promised son of Jerusalem by the Word of Elijah

Israel was jealous of Isaac as heir of Elijah and looked for a chance to take Isaac to the mountain. When he got to the mountain he seduced Abraham to build an altar and bound Isaac unto the altar and took out his knife, and as he was about to stab Isaac to death so Isaac doesn't populate the earth with immortal spirits in Jerusalem flesh, Elijah said: Abraham, lay not your hand on Isaac, for I know you are seduced to kill him by God whom you fear (22-12). My only son is with thee. If you want to slay, look, there is a goat in the thicket. Offer it as a burnt offering to God in thee whose spirit you do not know, and want to provoke me by killing Isaac because he is my son with Jerusalem by the WORD in righteousness.

Elijah said to Abraham: your seed shall multiply on earth because you have obeyed my Word. You shall have rest (18). Abraham called the mountain Elijah of the Lord in Heaven, and Abraham brought up Isaac. Israel's spirit and Hadassah's spirit fled from Abraham and Jerusalem in Sarah. Jerusalem's spirit had rest. Abraham brought up Isaac. He got married to Rebecca, then Abraham died.

Isaac and Rebecca

From Isaac and Rebecca many children were born from the seed of Isaac as the promised people. They are the righteous people and beautiful with great wisdom, magnificent with knowledge of the higher science to the way of life above. These are the people of Isaac of Jerusalem and Elijah by the Word. Jerusalem's spirit went to sleep till she awoke (**XXXII2–XXXIIII6**).

Isaac separated his people from the people born under the law, who were jealous and persecuted them because they were people of Elijah and Jerusalem (**XXXII 7–11**).

The people of Isaac have good appearance in likeness of the people of CHRIST in the first civilization and they are immortal spirits in the Light like their mother Jerusalem and Elijah, the king of the earth who protects them.

There was famine in the land. Elijah said to Isaac: come, my son, I'll show you a land where you and my children shall dwell, and Elijah took Isaac on a trip around the earth and brought him to an island separated from the mainland.

13–14 Elijah said: my son, from here children from your seed shall multiply and travel in many nations on the earth with blessed beautiful children to the west and east and south. All families from your seed shall be the blessed people of the earth (26–1).

Elijah and Isaac stayed there in the woods discussing the New Testament to salvation. At sunset Elijah took stones of the place and made a circle with the stones as a landmark for future generations as their heritage with the new testimony that spirits from his seed will ascend to Heaven after they depart from the kingdom (28–11).

Elijah said: Isaac my son, this land shall be yours and for all children from your seed to live from all who hate thee (27). When you return you shall build a vessel (26–24) and I will be with thee in all the places thou go until you have established all I have said unto thee and return to this land which I have given thee (28–18) for my people on earth.

The united kingdom

When it was sunrise Elijah set pillars of stones on top of the circle of stones as a monument for his people on the land of Light. Isaac vowed to keep the way of his father Elijah and called the monument the house of Elijah, to be the united kingdom for thc pcople of Light.

Isaac returned and built the vessel and all his people took their belongings and their livestock to sail to the goodly land of light. The kings in the nations came after the people of Isaac to slay them. Elijah spoke the Word and stones started to fall on them from the sky, and they stopped pursuing the people of the Isaac going to the vessel.

The winds came, rain and stormy seas came ashore on the land where the vessel was built, and it lifted the vessel and brought the vessel to the sea and it was on course until it was out of sight, to the land of milk and honey. The people praised Elijah for his greatness to be in his hand for ever.

Isaac brought them to the goodly land of light to establish themselves to populate his people, and spread out in the nations.

Isaac said to his children: kings shall come out of your seed in this land I have brought thee by our father Elijah, who has given it to thee from His son Isaac (35–11).

The death of Isaac united the kingdom with immortal spirits from his seed

Isaac lived to old age and saw people from his seed populate in the kingdom with immortal spirits like himself to be the chosen people of Elijah and Jerusalem on earth, and fell asleep.

The spirit of Isaac is called Elisha. he directed his people from the united kingdom and spread them out to populate on earth until Elijah begin to establish kingdoms of Mankind in salvation for creation of immortal spirits through CHRIST (29) so there is no division in kingdoms on earth. So all immortal spirits created in salvation be equal with the chosen people of Isaac, perfect in the name of CHRIST, to be among angels in Heaven.

Hos.6:11 O Judah, Elijah has set a harvest for thee from Jerusalem's flesh in the multitudes. **Mt.9:37; Jer.9:22; Mt.26:56**

Israel, thou have transgressed in holy flesh and your godly spirits are seducing the spirits of gods in Mankind to have no faith to fall. The end of all spirits from the seed of god in the kingdom shall come to an end in the final judgment in for ever (**XVIIIXVIII, XIXI**).

The spirits from the seed of Isaac are immortal spirits in the Light and are different from the spirits of seed of God of god of the devil, who live to death under the law to fall like devils after death (**XXII 7:11**). The spirits of gods that have faith will sleep in the earth in peace and escape the everlasting fire in the sun for eternity with the devils. The spirits of gods in the body of Mankind have a choice to have faith in Elijah to save them, or fall. Simple judgment: no spirit of god in the kingdom as a priest, a doctor in religion, witch doctor or evangelist can save a spirit from the seed of god if they don't have FAITH. Rather tell them about the choice that is available, free of charge, to sleep or fall and move on to the next one who wants to know of the choice. It is simple teaching.

Blessed are the immortal spirits in the Light through Elijah and CHRIST to be in the world in the Light for ever (**XXIV:14**).

After hundreds of years James wrote:

My dear brother, do not try to confuse Jesus to be the creator CHRIST. Make this distinction between CHRIST and JESUS clearly when you refer to the creation of immortal spirits in kingdoms in salvation by CHRIST through Elijah to the final judgment on spirits of gods in the kingdoms.

As soon as you can make this distinction you will know the godly spirit entered the kingdom, with Jerusalem, to commit sin as he did in Babylon and is a godly spirit condemned after death and came from captivity.

14. I make this case. My brother Judah/Israel the son of god (Cain) did

not do anything good but claims that he is a disciple of Jesus in the body of Peter.

Would you save him? This disciple in the body of Peter said: I will keep myself warm by the fire and through the mouth of Peter denied knowing Jesus three times.

He had no faith and fell after death because he followed the laws of ancient devils. Spirits of gods, your life in the kingdom is for a short time and when you leave it you will not return. Beware of the false prophet to make you fall through religion.

Many have tried to understand what connection they have with the devil and what can be done to correct what went wrong so the matter can be settled peacefully in accordance with the new testimony of CHRIST for their peace in the world.

The godly spirits were brought back from captivity in that generation to repent and ask Zion and Jerusalem to have mercy on them for their sin in their flesh. It seems good to me to write so the reader may know they have two choices while they live in the kingdom – faith in Elijah or fall.

Mankind and Israelites after the flood populated the earth with multitudes in the nations including people of Elijah and Jerusalem. After many hundreds of generations the time had come to reveal to Mankind what was hid from them and to teach the way of life, salvation for kingdoms with spirits of gods to prepare their bodies to have spirits of creation in the Light to continue in the kingdoms to populate the earth under the New Testament of CHRIST.

The Two spirits Zion and Jerusalem awake from asleep on earth

The two spirits Zion and Jerusalem awoke from sleep in that generation. Zion's spirit sanctified in an old woman in the name of Elizabeth, and Elizabeth's spirit was put to rest according to the plan.

Spirit Jerusalem awoke from sleep and sanctified in a body she called Mary, and Mary's spirit was cast out to rest according to the plan in that generation.

Godly spirits released from Hell in that generation

The multitudes of godly spirits were released from captivity to warn their children of the chaos in Hades and to teach them to prepare their kingdom for creation and to put their faith in Elijah to save them.

The godly spirits entered the bodies of Mankind in the nations and instead of doing what they were let out to do, they began seducing the spirits of gods in the kingdom called Mankind with their lust to lose faith. The godly spirits seduced the spirits in the kingdom called Mankind and Israelites to make statues that looked like them so the spirits of gods in the kingdom could worship them as their god with their religion to death.

The godly spirit of Judah named Israel went in the same body Jerusalem had sanctified in the name of Mary. The godly spirit of god (Cain), Israel's father went in the body Zion had sanctified in the name of Elizabeth.

Jerusalem began to cry to Elijah, I am distressed. Israel is in the same body I sanctified in and he is threatening me and accuses me for making him not perfect and having to go to Hell to suffer for me making him.

Israel reviles me because I made gods for the devil. He is angry with me. Elijah, the terrors of the devils frighten me if I go to Hell.

Elijah, I'm in fear and my spirit is trembling in this body I call Mary with his horrible spirit from captivity. Israel wants me to be his queen like when I was his queen in the body of Babylon to rule the earth with his godly spirits.

O Elijah, I want to be joined to you again like when I sanctified in the body of Noah with you to rest. I want to go back to Whykibully, to my island far away by the tempest.

I am fed up with this boaster with his talk of violence. It is stressful to me. He is malicious and base in this body.

All his godly spirits are seducing the spirits of gods in Mankind to lose faith in you with their deceit. One of his godly spirits insulted me and said I can't hide from them. **Ps.55:9–11**

Elijah, come quickly and take Israel by surprise and send him back to captivity with the devils for trespass in this body. I'll cry till you hear my distress. Elijah, I don't care if he assaults me for speaking to you in this body.

Jerusalem cried to Elijah and said: Israel said he will hold me in this body as a ransom till the last spirit from his seed leave my flesh. He calls me a whore of the earth and I'm his queen for ever and spirits of gods in kingdoms of Mankind and Israelites will know after death that he is their king.

Jerusalem cried: Elijah, Israel said he is my king with his godly spirits to attack spirits that have faith in you, Elijah, while they live in kingdoms from my flesh.

Israel said the godly spirits will speak through the mouth of rulers of Mankind to destroy the kingdom from my flesh by war. Elijah, only you can save the kingdoms from this wicked sucker in my flesh. All I want in my life is peace. Be merciful to me for making a blasphemer to pursue me after death (55:22).

You are my king, Elijah. Come and save me from Israel. I'm crying to you for help (5).

Zion began to cry: O Elijah, save me from god (Cain). He is holding me as a ransom. He is pestering me and blaming me for being born to suffer in devouring fire. He is jealous of you, Elijah, because you took his kingdom. Elijah, come and save me from god (Cain) of the devil. He is corrupt and deceitful in this body I call Elizabeth.

Zion said to the godly spirit (Cain): I rebuke you, god of the devil, and all from your seed is accursed. Cain said that all spirits on earth are from his seed from thousands of generations. Zion cried: I told him, Elijah, he is a godly spirit to his face and he is of the devil and all spirits from his seed in the kingdom in my flesh and will have to sacrifice kingdoms for salvation to CHRIST whom he hated before he was carried away from the earth to Hades. I told Cain he had no faith in CHRIST, and you, Elijah, will come and remove him from this body I'm in.

IN HEAVEN Rev11.4

CHRIST on His throne called Jesus and Elijah and said to them: the godly spirits (Cain) and Israel have entered the same bodies as Zion and Jerusalem, and they are making them cry. Both of you must return to earth to cast them out from Zion and Jerusalem, as salvation is far off. It is forbidden for godly spirits to trespass in the same body with holy spirits

The time has come for multitudes of godly spirits released from captivity to repent for their sins and ask Zion and Jerusalem to have mercy on them and for those born in sin to forgive Zion and Jerusalem for being born from passed on seed of devils by god and his son Israel.

Elijah to taste death

CHRIST said to Elijah: you have not tasted death in the flesh so this is the opportunity to return to earth to save Zion and Jerusalem from godly spirits before the inhabitants on earth, and you will be the judge before Mankind and Israelites.

CHRIST said to Jesus: you will have to return to confirm the New Testament Elijah gave the Israelites and Mankind in the vessel, Jesus, use this mission to teach about the kingdom and the way to eternal life so they can teach others to prepare their bodies for salvation. Tell Zion and Jerusalem to have a little patience for their resurrection to Heaven and to keep away from temptation by these godly spirits, who will make it difficult for them while they are on earth.

Jesus, you will have to sanctify to have flesh and sacrifice the body before these barbarous spirits to make an example for salvation, so all spirits of gods in Mankind and Israelites may know they have to sacrifice their bodies to have everlasting life to rest in peace.

Elijah, you will ask the godly spirits in the body of Mankind to repent and have mercy on Zion and Jerusalem for making gods, Mankind, and Israelites and to teach their children to do the same until salvation begins in kingdoms on earth from their flesh.

Christ said: Elijah, you will have no power with the Word until you are a spirit. Jesus will have the Word passed over to you before Jesus Sabbaths to resurrect him.

CHRIST said: Elijah, you will have rest from your work after you resurrect Zion and Jerusalem.

CHRIST said: Elijah, you sanctify with Zion and cast out god (Cain) from the body she is in and manifest in flesh to be seen by Mankind to start your mission for all spirits to repent for trespassing in the kingdom to pass on seed of god.

CHRIST said: Jesus, you sanctify with Jerusalem and cast out Israel and manifest in flesh in order to be seen by Mankind to begin your mission on earth.

Sanctification and Manifestation to be Among Humanity Rev. 12.2

Elijah and Jesus came down from Heaven to earth as spirits. Elijah sanctified with Zion in Elizabeth. The godly spirit (Cain) was in fear when Elijah entered. Elijah said to Cain: why are you in the body with Zion? Godly spirit (Cain) began to cry: have mercy on me. Elijah said: you are pestering Zion and making her cry because you are a god with no flesh. Elijah cast out the godly spirit Cain from the body of Elizabeth and his spirit went in the body of Judas. Elijah manifested in flesh and was separated from Zion, and then Elijah went to the wilderness to begin his mission among Mankind (13).

Jesus sanctified his spirit with Jerusalem in the body of Mary. Jerusalem cried: O Jesus, I prepared this body for thee. Great fear fell on Israel. Thinking it's CHRIST, he began to cry: have mercy. Jesus said: get out! And Israel's spirit went in the body of Simon Peter (25). Jesus manifested in the flesh so he could be seen on His mission, and was separated from Jerusalem in the body of Mary (38).

Jerusalem in the body of Mary went in haste to Zion in Elizabeth in the city. She entered the house and said: Mother, Jesus sanctified and he departed from me. Zion said: blessed are you, my daughter in this women you call Mary, and so it was with me with Elijah in this body I call Elizabeth. Elijah cast out god (Cain), who was pestering me in this body. I had no peace since he entered this body, with his grief making me sorrowful.

Now you shall see some action by Elijah against these godly spirits that returned to tempt us to lose faith. Zion said: Jerusalem, my spirit rejoiced with Elijah my saviour (17).

Jerusalem said: Jesus sanctified in this woman in my flesh. My flesh is in the hands of Elijah. From now on all generations of spirits shall know I'm a virgin spirit that is blessed for Elijah.

Elijah is mighty and has done many great things and has saved me from generation to generation. He is always merciful and he returned with Jesus my first brother when I was a virgin.

Jesus cast out Israel for his deceit in wanting to hold me captive again and threatening me because he was not born perfect, and hates me for suffering in Hades. I am a blessed spirit and not human any more (53).

Israel's spirit entered the body Abraham (35). Elijah gave me my promised son Isaac with my spirit by the Word. Israel is jealous of Isaac because Isaac is accepted above and not him from the seed of god (Cain) of the devil. Jerusalem abode with Zion for a few months and returned to her house.

God in Judas

The godly spirit of god (Cain) in the body of Judas went to Zion with hate and asked: where is the holy spirit Elijah that cast me out who brought up God-Israel (68)? Elijah brought us back from captivity so we can teach our children about salvation (69). Elijah has been with you since the beginning after I departed from the kingdom to save you from Israel who hates you (71).

The godly spirit (Cain) said: Zion's godly spirits are in fear of Elijah. He wants us to repent for our sins and ask Zion and Jerusalem for mercy before all godly spirits under the oath of the devils. We are in fear of Elijah (74).

The godly spirit god (Cain), now in the body of Judas, told Zion in the body of Elizabeth: Elijah warned the godly spirits released from captivity that if we don't come before you and Jerusalem and him to repent for our sin with Jerusalem when she was human, he will end our time on earth, and our children's kingdoms will not be worthy to be created by his Word (76) to have knowledge for the choice of our spirits to have to sleep in peace and not fall because of our sins to make gods in her flesh (77).

Jesus also came from Heaven (78) to teach our spirits in Mankind that the way to be spirits in the Light is by salvation and to tell them to have faith and not to fall like us to the devils.

The godly spirits asked Zion: where is Elijah? He cast out god (Cain) from the same body as you and now in the body of Judas? Zion said: Elijah left. They asked: what is his new name? Zion said: John. And god in the body of Judas began to praise Elijah and fear came in the godly spirits that possessed Mankind (65).

God (Cain) said: Elijah has come to rescue his people from godly spirits and to take away the spirits from our children's flesh to create spirits for Jerusalem.

In fear, the godly spirits in the body of Mankind went in haste to see Jerusalem and saw Jesus with her. Jerusalem kept her cool in the body of Mary. Israel in Peter said to Jesus, thinking Jesus is the CHRIST whose body Adam he hanged: now that I've seen thee, I shall depart before Elijah. Come after me to speak the Word to send me back in captivity for entering the same body as Jerusalem (26).

My eyes in this body can see you are a holy spirit who has sanctified and manifested before salvation begins in kingdoms for the children of Israel to have immortal spirits by the word (32).

In a bad temper, Israel said through the mouth of Peter to Jerusalem: if Jesus speaks one Word of the truth about us when you were queen in the body of Babylon and all the wickedness I've done to you, his body will Sabbath before multitudes of godly spirits (32).

The godly spirits will come against him for telling Mankind in this generation all that we have done in the world. I'll put a sword to this woman you are in for wanting to be the Queen Jerusalem, with Elijah as your king on earth.

Jerusalem looked and saw he was angry before Jesus and hated Elijah. Jesus departed and went on a journey according to the plan. Israel thought: why should CHRIST come in the name of Jesus? Thinking it is a trap, Israel kept away.

Israel was told he would not return to captivity before he had seen Jesus (26) face to face. He thought he had authority over Jerusalem under the law when she was his Queen Babylon. Israel begged Elijah to return from captivity for peace to prepare his children for salvation but instead threatened Jerusalem in the body of Mary that if Jesus told Mankind the truth of his abomination with her in Babylon, he would pierce the body she was in. Jerusalem was accustomed to threats all her life so it is no big deal. Her faith in Elijah is more important to save her from Israel and his godly spirits.

Jerusalem went looking for Jesus in fear that Israel in the body of Peter would do something cruel to Jesus because of his hate and killing her brothers when she was Queen Tamuze in Babylon.

Jerusalem met Jesus and said: I've been worried about you. Where have you been? Jesus said: the day I sanctified in the body you are in is come and gone; now we are separated. Jerusalem said: I love you, my brother, and my beloved Elijah of our father. Jesus said: Jerusalem, I came with Elijah to minister according to the New Testament of our father. **Jn.20:21**

Elijah called John

The mission according to the New Testament is that the godly spirits in the body of Mankind know Elijah's new name is John but Mankind and Israelites don't know John is Elijah the saviour of their forefathers in the vessel.

Elijah called John began his mission from the wilderness among local people and spoke to those about faith to rest in peace and to obey.

Elijah told the godly spirits in Mankind to repent for their sins. They began following Elijah from place to place. This excited the immortal spirits of Jerusalem who could hear but the godly spirits thought there was hope for them if they killed Jesus and Elijah.

Keep the faith

Multitudes of spirits of gods were brought up to have faith in the Great Spirit Elijah, and this was passed on from generation to generation after the flood.

In a similar way, John chose to guide the people in multitudes in the region to Jordan, where the devil came to attack Zion when she was human as Eve and was pregnant with god. Elijah concentrated on bringing everyone from the seed of god of the devil and godly spirits who commit sin in the kingdom to repent while they live in the bodies of Mankind to be witnesses of the sinners before their eyes.

Jesus

Meanwhile Jesus began to preach in temples and synagogues about the kingdom. This was to them who live by the law a new doctrine with much debate and confusion with the law to live to death.

Jesus explained and reasoned with them about the kingdom and the way to everlasting life is through sacrifice and faith to rest in peace. This was too simple for them to understand. They wanted something more spectacular than faith for peace.

This interested the spirits in Mankind but the godly spirits in their bodies seduced the spirits to ask Jesus to see signs and proof that they would not go to Hell if they had faith. The godly spirits in the body of Mankind asked Jesus all kinds of questions about how it could be done, seeing how much they can get out of Jesus.

Jesus knew they are godly spirits, who are in fear that Elijah would return them to Hell. Jesus could see the godly spirits in the body of Mankind just as they can see him as a Holy Spirit in the light, but spirits in their humanity could not see all what is being discussed because their ears were blocked. It is a parable to them as they are spirits in their humanity under the authority of godly spirits in them.

Jesus's mission was to cast out Israel from the same body with Jerusalem and confirm the New Testament to Mankind and to bring awareness to multitudes of Mankind that they are seduced by godly spirits to fall. Elijah meanwhile was concentrating on going from one place to another preaching repentance to spirits in the kingdom to get everyone in one place to repent to Zion and Jerusalem, and ask them to have mercy for being born in sin and passing the accursed seed to make gods in their flesh. Elijah started to draw much attention, saying all spirits of gods in the kingdom repent. The godly spirits began to fear Elijah will expose them in the bodies of Mankind.

Israel in the body of Peter 1.Pet.5:1; 1.Tim.4.1; 1.Pet.4:7, 16; Deut.27:22; Mt.13:57

The godly spirit Israel in the body of Peter, the prophet of the law of ancient devils, sent godly spirits in humans to try to expose John to ask him who he is before the multitudes, but Mankind was told his name is John to deny Mankind to put their faith in Elijah to have peace. A human cannot see a spirit only after death. The godly spirit can see Elijah just as Elijah can see them.

A godly spirit spoke through the mouth of a human and asked: John, are you CHRIST? John said: no! Are you Elisha (The spirit name of Isaac)? Elijah said: no! I am here to baptize in the water but when CHRIST comes it is to baptize who don't have faith in me in fire. Now go and tell your ruler what I have said and ask him to come and ask me himself who I am.

Satan was let out of captivity for an hour and was among the godly spirits in Mankind by the Jordan river. Elijah, seeing all the enemies in one place, began saying: All spirits in the kingdom in the flesh of Zion and Jerusalem, repent!

A human asked: are you Elisha? Elijah answered: I am the one who heard your father crying in the wilderness. He returned from captivity and he is now among you. You are children of the seed of god your father. Your wish is to do the desire of god your father. Repent while I am at hand.

Satan and the godly spirits were in fear Elijah would speak the Word, but the people in their humanity can't see the spiritual confrontation by the Jordan and are agitated hearing Elijah saying repent.

Elijah kept saying: he who continues to sin was a king in Babylon with the devils in the beginning. Repent!

god (Cain) in the body of Judas and Israel in the body of Peter and the devil kept silent in fear that CHRIST would turn up to send them back into the fire for raping His daughters.

Elijah called John (The Judge) **Deut.29:23; Heb.4:12; Ps.76:1-2; Lev.18:13; Act.5:6; Mic.7:3-6**.

Elijah stood in the crowd. Satan, Israel in the body of Peter; god (Cain) in the body of Judas; and multitudes of godly spirits in the bodies of Mankind by the Jordan. Elijah began saying to the multitudes: the time has come for all gods in the kingdom to repent for your sins

A godly spirit in the body of a human asked: are you Elijah? Elijah said: I am the Word and come to bear witness to two spirits in the Light who have been held captive in Babylon.

Another godly spirit in the body of another human asked through his mouth: are you the CHRIST? Elijah said: I am not. Are you Elisha? Elijah answered: no, I am the one who heard your father crying in the wilderness and brought him up on milk and honey by the rock. He is among you.

Elijah went on to say: children of the seed of god, your father is of the devil. Repent. If you don't, you wish to do the desire of god your father.

The godly spirits and Satan were in fear of Elijah with the Word. The spirits in their humanity can't see the spiritual confrontation in the Jordan and are agitated hearing Elijah saying repeatedly: repent while you are in the kingdom for your peace.

Elijah stood in the crowd and said: He who continues to sin was a king with the devils in the beginning. The devil, god (Cain) and Israel kept silent, in fear. Elijah said: CHRIST is coming to baptize in fire. Repent!

Zion in the body of Elizabeth, and Jerusalem in the body of Mary, came to the Jordan river and stood next to Elijah. Elijah said: repent! And there was silence. Zion looked at the devil, god (Cain) and Israel and all spirits of gods in the kingdom from their flesh. Elijah said: judgment has come this day before the multitudes that stand here to be a witness so it can be known all over the earth who are the sinners. **Rev.713–4**

Zion stood next to Elijah and said: who is mine adversary, let him come and let us stand together. Everyone began to look at each other. Zion said: come. Don't be afraid. Come unto me. This gave a lot of fright to Satan. Then Zion went on to say: hear ye. This day I am not speaking in secret. I'm before Elijah and CHRIST, who can see you.

Zion in the body of Elizabeth said: all spirits from the seed of the devils in the kingdoms will be removed from my flesh and will have no peace. Because of sin of Satan and the devils there is much wickedness on earth, with spirits of gods passing on the seed of devils to make gods in the kingdom.

Elijah is the judge between me; and all who want to contend and call me a sinner, come near me, who has waxed to old age, before a multitude of Mankind. He that came from captivity in Hades; let him come near me with his god (Cain) and (Israel). This put much fear in Satan and god

(Cain). Zion went on to say: ye from the consuming fire, compass the earth to stand in multitudes of kingdoms from my flesh. Come and stand next to me by my saviour.

All you have done is bring spirits in this world in my flesh to live in sorrow and die in your shame. All spirits in my flesh, let it be known Elijah is your saviour from falling after death.

Zion said: let it be known throughout all generations, I came to the Jordan and stand before multitudes to witnesses, I asked Satan to repent for raping me to make god (Cain) before multitudes of spirits in my flesh. And I asked god (Cain) and every spirit of gods who pass on his seed to forgive me before Elijah, who will judge between you and I that I asked for mercy.

Zion looked up to the Heaven and said: CHRIST and my holy Eternal Father and all angels in Heaven, forgive me for this sin to make a god in this world in holy flesh. I beg you for mercy. Satan and all godly spirits who stood there bowed the head of Mankind and Israelites in shame, and there was silence.

Elijah picked up Zion in his arms and walked in the Jordan river and dipped Zion in the body Elizabeth in the water, and Elijah told Zion: mercy is granted thee.

Jerusalem came forward and stood next to Elijah. Jerusalem looked at Satan and the multitudes of godly spirits in the body of Mankind and said: who is mine adversary, let him come and stand next to me. Let us stand together. Come ye near unto me in front of the multitudes gathered here in my flesh and boast of your power and your law. I am not silent and speak not in secret of all the cruelty I've suffered since I was held in captivity by you.

Jerusalem said to the crowd: first god raped me to make a god, then Satan and the devils and Israel held me in bondage under the law. All spirits from their seed in the kingdom who are from my flesh are standing in it before me. Elijah will judge between me and those who held me in captivity to make gods and Israelites.

First the godly spirit (Cain) raped me to make a god for him and his name is the godly spirit (Israel) who committed abomination to make

Israelites in the kingdom from my flesh, and Satan held me in captivity to make gods for devils in my flesh which belongs to Zion my mother and CHRIST my father.

Satan, I am ashamed to say your gods have brought no joy to me; and Israel, your abomination only brought sorrow to spirits born in my flesh to suffer after their spirits depart from my flesh to fall like god (Cain) after death if they don't have faith.

Godly spirits have no flesh Rev.19:20

Jerusalem went on to tell the crowd: Israel wants to have control over me? Come now and boast. Tell the multitudes of spirits in the kingdom before my face whether your abomination is true or false. Satan, with godly spirits in the body of Mankind, bow your heads in shame. Ye from captivity in the fire, come and stand next to me and show Mankind Satan and his god (Cain) who raped me to make him a mighty God so it can be known all over the earth. I ask the devil god (Cain) and Israel to repent for making gods and Israelites in my flesh to be born in sin. I ask all spirits that stand in kingdoms from my flesh for mercy for making them to be sinners while I was held in captivity, and to put their faith in Elijah to have peace, and not fall.

Jerusalem looked up to Heaven and said: CHRIST my father and Holy Eternal Spirit and all angels in Heaven, have mercy on me and forgive me. All I ask for is peace, and to all who have faith to let the matter rest in the hands of Elijah.

Satan, god (Cain) and God Israel and a multitude of godly spirits bowed the heads of Mankind in shame, for what they did to Jerusalem with hate and jealousy because Jerusalem is saved by Elijah and accepted above.

Water baptism

Elijah picked up Jerusalem in his arms and walked in the water and dipped her in the water. Then Jesus came to join them. Then there was thunder and lightning and the multitudes began to run away in fear of the Word. **Is.13:3–4; Is.12:6; Mic.4:10**

The spirit of the sun pulled up the devil from the earth to wait for the final judgment.

Can spirits from the seed of god in the kingdom foretell their future? Is.43:8–10

Zion and Jerusalem asked the devil god and his son before multitudes of spirits in the kingdom as witnesses before the judge of the earth to repent for making gods in holy flesh created to have immortal spirits and not gods to set an example for all spirits in the kingdom to have faith in Elijah and prepare their kingdom for creation for peace.

The baptism by water is a symbol of removing all the spirits of gods from the earth to make a clean break in the kingdoms on the earth for immortal spirits. No spirit from the seed of god can be born again; don't be deceived while you live in the kingdom.

Zion and Jerusalem are immortal spirits in the Light. There was no need for baptism, but to ask the spirits in the kingdom to forgive them for being born in sin and to have mercy on them, and prepare for salvation for peace. Every spirit is born in sin. Elijah will save spirits of gods from falling in fire in the time of salvation if they have faith in Him.

The meeting of godly spirits

The godly spirits had a meeting and were complaining about their fear of Jesus.

One said: no preaching is done by Elijah since he baptized Zion and Jerusalem, but Jesus is casting out our godly spirits out from the bodies they possess and making us cry. We tremble when we have no flesh on our spirit.

Israel, you are our king. What can you do? We begin to fear Jesus. He makes us tremble and we are in fear that when we see him he will cast us out from the bodies we are in, and we will return to the devils in captivity.

Another spirit said: Elijah is only preaching repentance and warning the spirits in the kingdom in their humanity to have faith so they don't fall like us. Sooner or later Mankind will get wise and know we possess their bodies and will lose the joy we have in seducing them to fuck while we live in their bodies.

Another godly spirit said: Elijah has a large following and he wants to save all the kingdoms of Jerusalem's flesh. CHRIST will come to send us back to the devils.

Much fear came on the godly spirits in the council. Israel in the body of Peter said: according to the covenant, who has the Word has power over the devils and us. We call Elijah John and we can see him as he can see us and we fear him because of the Word, but I think the Word is switched over to Jesus who we know not much about. He is the spirit that kicked my ass out of the body with Jerusalem.

A godly spirit said: according to the complaints we have, it seems Jesus has the WORD when he tells our spirits to come out. There is much fear by the Word, so if we capture Elijah while he is preaching repentance and to keep the faith, there will be one holy spirit less on earth to deal with and you will be king again on earth when we capture Jerusalem for you so she can be our queen instead of Hadassah in the body of Magdalena.

A godly spirit said: yes King Israel, we cannot have two kings to rule the earth. Mankind will want Jesus to be king and worship him as their king and not you.

God (Cain) in the body of Judas said: I stoned Abel to death in the beginning when Jesus was human. I will not have Jesus to be king over me on earth. I was born first. The earth is for us. This is the law. God (Cain) said: I'm the heir and all of you godly spirits are from my seed are under the law.

King Israel said: but it's through my abomination and lust the earth is full of spirits from your seed. I should be king.

An Israelite godly king said: yes, Godfather, we were kings in Babylon and we want to be kings of the spirits. We will fight with you for the earth to death and not god (Cain), who is the unknown god by Mankind.

God (Cain) in the body of Judas said: it is I who took more heat and if it were not for me, you would not be born to be a godly spirit like me. I should be king. There was much division and debate who should be king to rule the earth.

Israel in the body of Peter hates Elijah for telling him he cannot have Jerusalem; it's abomination if you go with your mother. Elijah had my faith tested in temptation when I saw her in captivity by Satan.

Jerusalem called Israel in the body of Peter a serpent and a dragon

Israel said to god (Cain) in Judas: my godly father Elijah took your kingdom from you and you want to be king of the spirits? Israel said: we are godly spirits with no flesh of my mother. If you want to be king of the spirits you must capture Elijah for casting us in the heat and kill Jesus and you will be king of the earth. You hated Jesus in the body of Abel; prove to us you hate your brother, whose spirit is Jesus the righteous son of CHRIST who was in the body of Adam and not you. We were not born when you killed Abel. We can see he is a spirit who returned to earth. If you want to be king, you must kill him, if you want to be king of the spirits on earth.

The godly spirits voted and said: it is fair. Prove to us godly spirits you can take the kingdom from Elijah to remove this fear from us, and if you kill Jesus, you will be king and you will have the authority in the kingdom, which you did not have, so our spirits don't complain and tremble with fear before Jesus.

The godly spirit Cain in the body of Judas said: if I kill Elijah, I want Jerusalem. Israel said: you were the first to rape Jerusalem to make me. You can have her for thirty pieces of silver. It's all yours as a starter and you will be king of the earth with Jerusalem.

No work is done by Elijah called John at the moment

The godly spirit (Cain) in the body of Judas did not know as much about scripture as Israel in the body of Peter, who was brought up by Elijah to know scripture. He took the bait and wanted to have Jerusalem. He took seven giant godly spirits and they began stalking (John). Elijah to achieve his part of the plan to be king of the earth spirits and told the godly spirits to concentrate on everyone to follow Jesus, to hold Elijah as the WORD is switched.

Multitudes began following Jesus to hear about salvation and the way to have everlasting life. This inflamed god (Cain) with much jealousy seeing Jesus doing miracles openly and he cannot be seen like Jesus and hated Jesus more and wanted, for to kill him because no one liked him he is the unknown god to Mankind. When Elijah was alone he and the godly spirits arrested Elijah. Elijah said: is it for doing good?

Celebration

They laid hold on Elijah and bound him and chained him in prison and there was much excitement among godly spirits. The news went about that Elijah was bound in prison. (Cain) began to torment Elijah, saying to the godly spirits: he took my kingdom, and he began to flog (John) Elijah. The other godly spirits began kicking Elijah, saying: it's because of you we suffered in fire, dying of thirst.

The taste of death

Israel in Peter began to torture Elijah: You want my mother for yourself? You gave her Isaac and don't accept me. I hate thee to death. Elijah said nothing. Israel spat on him and slapped (John) him and said: look at me. You cast the devils out from the face of the earth and can't open your mouth to say one word to save yourself. Look at me. You put fear in godly spirits and sent us in devouring fire and humiliated us before Mankind to repent for our sins with Jerusalem and Zion. Show us your power to save yourself. They began to kick and curse and spit and break his bones. Elijah was in much pain. Elijah put up no resistance. He didn't say a word, and they left him in the dungeon.

Hadassah, queen of the godly spirits in the body of Magdalena, prepared a banquet to celebrate the capture of Elijah. She hated Elijah for her fall in the rubble in the tower of Babylon for burning the bodies of Zion and Jerusalem. The godly spirit god (Cain) entered the body of Herod, and Israel entered the body of Philip. The other godly spirits entered the bodies of government officials to feast and celebrate the capture of Elijah.

The music started and Hadassah in the body of Magdalena seduced her to dance for Israel, now in the body of Philip as in the days of Babylon, belly dancing and shaking her ass before Israel her king and father. She said: now we will be king and queen again on earth.

Israel sat with the guests. His plan with Hadassah in the body of Magdalena was pre-planned what she should say and ask for before the guests with god (Cain) in the body of Herod.

Hadassah in the body of Magdalena began to dance for god (Cain) in Herod, getting him excited and tormenting him like a cobra snake charmed by a flute to get him involved with the killing of Elijah. god (Cain) thought if he kills Elijah, Elijah would send god (Cain) back to Hell and they will be king and queen of the earth spirits. When the music stopped Hadassah seduced Magdalena to fall at the feet of Herod. god (Cain) spoke though the mouth of Herod. He said to Hadassah: ask me whatever thou wilt and I will give it thee.

Hadassah said: will you swear before all the guests that whatsoever I ask thee, thou wilt give it? And god (Cain) in Herod said: I will give thee unto half of my portion on earth.

Hadassah went to Israel in Phillip (Peter) her father and said: what shall I ask? As planned she returned in haste unto god (Cain) in Herod and said: give me the head of John on a charger.

And god (Cain) in Herod had a choice if he wanted to be king of the earth and have Jerusalem he would have to kill Elijah. He swore by oath before godly spirits to kill Elijah for taking his kingdom. He could not back off to reject her request. He commanded that the executioner beheaded (John) Elijah and brought his head on a charger to him and he gave the head of John to Hadassah and she gave it to her father Israel in Phillip (Peter).

HOLY SPIRITS DON'T DIE, THEY SLEEP IN CHRIST 1.Thes.4:14

The followers of John came and took the body of John and laid it in a cave and the spirit Elijah slept until he heard the Word from Jesus to wake up to receive the Word. According to the plan, Jerusalem went to the cave crying for Elijah to wake up from sleep and went back to her house, crying for Elijah. Isaac's spirit, sanctified and manifested, was with Jerusalem his mother to give her support. He followed Jesus as the apostle John.

SPIRIT ELIJAH SLEPT, WAITING FOR THE WORD BY JESUS TO WAKE HIM UP Ps.4:8

I will lay me down and sleep in peace.

The Word wakes my spirit from sleep. Jerusalem cried: awake. Thou that sleepest, arise. **Cant.5:2**

I laid me down and slept. Jerusalem cried: awake, Elijah my husband. **Ps.55:3**

JESUS

The pharisee asked Jesus if he could show them the spirit of CHRIST in Heaven.

Jesus replied: Ye hypocrites want to see the face of CHRIST and want to know when HE is coming in the kingdom. You will not see him; your children's spirits will see HIS spirit in the kingdom when he comes in salvation.

Jesus said to Mankind who followed him: take heed of the doctrine of the pharisee of Israel. He is a godly spirit with no flesh.

Then Jesus asked them: who do you think I am? Israel in Peter said: you are the son of CHRIST. Jesus said: you know so because you are a godly spirit.

I say unto you, Elijah will establish the kingdom from Jerusalem's flesh, not you. When you are in the gates of Hell you will receive your spirits, as Elijah has promised you.

And whatever kingdoms CHRIST creates are through Elijah from your seed, and spirits that have no faith will return to you in the gates of Hell after death.

Israel in the body of Peter said: ye shall be far away when salvation begins in kingdoms.

Jesus said: you and the devils are afraid of Elijah for your abomination. You are a godly spirit without flesh of Jerusalem.

Jesus told the other godly spirits: tell Israel he don't follow me. He committed abomination with his mother. He wants to crucify me for telling the world the truth about him and what he did to Jerusalem.

Jesus said to Israel: when you leave the body of Peter you will have no one to save you when you enter the gate.

Jesus said: Israel, what did it profit god (Cain) your father, who raped his sister to make you and ended in the flames of devouring fire? The both of you are godly spirits with no flesh of your mothers.

Jesus said: Israel, I say unto you, spirits in the body of Mankind in this generation shall see CHRIST when HE comes in the kingdom of your children, and if they have no faith in Elijah to save them after death, they shall join you.

When Elijah presents kingdoms for salvation it will be in multitudes in all nations on the earth to CHRIST. god (Cain) in Judas went on the knee and said: Jesus, have mercy. I just came from Hell and there is no water.

Jesus said to god (Cain): if you had faith, you would not be there, you perverse lunatic. I won't be on earth to suffer you much longer. Go away from me.

A godly spirit in Mankind said through his mouth: why could we not tell god in Judas to go away from us? Jesus said: you are a spirit from his seed of the devils. You can't command him to return to the devils. You are from his seed.

A godly spirit asked Jesus: who is the first – Israel or god (Cain)? Jesus said: god (Cain) passed on his seed to Israel. Jesus said: they were born in the kingdom not by the Word. CHRIST in Heaven will not accept them They are godly spirits who trespassed in holy flesh and had no faith to rest in peace. When the kingdoms of your children are created with immortal spirits by the Word they will be accepted

A godly spirit said: woe is unto all spirits of gods that transgress in holy flesh. Their spirits will come after them in Hell. Jesus said: take heed you don't tempt your children to have no faith in the saviour Elijah. He will save who have faith in him and they will not fall.

Jesus is tormented by godly spirits

A godly spirit said: your sister went astray and was held in captivity by devils.

Another said: god (Cain) raped your sister.

Another said: she was in bondage on earth by devils.

CHRIST sent Elijah and Jesus to confirm salvation to Mankind according to the New Testament in Heaven Jn.28:28; 1 Pet.1:12; Ro.8:28; Rev.11:10; Mt.15:19; Jn.8:17; Eccl.12:7

Israel said: Jesus, how can I forgive god (Cain) for raping my mother? She conceived and passed on his accursed seed to me. I am born not perfect to go above. Jesus said: you had a choice to have peace or fall.

God (Cain) had the head of (John) Elijah cut off to rule as king of the earth. Jesus was the only one left on earth. God (Cain) imagined that if he got rid of Jesus he will be king with Jerusalem, so he began to provoke Jesus to leave the earth to go back to Heaven.

The spirits of gods in the kingdom can't see godly spirits of the dead until after death. The godly spirits use this as their advantage to seduce Mankind to kill Jesus. Israel knows Elijah is somewhere, and has experience of judgment when Elijah speaks the Word. Israel planned with the godly spirits to imprison god (Cain) after he killed Jesus, so he and Hadassah can be king and queen on earth.

Elijah is patient to catch them in the act of murder, and took his rest. Jesus knew his enemies. He can see them just as they can see he is a holy spirit manifest in flesh so Mankind can see him as a human. He told Mankind the truth and salvation to rest in peace is through faith in Elijah. There is no more Jesus can do for the spirits of gods in the kingdom of Mankind, as everything is in the hands of Elijah.

Jesus said to the godly spirits: the kingdom of your children will be for creation. blame god (Cain) and the devils for passing on the accursed seed to you in the flesh of Zion and Jerusalem. Why are you tormenting me? You are the transgressors

The godly spirit (Cain) was in fear of returning to Hell to suffer in fire. He said to Jesus: is it right for my king to give up his queen mother in the body of Babylon even if he commits abomination with her?

Is it not his right for his spirit to enter in the same body as her in the body of Mary? Why did you kick out my king from his wife?

Jesus said to the god (Cain): when you were in the body of Aaron, and Israel was in the body of Moses, Jerusalem was in the body of Miriam in the palace of Pharaoh in Egypt. You gave her a divorce so you could rape her again.

The godly spirits shouted at Jesus through the mouth of Mankind: she is no good to have eternal life above. We had to go to Hell because of her for our sins. Jesus said: the whole lot of you are damned. Hell is the place for you.

They backed off in fear of returning to captivity and what the devils would do to them.

Israel began to blame god (Cain): it is you who passed on this seed of devils to me. If you did not rape my mother to make a god like you, I would not be born to live in fear of Elijah and CHRIST, because of your wickedness to kill Abel to have her.

Jesus said: Israel, it is impossible to change your nature. You can't be born again. You are all wicked because Cain followed the devils' way in wickedness. Israel said: Jesus, I wish I could be born again with flesh to have faith in Elijah.

The godly spirit (Cain) said: you motherfucker and backslider, are you getting soft like the devils for flesh. We are godly spirits without flesh and the earth is ours to take. You are under authority to tempt Jesus and torment him to leave the earth so we can have power in the kingdom.

The godly spirits did not like the way god (Cain) spoke to Israel and wanting to have authority over them. They began to beat god (Cain) with chains for wanting to be their king.

Jesus stood there amazed and said: but you will receive a hundredfold of spirits from His seed when CHRIST comes in kingdoms. Elijah will send them back to you as he has promised your God Israel in the beginning if he had no faith in him to have peace.

A godly spirit cried: Jesus, who can be saved among us? Jesus said: it is impossible. Elijah is strict. god (Cain) said: that is why I cut the head off John, thinking he would not come back. Israel said: Elijah is cunning, slippery like soap. Jesus, I know Elijah is somewhere waiting for you to speak the Word to him to send us back.

Jesus said: if you want to remain on earth, go in the kingdom of your children in all nations on earth and warn them of the chaos in Hell and preach the truth of salvation and to have faith in Elijah to rest in peace. **Lk.24.39**

God (Cain) wants to be king of the earth. Israel, you have declared war for the earth against the Word of Elijah and CHRIST. You are the prophet with the law of devils by the oath to death.

Jesus said: it is either war or peace. godly spirit (Cain) said: I am the heir of the earth. I was the first to be born on earth. I should be king. Israel said: I did all the hard work to pass on your accursed seed under oath to the devils after death.

Elijah promised Jerusalem children in kingdoms from her flesh

Jesus said: Israel, you can have all the spirits from your seed, but not the kingdoms from the flesh of Jerusalem. Elijah has promised to give her children from kingdoms that are healthy so spirits created by CHRIST will live in the same resemblance to continue on earth, and not by your seed in her flesh.

The godly spirits insulted Jesus and said: we are not accepted above. Jesus said: don't you like the spirits of your children? They will return to you, but the kingdom of your children from the flesh of Jerusalem look right in my eyes for creation. It is her inheritance for her, grief, and crying by you bastards. The godly spirits got angry because Jesus was revealing the truth to the hearers. They took council to find a way to Sabbath Jesus for the earth. **Mic.7:2 Essek.13:13–20**

The godly spirits in the body of Mankind began to mix with the people of Isaac, following Jesus to hear the good news for them and their children that after they Sabbath they will resurrect and many mansions are made available for them in the heavens after their spirits leave the earth by Elijah, and they should have no fear of death, and should populate the earth for Jerusalem and Elijah. Jesus told the people of Isaac: the godly spirits want to kill me for telling Mankind in this generation the truth, but when he returns to Heaven He will celebrate with them. The violent and most wicked king of godly spirits wants to kill Jesus to possess Jerusalem to provoke Elijah for war. **Essek.13:21**

Jesus said to the godly spirits in the crowd: Zion and Jerusalem will receive kingdoms from their flesh in the nations on earth and it will again take root with perfect spirits of creation by CHRIST through Elijah for Mankind to be perfect with spirits to go above.

Jesus said: you godly spirits seduce the spirits to fornicate while you are in their bodies to lose faith to fall like your king. Christ will cast out multitudes in the time of salvation for you to rejoice with spirits who have no faith like you when they enter the gate.

You have done all the hard work making kingdoms for Elijah to give Jerusalem perfect children in the kingdom through CHRIST. You have wasted your strength like the devils that were removed from the earth by Elijah to everlasting death for ever. When CHRIST comes in salvation of kingdoms, it will be the battle in the kingdom.

Jesus said to the crowd: the truth was hidden from you in this generation. Keep the faith; it's your guarantee for peace unless your desire is to go backwards to the old way to death. be wary of those who do the work of God to lose faith in the only saviour Elijah, who will save only who has faith in him before CHRIST comes to cast out spirits of gods for the final judgment on earth.

The final judgment for all devils and godly spirits in the fire of the sun

Preachers are vain with their vanity in religion. They are interested in gifts and collecting silver coins and care not about a body well prepared for salvation. Neither do they tell Mankind about Elijah and CHRIST and the Word, but preach about god (Cain) in Judas and in the body of Paul and his son Israel in the body of Peter and what they did and what they said to make Mankind worship godly spirits as saints to lose faith for peace.

The power of Elijah Rev.11:3; Ja.3:16

If you have faith in your god after death you expect your god to save you from fire, and not Elijah. Your kingdom is your gift. Don't be ignorant any more; you need no one to teach you what you should do. Faith in

Elijah is all you need, and peace be with you. It is the choice you have while you live in the kingdom in the flesh of Jerusalem.

Elijah Rev.4:11

The godly spirits released from captivity in this generation have knowledge of Elijah with the Word with excellent judgment. Elijah keeps to his promise he made to the people in the vessel for the kingdom of their children to be created with immortal spirits by CHRIST, who is on the throne in Heaven.

The spirits of gods in the kingdom in this generation will have to wait for the promise for Elijah to establish the kingdom of their children with immortal spirits by CHRIST in the time of salvation. **Ro.4:20**

Luke wrote: the godly spirits from captivity are against any spirit of god in the kingdom that has faith in Elijah. godly spirits make spirits in the kingdom suffer to lose faith to possess their bodies. **Lk.23:47** Israel in the body of Peter seduced Peter to write: we godly spirits serve Elijah in fear and don't want Him to send us back to the devils in fire. **1Pet.4:16; Is.58:13; Col.126; 1.Tim.41**

CHRIST creates immortal spirits in any kingdom that is prepared and presented to him by Elijah for salvation to continue in the same resemblance of the spirits cast out.

Elijah is a spirit. He can see you. You can't see him unless you are dead.

41. Jesus showed his authority over the godly spirit, then left the synagogue and went to the house of Jerusalem. Many people went to Jesus in the house of Jerusalem and Jesus cast out the godly spirits from the people they came out crying: You are CHRIST with Elijah.

Jesus teaches the crowd about the kingdom and the New Testament Jn.17:42; Jn.1.6:8; Ro. 8.18:21

42. Jesus left the house of Jerusalem and went to the desert and people followed him and Jesus said: my mission is to teach about the kingdom with spirits of the seed of God. For this I am sent.

Godly spirit of God - Israel in the body of Peter 5:8

When the godly spirit of God/Israel in the body of Peter saw Jesus was teaching the crowds about the kingdom, Israel in the body of Peter was amazed to know the New Testament of CHRIST made the covenant between the Eternal with the devils obsolete and useless. Israel seduced Peter to kneel down at Jesus's feet and said through the mouth of Peter: I am Israel; I am a sinner in the body of this man.

Jesus said: fear not me. Elijah will catch you and multitudes of godly spirits and spirits from your seed in the kingdom.

Many people possessed with godly spirits came to Jesus and Jesus commanded the godly spirits to depart from the kingdom and told the people to have faith and they will leave you alone, else you will be seduced by godly spirits to sin if you have no faith (5:20).

A godly spirit in the body of a scribe in the crowd said: Jesus, only our God can forgive sin. Jesus said: God who you worship regrets he made you in sin and not perfect. The Son of Man has forgiven all born in sin as it's not your fault you were born sin, but have faith to have peace. (26).

Jesus told the people in the crowd; all spirits that are not in the light in the kingdoms in the time of salvation shall see CHIRIST and he shall cast them out for judgment by Elijah. The spirits that have no faith will be in fire (6) (9).

The people in the crowd who followed Jesus said: what shall we do? (10) Jesus said: every spirit of the seed of gods that has faith should prepare his kingdom for Elijah to present to CHRIST to create new spirits or be content in the nature you were born. Do not be violent, and love your neighbour as yourself (1) (14).

The Sabbath accusation. Reference to CHRIST in Adam

Israel asked Jesus: on Sabbath days why bo you do what is not lawful? (6:2) Jesus said: Israel, may I ask you one question – Was it lawful to do what that devil said to you to kill Adam? Did you save him or Sabbath his body, and also you eliminated all his holy sons from the earth. Was it lawful? (9)

The godly spirit in the body of a pharisee whispered to Israel in the body of Peter: Jesus is tempting us to speak the truth of killing the sons of Adam.

From this time they plotted to kill Jesus. (11)

Jesus departed from the pharisee and Israel, the godly spirit of King Judah.

Jesus went up to the mountain and stayed there all night. When he came down to the base, Jerusalem came to meet him with many who were sick with all kinds of disease.

Jesus began to heal the sick and cast out godly spirits and he looked at those who were stalking him and said to the god (Cain): the spirits that are cast out from the kingdom are from your seed. Jesus said to god (Cain): blessed are the kingdoms from the flesh of Jerusalem with immortal spirits. (18) (20) (21)

Jesus said to Jerusalem: Israel hates thee, and made you cry. When his spirits are cast out from your flesh, you will be above to see Elijah cast him out for being wicked like the devils for reproaching you for being born not perfect to go above. (22)

When the days of salvation come, you will be above, seeing kingdoms from your flesh created by our father in Heaven with immortal spirits and angels from the earth, and you will leap with joy when you see them come from the earth. In the final judgment, woe is unto the spirit of God (Israel). (23)

Israel can laugh and boast now, but he will cry later when he receives all the spirits he led astray to have no faith. (26)

He hates you, curses you (27) and threatens you and smites thee, and has no faith. (5:29)

The spirits of gods that worship him as their God will get no thanks from him for being born. Don't Mankind love their children to receive more children from them again? They do the same, passing on seed like him. Jesus said: Jerusalem, your reward shall be in multitudes of kingdoms for salvation.

Elijah is merciful and has not condemned thee. (37) Spirits will be created in the kingdom in the same resemblance, united in their body

(38) in salvation.

Spirits of gods in the kingdom that don't acknowledge the New Testament and who follow their own religion are like the blind leading a blind and will fall through ignorance (39).

48. Jesus said to Jerusalem: Israel (God) imitated the devils and wanted to build a foundation on earth from your flesh (49).

God/Israel wants to know if Jesus has power (7:2)

The servant of Israel was sick in a coma and he sent god (Cain) to ask Jesus to come and save his servant from death in the synagogue.

The godly spirit (Cain) in the body of Judas met Jesus and said: Israel built a synagogue for Israelites (4) in the nation. His servant is in a coma. He said he is not worthy to see you. Just say the Word and his servant will be healed. (7)

Israel wanted to know if Jesus has the Word. (Cain) said to Jesus: Israel has authority over multitudes of godly spirits. If he tells the godly spirit to go and enter in a body, he will do as Israel says and seduce the spirit in the kingdom

Jesus said to god (Cain): go and tell Israel to stop boasting, I have not met any godly spirit from your seed that has faith (9). Jesus told him to go away from him, and left Jesus in shame.

Jesus was returning to be with Jerusalem and saw a woman crying for her dead husband. Jesus said: Weep not. Then he said to the dead man: arise and speak, and fear was on all who saw the power of Jesus.

The fear of Elijah called John. The Word

Israel and god (Cain) wanted to know if Jesus had the Word and sent the dead man with this woman out of the city. Jesus, knowing it is a trap said: go back and show yourself. Say to your ruler that I know what he did, wanting to know if I had power to bring back a dead body back with life. (22)

(23) I hope your ruler who sent you is not offended in me for casting

him out from the same body with Jerusalem. A crowd of people gathered around Jesus. He asked them: what think ye of John? They answered: he came from the wilderness. Jesus said: he must have come from somewhere. Maybe by the wind. (24) Your ruler is inside a body of one clothed in gorgeous apparel, who was once king in Babylon. (25) Jesus said: Elijah came to tell you about him and to confirm the promise he made to your forefathers in the vessel in the flood for your children to prepare themselves for salvation and you as well.

Jesus said to the crowd around him: Elijah is the only saviour, and He is greater than God who is a godly spirit with no flesh, and all the people's ears were unblocked to hear what Jesus said. (29)

The godly spirit of God, Israel in the body of Peter shouted through the mouth of Peter in the crowd: don't listen to Jesus with this New Testament. It's against the law what Jesus is saying, and seduced Peter to the synagogue to have a council with the other godly spirits to Sabbath Jesus so he can return to Heaven.

The spirits of the seed of God live to eat

A woman in the crowd cried: Jesus, a godly spirit seduces me not to have faith. Jesus said: the kingdom will be created with spirits through Elijah much better than the spirit that is in your body, seducing you not have faith in Elijah. Have faith and the godly spirit will leave you and you will have peace. (12:23) (24)

If you have faith you shall not be tempted

34. Jesus went on to say to the crowd: on the day of salvation, children born will have spirits purer than lilies in the field and will have faith. (28) If you want your kingdom to be created to continue with everlasting spirits, seek ye King Elijah. (31)

35. Jesus told the men in the crowd: it is better you cut off your penis than to bring another god in the world to end in fire. The godly spirit of God Israel in the body of Peter said: Jesus, thou speak this against me and all godly spirits.

Jesus said: if you had faith and obeyed Elijah, your kingdom would have a wise son by Elijah to be his heir. Isaac is the promised son of Jerusalem and is Elijah's heir and all children from his seed are righteous on earth from birth in his mother's flesh. (42)

Jesus said to Israel in the body of Peter: Elijah is of creation and is the anointed blessed king of the earth and the judge as well when CHRIST comes to create spirits in kingdoms on the earth it will be according to the promise Elijah made to the people in the vessel in the flood on earth for salvation of kingdoms for their children who have faith to rest in peace.

Jesus told Israel in the body of Peter: don't be angry and go and beat up Jerusalem in the body of Mary because you think salvation is far off. CHRIST will catch you unawares for sure, and you will end with the devils for ever. (46)

Jesus told Israel in the body of Peter: the devils are waiting for you in the fire. You suppose I came to give you peace on earth? I tell you now; it's to warn spirits from your seed in the kingdom (51) born under the law to have faith for peace so their spirits don't fall after death. (53)

The signs of the end prophecy by Jesus for spirits who have no faith

Jesus told the crowd to tell their children to tell their children that when they see clouds all over the earth and rain in all nations on the earth, it is the beginning of salvation in kingdoms. It is the sign of the end of spirits in the kingdom.

The south wind will come and blow heat on the ice, to scatter clouds all over the earth. The ice will begin to melt because of the heat to make clouds all over the earth for CHRIST to come to create immortal spirits in salvation.

This is the time of salvation, when the ice begins to melt **12:56**

Jesus said to the crowd to tell their children to tell their children in the nations, highways, and jungles to have faith for salvation for their kingdoms to be created for their spirits to rest in peace. (22–23)

Jesus said to the crowd: tell your children to tell their children they will be tempted by seducing spirits of the dead to be lead astray to sin to live in bondage to have no faith to fall because of hate and jealousy.

Jesus told the crowd: Israel is not my disciple. He does not speak the truth. (27:26) Before he took the law, he knew his kingdom could have been created, to be a son of Elijah and not fall to the devils. He had no faith in Elijah who brought him up. The crowd asked Jesus: where is Israel? We can't see him following you. (28)

Jesus said: Israel has declared war against King Elijah and CHRIST with multitudes of godly spirits in the kingdom to rule the earth.

The end of the mission

The mission of Jesus was coming to an end. He told the people what was hid from them and told them the truth about the New Testament and exposed the godly spirit of God Israel in the body of Peter, and god (Cain) in the body of Judas. Jesus spoke about the kingdom, and the way to eternal life is through faith in the saviour Elijah for peace after their spirits depart from the kingdom and the coming of CHRIST to cast out spirits of gods from the kingdom.

The godly spirit Israel has multitudes of godly spirits under his authority from other nations, and ordered them to come to kill Jesus. They were in fear that Jesus had the Word and did not want to return to Hell. They thought Elijah returned to Heaven and left Jesus on earth. Israel and god (Cain) had a meeting with other chief of godly spirits on a plan under oath. If they Sabbathed Jesus his spirit would go back to Heaven and they would rule in the kingdoms earth to death.

Jesus was at the house of Jerusalem and she took some cream and poured it on his head. god (Cain) in the body of Judas came to the house and saw Jerusalem massaging the body of Jesus. Judas said: Jerusalem, you are wasting this cream on Jesus.

Jesus said: leave her alone. She is preparing my body for the Sabbath, so wherever the New Testament is preached about the kingdom, people will know they must prepare their kingdom before their spirits depart from the kingdom to rest in peace.

Jesus told god (Cain): you will always be a godly spirit with no flesh.

You are in the body of Judas as a seducer, and he went to tell Israel in the body of Peter. Israel got jealous with hate, since Jesus cast him out of the body of Mary. He felt Elijah is out of the way. Now is his chance to take revenge to kill Jesus to rule as king of the earth again, like when he was king in Babylon.

Cunningly they invited Jesus to feast before the Passover. Jesus, knowing his adversary, his mission had come to an end. There is no more he could do for the spirits of gods in the kingdom because he is not the saviour of spirits in the kingdom.

Jesus went to the feast. The godly spirits in the bodies of the disciples all sat at the table. Jesus stood up and looked at the hypocrisy of godly spirits in the body of disciples at the table and said: one of you shall betray me. I will depart according to the what is written in the New Testament, but woe unto the betrayer in a body at this table. It was better that he had not been born, because all of you are from his seed. **Heb.1:7–12**

The godly spirit (Cain) in the body of Judas said: Is it I? Jesus answered: thou hast said, and he seduced Judas to run outside to go and join the multitudes of godly spirits who were waiting to take Jesus by surprise.

Jesus took a loaf of bread and broke it in small pieces and gave it to the godly spirits in the disciples and said: eat; it will be in memory of my body from the flesh of Jerusalem, and told Israel in the body of Peter: I will Sabbath from her flesh in which you were conceived when she was held in captivity to make gods under oath while she was human.

Jesus took the cup on the able with blood and said: drink it, all of you, for the blood that will be shed from the flesh of Jerusalem's on the earth, it will be a testament against you for hanging the body ADAM/CHRIST and slaying all His sons on earth.

Zion and Jerusalem asked you to repent in the Jordan in front of multitudes of Mankind as witnesses and ask them for mercy and forgiveness for making a god to sin, in front of judge Elijah

Jesus said to Israel in the body of Peter: I will not drink blood with godly spirits in the body with spirits in the kingdom from the flesh of

Jerusalem that are not by Elijah through CHRIST.

You are offended because of what I say this night. Israel in the body of Peter answered through his mouth: I'm not offended if they are offended.

Jesus said: Israel, you will deny I cast you out of the body of Mary three times before the cock crows, that you never saw me in the kingdom with Jerusalem in the body of Mary.

Through the mouth of Peter Israel said: I am a godly spirit after I died. You are the spirit of Abel; I am a spirit from the seed of god (Cain) and not like you. In the Light I will not betray thee. Jesus left and went outside. Thcy followed Jesus.

Meanwhile multitudes of godly spirits were with Judas, waiting with a net.

Israel in the body of Peter followed Jesus with the disciples. Jesus said to the disciples: I am going a stone's throw away from you, and said to Israel in the body of Peter: don't be tempted as when you were tempted by the devils to hang the body of Adam.

The godly spirit in the body of the disciples was seduced to sleep. Jesus returned to the disciples and they were asleep and were told to wake up.

(Cain) in the body of Judas came with a multitude of godly spirits up to Jesus and said: Hail. Now you will know who is heir on earth. The godly spirits in the body of Mankind cast a net over Jesus and bound him in chains.

How else could people on earth know the truth of (God) Israel son of god (Cain) of the devils and know why CHRIST is coming to remove all spirits of gods from His flesh for killing all his sons from the earth to be justified in in the kingdom for peace on earth

The judgment hall

Israel entered the body of Pilate and the other godly spirits entered the bodies of Roman officials in the judgment hall. The centurion brought Jesus before Pilate.

Israel spoke through the mouth of Pilate and asked Jesus: who are you? Jesus kept silent. Through the mouth of Pilate Israel said: where did you come from? Jesus gave him no answer. Jesus knew it is the godly spirit Israel in the body of Pilate.

Israel said through the mouth of Pilate: why don't you answer me? Don't you know I have power over you for being against me? Jesus answered: you have no power over me. I am from above; you come from below.

You are the godly spirit who has committed abomination with your mother to sin, and want to judge me.

The godly spirit began to shout through the mouth of Mankind: if you let this CHRIST go, you cannot be our ruler and be the king of the earth. Jesus has spoken against thee.

Pilate had no idea what is going on. Israel seduced Pilate to be non-active. godly spirits were in the body of Romans and were seduced to be non-active and had no idea what is going on in this spiritual judgment.

Israel in Pilate sat before the godly spirits in the court and said to god (Cain) in Judas: shall I crucify your brother as the king? The godly spirits shouted through the mouths of Mankind: we will not have Jesus as our king. **Mt.15:13**

The godly spirits began to shout: Crucify Jesus; he is not the king of Israelites. Pilate got hold of himself and, dazed, said: I find no fault in Jesus.

Pilate was still confused and asked Jesus: who are you? Jesus kept his cool. Pilate said: tell me where you came from. Jesus just looked at him with piercing eyes.

Pilate looked at Jesus, dazed, and said: why don't you answer me? Then he ordered the soldiers to take Jesus away. The godly spirits removed the garments on Jesus. Israel in the body of Peter took a crown of thorns and stuck it on the head of Jesus and said: now you will know who is king of the earth.

The trial of Jesus by godly spirits in humans

Israel told god (Cain): tell the godly spirits to speak through the mouth of Mankind to be witnesses to make it look like it is Mankind who killed

Jesus.

(Cain) in the body of Judas asked Jesus: art thou a king who made Israelites in Babylon? Jesus kept silent before Mankind. god (Cain) said: why are you casting out their godly spirits? Jesus kept silent. The Romans returned Jesus to Pilate.

Israel in the body of Pilate said: Jesus the witness says you do many things against the law. Jesus gave him no answer. Israel said to god (Cain): what shall I do? God (Cain) said: let him be crucified! His blood be on our children. They brought Jesus in the common hall and stripped him of his clothes and stuck a crown of thorns on his head.

Israel switched and was in the body of Peter. He took a rod and smote Jesus like he did to Adam when he sat on the colt to hang his body on the tree, and began to mock Jesus and swear at him – fucking this and that, and told the godly spirits in the bodies of Romans: make Jesus carry the cross, and then nailed him to the cross.

AT THE CROSS

Jesus looked at Zion in the body of Elizabeth and Jerusalem in the body of Mary and with her Elisha (Isaac) spirit and said to him: look after your mother.

Then Jesus he looked at Israel in the body of Peter and said: look at what you have done to your mother because you have no faith. You will die of thirst for all the wickedness you have done. His spirit threw Peter on the ground and Mankind rushed to get some water for Israel in Peter on the ground.

They began to shout through the mouths of Mankind: thou sanctifed in Mary, save yourself. If you can un-nail yourself from the cross we will know you are the one who cast out of God/Israel from the same body with Jerusalem.

God (Cain) said: Jesus, you came to save Jerusalem and you cannot save yourself from Israel. (42) If you can save Israel from the devils, we will believe you. You put your faith in Elijah to save you. Tell Elijah to come and save you now!

Jesus shouted: Elijah, Elijah, wake up from sleep. My mission is over!

My spirit is in your hands. Jesus bowed his head and his spirit departed from the kingdom.

Mission accomplished according to the New Testament for all spirits of gods in the kingdom to live by the New Testament until the end of salvation in kingdoms for the final judgment when CHRIST Comes. Israel in Peter and god in Judas looked at the body of Jesus, whom they crucified on the cross, and had no faith to rest in peace on earth.

The synagogue building made of stone was split from top to the base, followed by an earthquake and the buildings began to collapse, to warn all who practice religion from the hierarchy at the top to the bottom to go out in highways, jungles and deserts to preach the faith in Elijah to save their spirits after death.

Elijah commanded multitudes of spirits from the people of Isaac that slept in the earth to wake up, and gather themselves under the clouds and follow Jesus in the clouds. multitudes of immortal spirits began to come out of tombs and began walking up to the clouds. When the spirits were in the clouds with Jesus, Elijah spoke the Word and a wind came unto the clouds and they were on their way with Jesus to the heavens. This was the first resurrection of the spirits of Isaac in the Light, waiting on Jesus to show them the way.

Jude 1

My dear children, I am writing to you about salvation in this present generation, and appeal to you to fight off temptation for your kingdom to receive the Word which has been taught to you since the flood to have faith.

The godly spirit of God/Israel is among you and has authority over his spirits. You have been told by Jesus to have faith to have peace. The same Elijah told your forefathers a long time ago that Israel and his godly spirits will want to tamper with the New Testament by Jesus to lead you astray to lose faith so you do not know Elijah and CHRIST, and to worship God. I write to remind you not to lose the faith.

Spread the good news of the New Testament and prepare yourself for salvation in your kingdom for peace.

ISAAC'S LETTER TO JERUSALEM HIS MOTHER, AND HER PEOPLE ON EART.

My mother, I love you very much and all our people through Elijah on earth to live in peace with you, from your son Isaac.

It gives me great joy, my mother, to know your children in the future will be spirits in the Light in the name of CHRIST.

My mother, love your husband who saved you from the beginning to live as the queen of the earth with your king Elijah, on earth in peace

Chapter 6

The resurrection of Zion to the heavens to see the battle in the kingdom Rev.12:14

Israel said to Zion: we will set a trap for you to fall to sin with the devils. Zion said: CHRIST rebukes you. Israel said: CHRIST is in Heaven. The earth is mine now and you are now living under the law of the devils, and everything continues as when CHRIST in Adam was hanged on the tree.

Zion felt threatened and cried: Elijah, wake up from your sleep! This blasphemer is threatening my life on earth to fall to the devils. Elijah appeared and Israel in the body seduced Peter to run away in fear of returning to the fire for provoking Zion.

Zion said: thanks, my saviour. CHRIST has chastised me with great measure. Now the godly spirits of God threaten me. I am afraid for my life. Let my spirit sanctify in your body so I'll be in your presence to have peace. O Elijah, save me from these godly spirits.

Elijah said: Zion, salvation cannot begin unless I resurrect you to Heaven. Zion began to cry daily to Elijah to make supplications to CHRIST to begin salvation in her flesh to remove spirits of god from her flesh.

Zion said to Elijah: speak to CHRIST to resurrect me to ask angels for mercy for making a god in the world.

If the devil did not come from Heaven to earth, there would be no god on earth to make gods in my flesh to threaten my life.

Elijah, I have taken the blame for the sin of the devil. The angels had the knowledge that if a god was born in the world it is death. I am disgusted, and feel unclean and humiliated and abused with this rape.

Jerusalem and I suffered death when we were tied together on a pile of wood set on fire. Our bodies were burnt to ashes.

Elijah, you snatched our spirits out of the fire and we are still on earth when we should be in Heaven in peace and happiness with angels. You are my witness on earth, Elijah. You have seen my suffering and humiliation. All I have is my faith in you to save me on earth, and my love for CHRIST. He is in Heaven.

The feast in the tabernacle in Heaven

Angels from all worlds gathered in the tabernacle to worship the Eternal Holy Spirit of Light and gave praise to CHRIST on HIS throne to put the world in the Light according to the New Testament.

The Eternal gave all angels HIS blessings. He created and blessed HIS CHRIST and angels from HIS seed in Heaven and children of Elijah and Jerusalem by the Word through Isaac.

The mercy seat was brought out in the tabernacle. The testaments in the ark of the New Testament were unveiled. CHRIST sat on HIS throne. Jesus and all his brothers and sisters, and Isaac and angels of Elijah and Jerusalem resurrected with Jesus sat as witnesses in the tabernacle before angels from all worlds.

CHRIST told Jesus to fetch the New Testament on salvation. Jesus began to explain to angels, saying: god (Cain) raped my sister Jerusalem when she was human and she conceived and made a wicked god.

The son of god committed abomination with Jerusalem when she was human and made Mankind and Israelites from the passed-on seed of god (Cain) of the devil. Now the earth is populated with Mankind and Israelites and they worship Israel as God their father to death.

The son of god has ill-treated Jerusalem and Zion and held them in captivity, just like the devils that held Jerusalem in captivity under oath to make gods from her flesh.

Elijah flooded the earth with water and multitudes of spirits were drowned to death. Elijah saved six thousand in the vessel and explained to them they would be on earth to make kingdoms for creation till salvation. They should have faith in Elijah to rest in peace.

The spirits that drowned became godly spirits and were held in captivity for a thousand years. Elijah released them to warn the spirits of their children of the chaos of Hell to have faith in Him to save them.

The godly spirits entered the kingdom and seduced the spirits to do the same evil to make war, shed blood on earth, steal, cheat, fornicate in holy flesh, commit adultery and lust in the body of Mankind, to be sinners and corrupt officials in governments to suppress and oppress all on earth with laws and declare war against the people of Elijah in the nations to exterminate them from the earth to rule in the kingdom.

Presently the godly spirits are seducing the spirits of gods in the kingdom to corrupt the testaments with many dots about Elijah and CHRIST and change the name of CHRIST to Christian to lead astray with their new religion. They preach Jesus is the son of god and they can be born again and Jesus will save them so they don't have faith in ELIJAH. These godly spirits seduce many to worship them with names of various gods to lead astray from knowing the truth of salvation and for peace on earth through faith in Elijah and, because of their religion, will cause multitudes to fall. The son of god declared war in the kingdom.

CHRIST has restrained and delayed war in the kingdom to give Mankind a chance to populate and make kingdoms for creation of immortal spirits with sciences of creation. These religions bring much conflict on earth to divert from faith for peace after salvation in kingdoms by our creator CHRIST for Elijah to save spirits who have faith in him from falling in the final judgment.

Jesus said to the angels: the plan for salvation is for CHRIST to create spirits in the Light so all spirits in the kingdoms on earth be holy spirits to live to old age until their time comes to resurrect to the heavens as angels among us in the Light.

Therefore CHRIST has to return to earth to remove spirits of gods from the kingdoms to establish the kingdom through creation in salvation by the Word of Elijah.

My mother made god in the world. She has suffered much for this sin and according to the testament, she must sit on the mercy seat to be judged by angels before CHRIST on the throne while the world still has gods of the devils for peace in the kingdom by divine justice to remove all in the kingdom for ever. CHRIST was created to finish the work the Eternal began in creation by the Word so the world be with angels created in the Light by the Word.

Jesus said: according to the Old Testament, for peace in the world, any angel who sinned with devils to make a god is death to the angel. The judgment would be dreadful. Angels had archangels to protect them from the temptation of devils.

Jesus said to the angels: the heavens are free from devils. They were cast out of Heaven and came to earth and committed sin with my mother to make a god on earth. The world cannot have peace until faith is put to the test from the throne of CHRIST.

The Old Testament, CHRIST has replaced by the New Testament in the tabernacle with a plan to put the whole universe in the Light and to establish the kingdom on earth to be everlasting when salvation ceases with spirits of gods to the last seed. Elijah saved my mother and Jerusalem on earth. They are no more humans, but angels on earth.

After Jesus was through speaking, Elijah stood on earth and looked up to CHRIST on HIS throne in Heaven. All angels looked at Elijah and he said: CHRIST, I stand here on earth before you as your servant in this world to serve you kingdoms and resurrect spirits to your throne in Heaven.

All angels in the tabernacle looked at Elijah in silence. The Eternal looked from the heaven of heavens and CHRIST said: what is your request, my son?

Elijah on Earth

Elijah said: the spirits in the kingdoms have populated the earth in multitudes and the godly spirits are threatening Zion. She cries daily and wants salvation in her flesh and asks for you to come and remove the spirits from her flesh and Jerusalem's as well.

Please have mercy and let her be on the mercy seat in the tabernacle to be judged by angels for this sin of devils in the kingdom on earth.

The devil assaulted Zion and committed sin by force to make a god to make Zion a sinner so she could fall before your eyes on the throne in the tabernacle. The devils knew under the covenant of peace that to bring a god in the world is death and took advantage of Zion's humanity to destroy you to bring the world back to darkness to be the ruler in the world like ancient times.

Zion was created free to put her faith in you. She is an angel. Let her be tried in Heaven by angels in the tabernacle for this sin in the world.

The spirits from the seed of god in Mankind have multiplied abundantly up to this generation and there is much corruption in governments and violence in the nations through godly spirits wanting to destroy the kingdoms in the nations with war, shedding blood, and putting fear on earth, and spreading disease in your flesh so there be no flesh left that is healthy to create in salvation. They boast that since you left the earth everything continues to be the same.

Zion cries: her faith in you is more than death and to be with you is more than happiness. She was deceived by the devil, whose intention was to do you harm, because he was in fear of you casting him out of the world.

Zion and Jerusalem have asked Mankind to forgive them for making a god with the devil and have put their faith in salvation for peace in the world.

Permit me, CHRIST, to resurrect Zion and Jerusalem to Heaven to ask angels to have mercy so justice can prevail. Zion is suffering for your love, just as you are for her. Both of you are no more human but created together as angels and have suffered death of your bodies living apart.

Jerusalem wants to stay on earth to live in kingdoms and wants to come up to see salvation and the final judgment on devils and godly spirits from her flesh. Accept my plea for mercy so there be peace in Heaven and on earth, so both of you can rule on your throne together and have dominion in all worlds through faith.

When Elijah was through talking, all angels looked at CHRIST on the throne. There was silence. CHRIST said: Elijah, my son, you have saved Zion and Jerusalem from the fire.

Resurrect Zion to sit on the mercy seat before the angels in the tabernacle. I'll send Jesus to show her the way. You have the plan and know what to do. Elijah commanded a pillar of cloud to come to where He was on earth waiting for Jesus.

Zion's spirit whispered in the ear of Elijah: thank you with my whole heart, my saviour. When I enter the gates above I'll rejoice and speak of your marvellous achievement and your righteous judgment and mercy on me since you saved my spirit and Jerusalem's in the fire after death unto our bodies.

I will rejoice with you and Jerusalem and all the children you give her in creation, and those through Isaac in the immaculate conception by the Word.

Zion said: Elijah, you have saved me and are worthy to be praised for saving Mankind in the flood to populate the earth to make kingdoms for salvation in my flesh for CHRIST to create immortal spirits in the kingdoms on earth by your Word to CHRIST and for spirits of gods who have faith in you to rest in peace.

Zion said: Elijah, my saviour, I am going forth from the earth to my CHRIST in the tabernacle in Heaven to tell the truth of this sin before angels, to put an end to spirits born to suffer Hell and to put a stop of the devils' hate for holy people.

I'll plead for salvation in my flesh to remove this deceit and offence of sin in the world, so kingdoms are undefiled to bring children in the world without sin.

I know CHRIST will listen to you to perform all petitions. I will rejoice when CHRIST creates immortal spirits from my flesh by your Word in salvation.

Zion in the cloud

Jesus arrived and waited on the pillar of cloud. Zion came out of the body, gave thanks to Elijah and began walking up on air towards the clouds. When she entered the cloud Elijah commanded the north and south winds to come unto the cloud, and it vanished out of sight to the heavens to CHRIST in the tabernacle.

Suddenly, as Zion vanished in the clouds there was a great rush of wind on earth and all leaves and branches of trees all over the earth began clapping vigorously for Zion's departure from earth to the heavens.

ZION ON THE MERCY SEAT

When Jesus and Zion got to Heaven, all the sons and daughters that Elijah resurrected after they were slain by gods and Judah when he was King Judah of Babylon were happy to be with Zion, their mother.

Jesus brought Zion to the tabernacle and she sat on the mercy seat. There was silence as she sat before the angels from other worlds before CHRIST. She began to cry And was ashamed among angels well groomed, thinking back when she was young yet still beautiful.

She cried: god has brought much sorrow in my flesh. god raped my daughter. She conceived from the accursed seed of the devil and made a god for him that became a tyrant and imitated the devils to do wickedly under the law of devils.

The son of god hanged Adam and slew all my sons on the earth. They are all angels in the tabernacle as my witnesses. Even my CHRIST on the throne will testify. He warned the son of god that if he hanged Adam all spirits from his seed would end in the gates in Hades. The devils made him king and he wanted to make a name for himself on earth by hanging Adam. He hated Elijah.

The son of god Judah made Mankind and Israelites after the devils were captured by Elijah, and had Mankind to worship him as God Almighty.

Zion cried: The devil deceived me, saying the Eternal sent him to earth to protect me and Adam from the enemy. He forced himself on me. I pushed him away. He slapped me and I fell on the ground and he forcefully raped me and took my virginity and I conceived from this accursed seed and his god was born in sin of Satan.

The angels were shocked to hear what the devil did. Zion said: I was very happy with my CHRIST. I love HIM all my life. I did not know what sin is. I never saw a devil to know he is the enemy of all angels. I did not know what was evil. I was created pure. I was created with good thoughts. I am innocent of this sin. I had no pleasure in this sin. I was sexually assaulted and raped to make a god that conspired with devils and brought me much sorrow. He was the first murderer on earth and stoned Abel-Jesus, whose body was unto death. He is my witness in this tabernacle. He turned out to be a wicked god.

The devil was the first rapist on earth and strangled god (Cain). Satan took my daughter Jerusalem in her humanity and held her captive while she was pregnant with the son of god who eliminated all my sons from the earth. My sons are all witnesses in the tabernacle of this Sabbath of their bodies.

The angels were in shock to hear what the devils did on earth with their lust for flesh to destroy the people of CHRIST, and tears began to fall from their eyes.

Zion cried loudly: I felt unclean in my flesh because of sin. Multitudes of spirits of gods are populating the earth to death in my flesh. Multitudes of godly spirits with the son of god as their ruler with authority over Mankind nailed Jesus's body on the cross for telling Mankind the truth about the way of salvation and peace. Jesus cast out the godly spirit of God-Israel spirit from the body with Jerusalem, then Jesus sanctified in flesh to manifest.

Elijah has saved me in fire and by water. The godly spirits know his work is in salvation and tempt me and Jerusalem to fall. It's my love for my CHRIST and faith in him and my saviour Elijah; I'm sitting on this mercy seat like a lamb for the slaughterhouse for the sin of a devil.

I have suffered more than I can bear and seen corruption and violence by godly spirits in my flesh and they began blaming me for sin and not the devil for rape. Elijah cast out the devils from the earth for raping my daughters to make giants to rule the earth and to make war to fight for the earth when they become godly spirits with no flesh.

All this wickedness the devils and the son of god have done in my flesh. My flesh is my heritage and it's burdened in sin like cancer. I ask you Lord – use your power to remove every spirit from my flesh to the last seed from devils. The devils waited after the son of god hanged Adam and slew all my sons with his battalion, even babies sucking milk on the breast so the seed of CHRIST in Adam doesn't take root on the face of the earth or the name of CHRIST to be heard of. After all my sons were slain the devils came in the nation and raped all my daughters and killed babies just born to make giants to rule on earth. All my daughters are angels in this tabernacle as my witnesses of what the devils did to them.

The kingdom from the flesh of Jerusalem and me and also my daughters who were raped is in abundance in multitudes all over the earth from the seed of god of the devil.

Zion looked at the angels sobbing in tears of this horror of the devils on earth and then said: CHRIST my lord, I want you to cast out every spirit from the seed of god from my flesh and do your holy work in salvation to give me children that are holy and pure in the kingdom that is worthy in salvation, or banish me for ever.

One sin by Satan has brought many problems to disturb the peace in the world in my flesh. Every time I see a child born from the seed of god I feel sorrowful, knowing it will not resurrect to Heaven and it will not rest in peace for eternity. This has become burdensome to me and stressful.

I was created under no law or covenant. The devils should respect creation of the Eternal while I was human and not come to earth and rape me to commit sin in the world to conceive from his accursed sperm to make god to be a sinner.

Zion looked at the angels, who were still in shock and said: look at me. What do you see? I am an angel of creation sitting before you, without flesh and blood, on the mercy seat. It is my first time in Heaven in judgment.

I was created good and pure and knew no evil and was quite innocent of sin. There is no wickedness in me. My spirit is holy, pure and spotless. I did not come to Heaven to commit adultery or sin to make a god to be a sinner.

All spirits from the seed of god should perish with him because of hate and jealousy for crucifying Jesus's body to death and when he was Abel and his conspiracy with the devils to kidnap Jerusalem to make gods in her flesh when she was human. CHRIST in his humanity in Adam warned god to keep away from the devil. He turned out to be a vagabond and raped my daughter to pass on his accursed seed of devils.

Zion bowed her head and began to cry, feeling all the sorrow and sadness flowing, remembering when Jerusalem was held captive by the devils, the strangled body of god by the devils, and the creation of Elijah by the Word of CHRIST His first holy created son in salvation in the kingdom of god by the word.

Wasting no time, Elijah and CHRIST went chasing after the devils and looking for Jerusalem. The whole tabernacle was inflicted with sorrow and the pain of losing a beautiful daughter most loved by CHRIST her father.

Elijah sent my CHRIST back to protect me.

Elijah went searching for Jerusalem to save her.

Up to this very day he is her saviour on earth. Zion composed herself and asked every angel in the tabernacle and angels in all worlds to have mercy on her before CHRIST on His throne.

Zion went on to say: if I am worthy to sit on the throne next to my CHRIST, forgive me. If not, banish me for ever and the kingdoms from my flesh on earth.

My desire is to sit next to my CHRIST to create immortal spirits in the kingdoms by the Word to be angels to live in all worlds and for spirits who have faith in Elijah to rest in peace so they don't fall to be with devils after death.

CHRIST sat in this judgment and looked at the angels in the tabernacle. They began to cry: O Zion, you are an angel of creation in Heaven like us. You have experienced good and evil we never knew existed. We forgive thee. You are worthy to sit next to your CHRIST as queen of the universe.

The angels cried: O CHRIST, put the crown on the head of Zion as our queen in the world without end and establish the salvation in kingdoms according to the New Testament to create spirits from her flesh to be one family of CHRIST, world without end.

Zion said: Holy Eternal, I am fully repentive for this sin to make a god in the world. Forgive me now and for ever. The Eternal Holy Father, creator by the Word, thundered from the heaven of heavens: My daughter, mercy is granted thee. Your faith and love for your CHRIST has saved you.

I created thee with CHRIST, male and female, to sit on the throne in Heaven to have dominion and rule the universe with my blessing. When CHRIST removes every spirit of gods from your flesh, it will erase this sin of the devil from your flesh for ever

Zion looked at CHRIST and said: if you forgive me, let all the world hear and love me for ever. CHRIST said: Jesus, bring your mother to me. CHRIST held her in His arms as when they were joined together in the beginning and all angels in the tabernacle shouted hallelujah after this long kiss.

CHRIST said: Jesus, look in the chalice and fetch me the ring made before we were created in Adam. CHRIST took the ring, glittering like stars, and put it on Zion's finger and said: now we are together, ever joined as angels in heavenly matrimony on the throne prepared for us before sin came in the world.

CHRIST said: Zion, sit next to me to see the battle in the kingdom to destroy the power of our enemy and his godly spirits who declare war against me and Elijah. They will be the first to be cast out of the kingdoms they possess in the nations on earth from your flesh.

The angels shouted: Amen. Bring on the battle in the kingdom before salvation begins for Mankind to have peace till salvation is established in the kingdom on earth from the throne of faith. Queen Zion, tell your Lord, let the battle begin to make beautiful angels like you.

CHRIST said: Zion, my love, now you shall see the battle in the kingdom until spirits of gods cease in the kingdoms, and see the final judgment on devils and godly spirits that have no faith in Elijah.

The Word came to Elijah: vengeance is mine. I want my enemy who hanged my body on a tree in my hand. Proceed with the battle in the kingdom. You know what to do, my son.

Mankind and the beginning of religion

The survivors of the flood passed on the faith of Elijah to their children and the elders in the nations to keep away from false worship and to keep the faith to rest in peace.

Elders warned their children not to go backwards and worship gods in the nations to fall like those in the flood and should hold fast the faith of their forefathers for Elijah to save them.

The godly spirits began to seduce Mankind in religion to worship God and punish any spirit that had faith in Elijah with disease, or seduce them with their lust to have control in the kingdom.

Godly spirits seduced Mankind to make images of themselves while they possessed their bodies to make gods of gold, gods made of silver, gods made of wood and stone to look like the godly spirits in their bodies for Mankind to worship them as their god in the nation to control Mankind in religion.

Mankind lost faith, being seduced by godly spirits to commit abomination, hooked on their lust and to live under the religious laws in the nations, godly spirits in their bodies controlling their lives and emotions and corrupting their spirits to fall to fight for the earth with the king of the godly spirits.

The godly spirits did not want to return to Hell to face the devils and made laws for all Mankind to worship their god's religion. All over the earth Mankind began worshiping their gods they made with carved images seduced by godly spirits in their bodies. They made gods of gold, silver, wood and stone and began putting curses on those who did not worship their god. They would say the spirit of their god would attack them and they would die through fear of death. They put their faith in statues which they made and prayed to them for help. Through this cult they lost interest in the New Testament for their salvation, saying the secret things belong to our god we worship to death. There for multitudes live in false hope by deception. **Ro.7:8; Ps.51:5; Eph.2:3; Mt.3:10; Ro.8:9; 1.Pe.5:8**

The battle in the kingdom

Judgment on the godly spirits in the kingdoms.

Elijah made his calculations to attack the godly spirits in the nations from north to west of the earth and commanded hailstones mingled with fire to fall on temples and houses in the fields. There was fire and smoke everywhere in the nations and the people began running out their homes to escape.

The godly spirits in the nations began to be in fear seeing fire everywhere, and began to separate themselves from the bodies they were possessing.

Everyone began to run here and there to escape from these hailstones with fire, seeing their homes blazing in flames and bushfires blowing in the wind. There was a great stampede to get away and the godly spirits tried to escape to the next nation.

Elijah commanded the sun to pull up the godly spirits trying to escape, like a magnet pulling up dust. The godly spirits were pulled up from the nations and were gathered together.

The spirits of Mankind and Israelites caught in the fire began to cry: God, save us from this fire! And spirits whose bodies were burnt to death became godly spirits with no flesh.

Elijah walked in the fire and the spirits that died saw Elijah in the Light and began to be afraid and said: if you are God, save us from this fire. Elijah said: I am not God who you worship; he will save you from the devils.

Elijah commanded the sun to pull up the godly spirits with no flesh in the fire in the nations and they were gathered together with the other godly spirits that was misleading Mankind.

Elijah commanded the tempest to come and it carried the godly spirits away and they began to fall in the mouth of the sea and began the journey to the gates of Hades. When the last spirits entered, the gates were shut, never to return to earth or to wait for the final judgment. Those who escaped were few to continue to make kingdoms till salvation.

This was the first victory over the godly spirits on earth. The angels began to sing: great and marvellous is the judgment of Elijah. Just and true is his way, thou king of the earth. Your magnificent judgment is according to the testimony in the tabernacle in Heaven by the Word for CHRIST to rule in the kingdoms. **Rev.5:5**

ELIJAH WILL NOT REST TILL HE ACCOMPLISHES VICTORY Job.20:50

The second attack was in the nations from west to south of the earth. Elijah commanded hailstones mingled with firestorms blowing in flames of fire everywhere. With this sudden attack everyone began running to exits to escape from the firestorms and everywhere they began running. Hailstones began falling and the godly spirits began to separate themselves from the body of Mankind.

Elijah commanded the sun to pull up the godly spirits in the nations. They were gathered together in one place. The spirits of Mankind whose bodies were burnt to death in the fire were now godly spirits without flesh and they began to cry: God, we trust you. The sun pulled all the godly spirits that shunned Elijah and joined the godly spirits. Those who did not cry slept in the earth in peace.

Elijah called the tempest and the godly spirits were carried away and fell in the mouth of the sea monsters and journeyed to the gates of Hades and spat out the godly spirits. When the last one entered the gates were shut. Those who escaped the fire in the nations were few to continue to make kingdoms for salvation.

The third attack, from south to east

Multitudes of godly spirits concentrated on building temples to bring back the days of Babylon to worship God in religion, according to the law. Every nation had a godly spirit that was their ruler in government, and enslaved the people to build pyramids to make a name for themselves on earth.

Elijah commanded lightning, thunder and earthquakes to break up all those monuments for false worship. Hurricane winds came blowing away houses, trees and branches began flying to block all exits. Rain came and flooded the rivers, bursting their banks.

There was a pause and Mankind began to hate God for breaking up their homes in the nations. The godly spirits began to attack those who lost faith in God with disease and madness, epilepsy, and enmity on every spirit in the kingdom who is against God, and there were dead bodies everywhere.

Elijah commanded hailstones mingled with fire to fall in the nations. The godly spirits began to fear, saying: it's Elijah, and began to separate themselves from Mankind and tried to flee to the north. The sun shone bright in the nations and the heat started forest fires in the nations.

Multitudes of godly spirits were trying to escape from the fire. The sun began pulling up multitudes of godly spirits from the nations like a magnet pulling up dust from the earth. When the godly spirits were gathered together, a tempest came and carried them away and they began falling in the mouth of the monsters in the sea. They journeyed to the gates of Hades, never to return on earth to await the final judgment. Mankind that survived continue to make kingdoms till salvation.

The fourth attack for the wicked god. The day of judgment. The day every man's work must be put to the test. If it's strong it will stand. If it's false it will fall Jer.38:28

GOD/Israel spread out his battalion in multitudes in the kingdom. He named the battalion the dragons of the earth – fierce killers with authority to rule in governments to destroy the kingdom by war to death to rule the spirits on earth.

Jerusalem lived in a house in a field

God/Israel was in fear. Elijah destroyed three-quarters of his godly spirits on earth, pursued Jerusalem, and found out she was living in a small house in a field. He entered the same body she was in to hide from Elijah.

Israel began to cry: O Jerusalem, my end has come. Let me stay in this body and we can live in peace together. Jerusalem said: did the devils have peace on earth for fucking in my flesh? How can I have peace with you in this body? You are like a devil.

I have acquainted myself with Elijah and I am at peace with him. Get out of this body and go in the body with your whore Hadassah who burnt my body in Babylon to death. Get out of this body, Jerusalem screamed at him. You are malicious, vindictive, stressful and violent, and want to be base in this body with your deceit with your law. Get out!

God/Israel said: if you don't let me stay, I'll have my battalion of godly spirits kill your people with Elijah and they will destroy their flesh like dragons to wipe them out from the face of the earth. While we live in the body of Mankind, we will threaten them to death and spill their blood as we did to your brothers, and they will have no seed to take root on earth.

You can't get away from me; it's either me or the devils. You can't escape. After this battle in the kingdom, there will be no flesh left on earth.

You will be on the earth with godly spirits and you will be in captivity like a bird without wings. You shall not escape the punishment by Israelites and Mankind for making them from seed of god (Cain) to suffer in Hades.

Jerusalem was in fear for her life and cried: get out! And she screamed in fear for her life and cried: Elijah, save me from Israel in this body! Israel is threatening me and wants to exterminate our children from the earth with his godly spirits.

Israel said: Jerusalem, you think your faith in Elijah will save you? Elijah will not save a sinner. You shut up in my presence. You are under the law as long as you live and have flesh on your spirit and also every spirit from my seed that lives in your flesh. You did not make us perfect like Isaac by your immaculate conception by the Word of Elijah.

I hate you for going with god (Cain) of the devils and for making me not perfect. I had to suffer in the heat for a thousand years because of his lust for you like a devil. When the spirits of Mankind become godly they will hate you after death for not being perfect to go above.

Jerusalem cried: Elijah, come and take this vagabond by surprise as you did to the devils to the consuming fire for sinning in abomination to make spirits such as him and god (Cain).

Jerusalem heard in her ear: now you shall see his shame going up like dust from under your feet, and all Mankind will know the truth about this boaster with the law of devils who deceived them to worship him and blaspheme CHRIST and ME and declare war for the earth.

The day Jerusalem requested judgment on God/Israel Ps.137:7

Like a bird caught in a trap, Elijah commanded the sun to shine bright over the house of Jerusalem in the field. Elijah said: CHRIST, the time has come to place Israel in your hand for judgment.

CHRIST said: my son, vengeance is mine for hanging my body on a tree and eliminating my sons from earth, and holding Zion and Jerusalem in captivity to sin with her according to his religion under the law of devils.

Elijah rode on his horse Faithful to the house of Jerusalem. When Jerusalem saw Elijah she ran out of the house crying: Save me, Elijah, from Israel. In this body he is threatening me and our children to death.

Elijah said to God//Israel: not by your power with your battalion with multitudes of godly spirits in the kingdom, but by the Word, and all your godly spirits will be cast out of the earth this day for ever.

Israel began to tremble in the body with fear. Jerusalem said: get out to face Elijah. Like a serpent in danger of being caught by an eagle, Israel separated himself from the body with Jerusalem and tried to escape.

Elijah commanded the sun to pull him up from the earth. CHRIST caught hold of Israel. He began to cry. CHRIST said: I warned you not to hang my body. Israel began to cry: the devils told me to kill you and I'll be a king with them on earth. Have mercy on me for my sins. Christ said: I warned you. Now it's too late. You are now a godly spirit. You had no faith while you lived in the kingdom. You became wicked like a devil and an antichrist and against the holy WORD with Elijah.

Israel cried: now I have faith, in fear of what the devils will do to him for going with Tamuze. His cries were so loud his battalion of godly spirits could hear him screaming for his life, and they began to tremble in fear of returning to Hades to be tormented by the devils.

CHRIST took Israel to the lower region and cast him in the lake of fire with the devils to be there till the final judgment on devils and godly spirits.

Elijah commanded hailstones mingled with fire to fall in the nations. The people began to run here and there from their homes. The seducing spirits began to panic and Mankind was screaming for God to come and save them from the fire.

Everywhere hailstones were thrown in their path. The wind was blowing smoke from bushfires in all directions surrounding the nations.

The eye of the sun began to shine through the smoke, and multitudes began to die from the smoke and fire. The godly spirits were left in open shame, without bodies. As soon as they got out of a body, the eye of the sun pulled them up. Multitudes of godly spirits were pulled up like dust from the earth and were gathered together until there were no godly spirits left in the nations.

Then the tempest came and carried them away and they fell in the mouth of the water to journey to the gates of Hades, never to return to earth, to wait for the final judgment will be on spirits of gods in the kingdoms before salvation begin. **Eccl.9:21**

The spirits of gods in the kingdom/Mankind that were saved to continue to make kingdoms to populate the earth for salvation according to the New Testament by CHRIST. **Zech.2:11–13**

Queen Helle

After the battle in the kingdom Jerusalem held Elijah and said: thanks, my saviour. Elijah said: I'll call you Queen Helle the beautiful, who destroyed the beasts of the earth like a dragoness for your flesh. I have put an end to godly spirits in the battle in the kingdom for kingdoms from your flesh to continue.

Elijah said to Jerusalem: now we shall have rest and let our people live side by side with Mankind for them to populate the earth till the time of salvation. **Zech.2:9; Da.2:44**

Elijah said: Jerusalem, when you wake up you shall resurrect to prepare yourself to be queen of the earth with perfect children. Jerusalem said: thank you, Elijah, and they went to sleep. Amen. **Eccl.1:4, 3:20; Jn.3:3–5; Ps.50:7–15**

Jerusalem resurrected to Heaven to see the final judgment on devils and godly spirits and salvation in the kingdom of Mankind Is.46:13

Final judgment is by the sun and Elijah before CHRIST on HIS throne in Heaven. What CHRIST, Elijah and the sun will do is not known through fear of spiritual death. **Is.30:26, 13:10, 23–24**

Salvation is every sixth day in the nations on earth by CHRIST. Elijah commands the wind to blow hot air on the ice to scatter mist and clouds in the nations on earth for CHRIST to come in kingdoms for salvation. **Job.7:7, 8:2**

Elijah presents multitudes of kingdoms for salvation in all the ations to CHRIST on His throne for CHRIST to come to remove the spirits of gods from the kingdoms for judgment and to create immortal spirits. **Ps.79:5–6, 9-13; Ps.83:16–18**

Within an hour, multitudes of kingdoms are created in the nations, then CHRIST waits for the spirits in the Light that sleep on earth to resurrect to CHRIST in the clouds. Elijah commands the wind to come unto the cloud to take up CHRIST and a multitude of immortal spirits to Zion on the throne in Heaven.

Jerusalem resurrects to Zion to see judgment and salvation Ps.76:19; Ps.80:14

Elijah woke up Jerusalem and said: the time has come, my queen, to resurrect you to be with Zion to see judgment in kingdom on the spirits CHRIST removed from your flesh. CHRIST our father is waiting in the clouds for you. They kissed, Jerusalem said: thank my saviour. Elijah said: lead the way so our children's spirits can follow you. Jerusalem began to walk on air to the clouds.

Elijah commanded the spirits of CHRIST that were asleep in the nations to wake up and gather themselves under the clouds to go to the heavens. The spirits of CHRIST from all nations woke up from sleep and looked and saw their mother Jerusalem. Elijah said: follow your mother to the clouds, and the spirits began walking on air towards the clouds. **Ps.48:2**

Jerusalem's spirit reunites with CHRIST Ps.48:2

When Jerusalem entered the cloud it was the first time She was reunited with CHRIST as an immortal spirit since she left her home as a human in the body of Tamah (Tamuze) (Babylon) when CHRIST was a spirit in Adam. She was held in captivity by the devils. This made CHRIST completely happy now they were holy spirits in the Light with her children of creation through Isaac entering the clouds to be with CHRIST their father by the Word. **Ps.48:5–6, 48:8** When the godly spirits saw immortal spirits going up in the clouds, they became terrified and were in great fear of judgment by Elijah.

Spirits of creation are angels with the mantle of light

When all the spirits of the children of Jerusalem and Elijah entered the clouds over the earth, Elijah asked CHRIST to let the spirits that had faith in him sleep in peace, and it was so. Elijah commanded lightning to flash its light on the spirits in the clouds, and they became angels with the mantle of light by the WORD.

The clouds vanish from sight by the wind Zech.5:6; Mt.8:27, 147:13–18, 104:3; Pro.26:1; Ps.104:4

Elijah commanded the winds north, south, east and west to go unto the clouds and take up the clouds with CHRIST with the multitude of angels to the heaven of heavens to the Eternal Holy Spirit in the Light to receive His blessing and for Him to bless CHRIST and Zion-Jerusalem and the multitudes of angels in creation from their holy flesh on earth.

Elijah commanded the devils and every godly spirit in the fire in the bowels of the earth to go on their knee and repent for taking Jerusalem in her humanity in captivity to make gods in her flesh.

Repent for hanging CHRIST's body Adam on a tree, repent for slaying all the sons from the earth, repent for raping the daughters of CHRIST to make gods and giants, repent for spilling holy blood to make Mankind to suffer grief and spiritual death.

Repent for misleading spirits in their humanity with the doctrine of devils with laws so the spirits don't know they must have faith to rest in peace, repent for forcing Jerusalem in the body of Babylon to marry under the law to commit abomination to provoke CHRIST and Elijah, repent for crucifying Jesus's body on the cross. **Ex.21:22; Lev.20:12; Num.30:3; 1.Sam.1:15; Mk.10:12; Gen.49:7; Pro.16:12; Lev.20:9–10; Deut.27:22—24; Lam.1:3, 7**

Elijah commanded the heat in the earth to increase until the devils and every godly spirit repented for their wickedness in killing holy people of CHRIST and Zion. The earth began to tremble from the cries of devils and godly spirits. **Is.6:6; Heb.3:6; Judg.5:4; SMH.2:1; Jer.10:10; Rev.8:19**

The devils and godly spirits began to cry: enough, enough. Elijah commanded: repent, and he increased the heat by the Word. God/Israel cried: Lord, Lord, save me from the devils. Satan grabbed him by his throat and screamed in his face: motherfucker, you are coming with us. You sinned more than us. While we were in the fire, you were enjoying yourself committing abomination with my Tamuze. **Gen.6:6; Ps.106:45; Jer.18:8; Ro.1:28; Lk.13:3; Jer.6:30**

god (Cain) screamed at Satan: if you did not rape my mother, I would not be here to suffer in this heat for your sin to make me in her flesh.

Satan screamed in the heat: you stupid bastard, I did not ask you to be born. It's because of you that I and all the devils were cast out of Heaven for my sin to make you, and you did the same as me. You are a murderer. You slew your brother Abel and raped your sister's virginity with lust for her flesh. Suffer like me for your sins. You were the first god to pass on my seed to make a god as wicked as you in her flesh. **1.Cor.9:27; 2.Cor.7:10; Dan.2:47**

The godly spirits began to shout and cry to god (Cain): you should not make our God/Israel to pass on this accursed seed to make us to suffer in this heat. Repent to Jerusalem for conceiving your accursed seed in her flesh to make us like scum of the earth. The earth began to tremble with much crying. The sea began to send up mountainous Tsunami waves to the nations, afflicting everyone on the coasts and doing much damage.

Satan said to the godly spirits: who is the Lord that I should repent for my sin with my Tamuze? The heat began to increase. Satan cried: I was in the world before the Lord. He should be here and I should be with my Tamuze. god (Cain) shouted in the devouring fire: you are a deceiver with your hope after death. You can't have her. Tamuze, she is a holy immortal spirit now; she is free from your oath and the law.

The other devils began to cry: this heat is by the WORD. Repent, Satan. We are all sinners. We followed your doctrine from Heaven and we are entombed in this fucking heat in the earth for our lust for the Eternal's creation. We are suffering for raping holy people in their nation. This heat is unbearable. Now all the angels in Heaven are laughing at us as scum of the world being punished by a Lord for flesh of creatures on earth to make gods

The earth began to quake in the nations on earth, sending earth tremors and making buildings collapse in the nations, volcanoes erupting and sending ash and boulders in the sky, putting fear in Mankind crying: what is going on in this world?

The godly spirits began to cry in the fire: if we had faith we would have rest. Satan shouted: you fucking asses had a choice while you had flesh to rest in peace. Your desire was to fornicate in holy flesh like me to death. That is why we are here; there is no peace with you bastards crying for your sins after death for passing my seed like god. You had no faith.

Go and cry to God/Israel who you worship. Ask him why he had no faith and took the law to do the same as us. He knew the law is to provoke Elijah and His CHRIST. You fuckers have made Israel a mighty god without the Word. Tell Israel to save us if he is a mighty god.

The godly spirits began to cry: God/Israel did not tell us about Elijah. We never heard about him to have faith to rest in peace from you fuckers who left the good life in Heaven to come to earth and screw like creatures with flesh to make gods in your nature to suffer after death.

The heat reached its maximum. Satan cried: this time I repent for raping Eve-Zion. He shouted: almighty God/Israel cry to Elijah 'it's enough'. Tell him to release the heat. Satan began crying: My Tamuze, My Tamuze, I brought shame on the daughter of Adam and Eve. I repent for raping Eve to make a deceiver to boast. He fornicated with my Tamuze under the law to make Mankind to worship him as almighty God. **Ps.100:4; Ps.100:3; Gen.6:4; Ps.106:42–43**

Satan cried: my lust for you, Tamuze, is more than Hell. O Tamuze, pray to Elijah for me to release the heat. It is killing me and everyone for our sin to make gods in your holy flesh. The devils shouted: Satan, this wrath is by CHRIST and Elijah the Lord. Repent. Satan cried: I don't know this Lord. Is he Elijah the judge? Satan began to cry: Tamuze, because of you I'm suffering for your fucking flesh in Hell. I, I, I, I, re, re, pent, repent. I've sinned in this world to make a god in the holy flesh of Eve and gods in Tamuze (Tamah).

Elijah commanded the heat to release and come through the waters and rise unto the clouds and made rain to fall in the nations on the earth to bless Jerusalem and every kingdom from Her flesh to be for creation with immortal spirits to live for ever.

Elijah commanded the devils and every godly spirit in the fire in the bowels of the earth to go on their knees again and bless the Eternal, the WORD, the spirit of the sun, CHRIST and Zion, Jesus, Jerusalem and all Her brothers and sisters in the Light. Bless all angels in the Light and spirits in the Light in their humanity. Bless Elijah to live in the world in the Light for ever.

Elijah commanded the heat in the earth to increase to its maximum until every devil and godly spirit blessed according to the Word. The devils cried quickly: I repent. I repent. We bless the Eternal, the WORD, the spirit of the sun, CHRIST and Zion to be on the throne for ever.

We bless Jesus, Jerusalem and Elijah and all angels in the Light and immortal spirits in the Light in kingdoms in the name of CHRIST to live for ever in the world.

Elijah commanded the heat to come through the waters unto the clouds and commanded rain to fall and bless the immortal spirits in the kingdoms on the earth in the name of CHRIST the creator, and much rain fell in the nations. **Gen.XXXIII; Deut.11:14, 32:9; Job .29:22–23**

God confesses the truth to the devils Jer.38:14

Elijah said to God/Israel: hide nothing from the devils. Tell the devils who is Eve. Israel cried: she is Zion. Tell the devils who is Adam. He cried: CHRIST, the creator of Elijah. Tell the devils who is Abel. He cried: Jesus. Tell the devils who I am. He cried: you are the Lord Elijah with the Word. Tell the devils who crucified Jesus on the cross. He cried: god (Cain) and myself.

Tell the devils who is Queen Tamuze: He cried: Jerusalem. Tell the devils who is Queen Babylon. He cried: Lord have mercy, she is Jerusalem. She is my mother and was Queen Tamuze. After you removed the devils from the earth, I was King Judah. I made her my queen in Babylon according to the law. Tell the devils who is Isaac. He cried: Lord, He is your son with Jerusalem by the Word. Tell the devils who is Tamuze's first god.

I am her first god by god (Cain), Satan from birth. You brought me up, my lord, and called me Ammon. **Gal.4:24; Heb.9:8–9; Dan.2:47; Sal.2:4, 9.3:10**

Satan and the devils rushed on God/Israel and called him a serpent, deceiver, a dragon for flesh, and a falcon for flesh of the dead. The devils began kicking God/Israel, screaming at him: you knew who is Elijah when we made you king, fucking with our queen while we are in the heat, to be the king of fuckers, to make kingdoms for CHRIST and Elijah from the seed devils for angels to laugh to us. Satan and the devils screamed: we committed sin to make this fucking god make us the scum in the world, and they began kicking the godly spirits in the fire. They began to cry: it's not me, it's him. God shouted: if you did not rape my mother I would not be in fire.

God/Israel cried: Elijah, save me. The devils are attacking me. Save me, Elijah, now I have faith. Elijah thundered: you provoked me with abomination with your mother; you were cruel to Her and forgot who brought you up from birth. When you saw your beautiful mother you lusted for her and joined the devils. After I cast out the devils from the earth you called yourself Mighty God. **Sam.2:47; Ps.76:1; Ps.5:4**

God/Israel cried: save me Lord, from the devils. I'm in trouble for hanging Adam on a tree. I'm in trouble with CHRIST for what I did to Jerusalem, not setting her free and killing all His sons. My spirit is trembling. The devils are kicking me in this heat. Lord Elijah, save me from Satan. He is angry because I made Tamuze my queen. Don't ignore my cries.

Elijah thundered in the heat for all to hear: your mother's beauty tempted you to lose faith in me. You had a choice to rest in peace but you disobeyed my words. You willingly chose to put your hope after death with the devils.

You oppressed my people in the nations. You wanted them to be your slaves, to rule them. You committed abomination with your mother. You became a tyrant on earth with your wickedness, putting fear in the people to rule on earth.

So save yourself from the devils with all the godly spirits that worshiped you when they had flesh, you made them live in your hope after death.

Multitudes who still follow your doctrine on earth and who have no faith in me are yet to join you in the fire. I warned you before you took the law of devils that if you committed abomination with your mother every spirit that has no faith in me will join you in the fire when they leave the flesh of your mother on earth.

The power of the WORD with Elijah

Salvation is between CHRIST and Elijah. The water that was on the earth that was blown to the north and south of the earth after the flood was solidified into ice by Elijah. On the days of salvation Elijah will command the wind to blow hot air of the sun on the ice to scatter mist and clouds all over the earth for CHRIST to come in salvation to cast out spirits of gods from the kingdom and create immortal spirits in multitudes in kingdoms for salvation on the earth.

CHRIST waits on the clouds after creating immortal spirits for Elijah to wake up immortal spirits that sleep in the earth after death to resurrect them to the clouds for CHRIST to take them up to the Heaven by the wind at his command by the WORD. **Zech.5:6; Eccl.11:6; Job.30:15; Mt.7:25; Pro.25:23**

The spirits of gods CHRIST cast out from kingdoms, that have no faith in Elijah, are passed on to the spirit of the sun for the final judgment to remove the godly spirits of gods after death from the earth to the gate of the sun. **Mt.7:25**

The final judgment on spirits of gods is by the spirit of the sun

The final judgment is through Elijah to pass on the godly spirits that has no faith for peace to the spirit of the sun to remove all godly spirits that have no rest on earth after salvation to the gate of the sun, to fall in fire (3.42). The spirit of sun works for six days and rests on the seventh day for salvation of kingdoms for CHRIST to cast out spirits of gods in kingdoms from his flesh for judgment by Elijah and the spirit of the sun after salvation.

There is no place to hide in the path of the sun from sunrise to sunset, from nation to nation, till the end of godly spirits after death of spirits of gods in the kingdoms on earth to establish the kingdom with no division to be as it was in the beginning with immortal spirits of creation for ever. **Act.8:7; Heb.11:4; SMH.IXXXVII; Job.37:21, 21:8; Ps.1:4**

AFTER SALVATION

The immortal spirits created in the kingdom of Mankind shall continue, in their resemblance, to populate the earth and to be with the righteous people of Queen Jerusalem with her king Lord Elijah as their subjects on earth till they go to Heaven to be among angels. World without end. **XXVII2–XXVII.3; Ps.98:11–12; Ps.9:4**

THE KINGDOM

Salvation is only in the kingdoms with spirits of gods in Mankind to create immortal spirits. According to the New Testament plan 9.9 the people of Elijah and Jerusalem don't need salvation. They are immortal spirits in the kingdom. **Gen.2:3; XXIV:14; Rev.15:2; Lev.19:19; PS.106:35** The spirits created in the kingdom from the spirits of gods will be in the same resemblance in the kingdom in the name of CHRIST and will be accepted above by the ETERNAL. World without end.

THE FINAL JUDGMENT IS BY THE SPIRIT OF THE SUN Job.31:26; Deut.17:3, 45; Ex.20:8–10; Dan.9:7; Dan.10:1

The spirit of the sun began work in the final judgment, removing godly spirits from the earth that have no rest from the first sunrise on earth every day for six days to the last sunset rest for salvation of kingdoms to be created with immortal spirits by CHRIST and Elijah with the WORD on the seventh day.

CHRIST AND ZION ON THE THRONE TO SEE JUDGMENT ON DEVILS AND GODLY SPIRITS

CHRIST and Zion had Jerusalem to sit with them on the throne with Jesus and multitudes of angels in the tabernacle to see the final judgment on the devils and godly spirits in captivity in the bowels of the earth. There was great excitement to see Elijah judge with the Word.

The spirit of the sun waits on Elijah for the Word for the final judgment on devils and godly spirits in chambers of Hades in the earth. **Job.30:15–22; Ps.50:1; Ps.113:3; Ps.98:3, 5–7; Dan.12:9–10**

For cruelty on holy people in their humanity and shedding their blood on earth. **Jov.30:22; Ps.50:1; Is.11:3.3; Ps.35–7**

Elijah commanded the spirit of the sun to pull up every devil and godly spirit that surfaced the earth, straight to the gate of the sun after he released them from their chambers in the earth. **XVIIIX VIIXIXI; Mt.13:40; Ph.3:19; 1.Tim.3:7; Ps.9:16; Rev.14:10**

Elijah commanded the chambers with devils and godly spirits in the earth to open. There was a great rush to get out of the fire. All the devils and godly spirits captured for deceiving the spirits of Mankind – rapists, perverts, murderers, thieves, deceiving preachers who scorned Elijah and CHRIST to lead astray for devils, greedy rulers and terrorists shedding blood to destroy the kingdom through envy, jealousy and hate began shout: freedom! hurry to get out of this fucking heat before the gate shuts. **Ro.8:9; 2.Pt.3:7; 1.Pet.3:4; Rev.14:18; 2.Cor.4.:16; Eph.3:16**

The choice is still before spirits of gods in the kingdom today to rest in peace through Elijah or be judged by the spirit of the sun to remove them from the earth to the gate of the sun. Don't wait after death to have faith in Elijah with no flesh for judgment. **Mt.3:40; Obd.9; Ro.1:11; 1.Pet.13; Ps.1.47:13–16; Is.30:26; Deut.11, 26:29; Dan.12:11–12; Mt.23:14–15**

The old covenant between the ETERNAL and the ancient devils of the dark world

The Eternal in the heaven of heavens with His archangels were looking at CHRIST on the throne in command. The Eternal thundered His blessing to CHRIST and Zion to rule the world prepared for them, and gave His blessing to Elijah: keep faith with the sun to make the Old Covenant with devils obsolete for the New Testament to begin in judgment by the WORD.

The final judgment began on godly spirits after death according to the New Testament between Elijah and the spirit of the sun to remove godly spirits from the face of the earth after death that have no exemption to rest on the earth to be pulled up to the gate of the sun to fall in the everlasting fire. **IXXXVI;Ps.148:3**

Judgment by the Word of Elijah Ex.20:8, 9, 10; Dan.9, 7, 11, 14

The Word of Elijah begins judgment on godly spirits cast out from the kingdoms by CHRIST to create immortal spirits in kingdoms for salvation every six days. The godly spirits that have FAITH in Elijah and not anti-CHRIST, Elijah will save and they will rest in peace on earth. This work is according to the New Testament between CHRIST and Elijah for salvation. After CHRIST has done his work the immortal spirits that sleep in earth will wake up and CHRIST will take them to Heaven with him. Then Christ will rest for six days.

The final judgment is by the spirit of the sun, beginning on godly spirits on the seventh day from the first sunrise to sunset, from nation to nation, as the earth rotates around the sun, and will pull up godly spirits that have no rest by the saviour Elijah to the last sunset on the sixth day and rest on the seventh day to let CHRIST come and create spirits in salvation in the kingdom in the nations on earth and to cast out spirits of gods for Elijah to judge the spirits that have no faith for the sun to pull up every godly spirit that has no rest as the earth rotates around to gate to fall in the fire of the sun.

This pattern of judgment is automatic till the end of spirits of gods in the kingdoms to the last seed of devils on the earth. The spirits of gods that sleep in the earth is for eternity and play no part in the world in the Light for ever. No purgatory, it's false hope. **Eccl.11:6; Job.37:21; Job.30:15; Zech.5:6; Pro.25:23**

Jesus and his brothers and sisters with multitudes of angels in the tabernacle from other worlds came to see the final judgment on the devils and godly spirits by Elijah and the spirit of the sun according to the New Testament of CHRIST.

EVERLASTING FIRE, GLOBAL HEAT, CLOUDS Ps.135:7; 1.Ki.23:4; Eccl.3:16; Rev.16:2

After the devils, God, god and multitudes of godly spirits went through the exit gate. Elijah commanded the exit gate to shut. **Gen.3:19; Is.226:2; Job.7:21**

Zion asked Jerusalem to sit with her as queen of the earth on the throne with CHRIST. Remembering her pain in being raped by god, held in captivity, pregnant and giving birth to a wicked god like god his father, Jerusalem cried: my father, tell Elijah to cast him out of the earth with the devils for forcing me to sin. I am ashamed of what he did to me.

Elijah spoke and it thundered in the heavens: Jerusalem, for abomination when he was King Judah, bringing shame on you, for his abomination and eliminating your brothers from the earth, I will punish him, for you and all in Heaven to see, for not having faith in me.

Jerusalem cried: Elijah, make this dragon from my flesh fall. He is a crooked serpent and led the spirits astray with his law to death. He denied Jesus cast him out three times before godly spirits in Mankind. He and god (Cain) were jealous of Jesus.

Jerusalem cried loud: O Lord Elijah, remove them from the earth for me. The angels began to clap: Hallelujah!

Jerusalem cried: Elijah, cast all in the fire of the sun for setting my body on fire, and I will be satisfied .

Sisters of Jerusalem, Elijah resurrected remembering the devils raping them to make gods. **Amos.52:2**

The angels in the tabernacle, hearing the devils raped the sisters of Jerusalem when they were human, shouted in anger: Your Excellency CHRIST, cast them in the devouring fire of the sun for us.

Elijah commanded the sun to pull up the devils and every godly spirit that emerged from the earth went direct to the gate of the sun to fall in the fire in the sun for bringing shame on Jerusalem and her sisters and eliminating the sons of CHRIST from the face of the earth to make gods in the name of Mankind and Israelites to live to continuous death for their sins. **Gen.3:16**

Jerusalem cried: O my lord Elijah, my children by our Isaac are multiplying. If the devils and godly spirits return to earth my children will have no peace with the bastards. They will hurt them. Let me see your judgment to give you praise among angels in Heaven.

CHRIST and Zion sat on the throne, looked at Jerusalem and her sisters and said: vengeance is mine for what they did to you and your sisters and brothers. Jesus took Jerusalem to sit next to him to keep her quiet with her brothers, who were slain by King Judah (the mighty God). The angels in the tabernacle looked intensively at CHRIST to bring judgment on devils and godly spirits according to the New Testament. **Ps.60:1; Ps.74:12**

THE ECLIPSE – THE SUN RESTED

The sun began to eclipse the earth while the devils and godly spirits were through the exit. Suddenly the earth was in darkness while the devils left the exit of the earth.

CHRIST commanded the comets to bombard the ancient planets of devils. With every hit, the ancient planets of the devils began to crack up, and the comets scattered boulders, bits and pieces and dust all over the universe. Some big boulders began to fall on earth, shaking the earth.

Every time a comet hit the planets of ancient devils, they began to crack up, breaking up planets of old civilizations of devils so no planets of devils can be in the world of angels created according to the New Testament of CHRIST.

The world returned to darkness with all this bombardment. The angels were in fear that the devils and godly spirits released by Elijah from the earth would make their way to Heaven to take vengeance for breaking up their planets.

The angels began to pray: Elijah, command the sun to bring back light in the world. There were loud explosions in the dark. Every time a comet hit a planet it shook the heavens. Chunks of planets began to scatter in the universe.

In the darkness, thunder was shaking the world. Because the sun could not be seen, the angels began to faint. Elijah felt weak and went in a deep sleep. CHRIST called: Elijah, Elijah, in the darkness. Wake up the sun. Wait for the Word for judgment.

Elijah was in a deep sleep and began to dream of Jerusalem in Heaven. CHRIST called by thunder: Elijah, Elijah, wake up. Elijah said: I'm having my rest with the sun. CHRIST commanded the place where Elijah was asleep to tremble to wake up Elijah. The place began to tremble vigorously, and Elijah sprang up and saw the world was in darkness.

Elijah said: CHRIST, I can't see the sun. Where is the sun? CHRIST said: the sun waits for thee for the Word. CHRIST sent a shooting star in the direction where the sun rested.

Elijah commanded the sun to come through the darkness. There were loud noises of spirits crying in the darkness: you can't bring judgment on us to death until Satan and his devils are captured with multitudes of godly spirits from our seed on the earth to rule the world without darkness.

Every time the sun showed a glimmer of Light, the spirits of the dark world would command darkness to cover the light of the sun to prevent it from lighting the world, suddenly there was a light flickering in the dark.

Elijah commanded the sun to let its light shine and let the dark be in the world till it cleansed the earth from all spirits of god to rule for ever under the New Testament.

Slowly and steadily, the sun began to eclipse to finish the work in judgment on godly spirits to the everlasting fire of the sun to rule.

Elijah commanded the sun to pull up every devil and godly spirit straight to the gate of the sun to fall in everlasting flames in the sun and to do the work from sunrise to sunset, from nation to nation, every six days, and rest on the seventh day for CHRIST to create immortal spirits in kingdoms in salvation, so CHRIST can have His rest for six days with Zion.

JUDGMENT BY THE WORD WITH ELIJAH AND THE SUN

From sunrise the devils and godly spirits began to submerge. The sun began pulling up the devils and multitudes of godly spirits direct to the gate of the sun and they began falling on top of one another in fire of the sun that can't be measured, to meet the unfaithful godly spirits that were judged by Elijah for having no faith in Him to save them to rest in the earth for ever in peace. **Is.24:20, 33; Ps.97:5; Gen.18:27; 1.Pet.1:9; Deut.32:20; Job.28:2**

CHRIST AND ZION ON THE THRONE

Jesus, Jerusalem and multitudes of angels in the tabernacle saw the devils and multitudes of godly spirits without flesh pulled up by the sun and saw them falling in the devouring fire of the sun.

They began to shout: Hallelujah! Hallelujah! in the heavens. Angels began to clap their hands and dance: we give CHRIST praise for your wisdom and your plan according to the New Testament to put the whole world in the Light with righteous justice for peace.

Jerusalem began to sing: Elijah brings on the final eclipse for CHRIST and Zion to have dominion and reign in all worlds. The angels said: Hallelujah, Jerusalem. **Ps.97:8, 97:4; Rev.14:15** You will be his queen on earth soon.

Angels in all worlds began to celebrate and sing: the devils are in the fire of the sun with multitudes of godly spirits We praise CHRIST and his son Elijah. We praise thee, O Eternal, for creating your CHRIST to remove devils from us for ever.

The godly spirits saw the devils falling in the sun, one on top of each other, in the flames of devouring fire. The godly spirits were in fear. The devils were confounded to see a multitude of godly spirits in the devouring fire there before them, thirsting for water and crying that they should have had faith in Elijah.

The devils asked the godly spirits: where did you come from? What evil have you done to be in this everlasting Hell, crying for water in the sun? They began to cry: we were doing all right having faith, then religious leaders came tempting us with doctrine of gods to worship God. We hoped he could save us after we die. Now we are in flames. We did not harm anyone.

Others spirits cried: we join the terrorists who spilled much blood in our nation, doing the work of God. Others said: we murdered innocent people. Others said: we stole and cheated. Others said: we are here for raping women, murder, etc.

The devils said: it was your desire to fuck and rape, steal, cheat and murder innocent people. You did the same as us. The fault is in our nature to be evil but while you lived like gods in the flesh, you had a choice to stop this desire and prepare your bodies to rest in peace. Why did you not take it?

Satan said: you decided to do like God and pass on our seed and worship him for making you not perfect, like us and god (Cain) his father who is with us in Hell for raping the daughter of Adam to make a wicked god who boasts he is a mighty god for making all kinds of images in the holy flesh of my queen. Satan said: while I'm in fire for my sin in the world to make gods I don't want to hear you fuckers crying for your sin. I have given up half my world for my sin. That can't be measured in flesh

Satan said: when you were fucking women and passing the seed of devils and having orgasms you said, O God each time and called him a mighty god for giving you such pleasure to pass on my seed, and worshipping him and giving him praise and paying tithes for not making you to fuck like devils. He is here in the fire. Go cry to him for passing on our seed to you to be in fire, and tell him if that he is a mighty god, save you and us from this fire in the sun, and we will give your God praise for making gods in the name of Mankind in holy flesh from seed of devils.

Satan said to the godly spirit: you followed a doctrine that was not yet tried by fire in the sun. **Is.50:11; 1.Cor.3:13** If the motherfucker is mighty, why is he crying in Hell for making you not perfect with his mother to suffer here after death? Get used to the idea that once any godly spirit goes through the gate of the sun, it is for ever for having no faith. **Deut.4:24; Deut.32:22; Ps.104:4; Jer.48:45; Ps 66.12; Ps.18:8; 2Thes.1:8; Dan.7:10; Dan.2:47; Is.6:4; Eze.1:4; Mk.9:44; Mt.25:41; Jer.23:29; Lk.12:40**

The earth was free from barbaric devils and uncivilized godly spirits to proceed with the New Testament and plan for salvation in kingdoms in the same resemblance of all Mankind from the flesh of Zion and Jerusalem.

The kingdoms of Mankind will be created by CHRIST in the same resemblance, to continue to be productive to make immortal spirits to be His subjects and Zion's on His throne in Heaven through Elijah, according to the NEW Testament.

The New Testament between CHRIST and Elijah after the flood is for salvation for the kingdom of Mankind to have immortal spirits to live in the New World in the Light under the New Testament.

Meanwhile the work in salvation between CHRIST and Elijah is going on in the kingdoms of Mankind in nations on earth, creating immortal spirits, and the final judgment between Elijah and the spirit of the sun to remove the godly spirits that have no exemption to rest on earth to the gate of the sun to fall in fire for eternity.

Jerusalem is making Herself ready return to earth to be queen in the kingdom with immortal spirits created for her to be her subjects on earth in righteousness with her lord judge King Elijah in the kingdom on earth.

His Excellency CHRIST and Zion are on the throne fulfilling what they were created to do – to rule the world with angels in the Light under the New Testament and to make the Old Covenant with devils obsolete for ever.

The spirit of the sun is removing godly spirits after death from the earth to the fire of the sun, putting an end to the old testament between the devils of Ancient World of Darkness and dissolving darkness in the world to death for their sin to make a god to sin to suffer after death.

The end of darkness will come suddenly. CHRIST and Zion wait for the spirit of the sun to remove godly spirits that have no rest by Elijah, for the sun to eclipse and dissolve darkness in the world for eternity, to be a perfect world with angels in the Light according to the New Testament by CHRIST and Elijah the WORD to remove the devils and spirits of gods from the earth for CHRIST and ZION to rule all worlds from the throne for eternity, as the ETERNAL prophesied HIS CHRIST will do after he took HIS rest from creation for a perfect world in the light for eternity By the WORD. **Eccl.11:4, Is.51:9; Gen.1:27, 2.1–3**

The letters left to by God/Israel, god (Cain) and Jerusalem

The hidden mystery of God/Israel of god (Cain) his father first god of the devils on earth is revealed to all Mankind, what they did to Jerusalem when she was human in the body of Babylon. Spirits of gods in Mankind, take heed of religious leaders that do the work of God/Israel of god (Cain).

God/Israel spoke through the mouth of Peter and said: Jerusalem was always sorrowful. Her faith in the Lord Elijah was more than spirits born from the seed of god (Cain) in the fire. When Lord Elijah says the word to the spirit of the sun is the final judgment on spirits of gods after salvation of kingdom by CHRIST. **1.Pet.16–9**

The happiness of an immortal SPIRIT created by CHRIST in the kingdom from the flesh of Jerusalem is through Elijah and is the misery of the spirit of the seed of God/Israel of god (Cain) that was cast out by CHRIST with no flesh to face the SPIRIT of the sun to fall in flames of fire in the sun. **Mt.25:46**

The truth by the godly spirit god (Cain)

The godly spirit of god (Cain) spoke through the mouth of Paul to the Corinthians: **(9.1–2)** I am a godly spirit. I am not an apostle of Jesus, and spirits from the seed of God/Israel are from my seed in the flesh of Jerusalem. God (Cain) said: God/Israel is a godly spirit and was in the body of Peter after Jesus cast him out from the same body Jerusalem was in.

The godly spirit (Cain) in the body of Paul said to the Corinthians: I am telling you the truth what Jesus did. Jesus cast out the godly spirit God/Israel in the same body with Jerusalem in the body she called Mary.

Jerusalem says farewell to spirits of gods of Mankind from the seed of God/Israel of god (Cain)of the devil.

Jerusalem says farewell to spirits of gods in Mankind

O ye spirits of god that dwell in the kingdoms from my flesh, God/Israel hath brought shame upon me. In the battle in the kingdom Elijah sent multitudes of godly spirits from the seed of God/Israel of god (Cain) crying into captivity.

No spirit of God/Israel of god (Cain) should rejoice over me. The godly spirits that were removed from the earth, they walked not in the statutes of new testaments while they lived in the kingdom in my flesh.

Elijah brought back God/Israel from captivity with multitudes of godly spirits from captivity and they went into the body of Mankind and seduced the spirits in their humanity with shameful passions to lead them astray so they did not know they must have faith Elijah to save them. Nor did they have any pity on Jesus.

In the battle in the kingdom they were captured by Elijah and carried away to fire for tempting the spirits in their humanity to go astray to fall like them. Elijah removed them from the earth to give spirits in their humanity a choice to have faith in him to save them or fall.

God/Israel and god (Cain) his father returned from captivity with a multitude of godly spirits with no flesh to warn their children of the chaos in Hell. Instead they did wickedly. They are your enemy so don't follow their way to be godly spirits with no flesh after death to suffer. Jerusalem said: no spirit of gods should pray to me. I can't help you.

I am going away to sce judgment in the kingdom, to be with immortal spirits created by CHRIST through Elijah with the WORD. It is Elijah who saved my spirit when my body was burnt in Babylon. Be of good cheer. Farewell. Have faith in Elijah to save you from the devils and Israel my enemy.

Elijah has given me everlasting children on earth through my son Isaac. I conceived Isaac by the Word with my spirit with seed of creation. Elijah is merciful. He is our children's saviour in the world. Have faith. in Him, my children.

When CHRIST comes in kingdoms for salvation it is to create immortal spirits. Spirits of gods, prepare your kingdom and have faith in Elijah to save your spirit after death so you don't go away crying without my flesh to blame me for not telling you the truth to save you from the fire in the sun.

Jerusalem wrote in her testament: Zion resurrected and has seen the captivity of God/Israel our enemy, who held us in captivity. I shall also see spirits created with everlasting life in kingdoms shortly by CHRIST through our saviour Elijah.

It is important spirits of god have faith in Elijah so you don't suffer after death to be in the gate with my enemies to persecute thee. Shortly, godly spirits who have no faith shall see him who committed abomination and his father who raped me to make a god to pass on his accursed seed to you. Spirits that don't have faith when you enter the fire, tread upon your father's neck for me for hanging the body of my father when he was a king under oath with the law and was with the devils in Babylon

God/Israel was disobedient; he had no faith. If you have no faith like him you will be carried away from the earth to be with godly spirits and the devils. God/Israel is a god of god (Cain). His father Elijah brought him up to do good in this world but he wickedly passed the accursed seed of god (Cain) of the devil to you.

God/Israel brought much suffering upon me and held me in captivity while I lived in body of Babylon in my flesh. If you have no faith you will be pulled up by the sun in final judgment to the gate of the sun to fall in the everlasting fire of the sun.

This is my testimony to all Mankind before I go to sleep. When I wake up it is to go forth to Heaven. I'll leave the earth from the affliction I suffered, to prepare myself for Elijah for when I return to earth to live among immortal spirits in righteousness that CHRIST created through Elijah to live in peace on earth.

Farewell, spirits of god in Mankind. Prepare your bodies for Elijah to direct to CHRIST to come and create immortal spirits in kingdoms to continue in perfection and populate the earth and to resurrect to worlds above for ever. My peace I leave with my children with immortal spirits in my flesh.

When I awake, Elijah will resurrect me, and I shall see salvation in kingdoms in all nations on earth, for their kingdoms to continue to give birth to immortal spirits in all nations on earth in the name of CHRIST through Elijah with the WORD.

Jesus's prophesy of the final end Mt.13:34–43

There will be much celebration on earth and in all worlds, CHRIST and Zion will go to the heaven of heavens to receive blessings from the Eternal to rule and have dominion in all worlds from the throne after the kingdom is fully established with immortal spirits by the WORD.

Salvation is on the countdown to the day and hour

While immortal spirits live among spirits of gods in the kingdom, the world is still between Light and darkness. Lord Elijah is prudent and deals strictly by the New Testament with knowledge, and has taken action to begin the final judgment with the spirit of the sun to remove the godly spirits on the earth that have no faith to establish the kingdom. to be the king in the kingdoms on the earth. **Pro.13:16, 14:18; Gen.1:11, 16, 18, 24, 27, 29; Gen. 2:1, 5:12, 5:17, 9:7, 9:11, 9:17**

If the spirits of gods don't live by the New Testament they we will be in the final judgment by the spirit of the sun after they depart from the kingdom. **Is.13:11**

On the day of salvation it take an hour for CHRIST to remove spirits of gods from the kingdom, to create multitudes of immortal spirits in the kingdom in the same resemblance to continue to populate the earth without shame in the world. **2 .Cor.3:8; 2.Cor.5:17**

Observation in salvation

The spirits of gods should observe the clouds in the nations, the sunset, rain in the nations, floods, drought, the ice melting (**Job.24:19**) earthquakes in various places, and the change taking place on earth according to the New Testament. **Deut.32:35; Ps.18:18–20; Pro.19:13; Job.24:19; Obad.13; Pro.16:15; Joel.2:2; Rev.1:7; Pro.1:7; Pro.26:1; Job.5:10, 36:27; Heb.7:12**

Daniel told Mankind in the nations, don't wait until you have no flesh to believe. If you have faith in Elijah, prepare your bodies for salvation to rest in peace, and for your bodies to have an immortal spirit with everlasting life in the same resemblance to continue in the name of CHRIST, equal as angels above to live in the world without end. **Dan.1:10; Ex.13:3; Zech.5:6; Eccl.11:16; Eph.4:14; xx.11:7; xx.10:14**

The spirits of gods who put their hope in God to save them after death will be in shock when they are godly spirits with no flesh to face the final judgment by the spirit of the sun. **XXIV.14; XX 11:7; P.53:19; PS.51:4**

The New Testament of CHRIST is for all spirits in the kingdom to be equal through creation by the Word to live in the world in the Light, through the TRINITY.

The TRINITY Jn.1–9

The ETERNAL with the WORD, CHRIST by the WORD and ELIJAH by the WORD with the WORD to do the work in the world through CHRIST the creator of immortal spirits in the kingdom to continue to populate the earth with perfect spirits in the light for ever.

Elijah, lord, judge and the king in the kingdom. His Queen Jerusalem made herself ready to be his queen in the kingdom with immortal spirits in the kingdom in her flesh in perfection in the name of CHRIST by the WORD. **Pro.13, 16, 14, 18**

Ask for peace and it shall be given thee. **Mt.7:7** The kingdom is righteous for creation. **Mt.6:33** Spirits of gods, be content with your nature. You can't be born again. Have faith and prepare yourself for salvation (**Mt.6:5**) so the immortal spirit created can make perfect children (**Mt.7:18**) to continue in the kingdom. **Mt.1:1–9** The immortal spirits of creation are righteous and need no repentance by priests in religion contrary to the New Testament, so close your door and speak to your saviour if you have faith. **Mt.9:13** The BATTLE in the KINGDOM is to give every spirit of god the free choice to decide their fate while they live in the kingdom.

Let there be immortal spirits in the light in the kingdoms and let their spirits be for signs, for days and to live in the world without END.

Let the kingdoms with spirits of gods be created with immortal spirits in the Light to be in Heaven from the earth.

And it will be so in the END.

When there are no spirits of gods in the kingdom from the flesh of Zion and Jerusalem on the earth, the world will be in the LIGHT. **Gen.1:14–15**

Through the two great SPIRITS, CHRIST and ELIJAH with the WORD (**Gen.1:16–17**) God Israel made kingdoms from the seed of god (Cain) of the devil for Elijah and CHRIST to create immortal spirits in the kingdoms on earth to be among angels in Heaven while the world is between light and darkness. **Gen.1:18–19**

God Israel repented he made Mankind not perfect from his passed on seed of god (Cain) his father because he had no faith in Elijah to rest in peace. **Gen.6:5–6**

The BATTLE in the KINGDOM is to give every spirit of god in the kingdom a free choice before CHRIST comes in the kingdom for salvation to have faith in Elijah for peace or fall. The earth has become corrupt and filled with violence. As it was in the beginning with God Israel, it is to date. **Gen.6:11**

Till the end of salvation of kingdoms with spirits from the seed of gods, for the kingdom to be as it was in the beginning with immortal spirits in the kingdom by the WORD of the ETERNAL with Elijah for CHRIST with Zion to rule all worlds from the throne in heaven.

Paradise will be regained, with no devils and no gods in the kingdom

The end, according to the New Testament.